THE PUCCINI COMPANION

THE PUCCINI COMPANION

EDITED BY

WILLIAM WEAVER

AND

SIMONETTA PUCCINI

W·W·NORTON & COMPANY

NEW YORK   LONDON

The text of this book is composed in 12/14 Bembo
with the display set in Centaur Bold with swashes
at 60% horizontal scale.
Composition and manufacturing by
The Maple-Vail Book Manufacturing Group.
Book design by Margaret M. Wagner.

Library of Congress Cataloging-in-Publication Data
The Puccini companion / edited by Simonetta Puccini and
William Weaver.
p.   cm.
Includes bibliographical references and indexes.
1. Puccini, Giacomo, 1858–1924.   2. Composers—Italy.
I. Puccini, Simonetta.   II. Weaver, William, 1923–   .
ML410.P89W3   1994
782.1′092—dc20
[B]   93-27718

ISBN 0-393-02930-1

W. W. Norton & Company, Inc.
500 Fifth Avenue, New York, N.Y. 10110
W. W. Norton & Company Ltd.
10 Coptic Street, London WC1A 1PU

  2 3 4 5 6 7 8 9 0

Alla cara memoria di Fedele D'Amico

CONTENTS

*I*NTRODUCTION

*I*n the most literal sense a companion is "a person who accompanies another" and—the dictionary adds—"a comrade." The book that follows is meant to be a comrade to those who love Puccini's operas and, at the same time, to accompany them along a journey of appreciation and, perhaps, of discovery. This *Puccini Companion* is not a disguised biography; and though much of it is written by scholars, it is not a work of scholarship, a treatise. The editors hope that certain chapters and appendices—the chronology, the *dramatis personae*—will be of use also to scholars; but the book is not a manual (a word that has, in any case, come into disrepute with the arrival of computers and their indecipherable, arrogant manual-prose).

There are, to be sure, chapters on each of Puccini's operas—some long, some short—but they are not intended as guides, or even as the last word on the subject. The individual authors were expected, simply, to write about some aspect of this or that opera, illustrating a particular facet of Puccini's genius. Thus the chapters are deliberately varied. It is no accident that one of the longest chapters in the book is devoted to the two least-performed operas in the Puccini canon, *Le villi* and *Edgar*. And similarly, one of the shortest chapters is devoted to perhaps the most popular work of all, *La bohème*.

Some of the chapters deal with Puccini's librettos, his dramaturgy, revealing complexities that earlier writers have ignored or dismissed. Other chapters emphasize the world around Puccini, the composers he heard as a youth, the interpreters he dealt with in the years of his triumph.

The Puccini bibliography is endless (and, at this writing, is the subject of a lengthy and learned work in progress); but it is only in the past few decades that musical scholarship has turned its attention properly to the Lucchese composer. Academic conferences are now regularly devoted to the composer and to aspects of his work. After Mosco Carner's pioneering study of 1958, Puccini—like Verdi before him—has gradually become respectable. Serious studies of individual operas have begun to appear, critical editions are in the offing, and, with them, we may also hope for some healthful changes in the performing tradition.

This volume is dedicated to that acute and impassioned Puccinian Fedele D'Amico, who, after granting us permission to use it, had intended to expand his article on *La bohème*. His fatal illness prevented him from making those revisions, which only his notorious perfectionism could have considered necessary. At any musical event, he was, in life, the most stimulating, demanding, and rewarding of companions. It is good to have him again with us here.

THE EDITORS

THE PUCCINI COMPANION

THE PUCCINI FAMILY

Simonetta Puccini

Simonetta Puccini, daughter of the composer's son Antonio, is the only direct descendant of Giacomo. After taking her degree in literature at the University of Milan (with a thesis on medieval literature), she taught literary subjects—Latin, Italian, history, geography—in the Italian school system. In 1973 she gave up teaching to devote herself to fostering understanding of her grandfather and his work. In 1979 with Mosco Carner, Fedele D'Amico, and Claudio Sartori, she founded the Institute of Puccini Studies, which is housed in the Casa di riposo "G. Verdi" in Milan. She has edited two volumes of Puccini letters: *Lettere a Riccardo Schnabel* (1980) and the *Lettere di Ferdinando Fontana a Giacomo Puccini* (1992). She has published numerous articles and has prepared two exhibitions: *Puccini e i pittori* (1980) and, with Franco Signorini and Maria Grazia Bajoni, *Puccini a Milano* (1979).

The Puccinis were a family of musicians who came from the little village of Celle in the mountains dominating the Serchio valley. This family, as Luigi Nerici writes in his *Storia della musica a Lucca,* "played a main role in the story of our music."[1]

1. L. Nerici, *Storia della musica a Lucca* (Lucca, 1879), 164.

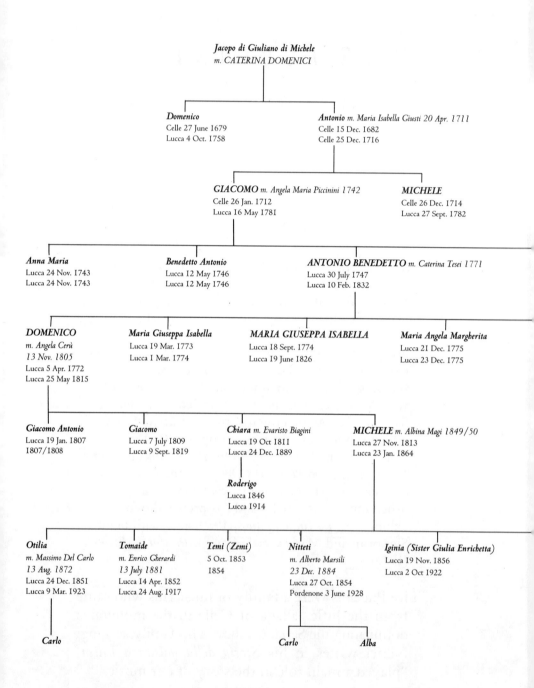

Jacopo di Giuliano di Michele
m. CATERINA DOMENICI

Domenico
Celle 27 June 1679
Lucca 4 Oct. 1758

Antonio m. Maria Isabella Giusti 20 Apr. 1711
Celle 15 Dec. 1682
Celle 25 Dec. 1716

GIACOMO m. Angela Maria Piccinini 1742
Celle 26 Jan. 1712
Lucca 16 May 1781

MICHELE
Celle 26 Dec. 1714
Lucca 27 Sept. 1782

Anna Maria
Lucca 24 Nov. 1743
Lucca 24 Nov. 1743

Benedetto Antonio
Lucca 12 May 1746
Lucca 12 May 1746

ANTONIO BENEDETTO m. Caterina Tesei 1771
Lucca 30 July 1747
Lucca 10 Feb. 1832

DOMENICO
m. Angela Cerù
13 Nov. 1805
Lucca 5 Apr. 1772
Lucca 25 May 1815

Maria Giuseppa Isabella
Lucca 19 Mar. 1773
Lucca 1 Mar. 1774

MARIA GIUSEPPA ISABELLA
Lucca 18 Sept. 1774
Lucca 19 June 1826

Maria Angela Margherita
Lucca 21 Dec. 1775
Lucca 23 Dec. 1775

Giacomo Antonio
Lucca 19 Jan. 1807
1807/1808

Giacomo
Lucca 7 July 1809
Lucca 9 Sept. 1819

Chiara m. Evaristo Biagini
Lucca 19 Oct 1811
Lucca 24 Dec. 1889

MICHELE m. Albina Magi 1849/50
Lucca 27 Nov. 1813
Lucca 23 Jan. 1864

Roderigo
Lucca 1846
Lucca 1914

Otilia
m. Massimo Del Carlo
13 Aug. 1872
Lucca 24 Dec. 1851
Lucca 9 Mar. 1923

Tomaide
m. Enrico Gherardi
13 July 1881
Lucca 14 Apr. 1852
Lucca 24 Aug. 1917

Temi (Zemi)
5 Oct. 1853
1854

Nitteti
m. Alberto Marsili
23 Dec. 1884
Lucca 27 Oct. 1854
Pordenone 3 June 1928

Iginia (Sister Giulia Enrichetta)
Lucca 19 Nov. 1856
Lucca 2 Oct 1922

Carlo

Carlo

Alba

THE PUCCINI FAMILY

Lucia Caterina	Michele Innocente	Giovanni	Giovanni	Giovanni
Lucca 12 Sept. 1748	Lucca 4 Jan. 1750	Lucca 29 May 1751	Lucca 30 Apr. 1752	Lucca 24 Jan. 1753
Lucca 22 Dec. 1748	Lucca 4 Jan. 1750	Lucca 29 May 1751	Lucca 30 Apr. 1752	Lucca 24 Jan. 1753

Maria Angela Margherita	Maria Margherita Rosalba Diana	Maria Teresa Paulina	N.N.
m. Gaetano Ghivizzani	Lucca 14 July 1779	Lucca 11 July 1784	Lucca 27 Dec. 1786
Lucca 6 Sept. 1777	Lucca 10 July 1792	Lucca 1785	Lucca 27 Dec. 1786
Lucca 26 July 1817			

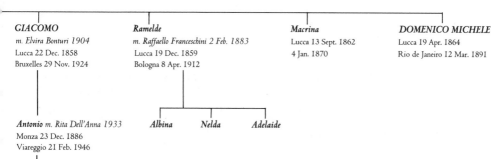

GIACOMO
m. Elvira Bonturi 1904
Lucca 22 Dec. 1858
Bruxelles 29 Nov. 1924

Ramelde
m. Raffaello Franceschini 2 Feb. 1883
Lucca 19 Dec. 1859
Bologna 8 Apr. 1912

Macrina
Lucca 13 Sept. 1862
4 Jan. 1870

DOMENICO MICHELE
Lucca 19 Apr. 1864
Rio de Janeiro 12 Mar. 1891

Antonio m. Rita Dell'Anna 1933
Monza 23 Dec. 1886
Viareggio 21 Feb. 1946

Albina   **Nelda**   **Adelaide**

Simonetta
Pisa 2 June 1929

The elder Giacomo was born in Lucca, 26 January 1712, and after finishing his studies in Lucca, he moved to Bologna where he became a student of Giuseppe Carretti, master of music in the church of San Petronio. When Giacomo returned to Lucca in 1739 he was appointed organist in the cathedral and the following year was named Maestro di Cappella to the most serene Republic. He wrote a great deal of dramatic and church music, in particular compositions to be staged on the occasion of the "Tasche";[2] also, between 1733 and 1780, he wrote the music for approximately thirty services for the feast of Santa Cecilia as well as numerous unrelated religious compositions. He was a member of the Accademia Filarmonica of Bologna and also an excellent teacher; among his pupils was the later famous musician from Massa, Pietro Guglielmi. François-Joseph Fétis describes him as a "talented organist" and records that his sacred compositions won him an "honorable" reputation. He died in Lucca, 16 May 1781.

On 30 July 1747 Giacomo's son, Antonio Benedetto Maria was born. He followed his father's profession and occupied with honor the same positions in the cathedral of San Martino and in the Cappella Palatina. He studied first with the abbé Frediano Matteo Lucchesi and in 1768 moved to Bologna to complete his studies with Giuseppe Carretti, who had also been his father's teacher. On his return to Lucca on 21 April 1772 he was called to take over his father's duties both as Maestro of the Cappella Palatina and as organist of the cathedral. Antonio Puccini was also a reputable organist and composer of both sacred and dramatic music. His *Messa di Requiem* was performed in the Lucca cathedral at the death of the emperor Joseph II of Austria; he also wrote thirteen stage works for the "Tasche" between 1768 and 1797. He married a woman from Bologna, Caterina Tesei (1747–1818), who was herself a gifted organist and often took over her husband's—and later her son's—duties in the cathedral until her death on 7 March 1818. Antonio and Caterina Puccini had eight children of whom a

---

2. "Tasche" of Lucca meant specifically the elections of the governing body of the Republic. For the ceremony connected with them, including its music, see Gabriella Biagi-Ravenni and Carolyn Gianturco, "The Tasche of Lucca: 150 years of Political Serenatas," *Proceedings of the Royal Musical Association* 3 (1985):48.

son, Domenico Vincenzo Maria, and a daughter, Isabella, survived.

Domenico, after studying in Lucca with his father, continued his training in Bologna with Father Stanislao Mattei before going to Naples for further study with Giovanni Paisiello. As Jacopo Chelini writes at the beginning of the nineteenth century, "Domenico Puccini surpassed all the others with his extraordinary lovely and harmonious style."[3] In 1796 he succeeded his father as Maestro in the Cappella di Lucca and as organist of the cathedral. In 1805 Elisa Baciocchi, sister of Napoleon I and ruler of Lucca, named him court conductor. During these years Domenico enjoyed a high and honored position, but when the court Cappella was suppressed, his economic conditions worsened so that in December of 1810 he was forced to address a humble petition to the Sovereign. In 1811 he took over direction of the Cappella Municipale and, along with his mother and his sister Isabella, gave music lessons in the Maria Luisa Institute, a girls' seminary.

Like his father and his grandfather, Domenico studied at the Accademia Filarmonica of Bologna and was secretary of the Santa Cecilia company. His sacred compositions include a *Psalm* in sixteen parts with double orchestra accompaniment, which he presented to Pope Pius VII. For the "Tasche" he wrote highly praised stage works in 1793 and 1797. Domenico Puccini was also the composer of four operas: *Le frecce d'amore* (The arrows of love), a pastoral opera in two acts; *L'ortolanella o La moglie capricciosa* (The gardener's girl or The capricious wife), performed in Camaiore in 1800; *Il Quinto Fabio* (Quintus Fabius), opera seria in two acts, first performed in the Teatro dei Floridi, Livorno, in 1810; and *Il ciarlatano ossia I finti savoiardi* (The charlatan or The feigned Savoyards), an opera buffa first performed in Lucca in 1815. He died suddenly on 25 May 1815, perhaps after eating a poisoned sorbet. He was forty-four and was survived by his elderly parents, Antonio and Caterina, as well as by his young wife Angela Cerù and their three young children: Jacopo, who was born blind and died at the age of nine, Chiara, and Michele.

3. Jacopo Chelini, *Zibaldone lucchese,* ms. 104, Fondo Sardini, Archivio di Stato Lucchese, 83–86.

After Domenico's death, the family moved from via di Pozzo Torelli to the house on via di Poggio, where the judge Arcangelo Cerù, Angela's brother, lived with his family. Michele Puccini, born in Lucca on 27 November 1813, was only two when his father died, and his grandfather Antonio acted as father to him, carefully guiding him in his musical studies but at the same time seeing that the boy also studied literature, philosophy, and mathematics. Iacopo Fanucchi, a former pupil of Domenico Puccini's, was young Michele's piano teacher, while the canon Marco Santucci taught him organ. On the latter instrument the youth's progress was remarkable, and he was soon considered the best and most versatile organist in the city. Eugenio Galli introduced him to the study of har-

The Duomo of Lucca, dedicated to San Martino, was a center of the city's musical life, and generations of Puccinis were the cathedral's organist and official composer, from the first Giacomo (1712–81) to Michele, father of the second Giacomo. (Courtesy of the Italian Government Travel Office, New York)

mony and counterpoint, which he pursued further in Bologna in 1834 with the famous musician and teacher Giuseppe Pilotti. In 1839, thanks to the financial assistance of the priest Stefano Cheli, he spent a year in Naples, studying composition at the Conservatorio S. Pietro a Maiella.

Upon returning home, Michele was named Inspector of the Royal Musical Institute, then directed by Giovanni Pacini; in 1846 he began teaching harmony and accompaniment at the Institute and was named director of the Cappella Municipale. His works include an *Ecce Sacerdos Magnus* for 32 voices, which he presented to Pius IX when the pope visited Lucca in 1857; he also wrote two Masses with orchestra and two stage works, *Antonio Foscarini* and *Giambattista Cattani*. An excellent teacher, he compiled a treatise on harmony and one on counterpoint. He was also organist of the cathedral of San Martino, where he introduced the fugato style, whereas Domenico, his father, had used the "sciolto e fantastico" style.

In 1850, at the age of thirty-seven, Michele Puccini married the nineteen-year-old Albina Magi. (A brother of Albina's, Fortunato, was Michele's pupil.) The couple settled in the Via di Poggio house where Angela Cerù, the widow of Domenico Puccini for thirty-five years, still lived. In the years that followed, the family grew steadily. Five daughters were born to Albina and Michele in rapid succession: Otilia in 1851, Tomaide in 1852, Temi, or Zemi, in 1853 (who lived only a few months), Maria Nitteti in 1854, Iginia in 1856. In 1858 a son was born and given the name Giacomo, after the founder of the musical dynasty. Then came two more girls, Ramelde in 1859 and Macrina in 1862. Michele Puccini chose unusual names for his daughters, sometimes derived from musical works. For his first son, he followed the family tradition, according to which first-born males were successively given the names Giacomo, Antonio, Domenico, and Michele. On 23 January 1864 Professor Michele Puccini died "di morbo dissolutivo" at the age of fifty-one, leaving his aged mother in poor health and his still-young wife with seven small children. An eighth, Michele, was born three months later, on 19 April 1864.

Michele Puccini's untimely death affected Lucca profoundly. The composer Giovanni Pacini read a funeral oration, in which he spoke of little Giacomo, who would grow up to continue the family tradition. The city authorities granted the widow a monthly pension of sixty-seven lire. At the age of thirty-one, Albina headed a household that comprised eight children, the oldest aged twelve, her elderly mother-in-law, and two maidservants. In 1865, a year after the older Michele's death, his mother, Angela Cerù, also died.

For some years, the family led a tranquil life: two of the girls entered the Collegio di San Nicolao, while the other children studied at home. But then in 1870 another misfortune struck: Macrina, the youngest daughter, died at the age of eight. Albina was a woman of courage and profound religious devotion; she also possessed a strong practical sense and an ability to make decisions promptly, a gift probably inherited from her merchant father. Her practicality proved especially valuable in a family of artists, who tended to live more in their imagination than in the world of reality.

No documents survive from the period of the infancy and childhood of the young Puccinis, except for a biography of Albina, written in 1906 by her daughter Ramelde at the request of her brother Giacomo for the magazine "La Scena Illustrata." Besides portraying Albina, the article tells about Giacomo's early years as well.

> Her first concern was the education and training of her older daughters; and, obedient to their mother's wishes, they were soon able to help support the family. All did their best, following a path illuminated by a great hope. This hope, for our good Mamma, was Giacomo, who was endowed with a very lively mind and a sensitive heart. But the darling boy, perhaps because of the extraordinary vitality and restlessness of his character, refused to take an interest in any kind of study. Mamma wanted her Giacomo to study the classics before devoting himself to music, because she sensibly believed and used to say: "pure music, pure jackass"; but the ebullient Giacomo, although he loved his mother deeply, was no good at sitting long at a school desk, and was frequently expelled, to be readmitted only through his mother's petitions.

Albina entrusted her son to her brother Fortunato Magi for his first musical instruction. Uncle and nephew, however,

apparently did not get along. Magi had little faith in Giacomo's musical gifts and one day actually advised his sister to
curtail the boy's studies. But Mamma did not lose hope and
refused to be persuaded; she used to say: "If he doesn't become
a worthy composer like his father and his ancestors, he'll still
be something! The important thing is to continue the generations of musicians." When the hours with Fortunato Magi
produced no good results, Albina sent her son to another
teacher, Carlo Angeloni.

This time, things went better; slowly Giacomo began to
make progress and regularly attend Lucca's Istituto Musicale
Pacini. At seventeen, when he had just completed his musical
studies, he entered a competition occasioned by the opening
of an exposition in Lucca: Giacomo's entry earned last place.
Mamma was distressed at this failure, but did not lose heart.
She decided that if Giacomo were removed from the atmosphere of Lucca, he would be able to have a career. She had
always believed that he would become a great musician, the
greatest of all the Puccinis, and she felt it was necessary for
him to go to Milan. There was the problem of finding the
financial means, since with her modest pension and the earnings of her daughters, who had begun to work, she could
barely manage to support the family properly. Thanks to the
friendships she had always cultivated, Albina found the right
solution. She called on the Duchessa Carafa di Noia, whose
two daughters, Mimì and Ninì, had been schoolmates of Iginia Puccini. The noblewoman was a friend of the Marchesa
Pallavicino, lady-in-waiting to Queen Margherita di Savoia.
In his book, *Immortal Bohemian,* Dante del Fiorentino quotes
an imaginary letter, which must have been fairly similar to
Albina's actual petition to the Queen:

Your Majesty!
You are the queen and the mother of all the poor, and you are
also the patroness of artists. I am a poor widow with two sons,
and it is my ambition to give them the best possible education.
My sons study music, and the older, Giacomo, shows great
promise. For five generations, the Puccinis have constituted a
musical dynasty, and if he has the opportunity, Giacomo will

continue the glorious tradition. He has completed his studies in
Lucca; he wishes to go to Milan, the capital of music. I myself
cannot pay the expenses of the Conservatory, as I have only a
small pension of seventy-five lire [actually sixty-seven, as we have
seen] granted me by the city authorities. The Duchessa Carafa,
who knows me well, has urged me to write to Your Majesty.
Could you, in your immense generosity, come to the aid of a
poor mother and an ambitious boy?

I kiss your generous hand, Albina Magi Puccini[4]

After some time the Queen's reply arrived, through her lady-
in-waiting, the Marchesa Pallavicino. Giacomo was granted a
scholarship of one hundred lire monthly for a year. Albina's
joy must have been very great, even greater than her sorrow
at being separated from Giacomo, who had never before been
away from home. The distance from Lucca did not, however,
mean a complete break with the family. Although he lived in
Milan, where his studies and the Conservatory occupied his
time entirely, Giacomo's ties with Lucca remained intact, for
there his mother, sisters, and brother represented his affective
world. Until the end of his mother's life, Giacomo was profoundly attached to her, and after her death, his sisters represented for him the link with his childhood, the family home,
and the ancestral tradition. On 10 November 1880, not long
after his arrival in Milan, Giacomo wrote to his mother: "As
I wrote you before, the examination went well. This very
morning I went to the Conservatory, and I saw that I did
better than the others, all modesty aside."[5]

When he suffered from homesickness, Giacomo would write
his mother about his life in Milan; thus, in February 1881:
"Dear Mamma, I'm here in Carlo's study [Carlo Biagini was
a cousin, living in Milan, who helped Giacomo in his early
days there], waiting until he has finished speaking with someone. I will make use of this time and spend a while with you,
dearest Mamma."[6]

The bursary from the Queen had been supplemented by a
loan from Giacomo's great-uncle Nicolao Cerù, but still the

4. Dante del Fiorentino, *Immortal Bohemian* (New York, 1962), 36.
5. Arnaldo Marchetti, ed., *Puccini com'era* (Milan, 1973), 15.
6. Ibid., 21.

young student was having financial difficulties. His mother often sent him money and also clothes, either new or altered for him. Giacomo missed Lucca's famous olive oil from the beginning and, in an often-quoted letter of 18 December 1880, he asked his mother to send him some:

> There is one thing I need, but I'm afraid to tell you, because I realize myself that you have no money to spend. But, believe me, it's a small matter. Since I have a great yearning for beans (in fact, one day they fixed me some but I couldn't eat them because of the oil, which here is made from sesame or linseed!), well, as I was saying . . . ; I need a bit of oil, the new oil, that is. I'd ask you to send me some. Just a little bit is enough.[7]

And, again from Milan, he wrote on 9 March 1881: "Dear Mamma, the money, the trousers, and the shoes [he uses the dialect words "sghei," "brae," and "ciocie"] have arrived. The shoes fit, and so do the trousers . . . soon I'll send my shirts to be let out. I'm short on money (think of me if you can).[8]

Albina, at home, must have eagerly awaited the letters from Milan. Giacomo tells her about his life, his studies, his excursions into the country, the Carnival season, and the great Universal Exposition of 1882 at Porta Genova, where the Milanese had actually constructed a replica of the banks of the Ganges.

The scholarship was not renewed at the end of the year, but, despite countless problems and thanks to the money his mother always managed to send him, sometimes incurring debts herself, Giacomo was able to finish his studies at the Milan Conservatory in June 1883. As Ramelde wrote:

> And so Giacomo could complete his studies with Amilcare Ponchielli: studies which culminated with the sensational success of a Capriccio Sinfonico which [Filippo] Filippi, critic of La Perseveranza, called "more than a promise of a glorious future." But the sad notes were not over: having won his diploma, Giacomo returned to Lucca and fell into a "dolce far niente" lethargy. This

7. Eugenio Gara et al., eds., *Carteggi pucciniani* (Milan, 1958), 3.
8. Marchetti, *Puccini com'era*, 27.

distressed our poor Mamma terribly, but on the other hand Giacomo could plead some extenuating circumstances that lessened his guilt. What was he to do? He did not feel cut out for teaching. Compose! But what? For whom? And anyway, where was the money to pay a poet to write a libretto for him?

Actually, this is not quite the way things went. From Giacomo's letters to his mother it is clear that, even before his final examination, he had been taking steps to prepare for his future. From Milan, on 20 June 1883, he wrote to Albina:

Michele Puccini (1813–64), Giacomo's father, was a gifted organist and composer and, by all accounts, an excellent teacher. He was also a theorist and wrote several treatises on harmony and counterpoint, which have not survived. Though he wrote two operas, now lost, his more numerous sacred works fared better. His untimely death was a blow not only to his family but to musical Lucca. The composer Giovanni Pacini delivered a grave-side oration at Michele's funeral. (Courtesy of the Italian Cultural Institute, New York)

The only surviving likeness of Michele's wife, Albina Magi Puccini, is this photograph taken during her widowhood. She is wearing some simple family jewelry: earrings and a little coral twig brooch holding her black mourning lace at her throat. The round, placid face suggests the purposeful determination that enabled her to bring up a large family in straitened circumstances. She was herself a trained musician, and her brother, Fortunato Magi, was Giacomo's first, not very successful teacher. (Courtesy of the Italian Cultural Institute, New York)

Dear mother, this morning, or rather, just now (11 o'clock), I have come from seeing Ponchielli, and we talked of many things, and he told me that the exams, both the 1st and the 2nd, went well . . . I am working furiously to finish my piece, which is now well along [this was the *Capriccio Sinfonico,* which he was to present as part of his examination]. After the examinations, I will concern myself with my future and will go to see Ricordi, though I don't have great hopes.[9]

The final examinations at the Conservatory went well, and the *Capriccio Sinfonico* was successfully performed on 4 July 1883 by an orchestra of Conservatory students under Franco Faccio. After the excellent critical reception of this work, the young composer was naturally expected to write an opera; but Giacomo was unable to pay for a libretto. Ponchielli came to his assistance, introducing him to the Milanese writer and poet Ferdinando Fontana. Ponchielli asked him to prepare a libretto for Puccini. The music publisher Sonzogno had established a competition for an one-act opera; the deadline was 31 December 1883. Puccini described the situation in a letter to his mother, written from Milan in July:

Dear Mamma, I went to visit Ponchielli and stayed there for four days. I spoke with Fontana, the poet, who was vacationing near Ponchielli, and we more or less arranged for a libretto; in fact, he told me he liked my music etc. etc. Ponchielli then also became involved and recommended me warmly. There is a possible good story that was given to another, but Fontana would be happier to give it to me, especially as it is something I really like very much, since it allows for much work in the symphonic-descriptive genre. This suits me very well, because I believe I would succeed. In this way I could participate in the Sonzogno competition. But the whole business, dear Mamma, is very unsure. Imagine: the competition is open to all Italy, not local and restricted, as I thought. And furthermore the time is short.[10]

Giacomo then returned to Lucca with the libretto of his first opera, *Le villi,* and, as his sister Ramelde narrates in her biog-

9. Marchetti, *Puccini com'era,* 32.
10. Gara, *Carteggi pucciniani,* 6.

raphy of their mother, it was once more his mother who helped him complete his first important work:

> Having returned to Lucca, Giacomo set to work with such ardor that it seemed the opera would soon be finished. But after a little while he was assailed by discouragement and doubt and, at the same time, inertia. However, a guardian angel was watching over his destiny, and this was his Mamma, who, thinking of her son's future, devoted all her strength to exhorting him, encouraging him, and acting as critic of what he was writing. Every piece of the work was passed to her to judge, and Giacomo accepted her judgment and revised and rewrote. His loving Mamma did not know music, but her opinion was valuable because, having lived among artists, intelligent as she was, and of sincere spirit, she had acquired taste and knowledge. What anxiety, what effort, what trepidation, how many nights she spent with her Giacomo! (Because Giacomo wanted to compose amid silence, as he does now . . .) Finally, the work was finished at midnight of the day set as deadline for the competition. The time between the submission of the work and the conclusion of the competition was one of terribly painful torment for our poor Mamma. It seemed never to pass: minutes were hours, hours were days. [The deadline was 31 December; the results were announced at the end of February 1884.]

It was in this period that Albina began to waste away: her anxieties, her terrible worries had undermined her strong constitution. The wait for the competition's outcome was unnerving, and when the results finally came, Giacomo was not among the winners. This news was a blow to both mother and son. Nevertheless, once again Albina's courage did not fail her.

Ramelde continues:

> Finally we read in the papers that the victors, or rather the prize-winners, were a certain Zuelli of Bologna and one Mapelli from Milan. Farewell, hopes!! The news was a terrible blow to Mamma and Giacomo, who, overwhelmed and dejected, shut himself up, in silent grief, within the walls of his home. It was a sad moment, and heroic resolve was necessary; and Mamma, with her vigor-

ous character, one fine day said to her son: "Giacomo, this vine-
yard's producing no grapes. You have won your diploma
honorably; now take the plunge. You're doing nothing in Lucca;
you must go back to Milan, and there you'll do something. Take
heart; the world doesn't belong to the pusillanimous." After this
exhortation, our good Mamma set to work. She sought and
obtained some letters of recommendation, she collected 200 lire,
and she sent her son to Milan . . . The first thing Giacomo did
was spend the 200 lire, then, broke, he had the idea of presenting
one of the many letters of recommendation. He chose the one
addressed to Giovannina Lucca, passionate music lover and
esteemed publisher, and he went to her, who received him most
amiably and invited him that same evening to a reception. Very
nervous, Giacomo went, but in that artistic atmosphere, he felt
very small, and was as awkward as a chick in straw. At that
gathering there were Arrigo Boito, Marco Sala, Alfredo Catalani, and many other prominent musical figures. The conversation turned to the outcome of the Sonzogno competition whose
judges [some of] these men had been. All of a sudden, Marco
Sala, perhaps through politeness or out of compassion, addressed
the silent boy in the corner, and asked him: "You're a student at
the Conservatory, why didn't you compete?"

"I did," the boy replied shyly, "but I didn't win."

"Come to the piano," Marco Sala added, "and play some of
your work for us."

Giacomo sat at the piano, but he gradually took heart, became
animated, and the score of *Le villi* flowed beneath his fingers,
which, once the first hesitation had passed, became very agile.
The listeners went from surprise to surprise, and from surprise
to wonder, until they exclaimed: "But this wasn't in the competition! Why, this music is new to us!"

(The contradiction of these competition judges was later
explained away with the pretext that the execrable writing of the
score had made it unintelligible.) The conclusion was that, after
they had heard the score played in that same drawing room, they
subscribed considerable sums to have it performed at the [Tea-
tro] Dal Verme.

Ramelde's story is surely affecting, though it does not reflect
exactly what happened. First of all, her biography of her mother

was written in 1906, twenty-two years after the events described above; further, the memory of her mother no doubt contributed to an emotional state that made Ramelde recall those events inaccurately. Thanks to surviving letters, we can give a more accurate account of those developments, which were so important in the lives of Albina and Giacomo. Word that Giacomo was not among the winners of the Sonzogno competition arrived towards the end of February. The family read it in the newspapers, as Ramelde writes. But Giacomo did not shut himself up in the house, or rather, he did not stay in Lucca. He may have gone there only for a short visit, for early in March he was back in Milan, and on 3 March Albina wrote:

> Dear Giacomo, I am writing so you won't be worried. Things are much the same, namely, I am weak and my stomach for the moment gives me no peace; but there's nothing to be alarmed about. This is what Cerù and Massimo both say [Giacomo's great-uncle Cerù and Massimo del Carlo, Otilia's husband, both physicians]. They say it's hysteria, but it is painful. They say a change of air will do me good.[11]

Le willis (as it was first called), after various vicissitudes that can be reconstructed thanks to Giacomo's letters from Milan to his mother, his sisters, and his younger brother Michele, was finally performed on 31 May 1884 at the Dal Verme, conducted by Arturo Panizza, with great success. All the reviews were favorable.

After his first opera's success, Giacomo returned at once to Lucca to embrace his mother. He found her condition much worse. From Milan he brought her the wreath he had been given after the final performance on 3 June. With this, Ramelde concludes her biography of their mother:

> He rushed at once to the sickbed of his beloved mother, and on it, with lacerated spirit, he put the first crown of laurels he had won; and the poor woman, overcome with emotion and her illness, unable to think of any other way to console him, took the only ring she possessed from her finger and slipped it onto her

11. Marchetti, *Puccini com'era*, 47.

son's. That ring symbolized, at that moment, the wedding of joy and grief. She lived only a few more days.

Giacomo Puccini had seven sisters: Otilia, Tomaide, Temi (or Zemi), Nitteti, Iginia, Ramelde, and Macrina. Temi died in infancy, and Macrina in childhood. Throughout his life Giacomo's relations with his sisters were affectionate: he was devoted to them and always very considerate with their families. Otilia, the oldest, was the first to leave home. In 1872 she married Massimo del Carlo, a physician, son of a grain merchant. Only one child, Carlo, was born of this marriage. As a girl, Otilia had studied music and apparently also performed in public. After her marriage, she led an uneventful life. For a certain period her husband was mayor of Lucca. In her last years Otilia suffered from a disease of the eyes, and this illness was accompanied by depression. Her daughter-in-law complained to uncle Giacomo, who answered her from Torre del Lago on 11 November 1919:

> Dear Assuntina, I'm very sorry Otilia is in such a dejected mood because of her eyes. I thought at once of Prof. Bardelli. You must accompany Otilia to Florence on a day I will tell you, and you will go together to the Professor for an examination and for advice on the cure to follow. Bardelli is a true scientist and I believe he will provide relief and remedy for Otilia's eyes, so her mood will change and you will all be pleased. Naturally, I will take care of the expenses of the journey, meals, etc. Many greetings to you and Carlo, and be patient with Otilia and I hope she, too, will try to bear her illness with greater serenity. Kisses to Otilia.

Otilia died in Lucca on 9 March 1923.

Tomaide, known as Tomina or Dide, was very serious from childhood. Diligent, studious, a bit severe, she so remained throughout her life. She was a teacher of French. After her father's death, she soon was able to provide valuable support for the family. In 1881 she married another teacher, Enrico Gherardi, a widower with two children. About this match,

Giacomo wrote from Milan to his sister Ramelde, on 4 April 1881: "I congratulate Tomaide on her forthcoming marriage. On the one hand, I am sorry because she was a great consolation for the family; but on the other, she too, poor thing, deserves this, as she has done so much for us, and it is time for her to rest and be happy."[12]

Tomaide was a very kind and generous person, always ready to help others. It was characteristic that she married a widower and father of two. Among the Puccini sisters she was the most willing to assume responsibility; her mother relied on her, more than on the others, for sending messages and instructions to the two sons in Milan when she was too weak to write herself.

Tomaide wrote to Michele (who had joined his older brother in Milan planning to attend the Conservatory): "Dear Michele, I would have written you also on my own, but today I am writing specially for Mamma. Poor Mamma, we must hope for the best . . . If only she no longer had troubles; but troubles never end . . . And you especially now have caused her some that I must reproach you for, at her bidding."[13]

As she had helped the family before her marriage, even afterwards, Tomaide on various occasions came to the aid of her brothers. In a very difficult period of his life, Giacomo found himself obliged to entrust to his sisters his little son Tonio, born in 1886 from the union with Elvira Bonturi. Tomaide came to his assistance. Giacomo wrote to Ramelde from Milan at the end of April 1891: "Thank Tomina, to whom I will write. I am sure that Tonio will have every possible and conceivable care. In that respect, thank God, I am easy in my mind . . . Tomina's very kind decision to keep him with her."[14]

There is no further information about the life of Tomaide Gherardi Puccini. She died in Lucca on 24 April 1917. On her gravestone is written: "Exemplary Teacher."

Maria Nitteti Noemi, born in 1854, the fourth Puccini sister, was short in stature, and nicknamed "Nano" (dwarf). In 1865, a year after the death of the senior Michele Puccini, his

12. Ibid., 29.
13. Ibid., 59.
14. Ibid., 160.

widow Albina decided to send her two daughters Nitteti and Iginia to the convent of San Nicolao, to the Augustinian nuns. Nitteti remained in the convent until 1873, when, at nineteen, she returned to the family. Like her sisters, she was given a good education. She wrote elegantly, in an excellent style; she was well-versed in Latin and apparently could even speak it. She was also, it seems, an expert embroiderer. She married the lawyer Alberto Marsili of Pisa and was the mother of two children: Carlo, born in 1885, and Alba, born in 1888. Nitteti was good-humored and likable and was able to retain her joviality for a long time, despite numerous misfortunes. Six years after her marriage, her husband died, leaving her in a precarious financial situation. Her son Carlo was ill for many years. Nitteti must have been charming and diplomatic. Her sister Ramelde called her also "prudent by nature." She was an excellent housekeeper and nurse, and as she was a widow and mistress of her own time, in free moments she would rush to Giacomo's house to lend a hand. When she was widowed, Giacomo assumed the responsibility of supporting her and her children, who considered their uncle a second father. Nitteti was the only one of the Puccini sisters who survived Giacomo. After the marriage of her daughter Alba, she followed her son Carlo first to Milan, then to Pordenone, where she died on 2 June 1928.

In writing of Iginia Puccini, one thinks immediately of Sister Giulia Enrichetta. The only information we have of her, in fact, concerns her life as a nun. Iginia entered the convent of the Augustinians in Via San Nicolao at the age of nine, in 1865, with her sister Nitteti. She remained cloistered for the rest of her life. She pursued teacher-training studies and, before taking her vows, she studied in Pisa, where she was awarded a elementary schoolteacher's certificate. She was also an excellent musician and played the organ in the convent chapel.

In 1887 many convents were expropriated, including the great property of San Nicolao. After various painful vicissitudes, the nuns were transferred to Vicopelago, a few kilometers from Lucca on the Pisa road. Sister Giulia Enrichetta was reverend mother of the convent for several periods. Though cloistered, she kept in close touch with her family.

Giacomo called Iginia "la mia suorina" (my little nun), and felt a special tenderness for her. From the surviving letters, it can be seen that Iginia Puccini, despite her secluded life, remained an active and practical person. In the convent she found complete happiness and satisfaction. In 1911 she wrote to Giacomo, who had apparently complained to her of the complications of his life.

> Thank you, thank you, dear Giacomo, for your dear and fond little letter! I truly appreciate all your affection for me, seeing that amidst all your headaches you remembered your poor little Nun, who, ignorant of the things of the world, lives alone in a convent at the foot of a mountain . . . I, too, rejoice in your successes, and I delight in the happy results of your works. I praise God and bless him for the talent he has given you. To be sure, you are right to say that I can have no idea of certain things: I, who came as a child to the Convent and have lived almost my entire life among four walls, cannot comprehend what the tumult of a big city is, or etiquette, the often boring formalities that surround a person of world fame like you, and yet, from what little I understand, it seems to me truly that all these things have been very burdensome for you and more boring than pleasant, therefore, while I congratulate you, I also feel sorry for you and sympathize with you.

In 1903, after a serious automobile accident, Giacomo was gravely ill for a while. Iginia was concerned that he legalize his cohabitation with Elvira Bonturi Gemignani, his companion since 1886. She wrote to her sister Tomaide:

> Your letter was the first I heard of Giacomo's accident. I can't tell you the effect of your letter on me with the dire story. Horror because of the danger poor Giacomo was in of losing in one moment both the life of the body and, even more, his soul, for which I have always had hope and these many years have prayed and yearned for . . . Listen, Tomaide, he opens his heart to you: Jesus has not sent this blow in vain. It could be considered a warning of His justice, but I believe, on the contrary, it is a sign of His mercy, for He loves him and does not want to lose him . . . "yes, yes, she was with Giacomo." You go to him, Tomaide,

some times, and tell also Ramelde and Otilia. All of you together, try to be missionaries. . . . Mamma blesses us from heaven. She loved her Giacomo so much. Is it possible that he should be lost? No, surely not; this grace is something we want, it is spiritual, and Jesus cannot deny it . . . With tears in my eyes, I beg you, Tomaide: help that poor boy, who is basically good . . . In confidence, I will tell you that on the very evening of the accident I learned that the person was dying.[15]

At that time, Giacomo and Elvira were not married. "The person" Giulia Enrichetta mentions was Narciso Gemignani, Elvira's husband. Iginia, concerned for Giacomo's salvation, in the name of their mother Albina asks her sister to persuade him to marry Elvira. At a certain point she obtained from the Bishop of Lucca a special permission for Giacomo actually to enter the cloistered convent. Soon he became the benefactor of the good sisters. A few years ago, in the Vicopelago convent, lived a nun in her nineties who, during Iginia's last years, was a young novice. She happily recalled those times and remembered the kindness and generosity of the Maestro. When he came, his sister went to meet him joyfully, and Giacomo actually would hand her his wallet, so that she could take what the convent needed. The good sisters still preserve some presents from the composer: the organ in the chapel, a bed and a chair for his sister in her illness. Surely the idea of writing *Suor Angelica* came to him during his visits to the Vicopelago convent. The aged nun remembered that, in those days, there was in the community a sister of extraordinary beauty known as Suor Angelica, who died young. Sister Giulia Enrichetta suffered from heart disease in her last years and died at Vicopelago on 2 October 1922. On 4 October, Puccini wrote to his friend Riccardo Schnabl: "My poor little nun-sister has died. I am sad, sad. . . ."[16]

Among Puccini's sisters, Ramelde was surely the one who understood him best. First of all, she was close to him in age, as she was born one year after him, on 19 December 1859. True, Iginia was only two years his senior, but the ascetic

15. Ibid., 265.
16. Simonetta Puccini, ed., *Lettere a Riccardo Schnabl* (Milan, 1980), 192.

older sister, much as she loved the family, had lived away from it since childhood. Giacomo and Ramelde grew up together. Both children were lively and fun-loving, and their affectionate intimacy is evident in their correspondence, which was virtually unbroken until Ramelde's death. They frequently use made-up words of their own, reflecting the close attachment of the Puccini home. Physically, Ramelde must have been fairly tall and sturdy and, as the years passed, she put on more and more weight. Some pictures of her survive. In his book *Puccini com'era,* Marchetti publishes the bulk of the Giacomo-Ramelde correspondence and also a picture of Ramelde, in the full bloom of her youth, wearing a light, flowery dress, a ribbon at her throat, her hair gathered and tied, with light bangs over the broad Puccini brow. Her face is round, a bit plump. At the time of the picture, Giacomo was studying in Milan and wrote her affectionate letters whose gaiety has an edge of homesickness. In addition to the details

Celle. In the modest ancestral home of the Puccini family a simple, affecting museum has been installed. Its exhibits include the handsome, capacious bed in which, according to tradition, the composer Giacomo was born in 1858. (Paolo Tosi)

of his own life, he wrote her about a wide variety of subjects: the latest female fashions in Milan, the works being performed in the city's theaters, the menus of his frugal meals. He wrote on 9 December 1880:

Dear Saint Thomas . . . here the women wear long capes, tight at the waist, dark, tobacco-colored, the hood lined with a lighter satin. Bocconi [a department store, later renamed "La Rinascente" by d'Annunzio] has them and sells them for 35, 40, and 50 lire. Fur hats with big talons of animals, the claws gilded, go very well. Then simple dresses of striped wool, pleated skirts, and for decoration they sell some big woolen scarfs with satin edges, that you tie below the hips fancifully, and they cost 3 or 4 lire each . . . Yesterday I went to hear *Carmen,* a very beautiful opera. Full house! This evening I'm going to eat beans at Marchi's with Santori, who is here, doing his military service . . . I've written a post card because it costs less, I'll write again soon. Make me laugh because I'm bored.[17]

On 4 April he wrote:

Dear Ramelde, I've received the suit that you, poor thing, have bought me with the sweat of your brow. You can't imagine the effect this sweet act of yours had on me. Tears came to my eyes. Poor Ramelde, how good you are to me, who don't deserve it! And how can I return your kindness? You know better than I how broke I am . . . Enough of this! One way or another, I'm going to send you the hat. However, not just yet, because now it would be absolutely impossible . . . Great preparations here for the Exhibition. You should see! They are preparing great theater performances: Carmen, Don Giovanni, Mefistofele, Ugonotti, Semiramide, Guglielmo Tell, Guarany, etc. Doesn't that seem something to you?[18]

As these letters show, Giacomo followed female fashion, remarking even the slightest details, and he could describe clearly the Milanese toilettes to his provincial sisters. Between Giacomo and Ramelde there was also a musical correspon-

17. Marchetti, *Puccini com'era*, 16.
18. Ibid., 29.

dence, a normal thing in the Puccini household, where music was always the most important thing. Ramelde, however was the only Puccini sister who could actually follow her brother's work, advising him in the choice of librettos. In her secret diary, she wrote:

> Through no merit of mine, I must confess that Giacomo pays great heed to my observations, though they are based only on common sense, and he proved this to me only recently when he gave up ipso facto the idea of Cyrano . . . Darling Giacomo! Because of the world he lives in he can no longer tell good from bad! He's promised to send me tomorrow Fanfani's libretto entitled Cecco d'Ascoli, and, depending on my impression, I will begin my work of demolition, as I did for the other, if I cannot give my approval.[19]

Ramelde was sensitive, intelligent, and able to express her thoughts logically and clearly. Very religious and without bigotry, in her mature years she became an eager student of theology. Despite her lively, jolly nature, her monotonous and sometimes petty life and her uncertain health gradually spent her enthusiasm and natural vitality. On 2 February 1883 she married Raffaello Franceschini, of an illustrious Lucca family. After the marriage, new responsibilities and interests assumed a dominant role in Ramelde's existence; still her profound tie with her family and, especially, with Giacomo, remained steadfast. Now that all the sisters had separate lives, it was Ramelde who kept up the contacts. It was she who gave Giacomo news of the old maidservants in the Puccini house, especially Assunta, who had brought all of them up since their early childhood. Giacomo wrote Ramelde from Milan in December 1906: "Poor Assunta. Give her my greetings . . . Poor Assunta! The memory of my early life is fading more and more."[20]

After a few years of marriage, Ramelde had to move to Pescia, where her husband directed a tax-collecting office. In the little city, which she always hated, Ramelde led a boring,

19. Ibid., 19–20.
20. Ibid., 325, 343.

Errata for THE PUCCINI COMPANION

Page   Entry should read:

327   Carner, Mosco. "The Exotic Element in Puccini." *The Musical Quarterly*
       22/1 (January 1936):45–67. In Italian in *Symposium: Giacomo Puccini*
       no. 2:173–99. Milan: Ricordi, 1959.

328   Gallini, Natale. "Gli anni giovanili di Giacomo Puccini." In *L'Approdo*
       Musicale 2/6:28–52. Rome: ERI, April–June 1959.

       Leibowitz, René. "L'Arte di Giacomo Puccini." In *L'Approdo Musicale*
       2/6:3–27. Rome: ERI, April–June 1959.

       Atlas, Allan W. "Newly Discovered Sketches for Puccini's *Turandot* at
       the Pierpont Morgan Library." *Cambridge Opera Journal* 3/2 (1991):
       173–93.

       Döhring, Sieghart. "Musikalischer Realismus in Puccinis *Tosca*."
       Analecta Musicologica 22 (1984):249–96.

329   Gavazzeni, Gianandrea. "La *Tosca* come campione esecutivo puccini-
       ano." In *Critica pucciniana,* edited by Comitato Nazionale per le ono-
       ranze a Giacomo Puccini nel cinquantenario della morte, 52–62.
       Lucca: *Nuova Grafica Lucchese,* 1976. Reprinted in *Quaderni Pucciniani*
       (1982):77–88.

       NOTE: the following entry, under Michele Girardi, should be on
       page 330, under Jürgen Maehder:

       _____. "Studien zum Fragmentcharakter von Giacomo Puccinis
       Turandot." *Analecta musicologica* 22 (1984):298–379. Reprinted in
       Italian as "Studi sul carattere di frammento della *Turandot* di Giacomo
       Puccini." *Quaderni Pucciniani* 2 (1985):79–163. Condensed and in
       English as "Puccini's *Turandot*: A Fragment—Studies in Franco
       Alfano's Completion of the Score." In *Turandot: Giacomo Puccini.*
       English National Opera Guide 27, edited by Nicholas John, 35–53.
       London: ENO, 1984.

330   Maehder, Jürgen. "Paris-Bilder. Zur Transformation von Henry Mürgers Roman in den *Bohème*-Opern Puccinis und Leoncavallos." *Jahrbuch der Opernforschung* 2 (1986):109–76. In Italian, as "Immagini di Parigi: La trasformazione del romanzo *Scènes de la vie de bohème* di Henry Murger nelle opere di Puccini e Leoncavallo." *Nuova Rivista Musicale Italiana* 24 (1990):402–55.

Maguire, Janet. "Puccini's Version of the Duet and Final Scene of *Turandot*." *The Musical Quarterly* 74/1 (1990):319–59.

331   Morini, Mario. "*Tosca* all'anagrafe della storia." *La Scala* 160 (March 1963). Reprinted in House program, Teatro La Fenice (1978–79): 129–37, and in *49o Maggio Musicale Fiorentino* (1986):57ff.

Torchi, Luigi. "*Tosca*: Melodramma in tre atti di Giacomo Puccini." *Rivista Musicale Italiana* 7 (1900):78–114.

Meyrowitz, Jan. "Puccini: musica a doppio fondo." Trans. Massimo Mila. *Nuova Rivista Musicale Italiana* 10/1 (1976):3–19.

332   Sartori, Claudio. "I sospetti di Puccini." *Nuova Rivista Musicale Italiana* 11/2 (1977):232–41.

Damerini, Adelmo. "*Suor Angelica* in una rare bozza di stampa." In *Giacomo Puccini nel centenario della nascita*, 84–88. Lucca: Industria Grafica Lorenzetti e Natali, 1958.

333   D'Amico, Fedele. "Una ignorata pagina malipierana di *Suor Angelica*." *Rassegna Musicale Curci* 28/1 (April 1975):5–14.

Santi, Piero. "nei cieli bigi . . ." *Nuova Rivista Musicale Italiana* 1/2 (1967):350–58.

334   Fairtile, Linda. *Giacomo Puccini's Operatic Revisions as Manifestations of His Compositional Priorities*. Ph.D. diss., New York University, 1996.

Ferrari, Franca. *Il linguaggio melodico di Puccini nella drammaturgia di "Bohème," "Tosca" e "Madama Butterfly."* Ph.D. diss., Università degli Studi di Bologna, 1989–90.

confined life, with difficult periods caused by some serious mismanagement in her husband's office. Raffaello Franceschini was born in Lucca on 17 April 1854; he was short, with black, curly hair; his distinguishing feature was his receding chin. Puccini thus describes him humorously in a letter from Milan on 5 January 1894, written to Raffaello himself: "Languishing, I see again your noble, yellowish countenance, I dream of your tall, slim form, your plump and provoking leg, your elusive chin."[21]

He must have been a good man, somewhat stubborn, touchy at times. Even if there were occasional ruptures and resentments between them, Giacomo got along with him well. Because of the special bond between Giacomo and Ramelde, and because Franceschini, like the composer, was an enthusiastic hunter and was always ready to accept his brother-in-law's sometimes heavy jokes, a comradely friendship grew up between the two men. And so, for many years, there was a fairly regular correspondence between Giacomo and the Franceschinis. For the composer, Ramelde and her family by now represented the most solid tie with Lucca. After five years of marriage, Ramelde gave birth to her first daughter, Albina, born in Lucca on 14 December 1887. Two other girls were born later, Nina and Nelda.

In the summer of 1895, to escape the heat at Torre del Lago, Puccini and his family moved close to Pescia, to the Villa del Castellaccio, property of Count Orsi Bertolini. He now was able to see his sister and brother-in-law often, and also to give Raffaello a number of little tasks, which the brother-in-law was always quite happy to perform: procuring wine, a lamp, a cap, trousers, blotting paper, pens—every day Giacomo seemed to need something. For Ramelde, Giacomo's visits were always a great joy, because of both her affection for her brother and this opportunity to meet new people and talk about music.

In 1903, while *Butterfly* was being composed, Giacomo and Elvira were involved in a bad automobile accident, and Giacomo suffered a severe leg fracture. At that time Giacomo was

21. Ibid., 181.

carrying on a fairly long-term affair with a girl from Turin known only as Corinna, who has otherwise eluded biographers' investigation. In April of that same year, while Giacomo was still convalescent and the fracture was proving slow to heal, Elvira's husband Narciso Gemignani died. An exchange of letters at this time between Puccini's frequent librettist and close friend Luigi Illica and Ramelde indicates their common effort to separate Giacomo definitively from Corinna and hasten his marriage to Elvira. In April 1903, Illica wrote Ramelde about a frank conversation in which he had clarified to Giacomo the legal situation, pointing out the risks he was running though his relationship with Corinna. Ramelde's reply of 21 April is as lucid and clear as Illica's letter, and it shows how eagerly she wanted to see her brother's situation properly settled. Finally, on 3 January 1904, Giacomo and Elvira were married in the church of Torre del Lago. The next day Giacomo wrote Ramelde: "Are you satisfied now?"

Ramelde's relations with Elvira, rather cold at the beginning, grew gradually more cordial, and at a certain point the sisters-in-law became good friends. In the last ten years of her life, Ramelde was constantly afflicted with various illnesses. A serious liver ailment was the cause of her early death. Her brother looked after her with affection and concern, seeing that she had the best doctors, defraying the expenses of hospital and operation. Despite excellent treatment, Ramelde died in Bologna on 8 April 1912, at the age of fifty-one.

Giacomo's brother Michele was born in Lucca on 19 April 1864; little or nothing is known about his childhood. He was surely much loved and cherished by his mother, his sisters, and by the two maids Assunta and Carola. In the family he was affectionately called "Mi'ele" (the Tuscan pronunciation of his name, and also the word for "honey"), Michelino, and also Belatti. As often happens with the last-born in a large family, they went on treating him as a baby when he was already a growing boy, and this upbringing contributed to Michele's prolonged immaturity. He remained a child for all his brief life. Giacomo mentions him for the first time in a letter to his mother from Milan in February 1881: "Tell Michele's gusciaro [joc. husk-maker] to work on Landi's overcoat,"[22] and to Ramelde on 24 March of that year: "Tell that shameless Belatti [Michele] not to forget that he only stopped nursing a short while ago: even fleas get the cough."[23]

This was when Michele was seventeen! Physically he was very tall and slender, with a long, thin face like his father's, whereas Giacomo resembled his mother. Following the family tradition, Michele also enrolled at the Lucca Conservatory and was still studying there when his brother Giacomo moved to Milan. As was natural, Michele also wanted to go to the Lombard capital, where there were greater opportunities. After a brief visit there for his army physical examination and for the entrance examinations at the Conservatory, in 1884 he moved to the city. He wrote to his mother from Milan, on 31 March 1884:

Dear Mamma, Saturday I had my [army] examination, it went splendidly, what's more the doctor told me I was a strong young man. Tell your doctor gentlemen that I have never been consumptive. They examined me for almost an hour. Tomorrow, Tuesday, I will have the first practical examination [at the Conservatory] and then Saturday, the second oral. Then Monday the written ones start. Giacomo couldn't put me up and I found a room for 50 centesimi a day. For dinner we go to Aida's and with 1.50 we eat soup, two courses and an 8th of a liter of wine.[24]

Giacomo found him a job in the music shop of Alessandro Pigna in the Galleria Vittorio Emanuele. Michele attended the Conservatory, but, though he studied there for three years, he never received a diploma. Giacomo's friends became his friends, and so Michele was admitted to the Milanese musical world. His brother treated him with affectionate superiority, always considering him a boy.

In fact, Michele's behavior was often childish, though he was now twenty. The sisters were more indulgent than Gia-

22. Ibid., 27.
23. Ibid., 28.
24. Ibid., 51.

como, and their reproaches were always mild. When their mother was already ill, Tomaide wrote from Lucca to Michele in Milan, 18 May 1884:

> Poor Mamma, you can't imagine how sad it makes us to see her like this. If only she had no more troubles, but they never end, and you in particular have caused her some now, for which I must reproach you at her instruction. The first is the *fuffigno* [little deceit] of the theater, which is not just talk, as you said, and the proof is the letter I enclose. Mamma absolutely cannot pay, especially now that she is ill. Though we all do everything we can, so much money has to be spent . . . Her second worry was the microscopes: you said you had pawned them for two lire, and instead we had to pay four. The third was the hat. Sor Emilio [identity unknown] said to Otilia: "Why did Michelino take that hat and then go off without paying for it?"[25]

These were boyish tricks, and yet Michele did take his job seriously at Pigna's and worked so hard that he had little time left for studying. Nevertheless, in June 1884, he took the Conservatory examinations.

After his mother's death, Giacomo stayed on in Lucca to work at his new opera *Edgar,* which had been commissioned by the publisher Ricordi. Michele, after the holidays, went back to Milan to continue his studies. It is not clear whether he resumed working at Pigna's. From Milan he wrote to his uncle Nicolao Cerù in Lucca on 6 December 1884:

> Dear Doctor, on your saint's day, though I am far away, I have not forgotten this fine day that, for so many years, we spent together . . . My health is very good, but the weather is so terrible that it's an effort to keep on one's feet: cold, fog, dampness are everyday matters. The temperature is zero. Still I work and lead a quiet life.[26]

Michele felt a special attachment for the old uncle, a bit gruff but always ready to help his nephews. The young man

25. Ibid., 59.
26. Ibid., 117.

probably felt in the other's austere honesty a paternal presence he had never enjoyed. Giacomo tried to act as a father to Michele, but he was still a youth himself and, further, beseiged by endless problems. From Milan, on 29 August 1884, Giacomo wrote his brother: "Do something. Think: you're old now! Ciao. 1000 kisses, Giacomo."[27]

And, from Lucca, he wrote Michele on 2 April 1885: "Dear Miele . . . Work. The exam is near, stay in the house a lot. Work a bit. You know you can do it! Ciao. Study, study!"

And again on 22 April of that same year Giacomo repeated: "Work, for God's sake."

In Giacomo's brief, telegraphic messages from Lucca, in which local news alternates with errands for Michele to run, the older brother never stops urging the younger to study. The examinations of 1884/85 went well; the report shows that Michele received good grades in harmony and also in the other subjects, though, because of absences, in the fourth trimester he was not given any grades.

Giacomo wrote Michele from Lucca on 22 June 1885: "Dear Michele, happy about the exam. My opinion is you should come to Lucca and not wait till 20 July."

Michele's studies continued irregularly until 1887 but did not lead to a final diploma. Almost all the time he shared lodgings with Giacomo (who, since the end of 1886, had been living with Elvira, after she had left her husband). Michele accompanied them on their summer holidays at Caprino Bergamasco and at Pizzamiglio, near Chiasso.

Michele also stayed with Dr. Cerù in Lucca, and with Ramelde at San Martino. But his relations with his brothers-in-law Raffaello and Enrico were not always good. Michele persisted in his childish ways and his little deceits, arousing the indignation of his brothers-in-law and also of Giacomo, who had his own problems. Michele's sisters helped him in secret, and for them he was always their beloved Belatti, the baby of the family. Still, Michele needed someone to take care of him steadily; and he also had his own sense of dignity. In spring of 1889, after a disagreement with Giacomo, Michele

27. This and the following quotations are taken from letters in private collections.

decided to go and live on his own, and he found himself a furnished room in Via Stella. He was still broke, and in May or June of 1889 he wrote to Tomaide:

> Dearest Tomaide, For the first time that I write you since leaving Lucca it is because of a serious nuisance which saddens me, too. But so many things happen in life, and luckily there are people we love, and who return our affection, so it isn't painful to have to ask for something once in a great while. Listen, I have had a disagreement with Giacomo, and I find myself very broke, with no income. But now I don't have time [to earn] because the exams are very near. I would need about twenty lire to fit out the room and pay for the piano I've rented . . . However, I will give it back to you in the month of August when I come to Lucca for *Edgar,* since I've already been engaged by Francesconi as assistant conductor and stage manager . . . If you can do me this favor, I thank you in advance, and believe me it is something that pains me very much, because as you have seen in the past I would never ask anyone for help . . . Don't tell anyone about it, please, because that would hurt me very much, don't even tell Otilia or Cerù.

But Giacomo's opera was not given, and Michele was therefore jobless. It is certain that Michele sat for the Conservatory exams in June of 1889, but the result is not clear. In the meanwhile, he had been coming to the decision to go abroad and seek his fortune in foreign parts. After living on his own for some months in Milan, he wanted to assert his independence and show his sisters and his brother that he could look after himself and perhaps even succeed. So he wrote to Giacomo in the spring of 1889: "I have now reached an age when I must commit myself, and if I never begin, when will I begin? Don't worry: I am working, and I hope to do well in the examination . . . I thank you for all your concern for me, which for various reasons of mine I would not have deserved."

In October 1889 with his Lucca friend Ulderigo (known as Ghigo) Tabaracci, he sailed for Buenos Aires. The ship stopped at Barcelona, at Las Palmas, and Tangier. After twenty-two days of navigation, the friends landed in Buenos Aires. Michele's letters demonstrate that he was a good writer, better than his brother. His descriptions of South American life are vivid and lively, and they give us a colorful picture of Argentina at the time. Though he always makes a show of being light-hearted and optimistic, things cannot have gone well for him. He immediately found work giving music lessons, and in his free time he worked as a journalist, contributing to the *Nazione Italiana* under the pen name of Serchio. Buenos Aires, however, was expensive, and his earnings disappeared quickly. There were many Italians in the city then, and Michele found numerous acquaintances from Lucca and Milan. His jovial nature made everyone fond of him; but alone as he was, so far from his family, he was very frightened at the idea of falling ill. Yellow fever was raging, and many immigrants were dying. From Buenos Aires, 22 March 1890, Michele wrote Giacomo:

> Yellow fever (brrr brrr) has put in its appearance in this country. In the street where I live, namely Calle Moreno no. 580, which is the post office, the first case of galloping yellow fever occurred, and as I write five people have died at 20 numbers from my house. I am a bit scared, because it acts very rapidly on the liver, and you know how I am fixed. Enough of that. I must be patient. I hope and believe, however, that I have certainly arranged a big deal and it will certainly be the beginning of my fortune. Because if I stay in Buenos Aires I won't put aside anything, nothing at all . . . They have asked me if I want to go to Cuccuy [*sic*, the actual name is Jujuy] in the north of the republic, near the Bolivian border. I would be professor in a state school for women, as singing master . . . The senator Juan José Lopez would take me there; he is the governor of the area . . . not a bad supporter . . . In this way I avoid yellow fever and the extra expenses I would have in Buenos Aires.

So Michele left Buenos Aires and set off for Jujuy. He wrote regularly to his brother, to his sisters, and to his uncle Cerù. The description of his journey, very vivid, was repeated, with variations, in several letters. He wrote to Giacomo from Jujuy, 30 May 1890:

I left B. Aires on Thursday 10 April at 8½ in the evening, and I arrived at Rosario de Sta. Fè at 9½ in the morning. Thirteen hours on the train. I stopped over in Rosario until the evening and at 9 I left again for Cordoba, where I arrived Sunday evening at 11½. I slept on the train, and set off again in the morning at 7, and arrived at Tuquman [*sic*] and continued the journey until 12 noon for Chilcos. But towards 11 in the evening, when I was traveling, a terrible storm, right in the *Pampas* meant that we could not continue the journey because the line was broken. What to do then? We had to spend the night in the *prairie* with no house or roof or anything to eat. In the morning the storm continued to rage more and more violently and there was no escape or way to continue. Finally, as God willed, at 2 P.M. we set off again on our journey and arrived at 9¼ in the evening of Thursday in Chilcos. And this is where the train journey ended; that is to say, the good and (for here) comfortable part.

I stayed in Chilcos Friday until 2 P.M. and set off again for Jujuy in the *Messaggeria,* a kind of medieval stage-coach drawn by 16 mules. Here it is called *galera* [galley, or prison, in Italian] the most appropriate name it could be given. We proceeded normally until 2 at night without hindrances, but when we were nearing the great Chaco desert, the mules could no longer continue the journey there, because the wheels of the *Messaggeria* sank into the muck. What was to be done? We were 8 travelers, all armed to the teeth. I had a revolver and a box of bullets, and a stiletto (which everybody carries here). We resigned ourselves to waiting till morning, but at just the right moment, after we had been in the *Messaggeria* for an hour, awaiting daylight, with indescribable cold, we were attacked by a band of *Cirnani,* terrible savages of the Chacco [*sic*], armed with arrows, spears, and daggers. I can't tell you how afraid I was at that unexpected visitation, with no possible escape. The night was very dark and hardly permitted us to see these Indians except at intervals when the lightning flashed. We 8 passengers and 4 drivers decided to put up a fierce fight. In fact, some shooting started, and the Indians, more furious than ever, advanced more and more. They howled like damned souls . . . As luck would have it, after all the revolver shots we fired, nobody was then heard from. Either they died or they ran off. Then, as a precaution, because others might return in greater numbers, we decided to leave before daybreak. But how? We couldn't stay in the *Messaggeria*. Jujuy was 54 leagues off (that means 284 kilometers) on the state road. But we couldn't take the road because we would sink into the thick mud. We couldn't turn back because we feared a return of the Indians. So? Danger threatened us from all sides, and we decided that each of us would take one of the *Messaggeria's* mules and ride, across the prairie, as best we could, to reach some place or other as soon as possible and buy a horse. And that is what we did. We 8 passengers and the 4 drivers set off and at 7 A.M. we arrived at a staging post, where we left the mules in the hands of the drivers, bought two horses for 20 escudos each and we set off again around noon. We had to start crossing the Cordillera de los Andes which, by this road, was much shorter, namely 38 leagues (190 km.) to arrive at Jujuy. That evening we were in the midst of the mountains in indescribable cold. We killed a *cordero* (ram) that someone from the country had caught along the way

San Michele in Foro in Lucca was the Puccinis' neighborhood church. Giacomo was baptized there and, according to family tradition, he received his first music lessons from his father on the keys of the little organ in the aerie-like loft. (Courtesy of the Italian Government Travel Office, New York)

with a lasso, we skinned it, put it on some coals, and so we fell asleep in a cave with a big fire in front of us, in fear of the fierce animals that are numerous in the Cordillera.

And Michele continues:

I'll continue, if it doesn't bore you. These things seem incredible, but you should see what these places are like. Buenos Aires is a European city, all wrong, without principle or taste of its own. It's like a Russian salad. Finally we resumed the journey Monday and arrived at last at Cobos, a village 18 leagues on. There we refreshed ourselves, I rested in the hide of a Lama (an American camel) stretched from one door of a room to another, like a hammock, and you sleep very well. In the morning we set off again, still on horseback, mind you, and we arrived at the pueblo Pericco del Carmen at 4 in the evening . . . We left Pericco and, after six days of riding, we arrived at five in the evening at Jujuy . . . Once in Jujuy I went immediately to the Hotel Universal and I stayed in bed for 2 days I was so tired.

Jujuy suited Michele at once. He was welcomed personally by Senator Perez, by the Mayor, and by the Directora of the National Female College. He began his lessons in vocal music and Italian language. He was also much in demand for private lessons, in music and in French. The Governor asked to take lessons on the cello—"where he got it from I never found out."

Michele also played the piano at dances, but accepted no pay." I would lose prestige," he wrote. "I may play all night, but they have greater respect for me . . ."

The Italian Consul, Dr. Antonio Baldi, from Barga (not far from Lucca), hired him as secretary at fifty escudos per month plus extras. Now for the first time in his life Michele was comfortably settled. He was working, making money, respected, and he was proud of his new status. He wrote to Ramelde on 8 August 1890: "I have nothing to complain of in my new residence in Jujuy. On the contrary, I am quite content to be here. I am the pet of the grandest houses of the whole province. And when I think that in Lucca you used to call me *pelandrone* [slacker]. How different things are now.

But there's a proverb that says: 'Eating teaches you how to drink,' and it's really true."

He also continued writing for the newspapers:

I am an editor at the paper "Ferro carillos" in Spanish. And how do I manage everything? I wrote an article the other day that has agitated all the Senoritas of the town. The title was *Soledad* (solitude), I will send it to you, along with another entitled "Nocturne," a "romantic" fantasy, and it came out very well. I am considered the Carducci of Jujuy. Sunday there was the great feast of the Savior, the patron of the city. I conducted the Mass in church, wearing full evening dress with white tie, and I composed a motet for soprano that I had one of my pupils sing. It was a state occasion. But I get along also with the Priests. I wrote a march for the inauguration of the *Ferro Carillo* (railroad) that everyone liked very much.

In that far-off little city in the Andes, Michele found himself, and he resumed the tradition of his Lucca ancestors, respected church composers and musicians, who performed their own works in church or in the Palace of Government. But he was always homesick for his family: "I am relegated here in a town surrounded by the Cordilleras de los Andes, wickedly cold, in the midst of the snow, and it often snows here: no fire in the houses, wood is a luxury for the shiftlessness you find in the sons of the town."

He always asked Giacomo for news of his music and his latest works. When Michele received a copy of Giacomo's string quartet *Crisantemi* he was delighted, and he actually made piano versions of it, for two hands and for four. When he speaks of his brother and his works, Michele always displays the greatest respect and admiration. Like his mother and sisters before him, Miele also sees Giacomo as a genius, but without any envy: his only desire is to be worthy of his older brother. But a sad fate lay in store for him. The news of his unhappy end was conveyed by Ulderigo Tabarracci, his traveling companion on the voyage out. Homesick and lonely, he had became involved with the wife of a very rich and powerful man. The affair was discovered by the woman's husband, who challenged poor Michele to a duel with pistols. The duel took place, and the husband was wounded in the shoulder. The woman's brother, who was chief of police, seeing that the guilty youth had not been killed, vowed that Michele would die anyway. Michele had to flee, without even going back to his house for his things. Pursued by gauchos and police, he made another, even more terrible journey to Buenos Aires, where he stayed for a while. Then he decided to emigrate to Brazil and seek his fortune again in Rio de Janeiro. Here he was taken in by his friend Tabarracci, but Michele was weak and dejected and, a few days later, he fell ill with the yellow fever he had so feared. Tabarracci called a doctor and took great care of his friend, but Michele finally had to be removed to a hospital, where he died on the night of 12 March 1891 at the age of twenty-seven.

Translated by William Weaver

THE MUSICAL WORLD OF THE YOUNG PUCCINI

Julian Budden

Julian Budden, the English musicologist, was educated at Oxford and the Royal College of Music, London. For some years he was the chief producer of opera on BBC radio. His books include the three-volume study *The Operas of Verdi* and a biography of Verdi in the Master Musicians series, for which he is currently writing a biography of Puccini.

Puccini grew up during an age of transition in Italian music, a time when the country's traditions underwent the biggest upheaval in their history. For two centuries Italy had maintained her supremacy as the ultimate source of the high style in music, even if she had not supplied the greatest composers. Bach perfected his art by copying the concertos of Vivaldi; Handel learned his operatic trade in the south; Haydn, his contemporaries said (though he himself denied this), owed something of his craft to Sammartini. Yet by failing to come to terms with those two great conquests of the late neighteenth century, the symphony and the quartet, Italian music drifted into a European backwater. From now on its empire was confined to opera, whose boundaries were in due course defined by Gioachino Rossini (1792–1868). For forty years the territory proved fertile enough, cultivated by Rossini himself and his immediate successors with the aid of the world's finest singers. But the lack of a symphonic tradition such as would sustain the Austro-German line from Mozart onward soon led to an exhaustion of the soil. Verdi, last and greatest of the post-Rossinian school, would hardly have achieved his prodigious self-renewal without having spent considerable time in Paris, where a far larger variety of music was to be heard than in Italy. If there were no great French symphonists active at the time, apart from the isolated figure of Berlioz, at least there was a public for symphonic music. When the young Mercadante first ventured on a large-scale vocal composition, a local critic advised him once and for all to abandon those sterile *sinfonie* that had won him the plaudits of his teachers and devote himself henceforth to the sublime, the only true art, opera.[1] This was a view that remained prevalent for half a century and more.

A glance at two of the chief novelties of 1857–58, about the time of Puccini's birth, will suffice to show the stagnation into which Italian opera, Verdi's *oeuvre* apart, had fallen. Mercadante's *Pelagio,* first given at the Teatro San Carlo, Naples, in February 1857, is an old-fashioned neoclassical drama of love versus patriotism of the type that the composer increasingly favored in his later years. Not only is it set out in the usual pattern of self-contained arias, duets, and multimovement ensembles but also the title role is written for a florid baritone, a vocal category that even Donizetti had abandoned in his mature works. Such a style inevitably imposes a basis of harmonic simplicity. Yet Mercadante was reputed the most "learned" amongst his countrymen and admired as such even by Liszt. In the north Errico Petrella presented *Jone* at La Scala in 1858. Based on Bulwer-Lytton's *The Last Days of Pompeii,* its forms are those of the 1830s and 40s extended and elaborated. If Verdi exaggerated in describing its composer as no musician, this opera, for many years regarded as Petrella's

---

1. B. Notarnicola, *Saverio Mercadante nella gloria e nella luce* (Rome, 1949), 18.

masterpiece, offers nothing more deserving of attention than a spectacular eruption of Vesuvius to bring down the final curtain.

But already the seeds of change were being sown. In 1859 Abramo Basevi, a doctor from Livorno, founded a quartet society in Florence whose public concerts were devoted to the classics of the repertory from Haydn to Mendelssohn. He himself published a detailed analysis of Beethoven's opus 18; its naiveté may make us smile today, but it heralded a serious approach to an art form that had previously been regarded as of no account in Italy. Five years later his initiative was followed up by the Società del Quartetto in Milan, of which Giulio Ricordi was secretary and Arrigo Boito chief propagandist. Verdi, it is true, viewed the enterprise with mistrust as a mere exercise in Germanization. Why not a vocal quartet society, he suggested, to perform the works of Palestrina? Nor can Boito's high-flown rhetoric have been much to his taste (". . . the sun is simpler than a carnation, the sea simpler than a brook; Mendelssohn's Adagio op. 87 is simpler than Mozart's Andante from K. 387"[2]); but it did not prevent him from enriching the treasury with an offering of his own.

Public orchestral concerts were slower to take root. Valuable pioneering work was done here by the Concerti Popolari of Turin, instituted in 1872 under the direction of Carlo Pedrotti. At first they hardly qualified as symphony concerts. The inaugural program consisted of five overtures, the prelude to Wagner's *Lohengrin* (a calculated risk, this), and the scherzo only from Beethoven's *Eroica* "since the symphony itself is rather long"[3] (so the public was advised). In his delightful and witty account of musical life in Turin, written in 1914, Giuseppe Depanis lamented that "the Italians of the nineteenth century, disowning their glorious traditions, neglected up until the last few years every form of music that was not operatic. With rare exceptions instrumental music did not exist in Italy other than display pieces for the piano or the violin, and symphonic music was confined to operatic overtures and pre-

2. "Mendelssohn in Italia," in Arrigo Boito, *Tutti gli scritti,* ed. P. Nardi (Milan, 1942), 1169–72.
3. G. Depanis, *I concerti popolari e il Teatro Regio di Torino* (Turin, 1914), 1:22.

ludes."[4] Nonetheless, in 1873 the promoters of the Concerti Popolari ventured on two full-length symphonies—Beethoven's First and Mendelssohn's Fourth (the *Scotch*). Neither was a success. Two years later the practice was discontinued, and it was back to overtures, Mozart's *Rondo alla Turca* orchestrated with extra percussion, Boccherini's minuet played by full strings, and the odd fantasy on operatic themes featuring instrumental virtuosi. In 1877 Mendelssohn's violin concerto made a solitary appearance, flanked by Glinka's *Jota aragonese* and a movement from one of Bach's flute sonatas arranged for orchestra. At the end of the year the organizing committee once more launched a four-movement symphony, namely Beethoven's Second, sugaring the pill with the prelude to *La traviata* followed by a Liszt Hungarian Rhapsody and an orchestration of Schumann's *Träumerei*. Not until 1880 did full-length symphonies become an established feature of the city's concert life. Yet Turin was already far ahead of the rival capitals in this respect. When Franco Faccio took the orchestra of La Scala, Milan, to the Paris International Exhibition of 1878, their *pièce de résistance* was Ponchielli's "Dance of the Hours."

Lucca too offered orchestral concerts during the 1870s given by the Società Orchestrale Boccherini under the direction of the city's violin teacher, Augusto Michelangeli. Here the fare, as might be expected in a provincial center, was still more meager, each program being diluted by piano solos, vocal and instrumental items with piano accompaniment, operatic fantasias galore, and the occasional trifle by a local celebrity. Never was there anything more substantial than one of the longer overtures. The first symphony to reach Lucca was Haydn's *Farewell* in 1881, in whose finale there is at least some action to sustain the spectator's interest. When four of the society's members presented a movement from one of Haydn's quartets, the critic of the *Provincia di Lucca* reproved them for sitting in a group and playing to each other rather than standing up and performing toward the audience.[5]

4. Ibid., 43.
5. *La Provincia di Lucca*, 5 July 1879.

In their respective calls for reform, Basevi and Boito agreed on one point: that the revival of Italy's instrumental tradition should have as its ultimate aim the regeneration of her national art form, the opera; and for both the supreme model was Meyerbeer, "whose works," Boito declared, "once appreciated, have caused Italian operas to collapse in their hundreds like the bricks of Jericho's walls: most of Bellini's, the greater part of Donizetti's, almost all of Rossini's . . . and some of Verdi's."[6] If Meyerbeer's operas had been slow to take root in Italy, the reason is that the right conditions for their performance were lacking. The rapid turnover of new works required at the principal theaters combined with the long-standing division of musical direction between the *primo violino* and the *maestro concertatore* to preclude adequate rehearsal. But by 1860 a new breed of professional conductor was in the ascendant led by Angelo Mariani, who could mount in a matter of weeks the kind of opera which in Paris had taken months to prepare. Nor was Meyerbeer the only beneficiary. In 1862 Gounod's *Faust* with recitatives added began its international career as an honorary Italian opera. Verdi's chief offerings of the 1860s, *La forza del destino* and *Don Carlos,* were both intended for foreign theaters and a wider, more sophisticated public than was to be found in Italy; yet the performance of *Don Carlos* at Bologna in 1868 under Mariani was by all accounts superior to its premiere in Paris the year before. With all this the long stagnant waters of native opera began to stir. In the north a generation of composers that included Antonio Cagnoni and Filippo Marchetti (author of a briefly popular *Ruy Blas*) made increasing efforts to absorb, however tentatively and often ineptly, ultramontane techniques. Boito went further, striking out in an entirely new direction with his original five-act *Mefistofele* of 1868—a monumental fiasco, as it turned out, but nonetheless a sign of the times.

The most influential of all foreign operas during that decade was Meyerbeer's *L'africaine.* First given in Italy in the autumn of 1865 under Mariani, it was performed in all the major theaters of the Peninsula during the next five years. It was suffi-

---

6. Boito, *Tutti gli scritti,* 1122.

ciently popular to rate a quotation in Lauro Rossi's theatrical satire *Il maestro e una cantante* (1867), along with "Casta diva," the *Guillaume Tell* overture, and a couple of numbers from *Il trovatore*. From it Italian audiences acquired for the first time a taste for the exotic, for folk idioms real or invented that reached beyond the borders of Spain or Switzerland. Antonio Gomes's *Il Guarany* and Verdi's *Aida* both carry the mark of *L'africaine*. On its shoulders, one might say, Italy entered finally into an era, however brief, of "grand opera," or "opera ballo," as it came to be called.

A name on everybody's lips at the time was Richard Wagner. Long before a note of his music had been heard in Italy, the theories propounded in *Oper und Drama* (1851) were cir-

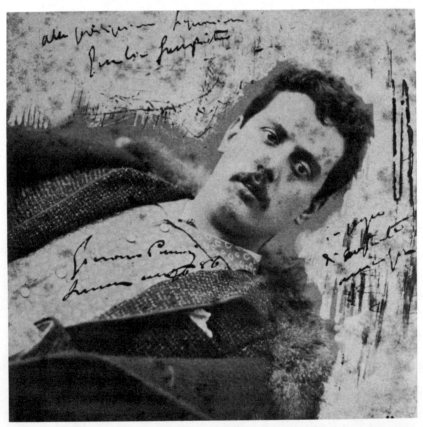

Giacomo Puccini's life coincides with the rise of photography, and so it is unusually well documented. This rare picture is one of the composer's earliest portraits. (Museo Teatrale alla Scala; Foto Saporetti)

culating at second or third hand, so that as early as 1859 Basevi felt able to accuse Verdi of out-Wagnering Wagner in parts
of *Simon Boccanegra* (1857).[7] The publicity, the spate of newspaper articles that attended Wagner's visit to Paris in 1861,
and the resounding fiasco of *Tannhäuser* at the Opéra echoed
throughout Italy, where "music of the future" rapidly became
a catchphrase. The resulting controversy found Basevi and
Boito once again on the same side. To the former it seemed
that Wagner was sacrificing melody to declamation. For Boito
he was the "Bar Jesus of the art of his time. But by great good
fortune his time has now passed. Wagner's first words," he
continued,

> we admit it, had moved us; we had all apprehended the courage
> of his thought, even further than the obscurity of his explana-
> tions allowed us. Wagner was promising to widen the bound-
> aries of rhythm and melody, Wagner in his triple capacity as poet,
> musician, and aesthetic philosopher seemed to us the man born
> and predestined to accomplish the mission of innovation. It was
> a lie. However, it would be somewhat merciless on our part not
> to recognize in his music a certain masterful instinct, a certain
> muscular vigor; but his dramas are feeble, low, and ridiculous in
> relation to the supreme task they are called upon to perform.[8]

One wonders how much of this powerful, muscular music
Boito had heard at the time of writing, or whether he had seen
a single one of the dramas that he so despised.

At any rate the huge prejudice that had built up against the
German master was at last put to the test in the autumn of
1871 when *Lohengrin* was given at the Teatro Comunale,
Bologna, under Mariani, the first Wagner opera ever to be
performed in Italy. Its effect was to plunge the country's musical
life into a turmoil. Many who had expected a tortuous, the-
ory-bound monstrosity found an opera more grandly and
spaciously conceived, more instrumentally orientated than they
were used to, but still an opera; having come to mock they
stayed to cheer. Others maintained an entrenched hostility from

7. A. Basevi, *Studio sulle opere di Giuseppe Verdi* (Florence, 1859), 270.
8. Boito, *Tutti gli scritti*, 1257.

the start. Verdi's appearance in the theater for one of the performances sparked off a demonstration in his favor. "Barbar-
ians out!" thundered the voice of a local dignitary at a concert
in Turin in which Pedrotti had introduced the overture to
Tannhäuser; and a large part of the audience applauded him to
the skies.[9] When *Lohengrin* was mounted at La Scale in 1873,
a persistent claque succeeded in forcing it off the stage after
seven performances. During a particularly stormy "replica"
the composer Antonio Smareglia rolled down the theater's
principal staircase locked in combat with an anti-Wagnerian.
In the columns of the firm's house magazine, the *Gazzetta
Musicale di Milano,* Giulio Ricordi kept up a relentless campaign against the Master of Bayreuth mostly through the
spokesmanship of the aged Francesco Florimo of Naples, who
constantly reiterated Verdi's famous adage: "Torniamo all'an-
tico, e sarà un progresso."

But the Wagnerian tide was not so easily stemmed. Bit by
bit the early canon made its way into Italy—*Tannhäuser* (1872),
Rienzi (1874), *Der fliegende Holländer* (1877). *Lohengrin* lost no
time in becoming a repertory opera. A performance of *Rienzi*
in Bologna in 1876 with the composer himself in attendance
scored a resounding success, despite all Ricordi's attempts to
prove the contrary. In a word, Wagner had come to stay.

Boito, whose wild theorizings had been considerably deflated
by the initial failure of his *Mefistofele* in 1868, allowed himself
to become part of the Wagner industry in Italy. Having paved
the way for *Lohengrin*'s favorable reception in 1871, he was
rewarded with an open letter from the Master himself addressed
to "a young Italian friend" and predicting a possible marriage
of Italian and German art "for which my poor *Lohengrin* may
act as broker."[10] Later Boito would provide translations of
Rienzi, Das Liebesmahl der Apostolen, and *Tristan und Isolde.*
Although he could never subscribe to Wagner's dramatic
methods (he would describe *Die Walküre* as a string of duets

9. Depanis, *I concerti popolari,* 28.
10. Richard Wagner, "Letter to a young Italian friend," cited in Franco Abbiati, *Giu-
    seppe Verdi,* 4 vols. (Milan, 1959), 3:431–34.

that moved with the speed of a stopping train),[11] he claimed that "this Teutonic creator, adorable and odious, will always return to our spirit whenever we are in contact with the vast serenities or spasms of nature or of the heart."[12]

Verdi too would admit that "there is melody in Wagner if you know where to look for it."[13] Puccini and his generation would be Wagnerians to a man, even if many years would pass before the Italian premiere of *Tristan und Isolde* in Bologna in 1888 afforded them the opportunity to come to grips with the composer's mature style, other than in the "bleeding hunks" (Tovey's phrase) that were to be heard in orchestral concerts. "The father [Papà] of all composers present and future"[14] was how Mascagni rated him—which is not to say that either he or his contemporaries ever attempted seriously to follow the doctrines of *Oper und Drama*. What appealed to them above all was the Wagnerian sound.

Indeed the general diffusion of the early Wagner canon had the effect of reinforcing a taste for grand opera, a form against which Wagner himself had firmly set his face from *Das Rheingold* onward. Halévy's *La juive*, Meyerbeer's *Le prophète*, Ambroise Thomas's *Hamlet*, Goldmark's *Die Königin von Saba*, and Gounod's *Cinq Mars* would rub shoulders with *Lohengrin* and *Tannhäuser*. Throughout the 1870s and beyond, foreign works enjoyed pride of place, thus seeming to confirm the gloomy predictions of Verdi and others that Italian opera was set on a decline. When in 1872 Ponchielli's *I promessi sposi* reached the Teatro dal Verme, Milan, in a revised version, sixteen years after its premiere in Cremona, the hitherto neglected composer found himself hailed in certain quarters as the savior of national music for whom Italy had been waiting (not by Verdi, however, who noted a stylistic discrepancy

11. Letter to Verdi, 31 December 1893, in *Carteggio Verdi-Boito,* ed. M. Medici and M. Conati (Parma, 1978), 1:221.
12. Undated letter (1893?) to Camille Bellaigue in P. Nardi, *Vita di Arrigo Boito* (Verona, 1942), 625.
13. P. Fresnay, "Verdi à Paris," 29 March 1886, in M. Conati, *Interviste e incontri con Verdi* (Milan, 1980), 165.
14. Letter to Vittorio Gianfranceschi, 8 April 1887, in *Pietro Mascagni,* ed. Mario Morini (Milan, 1964), 1:273.

between the old and the newly added music, observing that both were behind their respective times).[15] Ricordi decided to groom Ponchielli as Verdi's successor, setting him to work first with Ghislanzoni on a dark medieval drama, *I lituani* (1874) and then with Boito on the highly successful Hugo-derived *La Gioconda* (1876) on which the composer's present-day reputation rests. Both operas, needless to say, are uncompromisingly "grand." The publisher could boast another triumph in the revised *Mefistofele* of 1875, which, though hardly traditional, is at least free from any identifiable foreign influence. However, he too decided to follow his rivals Giovannina Lucca and Edoardo Sonzogno and invest in a foreign composer. His choice was Massenet, whose *Le roi de Lahore* was given with great success at La Scala in 1879 and from whom he subsequently commissioned the opera *Hérodiade*. This was to have been an Italian opera from the start, but Massenet could only work to a French text, which was later translated. Even in its Italian form *Hérodiade* remains unmistakably a French opera; but the impact of its broad, emotionally luxuriant melodies and flexible verbal articulation on the style of music that came into being with Puccini and Mascagni is palpable. Ponchielli, Puccini's last teacher, records a visit to Verdi in which the conversation fell on his own former pupil, "whose type of music we don't like because he follows in the footsteps of Wagner, Massenet etc."[16] The same could have been said of all Puccini's generation, including his fellow Luccan Alfredo Catalani.

By a cruel paradox of history the age of grand opera in Italy coincided with a lean period in the country's economic growth. The 1870s were a time of recession throughout Europe, as Wagner found to his cost when faced with the reckoning for Bayreuth. Ever since the unification of Italy in 1861 there had been a reluctance by successive governments to finance the theaters by a state subsidy. This, they felt, should be the business of the local councils. If the task had been difficult in the 1860s it was ten times more so at a time when operas demanded

15. Letter to Opprandino Arrivabene, 7 March 1874, in Annibale Alberti, *Verdi intimo* (Milan, 1931), 168–69.
16. Undated letter to his wife (April–May 1885?), in Abbiati, *Giuseppe Verdi,* 4:261.

a far larger orchestra and chorus. The result was that by the late 1870s some of the major theaters were having at least temporarily to curtail their seasons and even close their doors. If such was the fate of Venice, Genoa, and Florence, one could hardly expect a flourishing state of affairs in Puccini's Lucca.

Like every Italian city of its size and importance, Lucca boasted an opera season of its own. This was given at the municipal Teatro del Giglio during the weeks surrounding the Festa della Santa Croce in mid-September, thereby allowing the same team of soloists to participate in both events. Under the reign of Duke Carlo Lodovico of Bourbon, an art-loving if irresponsible ruler who could have formed the model for Verdi's Duke of Mantua, the theater achieved considerable distinction. In 1831 it mounted the first Italian production of *Guillaume Tell*. Many of its seasons were managed by the great impresario Alessandro Lanari, who secured a roster of high-ranking soloists that in 1834 included Maria Malibran. This period of glory came to an end in 1847 with the absorption of Lucca into the Grand Duchy of Tuscany, which effectively reduced the city to a satellite of Florence.

With the unification of Italy in 1861 Lucca dwindled even further into provincialism, and its opera season became intermittent, being reduced to two operas at the outside with soloists for the most part recruited locally. The year 1871 offered *La Cenerentola* and *Faust* (judged too severe and abstruse for Luccan taste); 1872, *Lucrezia Borgia* (cancelled after two performances) and a truncated version of *I vespri siciliani,* marred, it seems, by continual chatter from the boxes. In 1873 all resources were devoted to *La forza del destino* ("for the first time an opéra-monstre," declared the *Provincia di Lucca*).[17] The following autumn season passed without any opera, but in June a travelling company gave a few performances of *Crispino e la comare* by the brothers Luigi and Federico Ricci. For the next three years one opera only was the rule: *Maria e Fernando* by the Luccan composer Ferrari (1875), Gomes's *Il Guarany* in the presence of the composer (1876), and a performance of *Guglielmo Tell* (1877), which a local critic declared

17. *La Provincia di Lucca,* 23 August 1873.

unrecognizable.[18] After a year's gap, activity was resumed in
1879 with Petrella's *Jonè* and Donizetti's *Maria di Rohan*. 1880
brought another work by Ferrari, *Maria Menzikoff,* together
with that daring novelty, *La traviata,* last heard at the Giglio
in 1864 in its bowdlerized form as *Violetta*.

More enterprise was shown at the Teatro Pantera, managed
by an association of the local nobility, which usually offered
an opera season during Carnival. The *cartello* for 1871 contained in addition to Donizetti's *Poliuto* two operas by contemporary composers: Pedrotti's *Isabella d'Aragona* and *Asraele
degli Abenceraggi* by Puccini's teacher Carlo Angeloni—"a work
by no means lacking in spontaneous melody," opined the
Luccan critic, "but too many of the situations recall those of
Il trovatore"[19] (clearly a dangerous resemblance). Verdi
monopolized the playbill of 1872 with *Rigoletto* and *Un ballo
in maschera* (". . . the master's best work to date, except, we
are told, for *Aida*".)[20] The next year Cagnoni's *Giralda* was
followed by *Don Pasquale*. Then, after a year's gap, activity
resumed with two tried favorites, Pacini's *Saffo* and Mercadante's *La vestale,* which Puccini recalled having seen and
admired "while I was a student in Lucca."[21] Petrella's *Marco
Visconti* opened the season of 1876, which closed with *Ernani*.
1877 featured a double bill consisting of De Ferrari's *Pipelè*
and Lauro Rossi's early *I falsi monetari;* the other offering was
Le educande di Sorrento by Emilio Usiglio, better known as the
conductor to whom Verdi communicated his alternative ending to "Celeste Aida," designed for tenors who were unable
to sustain a high B-flat pianissimo. Then the Pantera too fell
upon evil days. *La favorita* in 1878 was a frost, while *La traviata* had to be cancelled for lack of suitable singers. In 1879
the *habitués* had to be content with a visit by the Franceschini
operetta company giving performances of works by Offenbach, Lecocq, and Johann Strauss. The following year the
management rallied to the extent of presenting Verdi's *Mac-*

18. *Il Progresso,* 16 September 1877.
19. *La Provincia di Lucca,* 11 February 1871.
20. Ibid., 10 February 1872.
21. Letter to Avvocato G. De Naple, 9 April 1910, in the possession of the Associazione
    Civica Saverio Mercadante, Altamura.

beth (whether in the old or the new version is not specified) and *Nabucco;* but although the Società Orchestrale Boccherini gave its services free of charge, the season ended with a massive deficit.

Another theater at which opera was sometimes heard was the Goldoni. Established in 1829 primarily as a venue for spoken drama, it offered the occasional opera season after Easter, usually drawn from the lighter side of the repertory—Pedrotti's *Tutti in maschera* and Donizetti's *Linda di Chamounix* (1872), Cimarosa's *Giannina e Bernardone* and an unnamed work by Pietro Guglielmi (1873). In 1875 it aspired as high as Donizetti's *Maria di Rohan* and Verdi's *Il trovatore,* only to relapse thereafter into the sporadic *Don Pasquale* or *Crispino e la comare*.

Contemporary accounts, however inspired by local patriotism, make it clear that at all three theaters standards of presentation left much to be desired; and one scours the cast lists in vain for a single singer of whom one has heard. The nearest *teatro di cartello* was at Pisa, and its activities were regularly reported in the Luccan press. An event of outstanding importance was a production there of *Aida* in March 1876. The newspapers announced a special train to carry ticket holders along the newly built Lucca-Pisa railway in time for the performance and another to take them home afterwards. The first of these, however, was cancelled, which may explain why Puccini and two of his friends decided to make the nineteen-mile journey on foot. Adami's statement that this was the first time Puccini had ever seen an opera on stage, apart from being most unlikely, is specifically refuted by his reference to Mercadante's *La vestale* quoted on p. 51. But that it first revealed to him the full possibilities of the genre need not be doubted. Less credible is Adami's tale (omitted from the first edition of his *Puccini*) of how the three friends obtained entry into the theater under false pretenses; likewise his account of the young composer's weary homeward trudge, his head filled with the magic of Verdi's Nile.[22] Why should he not have taken the special train back like everyone else?

22. Giuseppe Adami, *Il romanzo della vita di Giacomo Puccini* (Milan and Rome, 1944), 23.

With regard to sacred music Puccini was far better placed. This is an area that has received little attention from scholars of nineteenth-century music; although a vast number of Masses and motets were still being produced for the various feast days of the church calendar, they were no longer commercially profitable and therefore remained for the most part unpublished. The days were far distant when Pergolesi's *Stabat mater* could qualify as the most frequently printed composition in Europe. The Italy of Puccini's time had no great choral festivals like those of Leeds, Birmingham, and the Three Choirs in England, with their orgy of oratorios to which distinguished foreigners such as Mendelssohn, Gounod, and Dvořák were happy to contribute; nor was there a firm such as Novello and Co. to make the great classics from Palestrina to Haydn available to amateur choral societies. But as the recently exhumed composite *Messa per Rossini* of 1869 has demonstrated, there was no lack of musical science among Italian church composers, though the current style varied from city to city and occasionally bore the marks of the opera house. In Rome in 1850, Pietro Raimondi had produced three oratorios which could be performed separately or simultaneously. His favorite pupil, Pietro Platania, organist and choirmaster at Palermo Cathedral, provided the Sanctus for the *Messa per Rossini,* a choral *tour de force* of vigorous part-writing and contrapuntal brilliance, even if this is counterpoint that the experience of Bach and Handel seems to have bypassed.

But for his early death in 1864 another contributor to the *Messa* might well have been Puccini's father, Michele, whose fame as a composer of sacred music had spread far beyond the walls of Lucca. In Arthur Pougin's supplement to the *Biographie universelle des musiciens* by the Belgian musicologist François-Joseph Fétis, we read that Michele Puccini was "a learned harmonist, a highly skilled master of counterpoint," and that if his compositions lacked imaginative power, he was an excellent teacher, "able to expound the principles of his art with clarity and to smooth the path for young artists."[23] This was no exaggeration. Under his directorship the Istituto

23. Cited in G. Musco, *Musica e teatro in Giacomo Puccini* (Cortona, 1989), 1:39.

Musicale Pacini produced a number of technically proficient musicians, among them Carlo Angeloni, who became Puccini's first professor of composition, and his uncle Fortunato Magi, from whom he learned the first rudiments of music. Unfortunately there was no love lost between Magi and his nephew, whom, it seems, he nearly managed to turn against music altogether. This is not altogether surprising; for though Magi shared his brother-in-law's ability as a teacher (his pupils included Alfredo Catalani and, much later, Alberto Franchetti), he was clearly a difficult character with a flair for creating trouble wherever he went. In 1872 Magi resigned the directorship of the Pacini Institute over a dispute with the municipal authorities. He then moved to Sarzana to take over the local music school. Two years later he was appointed director of Istituto Musicale of Ferrara. In 1875 the city was rocked by the "vertenza Magi." The cause was a prestigious performance of *Aida* at the Teatro Comunale. Magi had been invited to conduct, but the orchestra held out for their own *primo violino*. The matter was referred to Ricordi, the publisher, who opted for Magi. However, it was the prima donna, Anastasia Pozzoni, who resolved the issue by insisting on Emilio Usiglio. Magi at once offered his resignation from the Institute, but was persuaded to withdraw it. The year 1877 found him at La Spezia, from which he passed to the directorship of the Liceo Musicale "Benedetto Marcello" in Venice. Here his conducting of Massenet's *Le roi de Lahore* at La Fenice won him ovations and a tribute from the critic of *La Venezia* to his ability to overcome the "camorrist pox" and the "manoeuvres of the envious, the malevolent, and the impotent."[24] Clearly Magi had not lost his gift for making enemies. He died in 1882 at age forty-three from "a painful illness"[25]—presumably the same that would carry off his sister and his nephew.

If Puccini never benefited directly from the tuition of his father or uncle, he would have had plenty of opportunities for hearing their music, which was still regularly performed in Lucca during his adolescence. A stronghold of Catholic

24. *La Provincia di Lucca,* 22 February 1879.
25. Ibid., 27 May 1882.

orthodoxy, the city abounded in religious festivals. Of these the most important was the already mentioned Festa della Santa Croce, which required the composition of two sets of Vespers, a Mass, and a "motettone" for double-choir soloists and double orchestra. "Sopranisti" were sometimes hired from the Vatican, and the occasion was often graced by the presence of the great Teodulo Mabellini, organist of Florence Cathedral, to conduct one of his own compositions. Himself a contributor to the *Messa per Rossini,* he had a bland, richly textured style that is reflected in that of Puccini's teacher, Angeloni. To the usual festivities at Christmas and Eastertide must be added the Feast of Santa Cecilia on November 22, its music provided by a long-standing Confraternita of which Magi and the musicians of the Puccini family had all been members, and the more recently instituted Feast of San Paolino, the city's patron, where the outstanding pupils of the Pacini Institute were

Puccini began frequenting Teatro alla Scala in his student days, and his first letters to his family contain irreverent comments on performances there. His own operatic debut, in 1884, was at a smaller Milanese theater, the Teatro Dal Verme; but a few months later, that first opera, Le villi, reached La Scala, where the composer's second work, Edgar, had its premiere. Though the later operas were usually introduced elsewhere, La Scala remained a fixed point in Puccini's life and, two years after his death, Turandot was presented there in 1926. (Courtesy of William Seward and Mary Jane Phillips-Matz)

allowed an opportunity to display their talents. Religious music also figured in the students' concerts held at the Institute itself.

Thus it was that on April 29, 1877, Luccans were able to hear a motet in San Paolino's honor, *Plaudite, populi* for baritone, chorus, and orchestra by the eighteen-year-old Giacomo Puccini. "On listening to this music," remarked the critic of the *Provincia di Lucca,* "we are put in mind of the ancient proverb, 'The sons of cats catch mice.' In fact Giacomo Puccini represents the fifth musical generation of his family; he has before him excellent examples to imitate and could become a young composer of rare ability, since he is by no means lacking in considerable talent."[26] It was not his first composition of substance. In 1876 he had already written a Prelude in E minor for orchestra, though there is no record of its having been performed. The motet, however, was repeated the following year on the Feast of San Paolino, together with a newly-composed Credo, which in turn was incorporated in the so-called *Messa di Gloria* of 1880, Puccini's graduation piece from the Institute. This too was first given at the Church of San Paolino on the saint's feast day; and once again the motet was to be heard inserted between the Credo and the Sanctus—a fact which may account for Carner's statement that Puccini had recycled its music in the body of the *Messa* itself.[27] Of the work as a whole the local critics were unstinting in their praise, and with good reason, for its level of craftsmanship is remarkably high. If the material is not always distinguished, Puccini's control of it is complete. Both the Gloria and the Credo show an attempt at large-scale organization rare for the time; nor would one quarrel with the *Provincia di Lucca*'s description of the "Cum sancto spirito" as a "fugone coi baffi"[28] (grand fugue with mustaches), embellished as it is with every contrapuntal device in the schoolbook, including a reprise of the opening strain of the Gloria by way of a countersubject. Stylistic fingerprints are already in evidence in the "Gratias" with its doubling of outer parts, its leaning towards the subdominant key, and an overall tonal plan which anticipates that of

26. Ibid., 4 May 1877.
27. Mosco Carner, *Puccini: A Critical Biography,* 2nd ed. (New York, 1974), 19.
28. *La Provincia di Lucca,* 24 July 1880.

"Che gelida manina." Both the Kyrie and the Agnus Dei would find their way into *Edgar* and *Manon Lescaut* respectively.

It is clear from all of this that had Puccini been disposed to follow his father's example and specialize in religious music, he would hardly have needed to stray outside the walls of his native Lucca. Given his actual aspirations, a further period of more general training was necessary, such as was available only at one of the great conservatories.

True, it had not been available for very long. In the pedagogical sphere, as in so many others, musical Italy had fallen behind the rest of Europe. Bologna and Naples, where Puccini's ancestors had studied, were no longer the centers of musical learning that they had been in the previous century. In 1870, however, the government appointed a committee that instituted a number of reforms, broadening the curriculum and bringing it up to date. Even before that time, Milan, one of the younger conservatories, having been founded in 1807 under the vice-regency of Eugène de Beauharnais, had already made notable progress thanks to the efforts of successive directors. During the 1840s Nicola Vaccaj added a new choir school to present works by Bach and Handel, but resigned when the government forbade the performance of *Messiah* as part of the celebrations of Holy Week. After a hiatus caused by the Austrian occupation of 1848–49 the conservatory was reopened under the direction of Lauro Rossi on a still larger scale, with extra classes for organ, harp, and musical history and philosophy. Rossi, who remained at the helm for twenty years before succeeding Mercadante at Naples, was the author of a *Guida ad un corso d'armonia practica orale* (1858), which is remarkably comprehensive for its time and place; he also initiated however tentatively a revival of Italy's Renaissance heritage. His successor, Alberto Mazzucato, managed after several years to form a symphony orchestra among the students.

Similar policies were pursued by Boito's teacher, Stefano Ronchetti Monteviti, during whose directorship Puccini was admitted to the conservatory, having passed the entrance examination without difficulty. He proceeded at once to the senior composition class, where he had the good fortune to come under the tuition of Antonio Bazzini, one of the few

Italian musicians of the time with a cosmopolitan background. Born in 1818, at twenty-two he embarked on the career of a violin virtuoso, playing in the various European capitals and winning the praise of Schumann. From 1852 to 1864 he lived in Paris, where his friends included Gounod and Saint-Saëns, both of whom he greatly admired[29]—indeed something of Gounod's influence can be traced in the *Dies irae* that he wrote for the *Messa per Rossini,* with its taut construction and abundance of sequences. In 1864 Bazzini returned to Italy to devote himself to composition. His only opera, *Turanda* (*sic*), given at La Scala in 1867, was a failure; but in the meantime he had plunged into the activities of the Società del Quartetto, to which he contributed several by no means negligible works of his own. He even took the unprecedented step of forming his own permanent quartet to give regular concerts. By 1870 he was Italy's foremost exponent of instrumental music, followed at some distance by Liszt's pupil Giovanni Sgambati. Three years later he was nominated professor of composition at the Milan Conservatory, succeeding to the directorship in 1882.

For Bazzini Puccini wrote a Quartet in D Major of which only the first movement survives—an elegant, beautifully crafted, but utterly uncharacteristic piece in Mendelssohnian style that at least bears witness to his technical prowess. However, it was in orchestral music that the young composer first began to spread his wings. A *Preludio sinfonico* in A Major, of which a copyist's manuscript score in the conservatory bears the date 1882 but which all biographies ascribe without the slightest justification to 1876, is recognizably Puccini from first note to last. The wealth of elegiac, soft-grained melody, the richness and variety of the scoring, the irregularity of detail masking an organic construction all point forward to *Manon Lescaut* and *La bohème*. Still more characteristic is the *Capriccio sinfonico* of 1883, his final exercise for the conservatory, whose central section would furnish the opening of *La bohème*. At its performance at a students' concert under Franco Faccio on

29. See letters to G. Franchi, 2 January 1878 and 8 May 1879, in Claudio Sartori, *L'avventura del violino* (Turin, 1978), 413, 418.

July 14, Milan's leading critic, Filippo Filippi, noted in the composer "a specifically symphonic talent"[30]—by which, like many Italians of his day, he probably meant no more than an aptitude for developing orchestral material. Nevertheless the term would remain attached to Puccini for many years during the start of his career.

No less important for him was the wide diversity of music to which he was exposed during his stay at Italy's most progressive capital with its four theaters—La Scala, the Dal Verme, the Manzoni and the Castelli: Verdi's revised *Simon Boccanegra,* Thomas's *Mignon,* Gounod's *Redemption* ("which bored me to distraction"), Catalani's romantically inspired *Dejanice* ("It doesn't send the public into ecstasies, but artistically speaking I think it's a fine work, and if they do it again I shall go back and see it"), and, not least, *Carmen* (". . . a most beautiful work").[31]

The significance of this last for the future development of Italian opera cannot be overestimated. Its composer intended it as an *opéra comique* in total contrast to the bland tradition represented by that hardy perennial, Boieldieu's *La dame blanche* of 1825. Unfortunately the Parisians were not amused. Bizet died within months of the premiere and the theater went bankrupt. But with the aid of Guiraud's recitatives the opera began to penetrate abroad, first to Germany, then, by the back door, to Italy, where the rights had been bought up by a newcomer to the editorial scene, the enterprising and unscrupulous Edoardo Sonzogno. First performed without fanfare in 1880 at the Teatro Bellini in Naples, it made rapid progress throughout the major theaters of Italy. Its importance was twofold. It accomplished the first step in breaking the cast iron framework of grand opera that had dominated Italy for the previous ten years; and it started a new trend in opera

30. Carner, *Puccini,* 32.
31. Extracts from letters to his family written over a period of three years (1881–83) and first published in Carlo Paladini, *Giacomo Puccini: Con epistolario inedito,* rev. ed. (Florence, 1961), 33. Other works mentioned by Puccini in connection with the Great Exhibition of 1881 are *Don Giovanni, Mefistofele, Les Huguenots, L'Étoile du Nord, I puritani, Belisario, Faust, La forza del destino, La favorita, Semiramide, Guglielmo Tell.* See letter to Ramelde, 4 April 1881, in Arnaldo Marchetti, *Puccini com'era* (Milan, 1973), 29–30.

toward that concept of realism that had already gained a firm foothold in Italian literature. After a performance at Rome's Teatro Argentina, the critic D'Arcais, who had already declared Bizet to be infinitely Massenet's superior, wrote, "Some would like to consider the composer as head of some school or other of realism in France—a judgment which doubtless Bizet, were he still alive, would have been the first to repudiate."[32] Be that as it may, it was the realistic element in *Carmen* that would prove decisive for D'Arcais's countrymen.

Correctly foreseeing the course of future events, Sonzogno announced in the columns of his journal *Il Teatro Illustrato* in 1883 a competition for a one-act opera, the winning piece to be performed the following year at the Teatro Dal Verme. Puccini, now in his last year at the Conservatory, decided to compete. After Bazzini's nomination to the directorship, he had passed under the tuition of Amilcare Ponchielli. At first sight this might seem a backward step. Ponchielli was a traditionalist who had not set foot outside his native country, having been for sixteen years a bandmaster in Cremona and Piacenza. But he was an excellent musician. At the age of thirty-four he had competed for the professorship of harmony at the Milan Conservatory, and though he was adjudged the winner, the post went to Franco Faccio. Happily his growing reputation during the 1870s eventually resulted in the *amende honorable;* and in 1881 he was granted the position that had been so unfairly denied him. By now *La Gioconda* had established itself as a modern classic, some of whose qualities find an echo in Puccini's work: the ability to evoke a particular ambience; the seamless incorporation of a recurring motif (e.g. "the rosary") into a closed number; and, more especially, the effective use of an orchestral peroration based on the principal melody of an act. This device, seemingly so obvious or even commonplace, first occurs in the definitive version of *La Gioconda* of 1880 at the close of Act III and was at once seized upon as a novelty by critics of the time. Puccini is often charged with abusing it; but in his hands it never fails theatrically.

Of a modest, generous disposition, Ponchielli was much

32. F. D'Arcais, "Rassegna Musicale," *Nuova Antologia* (March–April 1884):717–26.

loved by his students. With Puccini he shared a clownish sense of humor that expressed itself in doggerel verse. Informed of his pupil's decision to enter the Sonzogno competition, he took it upon himself to find him a suitable librettist. This would be Ferdinando Fontana, a young *scapigliato* poet and journalist, whose political activities would before long send him into exile in Switzerland. "With the success of his *Capriccio sinfonico* still fresh in my memory, "Fontana recalled, "I thought the young maestro would need a fantastic plot, and I unfolded to him the outline of *Le villi*."[33] Puccini confirmed his judgment. "It should be a good little subject," he wrote to his mother, "one that I like very much indeed, as it will mean working quite a lot in the symphonic-descriptive genre, and that will suit me very well, because I think I can succeed in it."[34] Alas, as far as the competition was concerned, success eluded him. The prize went elsewhere and *Le villi* was not even awarded an honorable mention. Nonetheless a subscription was set up for its performance, which took place at the same Teatro Dal Verme on 31 May 1884. Reviewing it in the *Corriere della Sera,* the music critic Antonio Gramola wrote, "We honestly believe that Puccini could be the composer for whom Italy has been waiting for a long time."

He was not mistaken.

33. Leonardo Pinzauti, *Puccini: Una vita* (Florence, 1974), 16.
34. Letter to his mother, 20 or 21 July 1883, in Eugenio Gara et al., eds., *Carteggi pucciniani* (Milan, 1958), 6.

*L*E VILLI, *E*DGAR, AND THE "*S*YMPHONIC *E*LEMENT"

M i c h a e l   E l p h i n s t o n e

Michael Elphinstone was born in Tasmania, Australia. After graduation from the University of Adelaide, he won an Italian government scholarship to do research on Puccini in Italy. He is a member of the Istituto di Studi Pucciniani, and author of several articles published in the Institute's journal, *Quaderni Pucciniani.*

> *If only I could be a purely symphonic writer! . . . But that was not for me . . . Almighty God touched me with His little finger and said: "Write for the theater—mind, only for the theater." And I have obeyed the supreme command.*[1]
>
> Letter to Giuseppe Adami, 17 July 1920

*I*t was not without a certain irony that Puccini's thoughts, during the difficult gestation of *Turandot,* turned to the "symphonic" music he had virtually abandoned in dedicating himself to opera

---

1. Giuseppe Adami, ed., *Letters of Giacomo Puccini,* trans. E. Makin (New York, 1973), 265.

composition. For it was as a composer of "purely symphonic music" that he had first achieved national success and notoriety; and, more important, it was as a composer of "symphonic" works that he had approached the task of writing his first opera, *Le villi* (It should be noted that the term "sinfonico" in late nineteenth-century Italy was practically synonymous with "orchestral" and thus carried few stylistic or formalistic connotations.) Unfortunately, this aspect of Puccini's creativity is rarely touched upon by his biographers, who persist in portraying him as a man destined from the very outset to pursue a career devoted exclusively to the composition of operatic works; such a view ignores both Puccini's earliest compositional objectives and the large role that chance or fortune had in initially directing his activities toward the stage. *Le villi* should *not* be regarded as the first logical and inevitable manifestation of Puccini's real destiny. Rather, it represents a tentative, albeit decisive step into what was then for him a fundamentally foreign territory, and as a consequence it bears, as does his second opera, *Edgar,* the unmistakable fingerprints of Puccini the "symphonist." Both compositions ultimately demonstrate how much he knew about music—particularly orchestral music—yet how comparatively little about opera.

No evidence exists to suggest that as a student Puccini had nurtured a particular interest in opera *per se.* The significance of his now-famous pilgrimage on foot to hear a performance of *Aida* in Pisa on 11 March 1876, has long been subject to exaggeration; many writers have blindly accepted Giuseppe Adami's assertion that the event in question in fact constituted the composer's first operatic encounter.[2] Considering the rich and varied musical life that provincial Lucca offered in the 1870s (symphonic concerts promoted by the Società Boccherini, frequent operatic productions at the local Teatro del Giglio, and various other musical events organized by the Banda Municipale di Lucca and the Istituto Musicale Pacini), together with Puccini's self-confessed study of the scores of *Rigoletto, Il trovatore,* and *La traviata,* it is difficult to believe that he

2. Giuseppe Adami, *Puccini* (Milan, 1935), 7.

would not have been well acquainted with opera before traveling to Pisa. The impression made upon the composer by *Aida,* as he later inadvertently confirmed, was due not to its general operatic features but to its particular grandeur, theatrical effectiveness, and "the splendor of its harmonies."[3] That he was particularly affected on an aural level—"When I *heard Aida* at Pisa I felt that a *musical* window had opened for me"[4]—is unquestionable, but it is likely that he was struck more by the important role given to the orchestra and the subtleties of the orchestration than by *Aida*'s harmonic language. The first Puccinian composition postdating the *Aida* performance is a *Preludio sinfonico* in E minor, his initial attempt at orchestral writing. Of this work, formerly in the Gallini private collection in Milan, we have Gallini's description:

> The most striking thing about this score is the accuracy of its orchestration, the clarity of the timbral combinations, the correctness of the instrumental writing. The Preludio begins with a simple idea exposed in pianissimo by the violins and violas, to which are added, during the development of the melodic phrase, a flute, then an oboe, while the other woodwinds complete the harmony.[5]

Even on the basis of these lines alone, it would not be unreasonable to assume that the prelude to *Aida* had provided the model for the instrumentation in Puccini's composition.

The references to Milanese operatic productions that punctuate Puccini's letters to his family from 1880 to 1883 have also frequently been given too much importance; these are, for the most part, reflections of the young Puccini's fascination and excitement upon finding himself in a new environment and surrounded by a multitude of cultural and artistic attractions. Consequently, the majority of such references are to be found

3. Arnaldo Fraccaroli, *Giacomo Puccini: Si confida e racconta* (Milan, 1957), 24.
4. Quoted in Mosco Carner, *Puccini,* 2nd ed. (London, 1974), 19.
5. Natale Gallini, "Gli anni giovanili di Giacomo Puccini," *L'Approdo Musicale* 2/6 (April–June 1959):29.

in the letters written between February and May 1881, wherein
Puccini, seeking to impress his family, enthusiastically outlines the various events programmed to coincide with the
National Exposition held in Milan from 5 May until 1
November of that year (Marchetti 3–7).[6] The number of opera
performances Puccini actually attended during his Milan student period would appear to be meager—his surviving letters
mention only *Carmen, Fra Diavolo, La stella del nord,* and
Dejanice—although an occasional condemnation of the La Scala
admission prices and his then penurious existence might lead
us to suppose that had he had the financial means, he might
have frequented the opera more often.

As far as can be ascertained, prior to commencing work on
Le villi, Puccini had expressed a direct interest in writing opera
on only one occasion. In a letter written to his uncle Nicolao
Cerù, 6 December 1882 (Marchetti 8), we find the following:
"Tell Michele to go and find Cappelletti Medarse and ask him
if he has still found nothing for me regarding that little libretto
he promised. I should need it very soon if I am to prepare
myself to do something." Here Puccini is referring to a certain
"Concorso Bonetti" organized within the Milan Conservatory, the details of which are outlined in a letter written several weeks earlier (16 October) by Pietro Mascagni to his former
teacher Alfredo Soffredini:

> I must tell you that in '79 a gentleman made a bequest to the
> Conservatory, which consists of an award of 600 lire for the best
> student opera in Rossinian, Bellinian, or Donizettian style. Every
> year the competition is open till May 30. The chosen opera is
> performed and the composer is publicly honored on the prize-
> giving day. Well, this year I too want to participate. But I don't
> have a libretto.[7]

6. Unless otherwise indicated, the letters cited in this discussion are taken from Eugenio
   Gara et al., eds., *Carteggi pucciniani* (Milan, 1958), and Arnaldo Marchetti, ed., *Puccini com'era* (Milan, 1973).
7. Quoted in Natale Gallini, "Mascagni a Milano," in *Pietro Mascagni,* ed. Mario Morini
   (Milan, 1964), 84.

Mascagni and Puccini were sharing lodgings during this period; it is quite possible that a certain degree of friendly rivalry prompted their decision to enter the Bonetti competition. It would appear, however, that Puccini's plans—perhaps because of Michele's inability to procure the libretto, perhaps because of waning interest—came to nothing (as did Mascagni's).

Nor had Puccini previously given any substantial indication of ability in the area of operatic composition. (We can disregard the two-page sketch for a "scenic cantata" currently in the possession of the Istituto Musicale "Luigi Boccherini," Lucca.) In fact, the majority of his student works are instrumental pieces and include a *Valzer* for band; two *Preludi sinfonici,* an *Adagietto,* and a *Capriccio sinfonico* for orchestra; three fugues; a *Scherzo* and a *Quartetto* for strings; plus various miniatures for piano and organ. An examination of Puccini's youthful compositions suggests that as the composer advanced in his studies, he increasingly devoted his attention to instrumental music—particularly of the "symphonic" genre—at the expense of vocal music.

The largest and most important vocal works emanating from Puccini's student period were therefore composed in Lucca and, with the exception of the song *A te* (1875) for voice and piano accompaniment, are religious compositions or choral works written to a set or given text: a *Mottetto* (1877), the missing cantata *I figli d'Italia bella* (1877), the *Vexilla Regis* (1878), and the *Messa a 4 voci* (1880, *Credo* 1878). In compliance with a rule established by Michele Puccini, Sr., all those final-year students of the Istituto Musicale Pacini who were candidates for the diploma of Maestro di Composizione were required to submit both an instrumental composition and an ecclesiastical or theatrical one to the examining commission; it is interesting to note that Puccini chose *not* to compose an operatic work. Despite being technically advanced and thoughtfully composed in terms of their treatment of the voice, the pieces mentioned above are far removed from the operatic world, having no dramatic component and therefore displaying no sense of the theater. Furthermore, the dominating feature of the *Messa* is not the music allotted to the soloists or the chorus, but the participation of the orchestra; almost every section of the work features an orchestral prelude, interlude, and postlude, providing evidence of the interests and ambitions of the young musician.

From Puccini's conservatory years in Milan only four completed vocal works exist. Three of these are simple songs for voice and keyboard—*Salve regina* (1882), *Storiella d'amore* (1883), and the now-missing *Melancolia* (1882; this apparently exists also in a version for voice with string accompaniment)—all set to verses by Ghislanzoni. The remaining piece, the dramatic scena and aria *Mentìa l'avviso,* represents the student composer's only operatically conceived work. Michael Kaye, in his authoritative volume *The Unknown Puccini* (New York and London, 1987), has shown that the text of this composition derives from the second scene in Act IV of Felice Romani's libretto *La solitaria delle Asturie, ossia La Spagna ricuperata,* a work set to music by several Italian composers during the 1830s and 1840s. And yet Puccini's setting of the scene in question—for tenor and piano—was composed to fulfill the requirements of his final examinations in 1883, and is therefore not indicative of an especially receptive attitude toward operatic composition.

Two final points serve to illustrate Puccini's limited interest in opera during his student period at the Milan Conservatory. The first of these concerns the subject "Poetic and Dramatic Literature," which was then a fundamental component of the general curriculum. Although one might assume that this subject would have been of practical value to any aspiring opera composer, Puccini initially found it tedious and unnecessary, as some remarks scrawled in the relevant notebook testify: "Alas!!!! Oh! Oh God!!! Help for Goodness' sake!!! Enough!!! It's too much; Bye, Professor . . . I'm going to sleep; I'm dying!!!" And a letter to his mother dated 9 March 1881 (Marchetti 5) echoes the same sentiment: "I'm here in my lesson of Dramatic Literature which bores me to tears." More revealing is Puccini's attendance record for this subject. His continued absence—not only in "Poetic and Dramatic Literature" but also in "Complementary Pianoforte"—eventually brought him before the Conservatory Council, and accordingly, his student record for the 1880–81 academic year contains the following observation: "Because of his continued unjustified absences, the Academic Council, at its meeting of 26 June 1881, inflicts the fine of 10 lire." Only after being subjected to such a disciplinary measure did he resume regular attendance.

The second point concerns Puccini's choice of composition for his obligatory graduation exercise—the most telling proof of his objectives as a composer in these early years. Fundamentally, such graduation exercises were composed with a view to being performed at the *saggi* that ended the school year. The *saggi,* in turn, were tickets of introduction to the greater Milanese musical sphere and beyond. It is extremely significant, therefore, that while students frequently presented operas or extended vocal works as their examination pieces, Puccini's composition was purely instrumental—the *Capriccio sinfonico.* We can assume that he deliberately chose to write an orchestral work—perhaps in an attempt to repeat the reasonably favorable reception afforded his *Preludio sinfonico* in A major when it was included in the *saggi* of 1882—since composition students had a certain liberty in the choice of their final composition; eight years earlier, in 1875, Catalani had presented his first opera, *La falce,* as his graduation exercise.

Needless to say, the highly enthusiastic critical acclaim for the *Capriccio sinfonico*—especially the preeminent critic Filippo Filippi's comments about the composer's "decided and extremely rare musical temperament, specifically symphonic"[8]—together with an offer to publish the work (albeit in a version for piano, four hands) from the publishing house of Giovannina Lucca and the probability of further performances of the *Capriccio* under noted conductor Franco Faccio's direction in Turin and at La Scala only reinforced Puccini's aspirations of succeeding as a symphonic composer.

Taking into account this particular background, we cannot fail to be pleasantly surprised by *Le villi* and *Edgar,* works that undoubtedly proved to Puccini that his real future lay in another direction. Likewise, we can understand why these operas give such prominence to the orchestra, and why on a dramatic level

8. Filippo Filippi, in *La Perseveranza,* 15 July 1883.

they exhibit several flaws—flaws the young composer, at this stage in his musical and artistic development, could not have hoped to correct.

𝕿he "symphonic element," which according to Puccini's earliest critics and supporters was a dominating feature of his character, manifested itself not only in the score of his first opera but also in various biographical details of its composition. *Le villi* (or *Le willis,* to give it its original title), as is well known, was Puccini's entry in a competition for a newly composed one-act opera. The competition was advertised in the Milanese periodical *Il Teatro Illustrato,* 1 April 1883, and was organized and sponsored by local industrialist and newspaper magnate Edoardo Sonzogno in his capacity as founder and director of the Casa Musicale bearing his name. The closing date for the submission of manuscripts was 31 December, the competition was open to young Italian composers, and the prize consisted of two thousand lire plus the presentation of the winning entry at a Milan theater.

It would seem, however, that Puccini was initially unaware of, or uninterested in, the Sonzogno competition. Carner asserts that "no sooner had the announcement of the competition been published than he decided to take part in it,"[9] but this statement is patently without foundation; had Puccini decided to enter it as early as April, he would surely have taken immediate steps toward procuring a libretto. In addition, he would not have been able actively to participate in such a competition until the latter part of July; at the time of the aforementioned advertisement he was three and a half months away from completing the final year of his Conservatory studies in Milan under Amilcare Ponchielli. Apparently, this last year was particularly demanding; the majority of the extant sketches and pieces that belong to his student days in Milan are now known to date from the 1882–83 academic year. Therefore, until his graduation, the various requirements of his course

9. Carner, *Puccini,* 36.

would have prevented him from working on a large-scale extracurricular composition.

In any event, we know from a letter to his mother dated 20 June 1883 (Marchetti 10) that less than a month away from his graduation Puccini still had no definite plans for his immediate future beyond making himself known to Milan's most important music publisher, Giulio Ricordi: "I'll worry about my future after the exams, and I'll go to see Ricordi but I'm not hopeful." In the following two letters to his mother, dated 1 and 3 July respectively (Marchetti 11 and 13), Puccini once again spoke of his intention to call on Ricordi but now had hopes of being formally presented to the publisher by a mutual friend—anonymous, but without doubt Ponchielli. Ricordi, however, had already left Milan for his summer retreat at Bellano, on the shore of Lake Como; Puccini would have had to wait until the end of the vacation period to see his plan realized.

Wanting to be certain that the introduction to Ricordi actually took place, Albina Puccini wrote almost immediately to Ponchielli (8 July):

> I'm thinking about this boy's future. What will he do? How and where will he be able to find the means of earning a living, now more than ever necessary since I have used the little I had put aside to keep him . . . if you were thinking of recommending him to the two publishing houses of Ricordi and Lucca, I'm sure that he would obtain something; I know how much you're respected by Signor Ricordi and Signora Lucca.[10]

As it so happened, Puccini's contact with the music publishing firm of Giovannina Lucca was established not long after 14 July, but it is doubtful that Puccini was personally introduced to Lucca herself on that occasion. When the *Capriccio sinfonico* received its first public performance in the conservatory *saggio* of 14 July, its success was such that the composer was subsequently awarded a scholarship from Lucca's firm; every year this scholarship was given to the most promising

---

10. Quoted in Gallini, "Gli anni giovanili," 39.

final-year student, and it included publication of his or her major composition. And yet Puccini's letters that date from after 14 July repeatedly refer to his attempts to meet Lucca in person—like Ricordi, she was already at her summer villa in Stabio (Switzerland)—which suggests that he had hitherto spoken only to her representative regarding the scholarship. It is certain that after being granted this award, the composer pinned all his hopes on receiving further immediate assistance from Lucca, possibly in the form of a commission. (Ricordi is not mentioned again in Puccini's letters until February 1884.) But she was not expected to return to Milan until the end of the summer.

At this point Ponchielli came to the aid of his student. About 17 July he invited Puccini to spend several days at his villa at Maggianico, near Lecco—not far from Lucca's retreat; both Ponchielli's and Lucca's villas could be reached via the same railway line, therefore Puccini planned to call on Lucca before commencing his sojourn with Ponchielli (Marchetti 18). About 20 July he left Milan; unfortunately, he was to discover that Lucca was now in Bayreuth attending a production of Wagner's *Parsifal*.

It can be assumed that during the few days spent at Maggianico, the two men decided that Puccini would enter the Sonzogno competition. The crucial problem of finding a librettist was solved by a stroke of fortune. Ferdinando Fontana, a young dramatist, critic, minor poet, journalist, occasional librettist, and member of the Milanese *scapigliatura*, happened to be among the guests of Antonio Ghislanzoni (poet of *Aida* and, as we have seen, several of Puccini's early vocal pieces) at the latter's pensione, "Il Barco." This pensione was regularly frequented by musicians and writers and was situated at Caprino Bergamasco, also in the vicinity of Ponchielli's villa. By sheer coincidence, Puccini and Ponchielli met Fontana at the railway station at Lecco, and they traveled together for the short distance to Maggianico, where the two composers alighted. During this journey, Ponchielli broached the subject of the Sonzogno competition and apparently succeeded in persuading Fontana to prepare a libretto for Puccini. However, the financial question was not resolved then, nor was a subject for the opera decided upon; although Fontana had recently begun preparing a libretto on the legend of the *willis,* which he considered entirely suitable for Puccini on account of its "fantastic" subject,[11] a certain "N.40" (Maestro Francesco Quaranta) had expressed an interest in eventually using it and would have to be dissuaded from doing so before Puccini could acquire the rights to it.

Nonetheless, Puccini was optimistic, and upon his return to Milan, about 25 July, he wrote to his mother to tell her of the meeting (Gara 6):

> I went to Ponchielli's and stayed four days. I spoke with Fontana, a poet, who is vacationing there near Ponchielli, and the matter of a libretto was nearly settled; in fact he said he liked my music etc. etc. Ponchielli then intervened and recommended me warmly. There's a good little subject that someone else is considering, but that Fontana would prefer to give to me; all the more so since I like it very much. There is ample scope for writing music of the symphonic genre, which suits me well because I believe I should succeed in it. In such a way I'd be able to take part in the Sonzogno competition. But the whole affair, dear Mother, is very uncertain. Just think, the competition is Italian, not restricted and local as I believed, then the time is short.

This letter contains Puccini's first known reference to the Sonzogno competition; although it would appear that he had already mentioned the competition to his mother, it is obvious that he had not previously informed himself of its "conditions." (And it is especially noteworthy that he here gives no details concerning the proposed subject of the opera beyond noting that it will provide him with the opportunity to write descriptive symphonic music—by this time considered his "specialty.")

Meanwhile Ponchielli had written to Fontana (25 July [Gara 7]), reminding him of the agreement made on the train and asking him to take Puccini's impoverished financial situation

---

11. Fontana, in an article titled "Giacomo Puccini" (*La Gazzetta Musicale di Milano,* 19 October 1884), stated: "With the vivid recollection of the *Sinfonia-Capriccio* [*sic*], it seemed that a fantastic subject was necessary for the young maestro, and I displayed to him the plot of *Le villi.*"

into account when drawing up his librettist's fees. In Fontana's reply of 26 July these were fixed at "100 lire upon consignment of the libretto; [with an additional] 200 lire if Signor Puccini wins the competition."[12] Finally, on 2 August, Fontana was able to inform Puccini that "N.40" had renounced the rights to *Le willis;* Puccini was thus free to use the "good little subject" for his own opera (Marchetti 20).

Puccini returned to Lucca on 7 August and remained there to work on his opera; the libretto, completed by early September, was sent to him there. It is extremely doubtful that he immediately threw himself into the composition of *Le willis,* or that he worked as intensely on the opera as is continually attested to by his biographers. A little-known letter written to Ponchielli, dated 29 October, illustrates not only a self-confessed laziness and the boredom that Puccini was apparently experiencing in Lucca, but also the order of his musical priorities:

> I hope that you will excuse my long silence, caused by both a slight illness and innate laziness . . . I hope that I might be given the chance to see you soon, since there's nothing to do here in Lucca, and I, instead, need to find something to do.
>
> As for the idea you showed me after the performance of my *Capriccio,* namely that you would have arranged for it to be performed in popular concerts, I cherish the hope that you will have the kindness to do this; I thank you in anticipation.
>
> I would also be very grateful if you could forward me the address of F. Fontana, as I need it for the correction of some spots in the little work I'm composing.
>
> When Signora Lucca promised to publish the *Capriccio,* she expressed the wish to have also the orchestral score, and so I had it copied here in Lucca; it is full of errors and lacking in bars, therefore I would ask you to approach the Director, so that he might agree to send me the score held in the Conservatory within a few days.[13]

And so as late as the end of October, Puccini had still not begun to work in earnest on his opera; although he continued

---

12. Ibid., 56.
13. Quoted in *Le Apuane* 6/12 (November 1986):56.

to follow the fortunes of his orchestral piece, *Le willis* was considered no more than a "little work." Moreover, it is very curious that he did not have an address for his librettist.

It would therefore appear that the major part of the work was composed within the space of a few weeks. Puccini sent the score to the Sonzogno commission at the last possible moment—31 December—and, according to Fraccaroli,[14] even had a post office official back-date it. He returned to Milan at the beginning of February 1884 to await the verdict of the judges, scheduled for the end of that month, during which period he was finally introduced to Ricordi by Ponchielli (Marchetti 29). But when the results were announced, Puccini's opera—one of twenty-eight—had not even received an honorable mention. It is generally claimed that the often illegible manuscript was responsible for the failure of the work in the competition. This may well have been a factor in the final decision, but the men on the judging panel—Amilcare Ponchielli, Cesare Dominiceti, Amintore Galli, and Franco Faccio (three of them Puccini's conservatory professors)—were all accustomed to deciphering his hand. (A fifth judge, composer Pietro Platania, had been obliged to withdraw from adjudicating owing to commitments in Palermo.) It is plausible that the late arrival of Puccini's manuscript automatically disqualified him.

Fontana, at least, did not intend to dismiss the worth of the opera. Largely through his *scapigliatura* connections, he arranged for Puccini to play excerpts of the work in the presence of various members of Milan's social and artistic elite. This event took place around 10 April at the home of Marco Sala, a wealthy eccentric, amateur composer, violinist, and author of light verses; the audience, besides Fontana and Sala, included Arrigo Boito, Giovannina Lucca, and Alfredo Catalani. The impression made upon these guests was such that it was immediately decided to collect the funds necessary to mount a production of the opera. Boito arranged for the use of the Teatro Dal Verme for the premiere (which was originally fixed for 27 May [Marchetti 45]), and Giulio Ricordi

14. Arnaldo Fraccaroli, *La vita di Giacomo Puccini* (Milan, 1925), 38.

consented to print the libretto free of charge—after being guaranteed that Puccini was not a "Wagnerian." Several other notables made generous financial contributions; a letter from Fontana to Puccini (April 1884 [Gara 9]) gives details of these sponsors and their respective donations.

Le willis finally reached the stage on 31 May, just a few weeks after the winning operas of the Sonzogno competition (the prize had been divided between Guglielmo Zuelli's *La fata del nord* and Luigi Mapelli's *Anna e Gualberto*) had received their premieres at the Teatro Manzoni. Consequently, Puccini's opera was publicized in the following unorthodox manner: "This evening at the Teatro Dal Verme, another of the operas submitted to the Teatro Illustrato competition—one which neither won nor gained an honorable mention—will be presented."

Nevertheless the theater was filled to capacity, and *Le willis,* described as an "opera-ballo" and given in a triple bill with Marchetti's *Ruy Blas* and a ballet entitled *La Contessa d'Egmont,* was a huge success. It was given four performances in all—not three as is often claimed and even indicated by a bill poster advertising the "third and final performance"—on consecutive evenings. At each performance the instrumental reprise closing the first part of the opera was repeated three times, and the "duetto d'amore" was encored on more than one occasion. Elated after the premiere, Puccini sent the following telegram to his mother: "Clamorous success. Eighteen curtain calls. First finale repeated three times. Am happy." And the critics wrote the following:

> The qualities that one encounters in *Le willis* reveal in Puccini a musical fantasy singularly disposed to melody. In the music of the young "maestro lucchese" there is the freshness of fantasy; there are phrases which touch the heart because they must have issued from the heart . . . we seem to have before us not a young student, but a Bizet, a Massenet. We sincerely believe that Puccini may be the composer Italy has so long awaited.[15]

15. Antonio Gramola, in *Il Corriere della Sera,* 2–3 June 1884.

We wish Maestro Giacomo Puccini a splendid artistic career worthy of his immense talent . . . as for the commission of the Sonzogno competition, we hope that its verdict on the work of Puccini is really "Mr. Pirota's last prawn [*sic*]." In our opinion, Puccini's opera is a small and precious masterpiece from beginning to end.[16]

In *Le willis,* that which emerges is certainly not the vocal part, the impassioned note; instead, the listener remains bewitched by the richness of the acoustic colors and by the harmonic boldness attempted by the young composer.[17]

[Puccini], when we talk about painting with instrumental colors, tends toward an imitation of the French school, particularly Bizet and Massenet . . . the composer Puccini has an essentially symphonic nature, and, as I said the day before yesterday, often abuses it, overloading the pedestal to the detriment of the statue.[18]

The enlightened comments of the last two critics cited here demonstrate that Puccini's disposition for "symphonic" music, and his skill in the handling of an orchestral medium had not gone unobserved. Indeed, it appears that the composer's early reputation was founded almost exclusively on his "symphonic element;" It is significant that a letter from Verdi to his friend Count Opprandino Arrivabene, dated 10 June 1884 (Gara 11), singled out this particular characteristic of Puccini's music:

I have heard much good of the musician Puccini. I have seen a letter which speaks very highly of him. He follows modern tendencies, which is natural, but sticks to melody which is neither ancient nor modern. It seems, however, that the symphonic element predominates in him! There's no harm in that. Only that it is necessary to go warily in that direction. Opera is opera; symphony is symphony, and I don't believe that in an opera it's good to indulge excessively in symphonic passages for the sole purpose of letting loose the orchestra.

16. Marco Sala, in *Italia (giornale del popolo),* 1, 2, 3 June 1884.
17. Amintore Galli, in *Il Secolo (La Gazzetta di Milano),* 1, 2, 3 June 1884.
18. Filippo Filippi, in *La Perseveranza,* 2–3 June 1884.

The same characteristic prompted Giovannina Lucca to pro-
pose that Puccini write a "grande sinfonia" in four movements, obviously programmatic, for her publishing house. This
proposal, made shortly after the final performance of *Le willis*
and referred to in a letter from Fontana to Puccini dated 9 June
1884 (Marchetti 55), was never taken up; the composer's
rejection of such an offer, which only ten months earlier could
have constituted the realization of his ambition, is extremely
revealing.

The success of Puccini's opera was naturally noted by Giulio Ricordi, who, sensing the presence of a strong new talent,
unhesitatingly took steps to acquire *Le willis* for his firm. On
8 June the publisher placed a notice in *La Gazzetta Musicale di
Milano* announcing that he had acquired world rights for the
opera and had furthermore commissioned Puccini to write a
new work, also to be set to a libretto by Fontana; Puccini
would henceforth receive a monthly stipend of two hundred
lire. At Ricordi's suggestion, however, the composer was first
to recast *Le willis* into a two-act opera, chiefly to facilitate its
acceptance by the larger opera houses. The premiere of the
new version—from now on to bear the Italianized title *Le villi*—
was fixed for 26 December at the Teatro Regio, Turin, and
was to be followed by a staging at La Scala in late January
1885. Ricordi never published the opera in its original one-act
form.

Also on 8 June, the day of Ricordi's announcement, Puccini
returned to Lucca to find the health of his mother—who had
been ill for some time now—seriously deteriorated. But he
went to Turin about 25 June to assist in rehearsals of his *Capriccio
sinfonico,* the previously projected performance of which took
place on 6 July (there was to be a second performance 26
October), then to Bellano for a meeting with Ricordi and to
Caprino Bergamasco to discuss the revision of *Le willis* with
Fontana, returning to Lucca only a few days before his mother
died of cancer, 17 July. The death of Puccini's mother undeniably slowed his progress on the modifications to the opera;
these were finally completed on 28 October, and the score
was dispatched to Ricordi by 2 November (Marchetti 91).

The Turin reception of the opera in its new guise was no

less enthusiastic than the Dal Verme premiere had been, although Fontana and Puccini had written to Ricordi on 24 December that rehearsals were disappointing (Gara 16). But when *Le villi* was given at La Scala, 24 January 1885, it did not quite repeat its earlier two successes, in spite of both Puccini's personal supervision of the staging and the orchestral direction of Franco Faccio, who was was already familiar with Puccini's music (i.e., the *Capriccio sinfonico* and possibly the *Preludio sinfonico* in A major). Nevertheless, it received thirteen performances in Milan, after which the opera was quickly taken up by other theaters both in Italy and abroad.

It was formerly believed that Fontana had drawn the subject for his libretto directly from Heinrich Heine's essay on German spirits and demons entitled *Über Deutschland II: Elementargeister und Dämonen* (1834), which outlines in very general terms the Slavonic legend of the *willis,* a legend dealing with young maidens abandoned by their betrothed shortly before marriage, who die of grief and then return as specters *(willis* or *villi),* appearing to their faithless lovers at night and forcing them to dance until they die of sheer exhaustion. (Heine's description had inspired Adam's ballet *Giselle, ou Les willis* [1841]). Recent research,[19] however, has revealed that Fontana's libretto was based on *Les Wilis* (1852) by Alphonse Karr, a little-known French romantic *littérateur* whose works were nonetheless familiar to the *scapigliatura.* Although Karr's story is itself an elaboration of the account contained in Heine, it conveniently provided Fontana with three stock characters: a young forsaken heroine, Anna (soprano); the swain who forsakes her, Heinrich (named Roberto in the opera—tenor); and the girl's father, Wilhelm (renamed Guglielmo—baritone), who, at the hands of the librettist, was to fulfill no real dramatic function, but merely to supply the contrast of a darker voice. Both the parts of the villagers and those of the spirits and *villi* lent themselves perfectly to the customary chorus. The opera is set, like Karr's story, in the Black Forest, and is divided into two parts ("acts" in the revised version).

---

19. Julian Budden, "The Genesis and Literary Source of Giacomo Puccini's First Opera," in *Cambridge Opera Journal* 1/1 (1989):82.

Since Fontana's choice of subject matter (and Puccini's enthusiastic acceptance of it) had apparently been based largely on "symphonic" and not dramatic considertions, it is hardly surprising to find that the scenario of the opera is somewhat weak. As stipulated in the conditions of the Sonzogno competition, the libretto was to have been tailored for a one-act opera, and yet Fontana handed Puccini a plot that by virtue of its time span alone should have necessitated a multiple-act opera—or the division of a one-act work into several chronologically separated episodes: the betrothal celebrations and Roberto's farewell; Roberto's seduction and ruin in Mainz; Anna's grief and eventual demise; Roberto's return and death. Surprisingly, Fontana did not exploit the most potentially dramatic of these episodes, Roberto's seduction and Anna's death. Nor did he take great pains in delineating his characters; Anna, Roberto, and Guglielmo are little more than conventional, both in their thoughts and actions.

For all that, however, Fontana's libretto is not as defective as many recent writers would have us believe. Filippi, the most astute Italian critic of his day, held the Fontana libretto in high esteem:

> The libretto, from that lively and congenial talent of Ferdinando Fontana, is elegant, interesting, theatrical, clothed with good verses—"rara avis."[20]

> Signor Puccini has been fortunate to have Ferdinando Fontana as his librettist, fervid and congenial talent, who has written a distinguished opera, full of life, of color, and of passion, using that German legend of the villi . . . This libretto has had the added advantage of offering Puccini the opportunity to indulge his bent for symphonic music, so accented and personal.[21]

And a critic for *La Gazetta Musicale di Milano,* while slightly less enthusiastic than Filippi, considered the libretto for *Le villi* more than adequate:

20. Filippo Filippi, in *La Perseveranza,* 1 June 1884.
21. Ibid., 2–3 June 1884.

Since the work had to be presented on the larger stage in Turin, it was necessary to alter the structure [of the libretto]; it had to be halved, it had to be expanded here and there, it was necessary to make up for the lack of action, because if the story was sufficient for one act, it was not sufficient for two. This explains why the first act—from the point of view of the libretto—is a little poor, indeed almost empty, while the second is stronger, more solid, more sustained. But after all it would be unjust to speak badly of the libretto. There are some flaws here and there, some blemishes that perhaps betray the author's hurry to complete the modifications, but in general the verses are good, capable of inspiring the composer, and there are one or two dramatic situations of more than reasonable dimensions . . . On the whole Fontana has performed his role of librettist well, since his libretto is human and—strangely enough—has comon sense.[22]

Whatever the verdict on Fontana's contribution to *Le villi,* Puccini's music is for the most part effective. Besides betraying, as one would expect, a certain indebtedness to the works of Ponchielli and Verdi—manifest particularly in its choral scenes—the score already displays many of the peculiarly individual characteristics found in Puccini's mature works. And the critics were not mistaken in detecting a French influence, noticeable primarily in the harmonic language—the effective and economical use of conventional harmonies, particularly of ii^7 and IV chords at melodic climaxes—and the orchestration.

And the influence of Wagner? It is the penchant of modern critics to find traces of Wagnerian influence on virtually every page of Puccini's earliest operas. Undeniably a very strong Wagnerian current pervaded Italian musical circles at the time of the composition of *Le willis.* But Nicolaisen's claim that Puccini was merely an eclectic who throughout his career constantly borrowed from the entire fund of contemporaneous musical devices seems right on target:

Not present at all in *Le villi* [or *Edgar*] was the evocation of certain passages from Wagner's music dramas . . . critics might well

22. *La Gazzetta Musicale di Milano,* 4 January 1885.

have pointed out the use of lengthy orchestral passages and leit-motives as Wagnerian elements, but these were actually common coin among the more progressive composers of the day.[23]

And it is significant that the ardent Wagnerian Filippi also defended Puccini from charges of Wagnerism:

> In his phrasing he is clearly Italian. I deny that he is Wagnerian, as many assert, because the shaping of his pieces, like the eur-ythmy of the melodies, doesn't have anything to do with Wag-ner. Yet Wagner is a huge mine, and I don't deny that Puccini has taken some colors, some expressions from him, as do all—even those who claim to despise him.[24]

Le villi is a "number" opera, that is to say, deliberately divided into well-defined musical sections. These sections, first indi-vidually numbered in the fourth edition of the two-act opera (1892), are as follows:

ATTO PRIMO	1. Preludio
	2. Coro d'introduzione
	3. Scena e romanza (Anna)
	4. Duetto (Anna and Roberto)
	5. Preghiera (Anna, Roberto, Guglielmo, and chorus)
ATTO SECONDO	6. Parte sinfonica—primo tempo—"L'abban-dono" (The abandonment)
	7. Parte sinfonica—secondo tempo—"La tregenda" (The witches' sabbath)
	8. Preludio e scena (Guglielmo)
	9. Scena drammatica—romanza (Roberto)
	10. Gran scena e duetto finale (Anna, Roberto, and chorus)

In spite of the numerical division, the majority of these sec-tions are linked either orchestrally or by passages of arioso.

As can be seen, the external structure of the opera is well balanced but old-fashioned; the format of the first act, with

---

23. Jay R. Nicolaisen, *Italian Opera in Transition, 1871–1893,* Studies in Musicology 31 (Ann Arbor, 1980), 234.
24. Filippo Filippi, in *La Perseveranza,* 2–3 June 1884.

its opening prelude, introductory chorus, and prayer, is strictly traditional, and demonstrates, as do many student works from this period (e.g., Mascagni's *In filanda*), a rigid adherence to the rules then perpetuated through scholastic studies. Yet it should be noted that the original one-act work, *Le willis,* was less logically conceived than *Le villi* since it lacked numbers 3 and 9. The opportunities Fontana afforded for effective characterization were thus practically nonexistent in the first version of the opera, and Anna and Roberto sang merely in the Act I love duet, the ensuing prayer, and in the final "gran scena," with the result that Guglielmo was the only character with a solo scene. Since he also had a small part in the introductory chorus, an important role in the prayer, and the line "E' giusto Iddio" (God is just) with which the opera originally finished (this line was removed when the opera was recast into two acts), Guglielmo, the least important character in the unfolding of the plot, was initially painted in slightly stronger colors than the two principals.

Certainly not traditional is the extent to which orchestral music dominates the score. In the first version of the work, the role allotted to the orchestra was even more prominent; three of the original eight numbers were purely instrumental—these, together with the prelude to Guglielmo's aria (No. 8), the instrumental reprise that preceded the intermezzi, and the extensive orchestral solos in the two choruses and finale, indicate that more than half of *Le willis*'s music was "symphonic." In view of this, both Verdi's comments about Puccini's symphonic element and the charges of "Wagnerism" leveled at the young composer after the triumph of *Le willis* are easily comprehensible.

The opening prelude (No. 1) introduces us immediately to Puccini's particular style of orchestration, featuring a heavy reliance on the woodwinds, especially in the opening seven bars, and already utilizing the harp—one of the fundamental ingredients of the mature Puccinian sound—to a remarkable degree. The outstanding feature of this short (forty-three bars) prelude is its orchestration; this was attested to after the first performance by Filippi: "The prelude of the little opera doesn't offer a lot of interest, but one notices immediately the vigorous and brilliant palette of the orchestrator."[25] The prelude is confidently written and is entirely constructed, following the then standard practice, on themes that reappear in the opera; of the five used here, two are later found in the love duet (No. 4) and three in the prayer (No. 5).

The two orchestral pieces, "L'abbandono" and "La tregenda" (Nos. 6 and 7), with which the second act opens "at Dal Verme served as nothing but symphonic intermezzi, but have since become an integral and dramatic part of the work."[26] The change of scene that would have occurred during these intermezzi in the one-act opera is now carried out during the interval between the two acts. Both pieces are accompanied by verses that explain the details of Roberto's betrayal, and Anna's death and the legend of the *villi*, respectively. These verses, written in September 1884 for inclusion in the revised two-act opera (Marchetti 84), were never set to music, and appear only in the score and libretto. When the opera was recast into two acts, a female chorus, which sings a funereal prayer, was also added to "L'abbandono" in order to render more obvious the significance of Anna's death.

The positioning of both orchestral pieces at the beginning of the second act (not between Acts I and II, as is often stated), where they are to be played with the main curtain raised, attests to their new role in the unfolding of the drama. During "L'abbandono," Anna's funeral cortege is seen moving behind a scrim; and "La tregenda," a lively tarantella, is now unquestionably a ballet for the *villi*. (Although *Le willis* was advertised as an "opera-ballo," there is no evidence to suggest that "La tregenda" was originally danced. For the Turin premiere of the two-act opera, however, Fontana and Puccini's letter to Ricordi of 24 December 1884 [Gara 16], speaks of the inadequacy of the dancers. And Filippi, commenting on the La Scala performances, declared that "the unrestrained dances of the *villi* make the music even more interesting."[27]) These two instrumental movements further demonstrate the young

25. Ibid.
26. Ibid., 26 January 1885.
27. Ibid.

composer's already sure grasp of orchestrating techniques: "Both pieces are admirable, as much for their invention as for their orchestral workmanship; in the first there are exquisite and tender melodies, in the second an overflowing rush of sounds, fine orchestral combinations, extremely talented polyphonic mixtures; then there's also a great clarity, as in all Puccini's music."[28] The movements also show attention to detail and effect—the dynamic levels, for example, range from *pppp* to *fff.* Even so, it is doubtful that Puccini, at this stage, realized the dramatic inadequacy of having explanatory verses (printed in the libretto and score but not recited on the stage) precede a symphonic intermezzo; he adapted the same piece of dubious stagecraft in *Manon Lescaut.*

The sixteen-bar orchestral reprise of the theme from the love duet (No. 4) with which the prayer (No. 5) and the first act close played an even larger role in the initial success of Puccini's score. This reprise, a heavily scored *tutti* dominated by the brass, caused quite a sensation not only at the first performance of the opera, but also at the La Scala season seven months later (in fact, it was this particular passage that was encored and repeated at each of the Dal Verme performances, and *not* one of the "parti sinfoniche" [intermezzi] as Carner and others testify). Filippi made no attempt to conceal his admiration for it:

> When the chorus is finished Roberto departs, and while Anna weeps, consoled by her father, inflamed sounds spring forth from the orchestra like a wave, so potent, so inspired, a phonic effect so novel that the audience remained enraptured by it, and wanted to hear once more the piece, and then another time, not only the first but the second evening.[29]

At the end of this very beautiful finale, there's that instrumental explosion so inspired that even at La Scala, as at the Dal Verme, the public went into raptures. When the piece was finished there was a real burst of enthusiasm and the clamorous repeat took place. . . . in these 16 bars there's a really extraordinary inspira-

---

28. Ibid., 2–3 June 1884.
29. Ibid.

tion, an immense sonorous effect, and, it should be noted, without offense from the timpani.[30]

While Puccini's early bent for "symphonic" writing is clearly
revealed in *Le villi*'s orchestral music, his technical preparation for and approach to composing opera are reflected in the
genesis of the work's choruses, ensembles, and arias. The
introductory chorus (No. 2) and the prayer (No. 5) both contain extensive self-plagiarism. No. 2, which celebrates Anna
and Roberto's betrothal, is divided into two parts. The first
of these, a lively F-major *allegro* in 2/4 time, was composed
expressly for the opera and contains not only Ponchiellian
echoes but shades of the Verdi of *Luisa Miller*. The second
part, however, is but a reworking of previously composed
instrumental pieces. As Carner points out, it is not a robust
Ländler as might be expected, but a capricious waltz "à la
Delibes"[31] in the key of A minor and in loose ternary form
(with introduction and extended coda). The A section is wholly
taken from the sixty-one-bar *Scherzo for Strings* in A minor
(1881); in the opera there is a slight alteration of some rhythmic cells, redistribution of the melody between wind and string
sections and voices, and a filling-out of the harmonic framework. Most of the B section (and the coda), which is in A
major, is derived from a twenty-three-bar *Adagio for Pianoforte*
(1881–82?) in the same tonality. The material in question is
given solely to the orchestra and accompanies first Guglielmo's dance and then his exit; not only has the original "adagio" tempo marking become "tempo di valzer," but the 12/8
time signature of the piano piece is now changed 3/4 and all
original note values are consequently augmented.

Both the orchestral introduction to the prayer scene (No. 5)
and the prayer proper, "Angiol di Dio, che i vanni rivolgi al
ciel stasera" (Angel of God, who spreads wings to heaven this
evening), are entirely derived from the thirty-five-bar *Salve
regina* (1882–83). This short work was written originally for
soprano and organ (or harmonium) and in the key of F major.

---

30. Ibid., 26 January 1885.
31. Carner, *Puccini*, 307.

In *Le villi* its principal thematic material is first given to Gug-
liemo (baritone), the tonality is lowered to E-flat major, and
the organ is curiously absent from the orchestra; and yet the
reverent character of the original piece is retained. With the

Based on a libretto by the bohemian poet Ferdinando Fontana, Le Willis *(as it was originally called) was Puccini's first opera, staged thanks to a fund raised among Milanese
music lovers, headed by Boito. The opera underwent considerable revision, before and after
its name was changed to* Le villi. *Though it has some ingenuous aspects, the work shows
the signs of future achievement, a fact recognized by even the usually skeptical Verdi.*
(Museo Teatrale alla Scala; Foto Saporetti)

entry of Anna, Roberto, and the chorus, the prayer develops into an effective ensemble scene, modeled in character and detail, if not in structure, on the grandiose ensembles of Ponchielli.

Puccini described his self-plagiarism as a "labor-saving device" (Gara 209)—we should recall both the haste in which *Le willis* was completed and the bouts of laziness that preceded its actual completion—but it also served as a means of reutilizing any earlier compositions he considered worthy of a wider hearing. And yet more than this his recourse to previously composed material, a practice begun with *Le willis* and then continued in all his operas up to and including *Tosca,* was symptomatic of his general approach to writing opera. Puccini's primary objective, more so in his later operas, was the establishment of a particular ambience, the realization of which was brought about by means of the orchestration, harmonic language, and the nature of the melodies. The composer always sought to use themes whose character accorded with the general atmosphere of the opera in question (hence his eventual employment of authentic Japanese, American, and Chinese melodies in *Madama Butterfly, La fanciulla del West,* and *Turandot,* respectively), most of his self-borrowings were thus taken from "descriptive" instrumental pieces; the original material was slightly modified only when required to accommodate a libretto. (Those few self-borrowings taken from vocal works showed little regard for the original text and/or dramatic context—for this reason Ricordi expressed his disapproval when Puccini used part of the discarded Act IV of *Edgar* in Act III of *Tosca* [see Gara 208].) The composer's occasional practice of asking his librettists to fit words to existing music (for example, "Quando m'en vo" in *La bohème*) can be regarded as a reversal of the same arguable working method; Puccini's themes were frequently conceived (or reused) as a means of projecting the ambience of his opera and so were not always directly inspired by the libretto.

The omission of solos for the two principal characters in the original *Le willis* betrays a curious disregard for standard theatrical and operatic convention; therein lies yet another possible explanation for the opera's rejection by the Sonzogno commission. Even if the responsibility for this dramatic over-sight must ultimately rest with Fontana, there is no reason to suspect that Puccini himself had initially considered giving either Anna or Roberto a "scena." The eventual inclusion of these in *Le villi* almost certainly came at the suggestion of Ricordi, who would have advised both composer and librettist about the nature of the modifications needed to transform *Le willis* into a two-act opera. (Indeed, several of Puccini's and Fontana's letters from August and September 1884 [e.g., Gara 8 and Marchetti 82] not only outline the various stages of composition of the scenes for soprano and tenor but also stress the importance of Ricordi's opinion on the progress made with these numbers.)

Anna's aria, "Se come voi piccina io fossi, o vaghi fior" (If I were tiny like you, o pretty flowers [No. 3]), one of the highlights of the score, is particularly notable for the orchestration of its introduction, where the flute melody, doubled by the piccolo and rhythmically punctuated by harp and bells, is set against a sextuplet countermelody in the first violin. As Nicolaisen says, such lightly scored passages in which the wind predominate are "simply not typical of the Italian style before Puccini."[32] Some sketches held at the Pierpont Morgan Library in New York in fact confirm that the composer's priority here lay with the orchestration: "In both parts of Anna's Scena e romanza and the lover's duet (No. 4), Puccini seems to have worked out the music for the orchestra before that of the vocalists. The sketches for these two numbers contain sections in which only the instrumental 'accompaniment' appears, with the vocal part not yet added."[33]

While the insertion of this aria gave Puccini the opportunity to improve upon his earlier characterization of Anna, the verses provided by Fontana, in which the girl addresses a posy of forget-me-nots, did not allow the composer much scope. Nevertheless, the music is more than competently written, and parts of the vocal line foreshadow the melody type given to Puccini's "little girls"—a predominance of both diatonic

32. Nicolaisen, *Italian Opera*, 197.
33. J. Rigbie Turner, *Four Centuries of Opera: Manuscripts and Printed Editions in the Pierpont Morgan Library* (New York, 1983), 88.

steplike movement that avoids chromatic inflection and intervals of fourths and fifths. Thus for Carner, "Anna is the first in the gallery of Puccini's frail heroines . . . she already shows the typical blend of *morbidezza* and *ardor*."[34] (For a more detailed analysis of Puccini's melodic structure, see Edward Greenfield's *Puccini: Keeper of the Seal* [London, 1958].)

Even though Roberto's dramatic scene (No. 9) was composed expressly for the Turin premiere of *Le villi*, its centerpiece, the aria "Torna ai felici dì dolente il mio pensier" (My sorrowful thoughts return to those happy days), was not written until after the commencement of the La Scala season (it appears that even in his modifications, Puccini had not envisaged an actual aria for the tenor); it is therefore not included in the first published score of January 1885 but appears in the second, May 1885. Fontana explained the circumstances of its composition to Natale Gallini in 1914:

> One evening, while he was attending a performance of the opera in the wings of La Scala, Ponchielli advised Puccini to cut a dramatic scene. Giacomo took me by the shoulder and literally pushed me into the dressing room. He sat himself at the pianoforte and commanded me to describe, in verse, the desolate emotional state of Roberto, the tenor. In an instant I improvised the poetry and he composed the aria. That "young rascal," instead of shortening the dramatic scene, as Ponchielli had advised, lengthened it, introducing a new piece in the middle. After a few days I went to Puccini's, and gave him the verses in a fair copy.[35]

The scene originally consisted of extensive arioso (curtailed in the successive editions of the opera) into which the aria was then inserted, and a prayer, "O Sommo Iddio" (O supreme God), toward the end. In the opening monologue leading to the aria, Puccini seems a little unsure of himself; there are thirty-eight bars of vocal line of which eighteen contain repeated E-flats—it is left to the orchestra to provide the main interest. Yet the aria is undeniably "Puccinian" in its craftsmanship (particularly in its melody) and provides a necessary dramatic

34. Carner, *Puccini*, 308.
35. Quoted in Gallini, "Gli anni giovanili," 45.

focus for the scene while engendering a certain sympathy for Roberto. In it we find yet another melodic fragment taken from one of Puccini's early compositions—an unfinished song (in the same tonality, B-flat minor) for baritone and piano-forte, *Ad una morta* (1882–83), with text by Ghislanzoni. The four bars in question, 21–24, accompany Roberto's words "ridean i fior / fioria per me l'amor" (the flowers were cheer-ful / love blossomed for me). Furthermore, the aria has an eight-bar prelude (and identical interlude), which is nothing but a reprise of Guglielmo's "dance" theme heard in the B section of the second part of the introductory chorus (No. 2) and itself taken from the *Adagio for Pianoforte.* It is now marked "Andante mosso," and is in 6/8 time, and in the key of B-flat minor.

The other point of interest in Roberto's scene, the prayer, presents no new thematic material but reemploys the melody heard initially in the opening prelude and then in the Act I prayer (No. 5); Puccini obviously considered it an attractive idea. The characteristics of its structure (sequences, descend-ing lines, and falling fifths) led Carner to classify this partic-ular tune as one of the composer's many "povera faccia" melodies, which "could have been penned by no one but Puc-cini."[36]

It is largely on account of its memorable melodic material that the love duet (No. 4), conventional as it is, has always managed to find such favor with critics and public alike; one noted opera authority even declared that the piece occasion-ally struck him "as the most caressing duet that Puccini ever penned."[37] The duet proper is strophic and commences after a brief section of arioso, to Roberto's words "Tu dell'infanzia mia" (You who from my childhood). Of the two verses, Roberto sings the first, and then Anna (accompanied by a more delicate orchestration and interjections from Roberto) the sec-ond, and the duet closes with both voices together. If on a dramatic level the piece displays little character delineation— it is a frequently voiced criticism of Puccini's early operas (especially *Manon Lescaut*) that the melodic material of the

36. Carner, *Puccini,* 310.
37. John W. Klein, "Puccini's Enigmatic Activity," in *Music and Letters* 46/3 (July 1965):196.

leading soprano and tenor is interchangeable, especially in duets of this type—the first critics, under the spell of Puccini's melodic invention, were oblivious to this. Filippi found that "in these two strophes the original character of the melody excels, sweet, flowing, impassioned, denoting in Puccini a theatrical temperament, melodic, suitable for expressing the amorous emotions."[38]

Guglielmo's prelude and aria "Anima santa della figlia mia" (Blessed soul of my daughter [No. 8]) betray a strong Verdian influence, not only in the character and high tessitura of the vocal line, but also in certain features of the orchestration— for example, the prelude's sinister opening melody played by the horns in thirds. In addition, the arioso contains the opera's first use of thematic recall in a dramatic context, when to Guglielmo's words "ed egli venne e / colla sua parola / d'amor le smanie in lei destò" (and he came / and, with his words / woke the longing for love in her heart) Puccini briefly quotes the woodwind motive that introduces the Act I love duet.

The final "gran scena e duetto finale" (No. 10) contains little new melodic material, since it is almost entirely constructed, as one would expect, from further use of thematic recall. It begins with motives taken from "La tregenda" and then "L'abbandono," which follow each other in quick succession; these accompany the voices of the *villi* and the appearance of Anna's specter, respectively. The ensuing duet predictably begins with the theme of the Act I love duet, which is, however, given a completely new orchestral guise in keeping with the altered dramatic situation. As Anna speaks of her "tremendo dolore" (terrible grief) the music returns to "L'abbandono." When the *villi* surround Roberto, there is a reprise of "La tregenda" accompanied by the voices of the *villi* (and other spirits)—ironically, to the words "Gira, balza" (Turn, jump), which had been merrily sung in the "waltz" section of the introductory chorus (No. 2). A triumphant "Osanna" from the *villi,* still to the music of "La tregenda," closes the opera.

38. Filippo Filippi, in *La Perseveranza,* 2–3 June 1884.

$\mathcal{G}$iven the resounding success of Puccini's first theatrical venture, his earlier aspirations changed. The composer no longer harbored ideas of dedicating himself to "symphonic" music (hence his apparent rejection of Giovannina Lucca's proposal) but he was determined to repeat the operatic triumph of *Le villi.* In his next opera he would attempt to capitalize on those musical elements that had been most crucial to the first work's success—the inclusion of purely instrumental pieces, the colorful orchestration, the particular emphasis placed on melody, and the individuality of the melodic turn itself—elements nurtured during his "symphonic" period. In the realization of this objective Puccini proved to be remarkably successful; there is scarcely a page of *Edgar's* score that does not reveal his orchestrating talent and/or melodic gifts. However, the simple dramatic situations and characterizations with which he had been confronted in setting *Le villi* had in no way prepared him for the complexities of the large-scale opera that was *Edgar,* and, almost predictably, the second work contains several dramatic flaws. If most of these can ultimately be traced to a problematic scenario and libretto, their very presence was still essential to Puccini's development as a musical dramatist.

By virtue of his contract with Ricordi of June 1884, Puccini was assured not only of a librettist and publisher for his next operatic composition but also of its eventual production. This does not imply, however, that the period in which *Edgar* was written was any less eventful than the preceding few years had been. The composer's private life, already affected by the death of his mother and worries for the future of his younger brother, now entered a new phase when Elvira Bonturi, wife of Lucchese wholesale merchant Narciso Gemignani, left her husband to live openly with Puccini, taking with her the elder of her two children, Fosca. Moreover, throughout this period Puccini had no permanent address, and movement between Milan, Lucca, Sant'Antonio d'Adda, Caprino Bergamasco (where he was a guest of Ghislanzoni), Monza, and Pizzameglio (Chiasso) can only have created an unwanted disruption to his work. And then in December 1886, while Puccini was still busy composing *Edgar,* his son Antonio was born; with four mouths to feed on a monthly stipend of two hundred lire (and scant royalties from *Le villi*), these were days of financial hardship.

Puccini was never a fast worker, but the composition of *Edgar* did not take as long as most biographers suggest. By the end of September 1884, a definite subject for the second opera had *still* not been decided upon (Marchetti 88), and almost a year later, in June 1885, Fontana had only just completed his libretto (Marchetti 98). And yet on 19 July 1887, Michele Puccini was able to write to his sister Ramelde that "Giacomo is at the end of *Edgar*" (Marchetti 120), and by 27 October 1887, Puccini had finished orchestrating the last act (Gara 26). Thus he spent just over two years in writing this work. Furthermore, it is probable that the composition of *Edgar,* like that of *Le villi,* was drawn out by Puccini's "innate laziness"—in a letter to Fontana of November 1885 (Gara 19), Puccini frankly admitted, "I am doing little work."

The sixteen months separating the completion of the opera from its premiere at La Scala on 21 April (Easter Sunday) 1889 are sketchily documented. It would seem that during this period, both the composer and his publisher were still occupied in finding a venue for the debut of *Edgar*. A series of negotiations for the staging of the premiere had been made as early as June 1887, if not before (Marchetti 119), but these were unsuccessful, as Puccini explains in his letter to Ramelde dated 9 September (Marchetti 122): "Plans to present my opera in Rome have been plunged into darkness because the Rome council has imposed an opera by a Roman composer upon the impresario Canori, and difficulties have arisen over mine . . . for the time being nothing has been arranged with La Scala." Once the details of the premiere had finally been decided upon, Puccini set about trying to secure celebrated tenor Francesco Tamagno (Verdi's first Otello) for the title role. Only two months before the long-awaited event (21 February 1889), he was still imploring Tamagno to take the part: "To live in hope is already something, at least it's better than a certainty that is lousy. There comes in the life of every man a decisive moment, and that is for me the good success of *Edgar*. I cling to him who can save me, as one who has suffered shipwreck clings to the last plank. And that plank is you!"[39] Much to Puccini's disappointment, Tamagno was already under contract for a long American tour.

According to Carner, the above letter demonstrates the profound apprehension with which Puccini regarded the opening night of his second opera, intensified by the fear of intrigues against him on the part of the enemies he had made through the success of *Le villi.* It more likely reflects an eventual coming to terms with the peculiarities of Fontana's libretto and the belief that *Edgar*'s salvation lay in revealing the quality of the music by means of a first-rate cast. Puccini had hitherto given no indication of discontent with his music—on the contrary, in his letter to Ricordi of May 1886 (Gara 23), he writes, "I am happy with my work, and I would like to hope that you, for your part, also remain satisfied with it."

And yet any forebodings Puccini may have had proved to be justified. The premiere of the work—"the biggest and most important event of my life" (Gara 29)—was not the success that Puccini, Fontana, and Ricordi had hoped for, and *Edgar* was consequently given only two more performances. The Romanian tenor Gregorio Gabrielesco sang the title role, the two female parts were sung by Aurelia Cataneo and Romilda Pantaleoni (the latter was a last-minute replacement for Giulia Novelli, who had suddenly taken ill), and the conductor was once again Franco Faccio. It must be stated immediately, however, that *Edgar* was not a fiasco—for all three performances the theater was filled to capacity, several pieces were encored, and Puccini had to take repeated curtain calls. The critics were divided. Some were unnecessarily severe:

[Puccini] desires those effects that were able to please the public when tastes were not yet as refined as it appears they are nowadays.[40]

[Puccini] has committed] grave sins against art; a lack of faith, of conviction, of well-defined ideals.[41]

39. Quoted in Carner, *Puccini,* 47.
40. Giovanni Battista Nappi, in *La Perseveranza,* 22–23 April 1889.
41. *La Lombardia,* 24 April 1889.

Others did not lose faith in the young composer:

> This young man from Lucca can be happy with his success; *Edgar* is something more than *Le villi* . . . the beauties of the new score, even if they don't yet indicate the extent of Puccini's talent, are certainly enough to confirm him a master.[42]

> *Edgar* is the fruit of a composer of genius, of a genius not yet mature, of a genius perhaps still unconscious of its own existence, and because unconscious, prodigal of its talents; of a genius not yet affirmed by pure and complete individuality—true; but still a genius, in other words, spark, facility, creation.[43]

They all, according to Giulio Ricordi, expressed the wish to have additional performances of *Edgar* included in La Scala's May program (these were not given).[44]

What, then, was the reason for the opera's mixed reception? It was generally accepted that the work was flawed by Fontana's curious scenario and libretto, with its lack of a logical plot, abundance of psychological and dramatic discrepancies, and puppetlike characters whose language was full of sham pathos. And yet a letter from Puccini to Ramelde's husband Raffaello Franceschini dated 4 May 1889 (Marchetti 134) states that the opera was seen on only three evenings because the standard of the performances had been very low! Puccini was likely attempting to conceal any hint of failure from the family; the composer had written to Franco Faccio on 25 April 1889 (Gara 30), thanking him for the "perfect and exceptional performances," and Giulio Ricordi had lavished high praise on the soloists, chorus, and orchestra.[45] Claudio Casini believes that the major defect of the opera—immediately identified by Ricordi—lay in Puccini's score and that Fontana was merely a scapegoat, sacrificed by Ricordi and Puccini.[46] In any event, Ricordi did not lose faith in his protégé and continued pay-

---

42. *Illustrazione Italiana,* 28 April 1889.
43. Alfred Soffredini, in *La Gazzetta Musicale di Milano,* 28 April 1889.
44. Giulio Ricordi, in *La Gazzetta Musicale di Milano,* 28 April 1889.
45. Ibid.
46. Claudio Casini, *Giacomo Puccini* (Turin, 1978), 94.

ments of the monthly stipend (which was soon after increased by one hundred lire).

The singular history of *Edgar* does not end here, however. Puccini was reluctant to admit that his opera could not be successfully revised, and he began to work on the score almost at once. When La Scala announced the inclusion of *Edgar* in its spring 1890 season, there was renewed expectation of a success, but, as fate would have it, the projected performances were canceled when the tenor fell ill. And yet *Edgar* was given thirteen extremely well-received performances beginning 5 September 1891 at the Teatro Giglio, Lucca; the score by this time contained even more modifications (Gara 57).

Puccini now set about reducing the number of acts from four to three. Contemporary reviews show that the three-act version of *Edgar* was first performed on 28 January 1892 (and *not* 28 February, as is invariably claimed and even erroneously stated in the second edition of the piano-vocal score) at the Teatro Comunale, Ferrara. Here it had a run of four performances, described by Ricordi as "a most brilliant success" (Gara 66); Puccini himself was the stage director, and the orchestra was conducted by his friend and colleague Carlo Carignani. This triumph was followed by a no less enthusiastically lauded production at the Teatro Regio, Turin (six performances, beginning 5 March, of which most biographers seem to be unaware), and then by equally successful seasons in Madrid (at the Teatro Real, opening 19 March) and in Brescia (at the Teatro Grande, opening 18 August). Just prior to the Madrid performances, contractual problems arose with the tenor, Eugenio Durot, and once more Puccini appealed to Tamagno, who, after much persuasion, finally agreed to take on the title role. The Madrid production featured a superb cast; in addition to Tamagno, the female parts were sung by Eva Tetrazzini and Giuseppina Pasqua, and the conductor was Luigi Mancinelli.

Edgar underwent further revision in 1901, when Puccini apparently contemplated reutilizing Act IV of the original version of the opera (which had been largely discarded in the reduced three-act version) and removing Act II. A handwritten note in the manuscript score (Ricordi Archives) reports that on 15 January 1901, the copyist's first three acts and Act IV of the autograph were sent to Puccini, and the composer remarks in a letter to his sister Dide on 6 March [1901], "I am going to set to work and cut down *Edgar,* completely recasting the last act and correcting the others. I shall take out the second act,"[47] and in another to Luigi Illica, March 11, 1901 (Gara 247): "I am tranquil, and reducing *Edgar*!!! in galvanoplasty [*sic*]."

The final changes to *Edgar* were completed in March 1905, in time for the opera's premiere in Buenos Aires on 8 July as part of a Puccini Festival. After this the work was largely abandoned, Puccini claiming that "it is warmed-up soup . . . what is wanted is a subject that palpitates with life and is believable—not trash."[48]

Since *Edgar* had enjoyed overwhelming successes in Lucca, Ferrara, Turin, Madrid, and Brescia, Puccini's persistent revisions to his score are not easily explained. There can be little doubt that his dramatic "instincts" were awakened during the composition of *Edgar,* and that he thereafter continued to discover flaws in the work that he felt capable of rectifying. But his relative inexperience in dramaturgical matters was evidently the chief determinant in the nature and extent of his initial modifications, many of which now seem ill-advised. Several of the later revisions appear to be attempts to correct earlier ones. And so, paradoxically, it was Puccini himself who sealed the fate of *Edgar.* His excessive alterations to the score, the more immediate success (and superior librettos) of the operas that followed, particularly *Manon Lescaut,* and, in later years, his own eventual dissatisfaction with *Edgar* were all in part responsible for the work's gradual neglect.

Before examining the changes made to *Edgar,* it is necessary to look briefly at Fontana's libretto. The story was taken from Alfred de Musset's five-act verse drama *La coupe et les lèvres* (The cup and the lips), which appeared in 1832 as part of the

---

47. Adami, *Letters of Giacomo Puccini,* 64.
48. Quoted in Fraccaroli, *La vita di Giacomo Puccini,* 61.

collection *Un spectacle dans un fauteil* (A performance in an armchair); Musset was another writer revered by the *scapigliatura*. Described by its author as a "poème dramatique," *La coupe* was intended for study rather than the stage and is in essence a psychological character study with melodramatic trappings, a drama of spiritual quest. Its hero is Charles Frank— the Edgar of Puccini's opera (the Frank of the opera is a different character)—who is a complex blend of misanthropy, ambition, pride, self-hatred, intelligence, impetuosity, and quick temper. Frank sets fire to his own house in order to demonstrate publicly his contempt for his fellow villagers, symbolically isolating himself from both them and his past. He foresakes Déidamia (Fidelia), the girl who has loved him since childhood, and leaves his village in the Tyrol to embark upon a life of adventure. He is lured on by the wild temptress Monna Belcolore (Tigrana), upon whom he then blames his own dissipation. After finally breaking free from Monna, Frank is acclaimed as a hero after a military victory yet is equally dissatisfied with worldly success. To vent his self-disgust, he arranges his own mock funeral, which also allows him to observe the reactions of his acquaintances to his feigned death and to his strong self-denunciation. When he finally arrives at the point of being reconciled with the faithful Déidamia, the world at large, and himself, Monna suddenly stabs Déidamia to death.

Why did Fontana resort to Musset's obscure play for his operatic subject? The answer undoubtedly lies not only in the French playwright's popularity among *scapigliatura* members but also in the resemblance of the plot of *La coupe* to that of *Carmen;* the parallels between Edgar and Don José, Tigrana and Carmen, Fidelia and Micaëla, Frank and Escamillo, are not difficult to detect. In addition, Musset's play allowed Fontana to introduce a theme of moral redemption reminiscent of *Tannhäuser* into his libretto; and in transferring the action from the Tyrol to Flanders in the year 1302 (date of the Battle of the Spurs), he was able to attempt to recreate the atmosphere of *Il trovatore*.

From Musset's conglomeration of "introspection and melodrama, of exalted lyrical poetry and rhetorical bombast,"[49] Fontana extracted what is undoubtedly its worst feature, the plot. With a strange regard for Musset's original characterization and the motivation underlying the hero's bizzare behavior, the librettist based his story around those episodes offering the maximum visual effect (Edgar's setting fire to his house, the mock funeral, the stabbing of Fidelia on the open stage). And yet it would seem that the concentration on such scenes was indeed intentional, and that Fontana sought to provide Puccini, as he had done with the libretto for *Le willis* (the betrothal celebrations, Roberto's farewell, "La tregenda," Anna's revenge, etc.), with as many opportunities as possible for exercising his "symphonic element." (A recently published collection of Fontana's letters to Puccini written between 1884 and 1916[50] reveals that in its initial stages, *Edgar* was to have also included a piece of symphonic music depicting "la battaglia" [Battle of the Spurs?].)

For his part, Fontana gave priority to the poetry of the libretto rather than to the finer details of the plot (*Edgar* is prefaced by a remarkable eight-verse poem: "Edgar are we all, for fate leads everyone to the crossroads—in alternate succession, shadow and light, love and death . . . Woe if, to the light of serene love, which can on mighty pinions lift souls aloft, we prefer the obscene flame that kindles the senses," etc.). Consequently, few of the first critics were able to comprehend Fontana's objectives with regard to *Edgar* or, for that matter, the resultant nature of his libretto. More recent appraisals of Fontana's work, however, have been surprisingly positive. Andrew Porter, for example, finds *Edgar* "an abrupt, violent, existentialist, and curiously modern opera—formal and symbolic, not veristic . . . a drama of small credibility, but, on a non-realistic plane, of high poetic power."[51]

Be that as it may, the libretto contains various dramaturgical flaws, the most serious of which is that no attempt was made to define Edgar's personality. Since in his dialogue he is little more than a conventional operatic tenor, his unconven-

49. Carner, *Puccini*, 312.
50. *Lettere di Ferdinando Fontana a Giacomo Puccini: 1884–1916,* published as volume four of the journal *Quaderni Pucciniani* (Milan, 1992).
51. Andrew Porter, *Music of Three Seasons, 1974–1977* (New York, 1978), 579.

tional actions cannot be understood by the audience. This was acknowledged after the first performances by Nappi, who was nonetheless unfair in extending the same criticism to all the other protagonists: "The situations are not enough to make us forget the improbability of the episodes and the incoherence of the characters who are lacking a special personality, clearly defined, original and sympathetic so as to impress upon the mind of the composer the true and absolute conviction of their 'musicability.' "[52]

While the first cuts and revisions (1889–92) made to *Edgar* should have borne testimony to Puccini's gradual development as a musical dramatist, many of these contrarily demonstrate how much he had still to learn about dramaturgy, particularly characterization. He may have succeeded in curtailing the excessive (?) dimensions of the four-act opera through the elimination of those scenes thought to delay the unfolding of the drama, but in the process he weakened his portrayal of the characters. Puccini's relative inexperience in this area was almost certainly a direct legacy of his "symphonic" background. If in *Le villi* this had been overtly manifested in the prominence of the orchestra and the unusually large quantity of purely orchestral music, in *Edgar* it was to be observed less in features of the original score, where the local writing was elevated in importance and generally on an equal footing with the orchestra, than in the rather haphazard nature of his earliest editing.

> Giacomo Puccini revealed himself, some years ago now, as having a musical character that is clearly symphonic. The second version of *Le villi,* of course, modified such an opinion—the voices merged together and sang of love with admirable clarity and simplicity. In *Edgar* these voices have been treated by the composer on the same level as the instrumental writing, and, owing to the natural preponderance that voices have over an orchestral accompaniment, the "singing," in the proper sense of the word, has shone with all its pomp and with all its splendor.[53]

---

52. Giovanni Battista Nappi, in *La Perseveranza,* 22–23 April 1889.
53. Alfredo Soffredini, in *La Gazzetta Musicale di Milano,* 28 April 1889.

The long-held view that Fontana stubbornly refused to alter his original libretto for *Edgar* is without foundation, as the aforementioned letters from Fontana to Puccini show.

The final changes (1905), although made by the now experienced, successful composer of *Manon Lescaut, La bohème, Tosca,* and *Madama Butterfly,* contributed little toward undoing the dramatic damage incurred in the first revisions—some of the new cuts were even more merciless than the original ones.

The total number of modifications to *Edgar* far exceeds that made to any of Puccini's other operas, *Madama Butterfly* included. It can be partially gauged by comparing the number of scenes into which the acts were divided in the first two editions of Ricordi's piano-vocal score, published in 1890 and 1892 (the third and final edition, 1905, is not divided into scenes):

1890: Act I = 9 scenes; Act II = 5 scenes; Act III = 6 scenes; Act IV = 7 scenes
1892: Act I = 9 scenes; Act II = 5 scenes; Act III = 4 scenes

As Hopkinson relates, "Such tremendous rewriting of the score took place that they [the first and second versions] might be treated as two distinct operas, apart from the story; and there were again a large number of revisions in the third version."[54] The most obvious changes include the following:

a) Act IV was discarded in the second and third versions, the stabbing of Fidelia being appended to the end of Act III (part of the music of the Act IV duet between Fidelia and Edgar eventually reappeared in Act III of *Tosca* ["Amaro sol per te"]).
b) Some of Fidelia's Act IV music was assigned to Tigrana (the Act II duet with Edgar).

54. Cecil Hopkinson, *A Bibliography of the Works of Giacomo Puccini* (New York, 1968), 5. A detailed list of all these modifications would be beyond the scope of the present study. However, two such lists can be found in Nicolaisen, *Italian Opera,* Appendix II, 291, and in Sergio Martinotti, "I travagliati avant-propos di Puccini," in *Il melodramma italiano dell'Ottocento: Studi e ricerche per Massimo Mila* (Turin, 1977), 504.

c) The original Act IV prelude, after being cut by thirty-four bars, functioned as a prelude to Act I in the second version of *Edgar* but was then completely discarded in the third version.

d) The lengthy banquet scene (Act II, scene 2) containing Tigrana's drinking song, "La Coppa," was drastically reduced for the second version and then discarded altogether for the third, and two of Tigrana's other major solos (Act III, scene 4 and Act II, scene 5) were deleted in 1892 and 1905, respectively.

e) The extensive ensemble scene in Act II (scene 4) was all but eliminated by 1892.

In addition to these alterations, many other pieces were reduced in size by the omission of repetitions or strophes, and several

Impressed by Le villi, *the influential publisher Giulio Ricordi gave Puccini a stipend and a contract for a second opera, which was to become the problematic* Edgar. *In later years, Puccini—like almost all critics and opera historians—had hard words for his piece, though sporadic recent revivals have led, in some instances, to a new and more favorable evaluation.* (Museo Teatrale alla Scala; Foto Saporetti)

that were cut for the second version were subject to yet further cuts for the final version.

The actual result of Puccini's revisions was an enfeeblement of Fontana's already confusing plot and, as previously mentioned, a mutation of some of the original characterization. This was due not only to the elimination of several solo scenes but also to the small amount of interaction remaining among the four principals. Fidelia's murder at the hands of Tigrana, for example, seems unprovoked when appended to the finale of Act III—Edgar has not had the opportunity to reestablish his love for Fidelia and thereby motivate Tigrana's revenge. As Puccini finally left them, almost all of his characters are unconvincing; the male leads, especially Edgar himself, are inadequately drawn. And yet in Fidelia we do encounter a satisfactorily realized character—much more than Anna, she represents the prototype of Mimì, Cio-Cio-San, and Liù, and is brought to life through the consistent quality of both her music and her dramatic treatment. Of particular interest in the second of her Act III arias, "Nel villaggio d'Edgar" (In Edgar's village), is the successful integration of coloratura writing with a typically lush Puccinian accompaniment, a device thereafter only rarely reemployed by the composer—for Manon (the Act II dancing lesson) and, to a lesser extent, for Musetta and Lisette.

The character most affected by Puccini's often ruthless editing was Tigrana. In the four-act opera she was adequately portrayed as a "she-devil," but then Puccini substantially distorted her character in eliminating roughly two-thirds of her music and in transferring part of Fidelia's Act IV music to her. The four large arias—one in each act—she originally sang were among the most impressive pages of the score; her Act III aria, "Ah, se scuoter della morte" (Ah, if to shake off death), was described by Carner as "an impressive piece of poignant dramatic expression."[55] Several writers, including Luciano Gherardi, see this mutilation of Tigrana's role as evidence that Puccini, on a psychological level, "could not manage to con-

55. Carner, *Puccini*, 314.

ceive a character as strongly negative as the librettist would have wanted."[56] But such a view fails to consider the "negative" characters of Puccini's mature operas and the relatively successful characterization of Tigrana in the original version of *Edgar:* "Tigrana's entrance is one of those instrumental devices of which Puccini knows the secret, and her first recitative makes us understand how that diabolic female character has been well-conceived by the maestro . . . the part of Tigrana astonishes on account of its truthfulness."[57]

Tigrana's musical "development" was no less complicated than her dramatic metamorphosis. By 1905 the tessitura of the vocal line in her remaining music had been altered—either lowered, as in parts of Act I, or raised, as in sections of Acts II and III—and such modifications have since created a great deal of ambiguity regarding the voice type that Puccini intended for that role. Because the 1890 piano-vocal score describes her as "soprano" (in the 1905 score this is changed to "mezzosoprano"), and because the first interpreter of Tigrana, as we have seen, was Romilda Pantaleoni (Verdi's first Desdemona and Puccini's third Anna), Nicolaisen believes that "certain commentators to the contrary, then, the evolution [of Tigrana's role] was from soprano to mezzo and not vice versa."[58] But a letter from Giulio Ricordi (after Puccini and Fontana, the person most familiar with the composition of *Edgar*) to Luigi Mancinelli, dated 29 August 1890 (Gara 44) offers a different version of the genesis of Tigrana's role:

The part of Tigrana is the most difficult, but the most characteristic; it calls for an excellent singer and a capable actress. In fact, at La Scala it was sung by Pantaleoni; however the part was altered here and there for this artist, who interpreted it extremely well. It was originally written for mezzo-soprano; Puccini doesn't want to sacrifice his singers, and if it is necessary will even make some changes.

---

56. Luciano Gherardi, "Appunti per una lettura delle varianti nelle opere di Giacomo Puccini," *Studi Musicali* 6 (1977):281.
57. Alfredo Soffredini, in *La Gazzetta Musicale di Milano,* 28 April 1889.
58. Nicolaisen, *Italian Opera,* 204.

It therefore seems that while Puccini conceived Tigrana as a mezzo-soprano, he felt obliged to raise the tessitura of her part when a soprano was unexpectedly chosen to interpret the role first. Such revision partly manifests itself in the 1890 score, published *after* the Scala performances, where Tigrana's vocal line is provided with numerous high alternatives. (Since it was Pantaleoni who created the role, Tigrana was designated as a soprano in the two earliest editions of the opera.) As Puccini gradually modified his score, he concentrated on redefining Tigrana as a mezzo-soprano, removing most of her high alternatives and transposing several sections of her music. By 1905, Tigrana was, by definition, a mezzo-soprano role.

Paradoxically, however, the list of the first Tigranas and their respective voice types reads as follows: Romilda Pantaleoni—soprano (Milan 1889; she substituted for Giulia Novelli—mezzo-soprano); Emma Zilli—soprano (Lucca 1891); Amadea Santarelli—mezzo-soprano, later famous as soprano in verismo roles (Ferrara 1892); Rosina Voenna—soprano (Turin 1892); Giuseppina Pasqua—mezzo-soprano (Madrid 1892); Emma Zilli (Brescia 1892); Giannina Russ—soprano (Buenos Aires 1905). Obviously, the pedantic distinction now existing between voice types was all but absent in the 1890s and early 1900s; roles were then generally entrusted to singers who could vocally manage them and often, as was the case with Tigrana, were further modified to suit the interpreters.

On a musical level, *Edgar* represents a marked advance on *Le villi,* primarily in its orchestration and extended harmonic language, suggesting that Puccini continued to give priority to the purely aural details of his work. *Edgar*'s formal structure is also more advanced than that of the earlier composition and does not subscribe to a traditionally set scheme of pieces. It is true that *Edgar* is a "number" opera, even if the various arias, duets, and ensembles constituting the musical fabric of the work, which correspond to the original scenes, are not numbered in the score. However, unlike *Le villi, Edgar* blurs the division between the individual pieces and, in addition, achieves a certain sense of continuity through the use of what

Nicolaisen terms "orchestrally-introduced signature motives."[59] These motives, which are given to each major character with the exception of Edgar himself, are often seen as proof of Wagnerian influence, but strictly speaking, they are not leit-motives; they do not serve as a basis for symphonic or dramatic development, nor do they have an added significance with each reappearance, as they usually recur in the same guise and with little or no change in the orchestration.

The instances of self-plagiarism in *Edgar* are more numerous than those in *Le villi*. In writing his second opera, Puccini took melodic ideas from five of his most successful early works, three of which were "symphonic" and thus understandably dear to his heart. These borrowings are as follows:

Act I   Sixty-five bars taken from the *Kyrie* of the *Messa a 4 voci* (1880), the first forty-two bars of which appear in the "seduction scene" at Tigrana's words "Tu voluttà di fuoco" (You fiery lust), and the remaining twenty-three bars at the chorus's "Dio non benedici che gli umili quaggiu" (God, bless only the humble here).

Act II   Five bars, a reprise of the theme from the *Kyrie,* occurring after Edgar's aria at Tigrana's words "Quel che sognavi un dì" (That which you dreamed of one day). Fifty-one bars based on two themes from the A-major *Preludio sinfonico* (1882) and contained in the large ensemble (Act II, scene 4) of the original four-act opera only; the first theme (ten bars) appears at Tigrana's words "Tentò sfuggirmi, speranza vana" (He tried to escape me, empty hope), and the second (forty-one bars) at the chorus's words "Sovra il suo pallido" (Upon his pale face).

Act III   A total of seventy-five bars taken from the *Capriccio sinfonico* (1883). The first sixteen of these are derived from the opening section (*Andante moderato*) of the orchestral piece and appear in the requiem scene, at

59. Ibid., 207.

the words "Del Signor la pupilla" (The eye of the Lord)—boys' chorus; after seven bars of "new" material, there are thirty-eight bars taken from the concluding section (*Tempo 1*) of the *Capriccio,* found at the syllables "riero" (*guerriero*)—tenors and basses of the chorus; at Edgar's words "Fu prode, è ver!" (He was gallant, it's true) there are twenty-two bars (nine bars, then thirteen bars separated by fifteen bars of unrelated motives) taken from the *Allegro vivace* of the *Capriccio.* Sixteen bars taken from the *Adagietto* (1883) for orchestra are found in the first of Fidelia's Act III arias at the words "Addio, mio dolce amor" (Farewell, my sweet love). Eleven bars (occurring twice) taken from the song *Storiella d'amore* (1883) are found in the terzetto "Bella signora" and are initially heard at Edgar's words "Io vi chieggo pietà per quei ginocchi" (I ask you to have pity on those knees).

In the first version of *Edgar,* Puccini's affection for "symphonic" music was shown not only in the self-borrowings from his early orchestral works, but also in the composition of extensive preludes for the second, third, and fourth acts, and many lengthy orchestral passages (e.g., Act I, scene 7; Act I, scene 9 ["duel" scene]; and Act II, scene 4). The importance the composer attached to the preludes is illustrated, moreover, by the following particulars: the Act III prelude was first heard at the third and final Scala performance in 1889 and was thus undoubtedly written after the "completion" of the opera; when *Edgar* was reduced from four to three acts, the former Act IV prelude was not abandoned but, as seen above, was slightly abridged and placed at the beginning of Act I; and for the important Madrid performances (1892), Puccini made further revisions to this Act I (ex-Act IV) prelude, including an additional cut of five bars, changes of rhythm at two points in the score, and slight alterations to the orchestration (e.g., string writing in the final nine bars). The existence of an autograph full score of this Spanish Prelude (dated 26 February 1892) has a logical explanation (the prelude was *not,* as Gallini affirms, composed in homage to the Queen of Spain, present at the opening performance of the Madrid season).[60] Several letters written to Luigi Mancinelli in the period from December 1891 to March 1892 (Gara 56–63) indicate that the music for *Edgar* was caught up in a complicated series of problems involving not only the copyists employed by Ricordi but also the Spanish Customs, as a result of which Puccini, wishing to carry out some modifications to the existing *Preludio,* appears to have been obliged to write out the score himself.

The orchestra Puccini employs for *Edgar* is slightly larger than that used for *Le villi.* There are now three flutes, the third of which doubles on piccolo (as opposed to the two flutes *and* piccolo required in the first opera), a bass clarinet, and four "new" percussion instruments—triangle, tam-tam, tambourine, and organ. There are also several instruments, including trumpets and drums, momentarily employed offstage along with the chorus. The presence of all these testifies to Puccini's ever-sharpening awareness of the tonal possibilities inherent in a large ensemble. If the employment of the tambourine was inspired by *Carmen,* Puccini's use of the organ is somewhat original; rather than following traditional dictates in providing an organ accompaniment for Edgar's requiem (the organ is also absent in the *Messa a 4 voci* and, as previously mentioned, the prayer scene of *Le villi*), Puccini uses the instrument in Act I to highlight Tigrana's seductive taunting of Edgar as the villagers enter the church. (After *Edgar,* Puccini's next operatic use of the organ occurs in the *Te Deum* of *Tosca*—here also it is found in a scene incongruously combining lust and religion.)

In *Edgar* we find many particularly imaginative demonstrations of Puccini's orchestrating skill. These are not restricted to the music allocated to orchestra alone (the Act preludes, the lengthy orchestral passages mentioned above, the preludes and postludes to the individual numbers), as was generally the case with *Le villi,* but are frequently to be found in the accompaniment of the soloists and chorus—an obvious example is Fidelia's first aria, "O fior del giorno" (O flower of the day), with its elaborate flute and piccolo obbligato. Other outstand-

---

60. Gallini, "Gli anni giovanili," 49.

ing examples of felicitous orchestration occur in the opening scene of the first act, where the pastel shades of woodwind and harp predominate; in Frank's only aria, "Questo amor, vergogna mia" (This love, my shame), characterized by the rich sound of divided strings with harp arpeggios; in the introduction to Edgar's Act II aria "O soave vision" (Oh sweet vision), in which the clarinet writing anticipates Cavaradossi's famous "E lucevan le stelle" by some thirteen years; in the prelude to Act III; in the requiem scene, which contains masterly choral writing; and in the music that accompanies Fidelia throughout the opera.

While the harmonic language in *Edgar* is basically conventional, there is a growing reliance on secondary seventh chords (for example, the opening twelve measures of Fidelia's Act I aria "Già il mandorlo vicino" [Already the nearby almond tree]); a marked increase in the number of chords of the ninth, eleventh, and thirteenth; the presence of long pedal points (e.g., Fidelia's same aria and Tigrana's Act I "Sia per voi" [Let it be for you]); unresolved suspensions; and parallel shifts of dissonant chords. These features bear witness to the modernity of Puccini's harmonic vocabulary in 1889 and explain how the composer was later able to transfer a section of the Act IV love duet from the original version of *Edgar* to *Tosca* without differences of style discernible in the later work. Roman Vlad[61] asserts that various facets of *Edgar's* harmonic language anticipate structures theorized by Messiaen and that pages of the score display a return to the Greco-Gregorian modes later adapted by Respighi, Pizzetti, Malipiero, and Casella and claimed as their own invention. Vlad also believes that with *Edgar,* Puccini prepared the way for Debussy, Ravel, Stravinsky, Bartók, and even Schoenberg; the particular characteristics of Puccini's harmonic language that earned him mention in Schoenberg's *Harmonielehre* (1922) are evident as early as *Edgar*. It is more likely, however, that these composers neither knew nor had the opportunity to examine Puccini's least

---

61. Roman Vlad, "Attualità di Puccini," in *Critica pucciniana,* Comitato Nazionale per le Onoranze a Giacomo Puccini nel Cinquantenario della Morte (Lucca, 1976), 165.

fortunate score, as it has always remained virtually unknown—even in Italy.

It is regrettable that *Le villi* and *Edgar* have never gained wider acceptance among the important opera houses; as with the majority of composers, Puccini's juvenile compositions and less successful works are little known. Yet the debatable quality of the librettos of these two operas should not justify neglect of Puccini's music. Not only are both works valid examples of Puccini's artistic expression and testimony to the state of his musical development in the 1880s, but when viewed from within the perimeters set by his initially naive concept of opera, nonexistent prior experience in writing opera, and dominating "symphonic element," they are also accomplished fulfillments of what must have then been his compositional objectives. Furthermore, these operas provide a fascinating documentation of the first phase in his artistic transition from "symphonic" composer to musical dramatist.

It is time for a critical reassessment of *Edgar* in particular. Far from being "that work in an artist's output that is recognized as being totally futile," that has "nothing to say and says nothing,"[62] *Edgar* represents a pivotal composition in Puccini's production, without which the stylistic leap from *Le villi* to *Manon Lescaut* would be unimaginable. In examining the score, we can understand why *Edgar* was initially described as a work of genius—no "run-of-the-mill" opera—and why it prompted a number of extraordinarily positive predictions, perhaps best exemplified in the words of V. A. Serrot:

> I believe that with a good libretto Puccini will be able to arrive, without difficulty, at the creation of a real masterpiece that meets the requirements of today's music and that has the expression of "that sweet new style" so much desired and longed for by the audiences of our theaters.
>
> However that may be, *Edgar* is a vital, extremely vigorous work of substance with a novel and original character, and so it

62. Claudio Sartori, *Puccini* (Milan, 1958), 223.

can be assured of a long and triumphant circulation in the principal theaters.[63]

If the first sentence surprises on account of its prophetic accuracy, the second causes us to reflect upon the largely unforeseen and unjust neglect of Puccini's second opera.

63. Quoted in *La Gazzetta Musicale di Milano*, 27 September 1891.

Puccini's Manon and His Other Heroines

William Weaver

William Weaver graduated from Princeton in 1946, after spending a year in North Africa and Italy as an ambulance driver with the British army. From the early 1950s he has lived in Italy (since 1965 in rural Tuscany), where he acts as Arts Correspondent for the *Financial Times* (London). He also contributes articles about the performing arts and about travel to many other newspapers and magazines. He has published several books on Italian opera, including *The Golden Century of Italian Opera* and *Verdi: A Documentary Study*. Some of his opera translations are collected in *Seven Puccini Librettos,* and he has written a brief biography, *Puccini,* as an introduction to the composer. He has also translated many contemporary Italian works of fiction, including novels and stories by Italo Calvino, Umberto Eco, and Luigi Pirandello.

Outside the busy inn at Amiens, the Arras coach arrives, and an idle little crowd gathers, curious to see, and comment on, the newcomers. As a number of travelers alight, amid colorful confusion, only one attracts the general attention and admiration: Manon Lescaut. And our attention, the audience's, is similarly focused on this charming young beauty. But the dusty diligence has not merely delivered its load of paying passengers. When randy old Géronte and Manon's unscrupulous, ambiguous brother help the girl alight, the opera has found its protagonist; and, with her, the whole series of Puccini heroines has begun.

Over the years—Puccini's early career dates back now more than a century—the words "Puccini heroine" have become a kind of abbreviation, a critical shorthand. We know what they mean, or think we do, and we use the expression because it is handy. But in reality, it is hard to paraphrase or define. It is true that in some ways most Puccini heroines resemble one another; they have certain qualities in common. And yet each is strongly characterized (often more individualized by Puccini than by the sopranos who interpret them with what has become a generic Puccinian pathos).

Take Manon, to start with (later we can look at the women in the two preceding Puccini operas, not to be lightly dismissed and not inapposite to the heroines of the composer's maturity). Manon arrives in Puccini's coach after a long journey: from an immensely successful French novel of the mid-eighteenth century, via an opéra-comique by Scribe and Auber and a more elaborate work (still defined opéra-comique) by Massenet. Also along the way, there was at least one successful dramatization for the spoken theater. In other words, Manon is one of those characters—like Don Juan—who steps outside of any literary frame, defies any specific author, and asserts an existence of his or her own.

Actually, even in the original novel of Abbé Prévost, the figure of Manon, at a first reading, does not seem especially interesting. Indeed, Des Grieux, the narrator, is more vital, more active, though no more admirable than his irresistibly beautiful and almost entirely unscrupulous beloved. Manon is largely passive. If a different set of people had met the coach in Amiens, she might well have gone on to the convent and taken the veil (the mind boggles at what the refectory atmosphere would have been like). It is Des Grieux who takes initiatives, shamelessly exploiting his friend Tibèrge, lying to his father, observing the murder of Lescaut with barely a comment, and finally becoming an unrepentant cheat and a would-be murderer.

Puccini knew the novel (its translation was very popular in Italy) and he knew the score, at least, of the Massenet opera, though it was not performed in an Italian opera house until after the premiere of his own work. Massenet's opera, in Puccini's view, was characteristically French, "with the powder and minuets. I shall feel [the story] as an Italian, with desperate passion." Puccini was oversimplifying: It is hard not to sense desperate passion in Massenet's seduction scene ("n'est-ce pas ma main"); and, though Massenet employs a lot of powder and minuet (or gavotte), Puccini—in his second act—did not disdain a generous, even overgenerous amount of "scene-painting" music and walk-on characters, those abbés, the dancing master, and so forth (one suspects the hand of Luigi Illica, future librettist of Umberto Giordano's *Andrea Chénier*).

But in his determination to avoid repeating Massenet's story line, Puccini made his librettists move from Amiens directly to Manon's grand Paris establishment (what composer would want to compete with Des Grieux's "Dream" and with "Adieu notre petite table" in Massenet?). Then comes the elaborate and successful Le Havre scene, and finally—as a coda—Manon's death in Louisiana, where the lovers are alone at last, but only, it seems, for a moment. The structure of the libretto has been much criticized; but in a sense, it is like its successor, *La bohème,* and could with justice have been entitled *Scènes de la vie de Manon Lescaut.* As in the later opera, these scenes, with huge narrative gaps between them, do not aim to tell a story in a traditional form; they illustrate a world. There is no good-versus-evil conflict, no demands are made by honor; the obstacles to be overcome are all external and, to some extent, self-induced. The simplicity of the characters measures exactly the depth to which Puccini wanted to delve.

In a typical Verdi opera, the heroine has to make big choices: between life and death (Gilda), between family loyalty and sworn love (the *Forza* Leonora and, in a sense, Violetta, though the honor is not her family's but his). Manon's decisions are all made for her. It is a family decision, passively accepted, that puts her on the Arras coach in the first place. A Verdi heroine may be driven by love; but that same love almost always causes her to bring about her own destruction. Puccini's Manon says, at the end, "ma l'amor mio non muore"; but the statement is ambiguous. Manon's definition of love would have to be all-embracing, allowing her to be deceitful, unfaithful to her lover. Her death, sad as it is, does not redeem her, as Violetta's does. She is more the victim of a stern legal system—deportation to Louisiana seems excessive punishment for her crimes—than of a tragic attachment. Violetta's death—like the deaths of the various Leonoras, and of Gilda, Aida, Desdemona—is a part of her character. Manon's end is due simply to bad luck.

As the Puccini canon grew, Puccini's characters, in particular his heroines, deepened, though nearly all his heroines maintained that special, pathetic melancholy that is adumbrated in Manon and perfected in Mimì. The heroine of *La bohème* is also the victim of bad luck; but her sad end seems implicit from the first act. Her autobiographical opening aria, in telling us that the flowers she lives among are false and have no perfume, is virtually an admission that nothing is going to come right for her. From a strictly moral point of view, she shares Manon's dismissal of conventional propriety; and she has hardly met Rodolfo before she is coyly seducing him. The shadowy Viscount, who makes eyes at her and with whom she runs off for an escapade, is given short shrift by the librettists (and presumably by Mimì herself); but none of the Bohemians raises an eyebrow, any more than they are shocked to see Musetta "working" old Alcindoro. Very few Puccini operas have two important female characters: the lighthearted Musetta is presumably intended as a foil for the melancholy Mimì; but they are much alike, and both have hearts of gold. In the end, it is Musetta who actually prays and calls Mimì an "angel," though a strict theologian would have to disagree with her.

Puccini's heroines may be good or bad, but they are seldom moral in any conventional sense. In a Verdi opera, the main characters may be murderers (like Otello) or adulterers or outright villains (Wurm, Iago); but they always act within a clear, if not conventional moral code, and they are aware of

After the quasi-failure of Edgar, *Puccini tasted genuine success with* Manon Lescaut, *which triumphed at the Teatro Regio in Turin in 1893, at about the same time that Verdi's final opera,* Falstaff, *was hailed at La Scala. With this success, Puccini seemed to assert his position as the legitimate heir of the eighty-year-old Verdi; at the same time, as* Manon Lescaut *was presented in one theater after another, the royalties meant economic security for the younger man and the ability to indulge his taste in elegant dress, motor cars, and speedboats. (Museo Teatrale alla Scala; Foto Saporetti)*

their departures from it. Their wickedness can be explained by thwarted love—like Luna's—or by insane jealousy—like Renato's—but it is not excused; and if it is not punished, it is at least acknowledged and may be pardoned. Verdi was concerned with the frontiers of morality, and so he sought out ambiguous figures like Azucena and Rigoletto and, earlier, Abigaille and Macbeth. None of these characters would have attracted Puccini, and when librettists suggested such heroines—like Verga's *Lupa*—he may have toyed with the idea of setting them to music, but then regularly turned them down.

At first glance, Tosca might seem the most Verdian of Puccini heroines: a woman who turns murderess and commits suicide for love. And yet, in the first act—when played sensitively—she reveals all her feminine vulnerability; and her big aria, after all, tells us that she has lived only for art and love, for personal concerns. The larger world, including the political world that costs her lover his life, is of no interest to her. And though she goes through the motions of her religion, putting flowers in front of the statue of the Madonna and making the Sign of the Cross with holy water, she has been happily living in sin for some time—and with a nonbeliever, at that! Even Tosca is faced by few choices, and when she has to make the crucial decision, to betray her lover or doom him, she chooses wrongly and must murder Scarpia to correct her mistake.

Suicide is an ingredient of all opera, from Monteverdi's Seneca to Shostakovich's *Katerina Ismailova;* but in several of Puccini's operas, self-destruction seems not the conclusion of a story but its supporting structure. Thus in *Butterfly,* the heroine talks about suicide (her father's) already in the first act; and, in *Turandot,* Liù's self-sacrifice, from the beginning, can lead only to one end.

Butterfly—as Arthur Groos so lucidly discusses in his chapter in this volume—is a victim of a cultural clash, a sign of Puccini's curiosity about exotic places and of his interest, which he shared with artists of the time, in local color, especially in faraway localities. Toward the end of his career, Verdi expressed a somewhat perfunctory concern about Egypt, for *Aida,* and about Cyprus and Elizabethan England for his last two works; but the actual evidence in his music is scant, and it is significant that he could set an earlier opera first in Stockholm, then in Massachusetts, without changing a note. Today, of course, adventurous productions may set *Butterfly* in Egypt and *Tosca* in Elizabethan England, but Puccini himself very much wanted his stories to take place in their specified settings, and Japan—even though it is a Japan filtered through two American writers and two Italian librettists—has an role in the opera. *Butterfly* is certainly Puccini's richest drama, and its heroine is his most complicated character.

Cio-Cio-San is, nevertheless, a "Puccini heroine" first and foremost. She shares the wistful melancholy of her sisters Manon and Mimì, the longing for a different existence. But, unlike them, she has a significant past and tells us about it (Pinkerton may not pay much attention to what she says, but the audience should). She belongs to a rigid tradition of belief and behavior, and, though she tries to reject it, her culture, in the end, tells her what to do. Examined closely, she is a double character; her cultural schizophrenia extends even to her speech. When she is around Westerners, she lapses into a kind of baby talk, becoming a "stage Japanese," as if that is what she thinks they expect of her (and she is probably right); but when she is with other Japanese—with Goro, or Prince Yamadori, or in particular with Suzuki—her language and her whole bearing change. She ceases to simper, to play the Japanese doll, and becomes a forceful, stubborn, brave woman. Often acted as the silliest of Puccini's heroines, she is probably the most thinking and the strongest-willed. Tosca kills herself on sudden impulse; Butterfly's fatal decision is carefully reached and her end is planned. In her autobiographical scene with Pinkerton, when she talks about the strongest oaks being uprooted by cataclysm, she suggests that she is the victim of external events; but she has clearly attempted to shape the events of her life, and she does, however tragic the shape may be.

If you read the Belasco play *The Girl of the Golden West,* you are tempted to think that here the setting is everything; Belasco's stage directions, in which every lighting effect is specified with fanatical detail, make you wonder if, at the time, Broadway audiences did not come out of the theater at least *trying* to whistle the scenery. Puccini, who saw the play on Broadway, was enthusiastic: he could understand the scenery, if not the words; and his enthusiasm lasted as he went through the long and painful (also for private reasons) period of composition. Several times he said this opera would be another *Bohème,* and there are, in fact, structural similarities—the many crowd scenes, the persistent japery, the endless little realistic touches (in both operas, foods are frequently named)—but there are profound differences, and the chief ones lie in the heroine's character and in the ending.

Puccini loved Minnie. She was to be a change from "Manon, Mimì, Butt., etc.," as he wrote in the midst of his composition, dismissing the three working girls who were bringing in torrents of royalties. Surely Minnie's entrance—she comes striding into the Polka Saloon, firing her pistol into the air— immediately sets her on a different plane from Mimì with her timid knock, and Butterfly with her toilsome ascent and delicate off-stage song. But as Minnie joshes with the miners and fights off the advances of the Sheriff (a Scarpia rerun, in a milder key), she gradually reveals her weaknesses. She is moral, all right, and with a vengeance; but her missionary zeal is on the surface, like Tosca's floral offerings to the Madonna: When Mr. Right comes along—a gentleman-Jack sort of bandit— she is easily persuaded to give him her "first kiss," which, it is legitimate to suspect, is Belasco's and Puccini's euphemism for her first something-else. She certainly has more good old American gumption than Manon and Mimì, but she also has that familiar Puccinian yearning (in this case, also for higher education); and when she browbeats the miners—pushovers, to a man—and wins her soon-to-be-reformed lover's release, the two of them set off for the East (strange place to take an ex-bandit) in what should be a happy ending, though it is drenched in the composer's typical and most heartrending melancholy.

If *La fanciulla del West* represents an attempt on Puccini's part to shatter the mold, to get away from the Puccinian world (did he see California as a kind of Allemonde?), the operas of

Il trittico are surely an even more strenuous effort to break new dramatic ground. One of the operas is comic, has a male protagonist, and even bears a male name as its title (count the number of Verdi titles that are men's names, then look at Puccini's *Manon, Tosca, Butterfly, Rondine, Turandot,* etc.). Lauretta, the closest we come to a heroine in *Gianni Schicchi,* has undeniable charm but little wistfulness. And even Giorgetta in *Il tabarro* lacks the pathetic melancholy of her older sisters; in the love-triangle plot, she is one among three equals, though she, too, has a "yearning" aria, much in the Minnie style, except that Giorgetta's dream is more mundane: what she misses is the bustle and even the routine of city life, existence in a working-class neighborhood, instead of her cramped, uncertain life on her unloved husband's barge. But she also dreams of passion with her clandestine lover. Unusual in the Puccini canon, she is, apparently, an older woman, oppressed by life; and also unusual is the character of her husband, one of Puccini's most developed male figures (even within the confined space of a single act).

Also unusual in Giorgetta is her remorse, an emotion almost totally absent from Puccini's dramaturgy. Curiously enough, the same emotion—or a close relative of it—appears in another opera of *Il trittico.* Suor Angelica would seem to be the Puccini heroine par excellence: young and vulnerable, victim of the cruel world, forced into a convent for having produced an illegitimate child, and yet—despite her sin—supremely innocent, even childish. The crux of her brief story is another encounter with the outside world: a visit from her stern aunt, the Princess (Puccini's only important contralto part, and, at that, hardly more than a comprimaria; the "Puccini heroine" is inevitably a soprano). The news of her child's death impels Angelica, crazed with grief, to commit suicide; but her sudden return to sanity as she is dying makes her realize and abhor her crime. Her remorse is then assuaged by a miraculous vision of the Madonna and of Angelica's child, who welcome her to paradise. This is one of the rare appearances of the supernatural in Puccini (the only other significant example is in his debut work, *Le villi*).

Often hastily dismissed as a saccharine tearjerker, *Suor*

Angelica is arguably one of Puccini's subtlest accomplishments. Setting himself the problem of confined time and space (he, who so liked panoramic visions and boisterous crowd scenes) and limiting himself to female voices, the composer managed to establish a hushed, but remarkably varied world, where whispered gossip has more impact than a crowd's shouting, and where the use of the litany in Latin at the end has all the power, but far more magic, than the grandiose *Te Deum* of *Tosca*'s first-act finale.

Now compare Angelica with Puccini's very first heroine, the ethereal Anna of *Le villi*. Anna is genuinely innocent; her encounter with the reality and treachery of the real world actually kills her. She, perhaps, is the emblematic "Puccini heroine," with her aria about dear little flowers and her immediate, free-floating melancholy, apparently unjustified. The successive heroines develop and complicate and vary this basic model: the outside world becomes more intrusive, more inventive. And no matter how hard the heroine tries to escape it—whether she takes refuge in a California saloon or a Tuscan cloister or simply in what seems an undying love—reality finds and crushes her.

In many ways an uncharacteristic Puccini work and probably the least performed of his mature operas, *La rondine* also has an uncharacteristic dramatic structure: when we first encounter the heroine, Magda, she is already firmly established in the real world, a courtesan, the kept mistress of a rich cynic, with a circle of equally cynical friends and peers. But she soon sings a typical yearning aria, telling of a youthful, innocent adventure with a student at a dance hall. And, reversing the usual Puccini process, Magda then escapes from reality into her dream. It seems to come true, but then reality returns and defeats her, in a sad, rueful, but not tragic conclusion.

Only two of Puccini's operas have double female protagonists: in the early *Edgar* the evil Tigrana is opposed by the innocent ("Puccinian") Fidelia; and in the posthumous *Turandot*, the gentle, long-suffering Liù is set against the icy Turandot. Fidelia and Tigrana, as their names clearly indicate, are symbolic, larger- (or smaller?)-than-life figures. Tigrana is allowed what seems a brief, sincere admission of love in the last act, but she is easily lured into betraying it by the offer of jewels (much as Calaf is tempted in *Turandot,* though he dismisses the bribe).

Tigrana can hardly be said to foreshadow the haughty Chinese princess, but Fidelia certainly suggests the faithful Liù (and, indeed, shares qualities with many other Puccini women). Puccini did not live to complete *Turandot* and, if he had, he would no doubt have made many changes, as was his habit, not only during rehearsals but also after the first performance; so it is risky to make too many or too firm assertions about the libretto.

But we know that *Turandot* is a fairy tale; its China is an unreal country, and—like the women of *Edgar*—the two heroines are emblematic. Without going into a Freudian interpretation of the two women (amply achieved by the late Mosco Carner in his now-classic study of the composer), and without drawing parallels from the composer's personal life, we can see that Liù—a character who does not appear in the Gozzi play that is the libretto's prime source—is the final expression of a Puccinian ideal: the humble, unselfish, loyal, submissive, but (when challenged) courageous love. The dream girl, in other words. The Princess, a truly fairy-tale figure, who has a short way with suitors and a firm view about men, is the character who must change. Her introduction to love is, paradoxically, also an introduction to reality. And, for once in Puccini, reality does not destroy, and love is not doomed. Turandot does not say, as Manon does, "l'amor mio non muore," but we are meant to assume that Calaf and his thawed ice princess live happily ever after. This is, remember, not only a fairy tale: it is an opera, where everything is possible.

Manon, Mimì, Artù

Harvey Sachs

Harvey Sachs's books include *Toscanini* (1978), *Virtuoso* (1982), *Music in Fascist Italy* (1987), and *Reflections on Toscanini* (1991). He has contributed to *The New Yorker* and many other periodicals and newspapers in the United States and Europe, and is currently writing a biography of Arthur Rubinstein. He is a native of Cleveland, Ohio, and a Canadian citizen, resident in Italy.

> *Via G. Verdi 4*
> *Milan*
> *2 February 1923*

Dear Arturo

You have given me the greatest satisfaction of my life! *Manon* as you interpret it is superior to what I thought it to be in those distant days. You have brought this music of mine to life with incomparable poetry, *souplesse,* and passionate temperament. Yesterday evening I truly felt your whole great soul and your love for your old friend and comrade at arms of early days. I am happy above all because you have been capable of understanding my young, passionate spirit of thirty years ago! Thanks from the bottom of my heart! . . .

> I embrace you fraternally
> your Giacomo Puccini[1]

1. L. Frassati, *Il Maestro* (Turin, 1967), 161.

𝒯he production of *Manon Lescaut* to which Giacomo Puccini's
letter to Arturo Toscanini refers was one of the high points of
the 1922–23 season at Milan's Teatro alla Scala. It was also the
high point of the long and sometimes difficult friendship
between the composer and the conductor.

We do not know exactly when the friendship began; perhaps in January 1890, when the twenty-two-year-old Toscanini conducted the thirty-one-year-old Puccini's music for the
first time—a production of *Le villi* at Brescia's Teatro Grande.
Four years later, when Toscanini was in Pisa to rehearse his
first production of *Manon Lescaut,* a year after the opera's premiere, he and Puccini were on friendly enough terms to address
each other with the familiar *tu.* "Tomorrow is the first ensemble rehearsal," wrote Toscanini to Puccini on 1 March 1894,

> with orchestra, solo artists, and chorus . . . If you want to honor
> us with your presence do so, and as soon as possible . . . We are
> counting on opening next Wednesday. I hardly need to tell you
> that the impresario is entirely at your disposal in regard to expenses
> etc. etc.—The tenor Rosati *is a cretin,* but he makes up for this
> misfortune of his with his beautiful, warm, and expressive voice.
> The baritone Bucalo, a present from [Carlo] D'Ormeville [a Milan-
> based agent], doesn't convince me at all, however he has already
> done it in Ferrara and it went well . . . If you heard him you'd
> know what I mean. The rest is going along all right.—
>
> Come quickly and let me know either by letter or tele-
> gram. . . .
>
> Ciao. Greetings from [Emilia] Corsi [the production's prima
> donna] and a handshake from yours
>
> Affectionately A. Toscanini[2]

That production was the beginning of the special relationship between Puccini and the man his biographer, Mosco
Carner, called "his favorite interpreter." It also inaugurated
the special relationship between Toscanini and *Manon Lescaut,*
which seems to have remained his favorite among Puccini's
operas, with the possible exception of *La bohème.*

These special relationships, however, were built over the

---

2. Autograph in the collection of Robert Hupka, New York.

grave of Toscanini's admired and admiring friend, Alfredo Catalani. Like Puccini, Catalani was a native of Lucca; their birthplaces are only two blocks apart, and Catalani was only four-and-a-half years older than Puccini. Catalani settled in Milan in 1873, at the height of the *scapigliatura*—with whose exponents he shared a taste for exoticism and morbid passion. The six operas he composed between 1875 and 1892 all have exotic or at least esoteric plots, settings, and protagonists and are mainly tales of love and retribution, jealousy and suicide, in which strong-willed but neurotic women of low social standing gradually destroy vacillating men of noble birth and/ or lofty vision.

Through most of his short life Catalani suffered from tuberculosis and a poorly lined wallet, yet his self-image as a particularly unfortunate, virtually accursed artist—an image posterity has accepted—is exaggerated. For each of his operas he managed to secure an expert librettist (Arrigo Boito, Antonio Ghislanzoni, and Luigi Illica were among his collaborators); all of his stage works were published by either Ricordi or Giovannina Lucca, the two most prestigious houses in the country; and all except the first—*La falce,* which was written as a conservatory graduation exercise—were promptly premiered either at Turin's celebrated Teatro Regio or at Milan's even more celebrated Teatro alla Scala. The young composer even enjoyed a moderate degree of international esteem: Mahler, for instance, considered Catalani's *Dejanice* (1883) superior to, or at least less bad than, Ponchielli's *La Gioconda.*

As Catalani's illness progressed, however, he became morbidly jealous of other young composers—Mascagni, Leoncavallo, and, above all, Puccini—and he was suspicious of anyone who helped them in any way. When he was a student at the Milan Conservatory in the early 1880s, Puccini had looked up to Catalani, who was already one of the city's better-known musicians; but by the fall of 1892, when Puccini was putting the finishing touches to *Manon,* his fellow townsman had persuaded himself that even Verdi was trying to destroy him by supporting Puccini. Verdi, who was then completing a rather important work of his own—*Falstaff*—was understandably offended by this unfounded accusation. "I have better things to worry about," he wrote to a friend, "than the little maestro from Lucca"[3]—meaning Catalani, not Puccini.

As the date of the world premiere of *Manon Lescaut* approached, fear that the work would succeed became an obsession with Catalani. He even took pleasure in a piece of secondhand gossip, according to which the composer Alberto Franchetti had told friends that Puccini's *Le villi* had been derived from Catalani's *Elda* and *Dejanice*. "This is what Franchetti said," Catalani reported thirdhand to his friend Giuseppe Depanis, who was the principal organizer of Turin's musical life,

> and it pleases me that he should have been the one who said it, because I myself, though thinking the same, did not have the courage to say it. I assure you, I believe in nothing more than in that truth expressed by Franchetti, and I could wish that one day when an opportunity offers itself, you would affirm it . . . By God! for twelve long years I have been working and fighting: should I now sit still and watch the ground being taken away from under my feet? Indeed no![4]

Manon was a success, as Catalani had feared, and his jealousy increased as Puccini's opera began to attract an ever broader public. But Catalani is to be pitied rather than criticized for his envy. He had read the cards correctly: Puccini was destined for lasting fame, whereas his own fate was virtual oblivion. Six months after the premiere of *Manon*, Catalani was dead.

Toscanini, who had helped to tend his ailing friend till the end, grieved deeply. He had made his Italian debut at the age of nineteen conducting the Turin premiere of Catalani's *Edmea*, thanks largely to the composer's confidence in his talent, and Catalani had helped him to mature as an artist. So great was Toscanini's esteem for Catalani that he named his first two children, Walter and Wally, after the protagonists of the composer's *Loreley* and *La Wally*. (By coincidence, Wally's daughter, Emanuela di Castelbarco, was born on Catalani's birthday,

---

3. Mosco Carner, *Puccini* (London, 1974), 30.
4. Ibid., 31.

19 June.) But Toscanini's grief over Catalani's death had artistic as well as personal causes. He believed that Catalani could have become a "third force" in Italian operatic life: Building upon what he had assimilated from Verdi and Wagner and upon his fundamentally refined tastes, he might have created much "nobler" works than the likes of Leoncavallo and Mascagni were capable of achieving, in Toscanini's opinion. Many years later, Toscanini said of Catalani: "I always think of him. The place he left will never be filled for me."[5]

Yet Toscanini, for all his loyal friendship, was also a canny man of the theater. He might never have gone so far as to say what Michelangelo Zurletti has said in his study of Catalani— that the composer "was already dead before he died"[6]—but he no doubt came to believe something similar, inasmuch as Catalani left no work strong enough to be worthy of enduring popularity. Toscanini remained active as an opera conductor for nearly four decades after Catalani's death, but in all those years he conducted only three productions of *Loreley* and four of *La Wally*—and the last of these, the American premiere of *La Wally* at the Metropolitan Opera, took place in 1909. He may have felt closer to Catalani's aesthetic point of view than to that of Mascagni or even Puccini, but he also understood that the younger composers had realized their ideas more convincingly than Catalani had managed to realize his.

Whether out of grief or for mundane reasons—both, more likely—Toscanini did not conduct for seven months after Catalani's death. In retrospect, it seems appropriate that his first engagement at the end of that period should have been the brief Pisa season that included *Manon Lescaut,* for the occasion gave a push to what was ultimately a more productive relationship than his association with Catalani.

Manon was warmly received in Pisa. Reporting the event in *La Nazione,* the Florentine daily, a Pisan music critic (using the pseudonym "Minimus") stated that "the public was unan-

---

5. Harvey Sachs, *Toscanini* (London and New York, 1978), 44.
6. M. Zurletti, *Catalani* (Turin, 1982), 52.

imous in its enthusiasm" and, curiously, expressed gratitude
that the staging had left a great deal to be desired:

> I could imagine a genteel, perfumed, powder-puff setting—which
> was certainly not to be seen in this tawdry little Pisan *mise en
> scène.* But if the setting were reproduced as it ought to be, who
> could concentrate on the drama?
>
>   . . . In Pisa as elsewhere, the last act, despite some stupendous
> musical segments, was not heard with the same degree of
> enchantment and admiration as the others, in which an infinite
> number of pieces had been encored.
>
>   In the performance of this opera, the conductor, Maestro Tos-
> canini, surpassed himself. Miss Corsi, too, stupendously brought
> to life the role of Manon. One cannot say as much, however, of
> either the tenor or the baritone, to tell the truth.[7]

Enthusiasm grew throughout the production's run—so much
so that on 20 March *La Nazione* gave the story front-page
coverage:

>   Maestro Puccini, who had been invited by the theater's admin-
> istration to attend a performance of *Manon Lescaut,* came this
> evening [the 17th] to the Royal Teatro Nuovo. From the first act
> through the last, he was continually applauded. He had to take
> twenty bows in the midst of all the enthusiasm.
>
>   The ending of the third act was repeated three times. All the
> artists gave their best, so that the performance came off excel-
> lently.
>
>   A popular performance at reduced prices has been announced
> for Wednesday evening.[8]

$\mathcal{A}$s the reports in *La Nazione* demonstrate, Toscanini had not
yet been able to enforce the no-encore rule that Italian singers
and opera house administrators had first tried to put into effect
a century earlier; he would manage to do so in Turin the following year and would fight a decisive battle over the issue at

7. *La Nazione,* 12 March 1894.
8. Ibid., 20 March 1894.

La Scala in 1903. Nor had he yet accumulated all the prestige that would eventually allow him to insist on a variety of other reforms in the lyric theater. We can only vaguely imagine how the Pisa production sounded, what with its catch-as-catch-can orchestra and less than first-class singers. For that matter, we can only vaguely imagine how the very first production of *Manon,* at Turin's Teatro Regio on 1 February 1893, had sounded, although it was widely reviewed and therefore reasonably well documented. The conductor was Alessandro Pomé—but only the most incautious of historians would attempt to estimate the extent to which Pomé was responsible for its success. Although he was only forty-two at the time, Pomé belonged to the old school of Italian conductors who believed in a division of labor between the *concertatore,* or "rehearser," and the *direttore d'orchestra,* or "orchestra leader." The *concertatori* were often barely competent time-beaters who, illogically, were entrusted with the main task—that of preparing productions; the *direttori* were better-known personalities who would take over the final ensemble rehearsals and, it was hoped, give the performances a certain *éclat.* (Toscanini himself, at the time of his above-mentioned Italian debut in Catalani's *Edmea* at Turin's Teatro Carignano in 1886, had initially been engaged only as Pomé's *concertatore;* not until he had shown his mettle was he told—less than two weeks before the production opened—that he would also conduct the performances. Having finished that task, he rehearsed a production of *The Flying Dutchman* that Pomé then conducted.)

The problems created by this system were accentuated by the highly transient nature of Italian orchestras in those days. Gino Monaldi, in his book *Memorie d'un suggeritore* (a prompter's memoirs), published in 1902, referred to the opera orchestras of his day as largely "adventitious." Players were engaged one by one, season by season, and this meant that

> things fall apart and rebellions are not infrequent. I remember having been present at many occurrences and disturbances of this sort, usually quelled by the moral authority of the conductor—if he has it. On other occasions, however, disputes over the order

of seating are exacerbated to the point of degenerating into violent altercations, and police intervention is necessitated; because
it is impossible to imagine to what an inordinate degree the spur
of self-esteem is honed in all these *virtuosi* who live in the theater.[9]

Such conditions often obtained even in the principal Italian
opera houses. Little wonder that Toscanini and other Italian
conductors of his generation were notoriously foul-tempered:
shock therapy was required to create even a semblance of order
among the troops. Throughout the second half of the nineteenth century Italian opera composers gave increasing prominence to the orchestra, and the need for reform increased
commensurately.

Whatever defects the early productions of *Manon* may have
had, however, this first of Puccini's mature operas was a great
success from the start. Moreover, it was impressive for its
musical qualities above all, whereas the instantaneous successes of Mascagni's *Cavalleria rusticana* in 1890 and of Leoncavallo's *Pagliacci* in 1892 were as much attributable to the
concise, shocking raciness of their plots as to their music,
undeniably fresh and original though that music was. Many
commentators have hypothesized, probably correctly, that
when he wrote *Manon Lescaut,* Puccini was not yet the sure-
footed man of the theater he was later to become. What is
certain is that he was working with a very uneven text. The
story line lacks both the slow-moving, cumulative force of
the Abbé Prévost's loquacious original version—which could
never have been squeezed into an operatic mold—and the quick,
hard-hitting impact that a masterly, incisive libretto would
have lent it. Having passed at various times through the hands
of Marco Praga, Domenico Oliva, Luigi Illica, and others,
including the composer, the *Manon* libretto could only have
come out botched—and so it did. As a result, Puccini had no
choice but to deemphasize the plot and to stake everything on
the musical characterization of the two protagonists. As in the

9. G. Monaldi, *Memorie d'un suggeritore* (Turin, 1902).

case of *Tristan und Isolde, Manon*'s plot *is,* simply, the fatal
attraction between the two main characters—a fact that may
help to explain why Puccini, perhaps subconsciously, leaned
heavily on the *Tristan* Prelude when he wrote *Manon*'s Intermezzo. Apart from the second act—atop which Puccini set a
periwig, just as Umberto Giordano was to set a periwig on
the first act of *Andrea Chénier* three years later—*Manon*'s action
could be transferred to other periods and places with no loss
of credibility. This is not true of Puccini's later operas. Insofar
as *Manon Lescaut* is more a "character opera" than a "plot opera,"
it is the most Verdian of Puccini's works. And Des Grieux,
tormented by and obsessed with his love for Manon, more
closely resembles Verdi's last four tenor-heroes—Don Alvaro,
Don Carlos, Radamès, and Otello—than he resembles any of
the male protagonists Puccini himself would later produce.

When Puccini attended the 1894 Pisa production of *Manon,* the
operatic world already knew that he was working on his next
opera, *La bohème,* and that Ruggero Leoncavallo was working
on an opera based on the same story—Henry Murger's *Scènes
de la vie de bohème* (1848). Puccini, however, was working on
another opera as well: *La lupa* (the she-wolf), based on a short
story by Giovanni Verga. For a time, according to Carner,
the composer gave more attention to *La lupa* than to *La bohème;* but after a visit to Verga in Sicily, a few weeks after the
Pisa episode, he decided to give up *La lupa* and to concentrate
on *La bohème.*

At that time, Toscanini had as strong a connection with
Leoncavallo as with Puccini. On 21 May 1892, at Milan's Teatro
Dal Verme, he had conducted the world premiere of *Pagliacci,*
as part of a short season whose main attraction was the participation of the celebrated baritone, Victor Maurel. (The other
opera performed there that season, also under Toscanini's baton,
was Ambroise Thomas's *Hamlet,* which was one of Maurel's
specialties.) Toscanini's engagement seems to have been
brought about by Verdi, who had been hearing good things
about the young conductor: He is said to have recommended

him to Maurel, who had been Verdi's first Iago in 1887 and was soon to be his first Falstaff. Maurel, in turn, recommended Toscanini to Leoncavallo's publisher, Edoardo Sonzogno, who called the shots at the Dal Verme.

Several people who knew Toscanini in later years have reported that he did not think highly of *Pagliacci;* nevertheless, the premiere went extremely well, and the following winter he introduced the opera to Palermo. In the meantime, however, he had incurred Sonzogno's wrath by withdrawing from the first Roman production of *I Rantzau*—the latest opera by Sonzogno's star composer, Mascagni, with whom Toscanini had had the first of many fallings-out. When Leoncavallo wanted Toscanini to conduct the premiere of his new opera, *I Medici,* at the Dal Verme in November 1893, Sonzogno told him: "If you are so fond of Toscanini, then go ahead; but I will not go to the theater that evening." In the end, the opera was conducted by Rodolfo Ferrari.[10]

All these factors may have contributed to Toscanini's lack of interest in Leoncavallo's *Bohème.* Two other factors, however, presumably led him to conduct the world premiere of Puccini's *Bohème,* which took place at Turin's Teatro Regio on 1 February 1896: He saw the score and liked what he saw; and he had recently become what would today be called the "artistic director" of the Regio and was expected to conduct all the operas scheduled for performance there.

The position at the Regio had been created for him by his and Catalani's old friend Giuseppe Depanis, a lawyer and music critic who functioned as the mainspring in Turin's musical life. Toscanini and Depanis had been influenced by direct contact with Verdi and by Wagner's writings on music and the theater, and they believed that certain reforms were long overdue in Italian opera houses in general and at the Regio in particular: The repertoire had to be internationalized, a permanent orchestra had to be formed, and audiences had to learn to attend opera performances in order to listen to and watch

10. Sachs, *Toscanini*, 40–45.

operas from beginning to end, rather than to use them as social soirées with musical accompaniment.

The Regio—more than 150 years old at the time—was refurbished at public expense during the fall of 1895; at Toscanini's insistence and under his supervision a new stage lighting system, a new organ, and the house's first orchestra pit were installed. The season opened on 22 December with the first Italian production of *Die Götterdämmerung,* which was successful beyond anyone's hopes: Twenty-one performances had to be given to satisfy public demand, and the entire Italian musical world took note of the event. Next came a production of *Falstaff* that elicited the congratulations of Boito, thus initiating a lasting friendship between the poet-composer and the conductor. There were some performances of the now-forgotten *Savitri* by Natale Canti, following which the attention of the Italian musical world was again riveted on the Regio for the world premiere of *La bohème* on 1 February 1896.

Puccini had initially opposed the choice of Turin. "I am not very happy with it," he had written to his publisher, Giulio Ricordi,

> in the first place because the theater is acoustically dead, secondly because encores aren't allowed in the same, thirdly because the conductor is an unpleasant man, fourthly because it's too close to the waspish Milanese who will certainly "make fun" of me. Naples, Rome should be the first [cities]—[Leopoldo] Mugnone writes that they're contracting him for Palermo—Try to have him engaged where *Bohème* will be given [as] he is more of an artist than any of the other conductors, he may be a scoundrel but he "has soul," which is something that "all the others" lack.[11]

Given the outstanding success that the Regio's audiences had bestowed on the newborn *Manon Lescaut* three years earlier, Puccini's opposition to the choice of Turin is hard to attribute to any cause other than sheer nervousness. His complaints about the acoustics can no longer be judged: The conditions to which he refers were altered by the construction of

11. G. Piamonte, "La Bohème, novità assoluta," in *La Bohème di Giacomo Puccini,* House program from 1974–75 season, Teatro alla Scala, Milan, 1975, p. 18.

the orchestra pit, and the theater burned down in 1936. His dislike of the no-encore rule is comprehensible, because in those days one of the measures of an opera's success was the quantity of musical numbers that had to be repeated. And his reference to Toscanini as an unpleasant man (*omaccio*) leads one to assume that he had had the sort of run-in with the notoriously outspoken, sharp-tongued conductor that befell nearly everyone in the business sooner or later.

But Ricordi insisted that Turin was the best site for the premiere, and Puccini began to calm down once he had arrived in town for the rehearsals. "I've found Toscanini very kind," he wrote on 6 January to Luigi Illica—co-librettist, with Giuseppe Giacosa, of *La bohème* and, later, of *Tosca* and *Madama Butterfly*. "The baritone [Tieste Wilmant] is vile! . . . The rest (excepting Colline, whom I haven't heard yet) are all right."[12] Four days later he wrote, again to Illica:

> This Marcello [Wilmant] is absolutely no good. He doesn't understand anything at all, and he wouldn't make it even if we rehearsed as much as at Bayreuth. [Cesira] Ferrani [the Mimì] is excellent, Musetta [Camilla Pasini] is excellent, [Antonio] Pini-Corsi and Polonini [the Schaunard and Benoit, respectively] are excellent. The tenor [Evan Gorga] has arrived but is still ill. I'll hear him tomorrow and I'll let you know. We still don't know about the Colline. They've told me that a bass from the *Götterdämmerung* will be doing it, but I believe he has a harsh voice, not right for the part. [The role was eventually taken by one Mazzara.][13]

Ferrani had also been the first Manon Lescaut, and Toscanini was to choose her to be Mélisande in the first Italian production of Debussy's masterpiece, at La Scala in 1908. Rumor had it that Puccini was in love with her; she, however, seems to have been in love with Toscanini. Gorga was a neophyte who had made his debut in the provinces the previous year. Puccini had invited him to Turin to sing Rodolfo, but Gorga proved unequal to the task: Virtually the whole part had to be

12. Eugenio Gara et al., eds., *Carteggi pucciniani* (Milan, 1958), 137.
13. Ibid.

At the age of twenty-nine, the Turin soprano Cesira Ferrani created the role of Puccini's Manon in her native city, with great success. Three years later, again in the Teatro Regio, she was the first Mimì in La bohème. *Her physical beauty and sensitive acting made her the ideal interpreter of these first Puccini heroines (she never essayed Tosca). She also sang many French roles, including the first Italian Mélisande at La Scala, and in that role she appeared on the opera stage for the last time: in Rome, 1909. (Archivio Storico Ricordi)*

transposed down for him.[14] (So much for the legend of the superabundance of great voices in the Good Old Days.) He was to perform for only ten years altogether, after which he would make a name for himself as an antique collector. Pini-Corsi had sung the role of Ford in the world premiere of *Falstaff;* under Toscanini he had already sung the title roles in *Falstaff* and in the first production of Franchetti's *Cristoforo Colombo* (1892).

Regarding the *omaccio* Toscanini, Puccini's diffidence soon turned to total admiration: "And the orchestra! Toscanini! Extraordinary!" he wrote, adding that he found the young conductor "highly intelligent," and describing a typically gruelling Toscanini-style rehearsal schedule: "today from eleven to 4:30 p.m. Tonight we rehearse from eight-thirty to midnight."[15]

A chronicle of the opening-night performance appeared in Rome's *Fanfulla* under the byline "Tom"—pseudonym of the well-known writer Eugenio Checchi.

> At eight-thirty almost all the seats were already occupied, and everyone gave visible signs of eagerness to be able to satisfy expectations at last. When Maestro Toscanini gave the first sign, anyone whose eyes had been closed might have believed himself to be in a perfectly empty hall.
>
> . . . Their Royal Highnesses the Duke and Duchess of Aosta were present, as were Princess Letizia and the Count of Turin, in their respective boxes. Mascagni and Ricordi were in orchestra seats; the Count and Countess Franchi Valetta [a.k.a. the music critic Ippolito Valetta and the violinist Teresina Tua] were in one of the first-tier boxes. [Boito was also present.]
>
> The first applause broke out after the tenor's tale in the first act. Although the Maestro [Puccini] was warmly acclaimed, he did not step forward. But when the curtain fell there was another resounding outburst of applause, and he was called before the curtain three times.
>
> The highly picturesque second act was liked for the great vivacity of its color . . . More applause and two curtain calls for the Maestro at the end of the act. The setting for the third act is

14. Carner, *Puccini,* 92.
15. Ibid., 93.

a wintry dawn at a customs-barrier in Paris. The good impression continued to grow, thanks to the well-worked-out contrast of emotions, efficaciously expressed with great melodic clarity . . . When the curtain fell a burst of applause exploded, and the Maestro had to take five bows.

The fourth act was liked even more. The contrast between Rodolfo's friends' noisy fun and the arrival of Mimì—pallid, languishing, and near death—was felicitous. Mimì's death scene, which was listened to with great attention and in total silence, made an enormously favorable impression. The audience rose to its feet, shouting approval with real enthusiasm. The Maestro took five more *curtain-calls,* for a total of fifteen.

During the last act Maestro Puccini had sat mainly in the box of Princess Letizia, who had invited him in to congratulate him on the growing success.

On the whole, the performance was considered good; Mmes. Ferrani and Pasini were excellent in the two women's parts and were much acclaimed. the men were judged deficient . . . The orchestra, conducted by Toscanini, was feeble here and there; the very lovely, dignified production was much liked.[16]

Most observers were harder on the work but treated Toscanini better. "BOHÈME FAILURE IT WON'T MAKE THE ROUNDS," read Carlo D'Ormeville's now celebrated telegram to his associates in Milan; other commentators, although not quite so drastic in their judgments, did not believe that the work would become a popular favorite. The orchestral performance, however, was described as "excellent, perfect," by one reviewer, while others referred to "the valor and the artistic conscientiousness that make [Toscanini] one of today's best," to the conductor's "elect spirit," and to his "aristocratic temperament."[17] Indeed, in no other review, however negative, of any Toscanini performance in his entire career, have I seen the word "feeble." Says Enzo Siciliano—commenting on "Tom" 's review: "We can only think that the Maestro [Toscanini] was the first to reveal the sound of Puccini's strings to the public: that imperceptibly trembling sound that imitates

---

16. Piamonte, "La Bohème, novità assoluta," p. 19.
17. Sachs, *Toscanini,* 51.

the violin of the *café-chantant*."[18] The only critic who seems to have perceived the opera for what it was, through the medium of its carefully prepared first performance, was the *Corriere della Sera*'s gifted young Alfredo Colombani, who died four years later at the age of thirty-one:

> [*Bohème*] has qualities that can win over people who only enjoy music superficially as well as those who are more demanding. The former will be satisfied with this or that brilliant, hummable tune, the latter with the chance to turn up this or that jewel in the orchestration and harmony; the former will say that the music is beautiful, the latter that it is well crafted.[19]

This or that hummable tune? Well crafted? Now that the world has had approximately a century to get to know *La bohème,* no one can doubt that the work has hardly any unhummable tunes or that it is built like a battleship. It stays afloat under even the most unpromising conditions, and, when handled by a crew that knows its business, it is the most agile of vessels.

The *Bohème* premiere gave the decisive impetus to what remained an outstandingly fruitful professional relationship—and a somewhat more fragile but nevertheless enduring friendship.[20] Puccini wanted Toscanini to conduct the premiere of his next opera, *Tosca* ("remember, you must be the one to deflower her," wrote the composer to the conductor in 1898[21]), but the first production took place in Rome under Mugnone; Toscanini conducted the Milan premiere at La Scala two months later. And Mugnone, who prior to the *Bohème* premiere had been Puccini's favorite conductor, was to drop lower and lower in the composer's estimation as Toscanini rose ever

---

18. E. Siciliano, *Puccini* (Milan, 1976), 156.
19. Ibid., 159.
20. For more detailed information on the ups and downs of that relationship see G. Barblan, *Toscanini e la Scala* (Milan, 1972), 203–209; and H. Sachs, *Toscanini,* 125, 138, 155–58, 160–61, 170–71, 177–79.
21. Gara, *Carteggi pucciniani,* 158.

higher. When Mugnone conducted *La rondine* in 1917, Puccini complained that the conductor's work was "truly deleterious: no *finesse,* no *nuance,* no *souplesse* . . . I was massacred."

Toscanini was not active at La Scala in 1904, when the disastrous first performance of *Madama Butterfly* took place there; looking back on the event years later, Puccini considered Toscanini's absence a partial cause of the disaster. Toscanini did, however, conduct the South American premiere of the opera—in its revised version—in Buenos Aires a few months later. *La fanciulla del West* had its world premiere under his baton at the Metropolitan Opera in 1910. He did not like and never conducted either *La rondine* or the *Trittico,* but he led the world premiere of *Turandot* at La Scala, two years after the composer's death.

Although Toscanini eventually conducted *Butterfly* more frequently than any of Puccini's other operas, *Manon* and *Bohème* seem to have remained closer to his heart. He conducted *Manon* at Milan's Teatro Dal Verme in 1897; in Buenos Aires in 1903, 1904, and 1912; in Montevideo in 1903; in Paris in 1910; regularly at La Scala between 1922 and 1929; and in Berlin with the Scala ensemble in 1929. Over the years, his Manons included Maria Farneti, Lucrezia Bori, Juanita Caracciolo, Gilda Dalla Rizza, Maria Zamboni, and Rosetta Pampanini; and his Des Grieux were Enrico Caruso, Edoardo Garbin, and Aureliano Pertile.

The Paris production of 1910 was the work's local premiere, with the Metropolitan Opera's chorus, sets, and cast (starring Bori and Caruso), but with a Parisian orchestra. It was an enormous success, and Puccini exulted: "I've never had such an organic, perfect ensemble for *Manon.*"[22] Toscanini had made some modifications in the orchestral score of the opera, with Puccini's encouragement, although the score he used in Paris has very few annotations in his hand: some accent marks, some changes in the use of mutes, a few remarks like

22. Ibid., 376.

leggerissimo and *en dehors,* and a few bowing changes.[23] Further alterations may have been made during rehearsals, for Puccini wrote to Toscanini shortly thereafter:

> The Ricordi Company has finally decided to print [a new edition of] the orchestra score of *Manon*. A copy will be sent to you [in proof] and you will want to make some revisions. Believe me, you couldn't do me a bigger favor. With the corrections you make in the [orchestral] coloring and efficacious bowings for the strings etc. etc. I'll finally be able to have a definitive *Manon* and to free her from the anarchy to which she remains in thrall. My soul is full of your performance and of the goodness of your spirit; I hope to see you soon.[24]

Then came the great Scala production of *Manon* during the 1922–23 season, which was the occasion for more touchings-up of the score on Toscanini's part, and which gave Puccini one of the most satisfying moments of his life. "*Manon* this evening," he wrote to Riccardo Schnabl-Rossi on 26 December 1922:

> a great *Manon,* and if the audience isn't stirred it will mean that we're living on Saturn rather than on the Earth—I assure you that Toscanini is a real miracle of feeling, of refinement, of sensitivity, of equilibrium—what pleasure I've experienced at the rehearsals—never but never have I so much enjoyed hearing my music.[25]

As to *La bohème:* In addition to the premiere production, Toscanini conducted the opera in Brescia in 1896, in Venice and Milan in 1897, in a revival at the Regio in Turin in 1898, at La Scala in 1900, in Buenos Aires in 1904 and 1912, in Paris (Act III only) and New York (Metropolitan) in 1910, and at La Scala in December 1924, one month after the composer's death. His Mimìs included Adelina Stehle, Emma Carelli,

23. Sachs, *Toscanini,* 111.
24. Gara, *Carteggi pucciniani,* 377.
25. Simonetta Puccini, ed., *Lettere a Riccardo Schnabl* (Milan, 1981), 209.

Rosina Storchio, Geraldine Farrar, Bori, and Zamboni; and his Rodolfos were Garbin, Caruso, Hermann Jadlowker, Giuseppe Anselmi, and Pertile.

$\mathcal{T}$oscanini resigned the directorship of La Scala in 1929; excepting appearances at the Bayreuth and Salzburg Festivals during the 1930s, he dedicated himself almost exclusively to symphonic music for the remaining quarter century of his career and never again conducted whole, staged opera performances. Between 1944 and 1954, however, he conducted the NBC Symphony Orchestra in concert performances of seven operas, including *La bohème*. The *Bohème* performance took place in two parts, on 3 and 10 February 1946, to mark the fiftieth anniversary of the premiere; Licia Albanese was the Mimì, Jan Peerce the Rodolfo. This remarkable performance—more buoyant and tragic than any other I know—was broadcast and recorded; it has been issued and reissued many times by RCA, and is now available on compact disc.[26] Parts of the rehearsals, too, were recorded, and ought to be made available for use by professional musicians and students. The excerpt in which Toscanini rehearses the orchestra in the accompaniment to *Musetta's Waltz* in the second act is, in itself, an extraordinary lesson in *tempo rubato*.

Nineteen forty-six brought another Puccini-Toscanini surprise—not so well known as the *Bohème* recording, but equally fascinating. Toscanini, who had not conducted in fascist Italy since 1930 and who had lived in exile in the United States from 1938 on, returned to his country after World War II to conduct the concert that reopened La Scala, which had been severely damaged during an Allied bombing raid in 1943. That concert—one of the most moving events in recent Italian musical history—took place on 11 May 1946; the program was all-Italian, and its centerpiece was an unstaged version of the third act of *Manon Lescaut* (including the *Intermezzo*), with

26. Interested readers are referred to a fascinating essay on this recording, "Comment faut-il jouer *La Bohème*," by the conductor René Leibowitz in his book *Le compositeur et son double* (Paris, 1971), 357–77.

Mafalda Favero as Manon, Giovanni Malipiero as Des Grieux, and Mariano Stabile as Lescaut. A poor-quality but nonetheless impressive recording of the performance exists. With luck it will someday be released, for the enjoyment of listeners and for the instruction of present and future generations of Puccini interpreters. It was Toscanini's last major tribute to the composer with whom his name was so often linked during their lifetimes and with whom it continues to be linked long after their deaths.

LA JEUNESSE QUI N'A QU'UN TEMPS: LA BOHÈME AND ITS ORIGINS

Fedele D'Amico

Fedele D'Amico (1912–90), though he published few books, was one of Italy's most influential music critics during the post–World War II period. Son of a leading drama critic, he grew up in the heart of Italian cultural life, and his interests ranged well beyond the strictly musical field.

Among critics there is almost universal agreement that Puccini's first "mature" opera is *La bohème,* whereas *Manon Lescaut* is considered a merely transitional work. But this opinion is open to question, for, with all its flaws, *Manon Lescaut* is a vital, original work, its popularity abroad (but not in Italy) limited only by the competition of Massenet's *Manon.* The Puccini work is not just an episode in its composer's apprenticeship. On the contrary, it defines a specific moment in the history of Italian opera, the moment when the Verdian world is rejected, though the unadulterated petit bourgeois ideology has not yet triumphed.

In *Manon Lescaut* love is no longer seen in the popular view of Verdi's risorgimento as the symbol of positive moral values, but rather, as in French opera, conceived as a value in itself. Still, Puccini's characters retain a heroic quality: the temperature of their passions is very high, there is an inevitably tragic background, and the raging dialectic of love and death is not impelled by bourgeois motivations. This intermediary position, in fact, is reflected in the opera's style and its musical forms, which combine elements both old and new, melodies of a traditional cast alongside symphonic outbursts and newer structures, and influences of various origin.

It is closer to the truth to see *La bohème* as the first example of the more specific Puccinian spirit: the spirit that makes his theater an authentic voice of the new society, so different from the Verdian voice. And *La bohème* is not only the first example, but also the most typical—"Puccini's essential opera," as it was defined by one of the keenest and most modern Puccini scholars, Claudio Sartori. It is possible not to agree with Sartori when, to emphasize his point, he demotes all the other operas of Puccini to the rank of not entirely successful works; but it is difficult not to agree with him on the definition itself (for that matter, classifications are often simply rhetorical figures used to underline what is in fact a definition). Puccini was an extraordinarily varied author, moving from the decapitated romanticism of *Manon Lescaut* to the twentieth-century aestheticism of *Turandot*. It is difficult to force him into a formula. And yet what makes the composer genuinely irreplaceable in the panorama not only of the music but also of the art in general of his time is *La bohème*—in this respect, truly the "essential opera."

Written between 1845 and 1848, Henry Murger's novel *Scènes de la vie de bohème* describes the Parisian world of the young artists of the period: a romantic and anarchic world, where poverty was a kind of boast, social nonconformity a code. The book's characters are numerous, almost all based on real people, and their lives are interwoven. They appear and disappear capriciously, observed by an eye that is at once nostalgic and ironic, tender and bitter, indulgent and sarcastic. The author may even make moralistic pronouncements or express social criticism. Indeed, the Goncourts saw the novel as "un triomphe du socialisme."

In the opera the number of characters is reduced to the minimum; any moralistic and critical tone has been eliminated, as well as any hint of bitterness. We are told that Mimì bares her ankle, but she is an angel. Musetta may not have too many qualms about her own behavior, but what matters is that she has a heart as big as a house. Evil, moral evil, plays no part in the story, so no actual drama is set in motion. The characters live only in the sentimental aura that envelops them; it is not so much a story as an atmosphere.

Puccini's *La bohème* is not a chronicle, like Murger's; it is a memory, a dream. Certainly Puccini enriched it with his own nostalgia for his own Bohème, for his student days in Milan. This, Sartori explains, is why the theme that opens the opera and circulates through it constantly, like the motive of Bohemia itself, is taken from Puccini's *Capriccio sinfonico,* the piece he wrote in those early days for his graduation from the Milan Conservatory. But the opera then transcends autobiography. As all the other elements of the novel fade, *La bohème* becomes valid as a straightforward, nostalgic picture of youth *überhaupt:* youth as the happy season of irresponsible freedom, without burdens or commitments, whose very adversities will reappear, in later memory, transfigured by an indulgent smile.

The only price of this happiness is its transience: It has to end. For youth, understood as irresponsibility, is not a step toward the future, a stage of human life; it is something destined to be consumed in itself. This explains why Murger, who was the critic, in his way, of that season, could bring his characters safely into port and show us, at the end, Rodolfo and Marcello as settled, comfortable members of the bourgeoisie. But this was impossible for Puccini. His Mimì had to die: not through external causes, or through any dramatic process, but rather as the spontaneous allegory of that youth that cannot survive, that has no future, except in memory (and that memory will be swathed in tenderness). "La jeunesse qui n'a qu'un temps," Murger wrote, and the words apply also to Puccini, but in a sense different from the moralistic "memento mori" tone that Murger gave it.

It is only too clear how distant such a position is from the themes of romantic opera. This was an attitude that could be born only in a society whose ideals were diverging from reality and were being transformed into a repertory of sentimental consolations offered to a world beginning to despair of resolving the problems it had set itself. In a word, this position could emerge only in a society on its way to being governed willingly by a petit bourgeois ideology. And yet it expresses a moment that, considered on its own, is an eternal moment in human life: a minor moment, not heroic certainly, but authentic, which to some extent is shared by everyone. Therefore it can also produce poetry; in other words, it can transcend the very ideology that generates it.

This is the case with the *Bohème* of Puccini, who employed an art perfectly suited to the situation, a new art. First of all, the structure of the libretto is totally new; it presents not a carefully constructed action, but rather some individual scenes linked by fairly slight narrative ties. There is still a precise calculation of symmetries and correspondences; but this calculation is purely theatrical, not dramatic. It aims, that is, at devising the various situations in such a way that each of them is given the maximum prominence in the spectator's mind, with no one scene objectively generating another. This also allowed the librettists, at a certain point, to eliminate an entire scene without compromising the whole. It is true that after the elimination of the courtyard scene, some speeches in the following scenes remain rather cryptic; but nobody pays any attention; nobody wastes time wondering about the identity of the little viscount who makes eyes at Mimì. Because it is the individual scene that matters, in accordance with the opera's basic assumption, which is to see the world as a series of "free" situations, as gratuitous flashes, not as "history."

The same idea is carried out in the music. The general musical structure is based on different atmospheres, each exactly marked out, and they alternate according to the "theatrical" levels delineated by the libretto. Thus the first and last acts, both of which take place in the garret, are symmetrical: Each is divided into two parts, of which the first is comic and brilliant, the second lyric or tragic (lyric in the first act, tragic in the last, which echoes the first, transfiguring much of the same thematic material into the new "tone").

Within these broad lines the musical texture, though connected with the "symphonism of conversation" of Massenet and the French composers in his genre, can be considered new, owing to a complexity and sensitivity of an incomparably higher degree. This texture is based on numerous brief thematic cells, each associated with a given expressive meaning; they are mingled to constitute ever-new situations, in a sort of highly refined mosaic technique. These little cells are almost all of vocal origin; they arise, that is, from inflections of the sung performance, and thus they irresistibly suggest words. The result is a highly mobile language, capable of suggesting the murmur, virtually the gossipy chatter of everyday life, but also capable of opening out in bursts of song, thus idealizing that same quotidian sound. The achievement is so absolute that it promptly consumes the tools it has employed; as a result, the simplicity and immediacy of the music are only apparent. Though we have become accustomed to defining its most famous pieces with the traditional terms—aria, duet, romanza— in reality they are entirely new forms, which, when analyzed, reveal extremely subtle complexities in every aspect: in the tonal system, in the harmony, in the orchestration.

Many listeners sensed all this when *La bohème* first appeared; but others, increasingly numerous, came to believe that the opera's values, assuming there were any, all consisted of the usual heart-on-the-sleeve that Puccini shared, in varying degrees, with his supposed colleagues of the so-called Giovane Scuola. But those days are now long gone. Now we know not only that *La bohème* is a masterpiece, but that in its creation critical intelligence, self-awareness, what in the days of Rossini and Donizetti was called "la scienza," play an outstanding role; that creation, even in strictly musical terms, is a miracle.

We do not know exactly when Puccini began thinking about basing an opera on Henry Murger's novel. The first reliable document is the brief series of news items and polemics published by two Milanese newspapers, *Il Secolo* and *Il Corriere della Sera,* on 20 March 1893 and the following few days. On 19 March, after running into Leoncavallo in a Milanese café, Puccini told the composer that he was working on a story derived from the Murger novel; and Leoncavallo, who was working on the same story, took umbrage. *Il Secolo,* property of Leoncavallo's publisher, Sonzogno, immediately communicated to its readers that Leoncavallo was composing a *Bohème;* and the next day the *Corriere* published a similar notice regarding Puccini. Then *Il Secolo* brought up the matter of priority, explaining that Leoncavallo's contract with Sonzogno dated back to December, and he had already for some time been negotiating with various singers. Puccini wrote a letter to the *Corriere* in which he claimed previous ignorance of Leoncavallo's intentions and deftly shifted the terms of the question: "For that matter, what difference can this make to Maestro Leoncavallo? Let him write his opera, I will write mine. The public will judge. Precedence in art does not mean that the same subject must be interpreted with the same artistic intentions."

But the matter must have been a bit more complicated, since Guido Marotti and Ferruccio Pagni, Puccini's inseparable friends at Torre del Lago, in their lighthearted little book *Puccini intimo,* tell a different and less edifying story: "Some time before, Ruggero Leoncavallo had proposed a libretto to him entitled *Vita di Bohème,* but Puccini had other ideas in his head and didn't know the Murger novel, so he cordially refused his colleague's work, without even glancing at it. But, a year later, having read the novel with enthusiasm, he raised such a tremendous fuss that Giacosa and Illica, with the paternal help of Giulio Ricordi, prepared the libretto of the famous opera." And yet "history" has accepted the story with a cynically indulgent smile. "Let him write his opera, and I will write mine." When the second *Bohème* was born (Venice, 6 May 1897), it was too inferior to the first for anyone to deplore the underhanded act, except its victim.

Luigi Illica had already had a bit of Puccinian experience, having collaborated on *Manon Lescaut* in 1893 (other collaborators included Leoncavallo, Marco Praga, and Domenico

The playwrights Giuseppe Giacosa (to Puccini's right) and Luigi Illica (to his left) had both played small roles in the tormented creation of the libretto of Manon Lescaut. *With* La bohème *they began a successful, if not always happy, partnership that was then to continue, with* Tosca *and* Madama Butterfly, *until Giacosa's death. Puccini himself and the gifted Giulio Ricordi also took an active part in the shaping of the texts. By and large, Illica was responsible for the dramatic structure of the libretto, while Giacosa turned Illica's draft into verse; but this division was not strict and there was considerable overlapping of tasks, and considerable friction. After Giacosa's death, Illica tried several times to write a libretto for Puccini on his own, but for one reason or another, these projects came to nothing. Meanwhile, the fertile Illica produced texts for Mascagni, Giordano, Franchetti, Montemezzi, and others. (Museo Teatrale alla Scala; Foto Saporetti)*

Oliva, not to mention Giulio Ricordi, the eternal gray eminence). And that experience had been extremely wearisome: Puccini, who had still lacked authority at the time of *Le villi* and *Edgar* and had accepted the librettos of Ferdinando Fontana without much discussion, had driven his *Manon Lescaut* writers crazy to such a degree that, in the end, he could not find one who was prepared to put his name to the text, which was then published anonymously.

Nor, as far as his eternal dissatisfaction was concerned, did Puccini ever change. Still, *La bohème* marked an important turning point, the debut of the writing couple destined—under the usual vigorous control of the publisher and the composer—to produce Puccini's three most colossal successes: *Bohème,* followed by *Tosca* (1900), and *Madama Butterfly* (1904).

The two writers had different functions. Giuseppe Giacosa was chiefly to be responsible for the literary quality of the text, though in principle he had a say about everything. To put it bluntly, he was the versifier. The scenario and the first draft were entrusted to Illica though with the thousand interferences of the others. And Illica, in fact, is the addressee of Puccini's letter acknowledging receipt of the initial sketch of *La bohème,* in which he expresses admiration for the first two acts (these correspond to the first three of the final version; Illica's original Act I had two scenes). The date is 22 March 1893, barely three days after the encounter with Leoncavallo. Giacosa immediately set to work on the first two acts, delivering the verses of Act I in May and those of Act II in July.

But then things did not move quite so fast. Murger's novel (published in installments in the *Corsaire* between 1845 and 1848 with the title *Scènes de la bohème*) was such a jumble of events and characters that it was impossible to read, even between the lines, any possible thread of a theatrical plot. The stage adaptation, entitled *La vie de bohème,* written by Murger with Théodore Barrière in 1849, was not overlooked by Illica and Puccini, but it could offer merely one possible solution among many. The libretto adaptation, therefore, posed problems, and the authors had to make important decisions about the personalities of the characters; in fact, none of the characters in the opera is drawn from a single specific figure in the

novel. Rather, each has only some aspects of a given character, or is a free blend of several. This is the case with Mimì,
for example. (For a more exhaustive study, the reader is referred
to Mosco Carner's biography of the composer.)

The first thing to be eliminated from Illica's projected libretto
was an entire scene, "The courtyard of the building in rue
Labruyère," centering around Musetta and repeating the fes-
tive atmosphere of the Latin Quarter. The scene was situated
between the present last two acts (it was published in the
magazine *La Scala,* edited by Mario Morini, in December 1958).
Other, fairly sharp debates followed concerning the rest of the
libretto; and in these discussions Puccini's ideas sometimes won
the day.

But not always. A letter from Illica to Ricordi written in
February 1894 may dispel, or at least diminish, the notion that
Puccini's librettists were only recalcitrant amanuenses. It con-
cerns the scenario of the last act.

Egregio Signor Giulio,
    Puccini is leaving, and meanwhile, from my bed, where I am
confined by a stubborn influenza, I am writing you, first so that
you will hold me excused from attending tomorrow's meeting
of the Society of Reciprocal Succor, and then . . . what could I
be writing you about then, if not *La bohème?*
    So Puccini is not at all pleased with the solution we found on
Sunday evening. He wants to begin, as he stubbornly insists,
with Mimì in bed, Rodolfo at the table writing, and a candle
stump illuminating the scene. In other words, no separation
between Mimì and Rodolfo! Now in this way we no longer have
a *Bohème,* and, what's worse, we no longer have the Mimì of
Murger! We have a meeting in a garret between a journalist-poet
and a seamstress. They love, they quarrel, then the seamstress
dies . . . The story is sad, but it's not *La bohème!* The love story
is pathetic . . . (and romantic), but Murger's Mimì is more complex! A bit of compassion is necessary also for librettists!
    Now what I say to you is this: it is already a mistake not to
allow the separation of Rodolfo and Mimì to take place before
the eyes of the audience: just imagine if the separation were not
to take place at all! Because the essence of Murger's book lies
precisely in that great freedom in love (supreme characteristic of

the *Bohème*) that governs the actions of all the characters. Imagine how much greater and more moving this Mimì could be if—in a position to live with a lover who gives her silks and velvets—realizing that consumption is killing her, she comes to die in the cold and barren *mansarde,* only so that she can die in the arms of Rodolfo. It seems impossible to me that Puccini refuses to understand the greatness of this! And yet this is truly the Mimì of Murger!

And think (this to me is virtually a new invention) how original it would be to begin the last act precisely as the first act begins. Only it is autumn, not winter. Through the broad window we don't see the rooftops of all Paris white with snow, but Rodolfo picks up a leaf, blown in by the wind, and the thought of Mimì returns to him. We could begin with Rodolfo alone—and thus inform the audience of the separation—this damn separation that is so necessary! (So far there is no solo for the tenor!)

In the whole drama our Bohemians do nothing but eat well and drink better. Here we could let the audience see them dining on a herring divided into four portions as they discover the flavors of a hundred dishes. Finally, if we like, there is a way to complete the libretto and heal the enormous wound inflicted on it by cutting the "courtyard." But here—more than Puccini—it seems to me that you should join our side. Believe me, the press will be excessively severe. They will say it was pointless to engage two of us to make a libretto—or rather—to extract an inconclusive little text from a book. This way, instead, while leaving Giacosa the greatest freedom and scope, everything is fixed, and more, this last act will become powerfully moving and poetic. In this way—as we agreed Sunday—we will also have some breathing room. For, if we had to cut the "courtyard" to fix up "nothing," it would be too little.

Forgive the tirade, but that Puccini causes certain frights . . . Unfortunately (and it must be confessed!) you almost always let him win! The truth must be said, and the poor ugly ducklings are always Giacosa and your most devoted . . ."[1]

That spring Puccini went to Sicily to meet the novelist Giovanni Verga, whose short story *La lupa* (and its dramatization) he wanted to make into an opera; he had already written some music for it. Puccini spoke with Verga and procured

1. Eugenio Gara et al., eds., *Carteggini pucciniani* (Milan, 1958).

photographs of locales and costumes; but he concluded nothing and once more concentrated his activity entirely on *La bohème,* incorporating some of the *Lupa* music (including Rodolfo's opening tune "Nei cieli bigi"). The composer accepted Illica's ideas about the last act (we do not know when, but on 7 September 1894 he wrote to Ricordi, "The last act is very beautiful," and it is the act as we know it). But then he found things to criticize in the second and third acts, and again many of his ideas prevailed.

According to the dates written on the autograph score, the orchestration of Act I, begun on 21 January 1895, was finished on 6 June; that of Act II was completed on 19 July; Act III on 18 September; and the last act on 10 December. But this does not mean that there were no further debates about the libretto: They continued up until a few weeks before the premiere. Many years later Puccini told how, having written the last note, he was overcome with an emotion unique in his whole career: "I had to stand up in the middle of the room, alone in the silence of the night, I started crying like a baby. I had the sensation of seeing a child of mine die."

There were arguments between Puccini and Ricordi over the choice of theater and conductor for the premiere. Three years earlier *Manon Lescaut* had triumphed at the Teatro Regio in Turin, but Puccini distrusted encores and he was not pleased with the Regio's acoustics. He wanted a city far from Milan, like Rome or Naples, and he wanted Leopoldo Mugnone to conduct. Ricordi persuaded him to change his mind, and he also persuaded the Regio to take steps to improve its acoustics. As for the maestro, the Regio had only recently named a twenty-nine-year-old musician as its permanent conductor, Arturo Toscanini. The cast included Cesira Ferrani (who had created Puccini's Manon), the tenor Evan Gorga, the soprano Camilla Pasini (Musetta), and Tieste Wilmant (Marcello). Schaunard was Antonio Pini-Corsi; Colline, Mazzara; Benoit and Alcindoro, Alessandro Polonini. At the rehearsals Gorga's high notes proved uncertain and Puccini wanted to have him replaced; but Illica, who was in charge of the staging, defended the tenor because of his acting ability, and Puccini finally gave in, lowering the key of "Che gelida manina."

The opera opened on 1 February 1896, exactly three years after the premiere of *Manon Lescaut*. Its success was not as great, though the reception was warm. The critics from out of town treated the work with admiration or respect, but the Turin papers were generally hostile. One opinion became famous: Carlo Bersezio (son of a well-known playwright) considered the opera "a momentary mistake," prophesying that it would not leave "much of a mark in the history of opera." And even more famous, in the same vein, was the telegram sent by the agent, librettist, and theatrical jack-of-all-trades Carlo D'Ormeville: "*Bohème* failure. Will not make the rounds."

There were also "technical" objections, particularly against the brilliant "parallel fifths" of the beginning of Act III (Verdi did not like them, either). But it would not be a mistake to infer that the opera was really a failure: These were minority reactions. By the end of that short month there had been twenty-four performances, almost one a day. On 23 February *La bohème* opened in Rome at the Teatro Argentina, conducted by Edoardo Mascheroni, with Pandolfini (Mimì), Storchio (Musetta), Apostolu, and Bensaude; and despite an initial coldness, the last two acts aroused enthusiasm. Then, in April, at the Teatro Massimo, Palermo, the success was total, this time under Mugnone. Here the curtain calls went on so long that Mugnone finally decided to encore the whole second half of the last act, despite the fact that the singers had begun removing their makeup and had shed their wigs.

The opera traveled quickly to every theater in every country, and was destined to become a mainstay of the standard repertory. Still it is worth recalling that the subscription audience of La Scala managed to boo it as late as 1900, when the Rodolfo was Caruso; Mimì, Emma Carelli; and the conductor, Toscanini. Poor Carlo D'Ormeville had finally found some disciples.

Translated by William Weaver

TOSCA AND
PESSIMISM

Franco Serpa

Franco Serpa, born in Rome, studied classical philology and the history of music at the University of Rome and took his degree with a thesis on Puccini. He is now professor of Latin literature at the university. He has published *La polemica sull'arte tragica* (writings by Nietszche and Wagner on tragedy, 1972), as well as translations of Schopenhauer's writings on music and the arts (1981). His Italian edition of the Strauss-Hofmannsthal correspondence is to appear shortly.

The idea of an opera based on *Tosca* by Victorien Sardou (1887) came to Puccini in 1889, a few months after the first performance of *Edgar.* It came to him, in fact, from Ferdinando Fontana, who until that moment had been his librettist (and who evidently wished to continue writing for him). Sardou's drama was at the time a novelty that Sarah Bernhardt, then at the apogee of her career, had turned into a major success on 24 November 1887 in Paris, at the Théâtre de la Porte Saint-Martin. (For the next twenty-five years, from 1887 to 1913, the drama was to be her almost exclusive property, and she performed it on the stages of Europe and the Americas). Perhaps it seemed to Fontana that Sardou's work, with its interperate theatricality, was well suited to his capacities (which were, indeed, those of an emphatic man of letters, as is evidenced by the hopeless libretto of *Edgar*) and that its enormous success would guarantee the success of an opera based on it.

For a while Puccini, after the partial disappointment of *Edgar*, was enthusiastic about the project, as he makes clear in a letter of 7 May 1889 to Giulio Ricordi:

> My zest for work, instead of leaving me, has returned more vigorous than before . . . I am thinking of *Tosca!* I beg you to take the necessary steps to obtain Sardou's permission before abandoning the idea, which would greatly sadden me, for in this *Tosca* I see the opera I need, one whose proportions are not excessive, either as spectacle or as something giving rise to the usual superabundance of music.

One infers that an agreement with Sardou was no easy matter; and one can see that Puccini was by now thinking in an original, mature manner and beginning to demand control of the libretto and realism in his texts (he was, therefore, ready to free himself from Fontana's collaboration and from late-romantic sentimentality).

About a year later Puccini saw Bernhardt perform *La Tosca* in Milan. (*La Tosca* was the original title of Sardou's drama, and it signified the name of a star prima donna—witness the Italian custom of referring to *la* Bernhardt, *la* Garbo, *la* Callas. The Italian title caused some confusion—even in Mario Cavaradossi—because without the definite article the surname looks like a given name; some early Puccinians evidently mistook it for such when they named their daughters Tosca.) Bernhardt was then touring Italy (her tour ended clamorously, requiring police intervention), and although Puccini understood little of the performance, which was in French, the experience rekindled his enthusiasm, both because of the effectiveness of the plot, which he was now able to verify on the living stage, and because of the star's new manner, which had become tormented and realistic as the result of the requirements of the play itself. This was to be the first time that Puccini shaped his inventiveness in part on a theatrical model; but later, with *Butterfly* and *Fanciulla,* the model exerted a much smaller influence on him (Puccini never saw Gozzi's *Turandotte* onstage; he only received an account of Reinhardt's production in Berlin).

For *La Tosca,* Bernhardt had made drier her famous, much-celebrated sung recitation, her *mélopée* (Victor Hugo had called it her *voix d'or,* others, *voix mélodieuse*), and had transformed it into a prosaic speaking voice, even a shouting voice ("Ce qu'épreuve la Tosca est si violent, que cela ne se peut exprimer que par des cris, des hurlements, des rugissements, des sanglots," wrote Jules Lemaître in *Impressions de théâtre*).[1] Many years later Puccini was still telling his friend Fraccaroli that though he had understood little on that occasion, he had been especially moved by the anguish with which Bernhardt had repeated in an undertone: "Malheureuse! Malheureuse!" Bernhardt's performance in October 1895 in Florence, however, pleased him less, and he wrote as much to Luigi Illica. The actress was in poor health, and Ricordi hastened to advise Puccini of this, to avert a change of mind; but the deeper reason for the disappointment was that by 1895, the composer was conceiving *his* drama, *his* protagonist.

And so in 1889, when Puccini had become quite taken with the subject, he and Ricordi found a way of dropping Fontana, who was deeply hurt; and they entrusted to Illica (a beginner in the field but promising and, besides, backed by Arrigo Boito) the very arduous task of turning the voluminous play by Sardou into a libretto.

Illica worked on *Tosca* for Puccini throughout 1891 and was still at work on it when Puccini began composing *Manon Lescaut.* The difficult *Tosca* project was taking a long time partly, perhaps, because of Sardou's uncertainty and diffidence. For example, in a telegram of December 1892, Sardou's agent for

1. "What la Tosca feels is so violent that it can only be expressed in cries, shouts, growls, sobs."

Italy informed Ricordi that Sardou did not like Puccini's music; in reality, he almost certainly knew not a note of it, since neither *Le villi* nor *Edgar* had circulated in France. More probably he opposed Puccini because the young unknown composer could not guarantee him a success.

Finally, at a certain point (precisely when we do not know), Puccini, in a turnabout not unusual with him, abandoned the *Tosca* project. We do know that in January 1893 Illica wrote to Ricordi: "Puccini's instability is nothing new. Just remember his enthusiasm for *Tosca* . . . And then? Was it not I that had to tell you he 'no longer cared for' *Tosca?*"

It is well known that the story of operatic subjects and librettos coveted and later rejected by Puccini is rich and full of incident (Illica's letter shows that Puccini was already famous for this in 1893), and there would be nothing extraordinary about the present infatuation ("the opera I need") and rejection. But it has not been noted before that *La Tosca* (which henceforth we shall call *Tosca,* as Puccini and his librettists preferred) is the only case of a project rejected by Puccini but then taken up by him again some years later and carried to completion. And we shall see that this singular episode has its source in the psychological makeup of the composer and furnishes a decisive insight into the significance and character of the music.

When was Puccini's interest rekindled? And was it really rekindled by a favorable opinion from no less a judge than Verdi? The story has been told many times but is by no means certain. After Puccini's rejection, the *Tosca* libretto prepared by Illica was offered to Alberto Franchetti, who accepted it (and gave up an *Andrea Chénier,* also by Illica, which went to the young Giordano; thus, in those years, Franchetti gave up two librettos that were later to become worldwide operatic successes). In October 1894 Franchetti and Illica went to Paris to obtain Sardou's consent for the definitive version of the *Tosca* libretto. At that time Verdi, too, was in Paris, together with Giulio Ricordi, attending rehearsals for the premiere of *Otello* at the Opéra. There was a meeting, probably arranged by Ricordi, at which Illica and Franchetti read their libretto to

Puccini's operas from Tosca *on coincided with a period of exciting new development in Italian graphic design; and the publisher Ricordi encouraged this movement, hiring artists like Adolfo Hohenstein, who, after creating the sets and costumes for the first production of Verdi's* Falstaff, *also designed numerous, colorful covers for piano scores and some striking posters like this one for* Tosca. *He was also responsible for the sets and costumes at the premiere in the Teatro Costanzi in Rome in 1900.* (Warder Collection)

Verdi, who reacted very favorably and praised particularly a tenor aria in the last act, a manly farewell to art and life in the form of a hymn.

It is hard to believe that news of Verdi's praise can have immediately made an impression on Puccini, who, among other things, had no use for Cavaradossi's hymn, since he later eliminated it altogether. It is more probable that the grand old man's reaction caused Giulio Ricordi to reflect and induced him to direct the project once more towards his favorite among the young Ricordi composers. Thus it does not seem there ever was a conspiracy motivated by envy and rivalry on the part of Puccini against his colleague Franchetti for the purpose of recovering *Tosca*. The dates confirm this: Franchetti wearied of the project in March 1895, and this was four months before Ricordi, in a letter of 26 July, urged Puccini to finish *La bohème* in order to devote himself to *Tosca*. A few days later, Puccini made up his mind (as he related in a letter to his friend Carlo Clausetti, Ricordi's Naples representative, on 9 August 1895).

And so Puccini spontaneously came back to the project of the powerful, dramatic opera; came to it, as we shall see, because of an inner psychological and aesthetic need. He had kept the idea within himself for nearly three years, meanwhile allowing his feelings and style to mature with *Manon* and *Bohème;* and now his intentions and goals with *Tosca* were clear. With *Tosca,* Puccini abandons the poetry of youth. (The exotic *Butterfly* is a special case, which, in terms of dramatic density, is much closer to *Tosca* than to *Bohème;* years later, the poetry of the young lovers in *Gianni Schicchi* and *La rondine* will be stylized and mannered.)

It is easy to see why the reworking of the *Tosca* libretto was a long, laborious process. At first Illica was engaged in writing other librettos as well; later, from the beginning of 1896, he devoted himself to the rehearsals for the premiere of *Andrea Chénier* at La Scala (26 March 1896). *Tosca* was not then, nor even later, his chief concern, as perhaps Puccini might have wished it to be, nor did the addition of Giuseppe Giacosa as collaborator improve the situation. Illica, who felt he was a dramatist and poet, did not welcome the participation of that cultivated man of letters, even though he was on friendly terms with Giacosa; and indeed, the situation he was forced to accept was anomalous, since his capacities as librettist were judged insufficient *only* in the case of the librettos intended for Puccini. Giacosa, to be sure, was a refined and sensitive writer, but he was also a difficult, touchy, and by now tired man. And if the subject and characters of *La bohème* had agreed with his own attitudes of introspection and elegiac realism, he felt distant and hostile towards the subject, situations, and characters of *Tosca*.

But Puccini knew what he wanted: the drama itself, reduced to its bare essentials and charged with as much tension as possible. And this he obtained, by dint of tenacity and amid constant disagreements. Indeed, even at the end, when all the music was completed, Puccini found ranged against him his faithful ally Giulio Ricordi, who thought the last act fragmentary and poor (letter to Puccini of 10 October 1899). Even if one considers that at that point Ricordi did not yet know the marvelous Prelude to that act (which Puccini completed on 17 October), the substance of what Ricordi found wanting remains unchanged. He felt a lack of solemnity and of an idealistic attitude towards death. He had expected a duet of some size and a heroic hymn, the so-called Latin hymn—everything, indeed, that Puccini had discarded (and labeled "academic" in the drafts of the two poets [letter to Ricordi of 11 October 1899]). And so, despite Ricordi's urging, Puccini added nothing and changed nothing.

Other contributors of small or minimal details to the libretto, in the words, stage directions, or scenic action, included Puccini's friend Alfredo Vandini, a Luccan living in Rome; don Pietro Panichelli, a clergyman who grew so fond of Puccini that he was nicknamed "Puccini's little priest" (don Panichelli obtained the music of the *Te Deum* sung in Rome, described the order of a solemn procession, and found in the Vatican a musician, Maestro Meluzzi, who could identify the pitch of the lowest note sounded by the biggest bell of St. Peter's, an E); and, finally, the Roman dialect poet Luigi (Giggi) Zanazzo, who furnished a graceful quatrain for the already composed music of the young shepherd's song (Puccini would have liked to obtain it from the famous Cesare Pascarella, who, however, was not in Italy at the time).

Tosca was produced on 14 January 1900 at the Teatro Costanzi in Rome, conducted by Leopoldo Mugnone, and sung by Hariclea (Ericlea) Darclée, Emilio de Marchi, and Eugenio Giraldoni; the public's response was occasionally warm (the two tenor arias, the *Te Deum,* Tosca's prayer, and the third-act duet were encored), but for the most part barely cordial. Prudence was the keynote of nearly all the newspaper reviews, together with some recognition of the work's theatrical effectiveness. (Because of the importance of the writer, the severe criticism by the Wagnerian Luigi Torchi[2] stands out and is still worthy of attention: It is a detailed analysis of the opera, written in an aloof and sometimes irritable manner, to be sure, but not without some intelligent insights.) On 17 March 1900, *Tosca* arrived at La Scala (conducted by Toscanini; with Darclée, G. Borgatti, and Giraldoni); and on 12 July at Covent Garden, London (conducted by Mancinelli; with M. Ternina, F. De Lucia, and A. Scotti). Ternina was the first soprano whose interpretation won Puccini's unbounded approval, on 4 February 1901 at the Metropolitan Opera in New York (with Cremonini and Scotti; the conductor was Mancinelli). Paris became acquainted with Puccini's *Tosca* in French (entitled once more *La Tosca*) at the Opéra-Comique on 13 October 1903 (conducted by A. Messager; with C. Friché, L. Beyle, and H. Dufranne). It was an authentic public success (*La Tosca* remained one of the most frequently played works in the repertory of the Opéra-Comique), but the opinions of critics and musicians (Vincent D'Indy and Paul Dukas, for example) were harsh, if not outright insulting.

Characteristics of Puccini's music, of his melody and the music's flow and color, include a secret, intense melancholy, a delicate sadness, and the constant premonition of pain and death in the sentiment of love, even in its very first manifestations (every listener has his favorite moment—"Donna non

---

2. *Rivista Musicale Italiana* 7 (1900):78f.

vidi mai," for example, or "Dammi il braccio, mia piccina," or Butterfly's entrance, or even the very melancholy first finale in *La fanciulla del West,* which happens to be the harbinger of a story with a happy ending). In life, which Puccini seems to wish to reproduce poetically and simply, he is never able to see innocence or happiness. These qualities are known to his characters only in the guise of nostalgia or desire. The primary energy of his art comes from an existential pessimism, not properly conceptual or moral, but sentimental, hence all the more desolate and blind.

Studied, alert simplicity is a highly refined quality of Puccini's dramatic forms, which ripened and became personal astonishingly early, thanks to his individual genius and his family tradition. The content of his drama, however, is another matter. In the final analysis, every Puccini drama can be reduced to just two components: the love impulse and the image of death. Puccini apparently perceived only eros at the origin of all existence, an eros devoid of vitality and moral hope. The idea was anything but delicate. On the contrary, it was a strong one common to nineteenth-century European decadent writers, an idea, we repeat, of the origin of existence but also of a destiny bereft of consolation. But Puccini, a bourgeois who mistrusted provocation and had an insecure literary background, came to recognize, and thus to express, the true nature of his melancholy only by degrees, through a successive deepening of his images of a negative eros, of loneliness, of death— through Act II and especially Act III of *Manon Lescaut* and through *Bohème,* an admirable dirge, composed of cold and tears, on the death of youth.

It was after he had understood how cruel his idea of life could be that Puccini returned to the *Tosca* project, that is, to the powerful, explicit drama: because he felt his psyche and mind were ready to conceive a destiny of the unfortunate and obsessed. *Tosca* is, then, a touchstone of maturity, psychological more than creative (indeed, not everyone agrees that the musical result is entirely satisfactory); and as such it really holds a central place in the Puccinian canon, because from it Puccini has excluded any reassuring or consolatory element. In *Tosca,* eros conveys only a negative image, an image of exasperation, irresponsibility, cruelty, and finally death. This was the image that ate at Puccini's soul and imagination, despite the efforts he made to mitigate or sublimate it.

This quality of the composer's work was first noted as early as the 1930s (hence at a period that was hardly partial to Puccini's music) by Austrian and German musical analysts, who rightly placed Puccini among the representatives of pessimist aestheticism. And if in the twenties the opinions of Adolf Weissmann and Julius Kapp regarding Puccini were still conventional and dismissive, beginning in 1931, with the fine monograph by Richard Specht (translated into English in 1933), the climate began to change. This is not the place to describe in detail the further course of Puccini criticism (it will be well to remember, however, that the author of the most exhaustive critical biography of Puccini, Mosco Carner, was also Viennese, though the book appeared in English); but we must note that in the tormented climate of postwar Germany in 1947, *Tosca* became the basic argument of an excellent book, built on Specht's foundations but with a psychological and cultural, rather than musicological, emphasis: *Puccini: Versuch einer Psychologie seiner Musik* by Frank Thiess. It was Thiess who, sympathetic to the music and the composer, proved that in *Tosca* stands revealed the profound nature of Puccini's art, terrified and disarmed in the face of the evil of existence.

Certainly the theatrical form insisted on and imposed by Puccini, often against the intentions or even the abilities of his librettists, concise and spare as it is (Sardou's original has been cut in half, yet nothing is missing), confirms for us at the outset that Puccini was intent on penetrating bravely to the core of the drama's concepts and impressions. Everything, every secondary character, every narrative thread, every event contributes to the presentation of a dry, macabre triumph of death.

Because of the tight unfolding of the drama and the particular type of vocalism it requires—i.e., dramatic declamation—*Tosca* has been ranked with the operas of verismo in a pejorative sense. It cannot be denied that in *Tosca* one hears some musical elements typical of verismo—for example, the declamation as well as the agitation and exasperation of the

The brief, lyrical open-
ing of the last act of
Tosca, with the off-stage
song of the shepherd boy,
cost Puccini a good deal
of effort. Finding a
Roman dialect poet to
write the text occupied
some time; then the com-
poser agonized over the
pitch of the bells that are
heard sounding matins.
This opening music,
finally, was a great suc-
cess, and, while Puccini
was in Rome for the pre-
miere, he signed this
photograph for Angelo
Righi, the boy soprano
who sang the shepherd
on that occasion.
(Museo Teatrale alla
Scala; Foto Saporetti)

singing (with leaps in registers and climaxes close to shouting; but this is also a degenerate form of certain aspects of Wagnerian vocalism common to nearly all European music up to the Expressionists) and a certain aggressiveness of sound designed to enhance the violence of the events onstage. But in Puccini's *Tosca* some of the prime hallmarks of verismo are absent: the emphasis on virility, the plebeian cast of characters, the lyricism of folklike simplicity, the realistic tableaux (in *Tosca* the Sacrestan is perfectly relevant to the world of Scarpia, indeed is one of its constituent elements), and, finally, the loosening of the musical fabric.

Instead in *Tosca,* whatever one might perceive unreflectingly, the expression is exquisitely controlled, and the musical forms are perfectly arranged (there is a thorough and intelligent, if not always persuasive, study on the subject, *Analytische Untersuchungen zu Puccinis Tosca,* by Hans-Jürgen Winterhoff [Regensburg, 1973]). The rigorous concision of the invention, wholly thematic, is the musical correlative, or better, the necessary consequence of the dramatic concentration. All the musical ideas in their various appearances and transformations tend to express the imminent supremacy of deception and death.

From the very beginning, two worlds confront each other in two musical styles. But the confrontation is the result not of a moral dynamic (the dynamic of good and evil, of damnation and redemption, as in the romantic theater), but rather of the clash of strong and weak psychic impulses. *Tosca* is not essentially a drama of the defeat of love, as were *Manon Lescaut* and *Bohème,* but a tragedy of the supremacy of terror. The two artist lovers are adults (the first in Puccini's oeuvre), and they are quite devoid of youthful innocence and intrinsic goodness. Their passion and the art that springs from it are fated, because of their rashness and blind exaltation, to be annihilated in a trap prepared with icy cunning.

In the music of *Tosca,* wickedness, which Puccini for the first time examines with dismay, takes on the characteristics of impassiveness, repetitiveness, and, more deeply, unmoving, unformed menace. It eschews the logic of human affections, just as the language that expresses it eschews the logic of tonal and chromatic harmony. Scarpia's theme, with which the opera has its noisy beginning, is made up of three unrelated chords (B-flat major, A-flat major, E major), of which the first and last stand an augmented fourth apart—that is, a "diabolic" tritone apart.[3] As is well known, this thematic cell recurs identically, concise and suggestive as it is, throughout the opera (up to the middle of Act III, when the two victims dare to hope and plunge into the trap); indeed, it attracts and, as it were, paralyzes any other meaning.

Puccini expressed evil with themes based on repetition (especially ostinatos, but also melodic cells that form a circle incapable of expansion) or on modal harmony. With modality, perceived as the absence of internal definitions and articulations, that is, as stasis and inhumanity, Puccini evokes the cold authority of death. But this characteristic and its meaning are not immediately explicit. The whole-tone mode on which Scarpia's theme is built is heard in its entirety for the first time only halfway through Act I, in a highly significant situation: when Cavaradossi tells Angelotti of the hiding place in the garden well, the "secure and impenetrable refuge." The two men imagine themselves safe and victorious, but the music tells us that they are already victims and condemned. The same thing happens at the beginning of Act II, with Scarpia's second theme. We hear three notes descending by whole tones: rather than a theme, it is an evasive gesture, the shadow of a thought. Then, in a highly tense and threatening context, the theme appears in its true colors, as the sinister completion of Scarpia's first theme, which it immediately joins (in Cavaradossi's first interrogation: "Where is Angelotti?" "I don't know." "You deny giving him food?" etc.).

But the symbolic capacity of the modal harmony is perceived above all in the masterly and hermetic way in which Puccini attracts to it and "distorts" themes having a well-defined tonal profile. For example, the theme of Angelotti's flight is transformed under Tosca's jealous words ("Where are they? If only I could catch the traitors"), and the scaffold theme

---

3. Note also that the theme of petrification, of shapeless stasis, in Strauss's *Die Frau ohne Schatten* is also characterized by the tritone relationship; it is almost like the inversion (in minor) of Scarpia's theme, from C-sharp minor to G minor.

("See? I stretch out to you my clasped hands," E-flat minor) is stiffened in the Phrygian mode, before and after Tosca's supplication (and in her narrative in Act III). Inexorably, the spell of wickedness attracts passions and dreams and annihilates them. Yet it would be necessary to analyze the entire score to show with what courage Puccini confronted the tragic idea of human cruelty and damnation, with what technical skill he controlled, *at all times,* his musical language (see the Winterhoff essay mentioned earlier).

Does this mean that in expressing twentieth-century pessimism, *Tosca* has the same cultural authority as *Salome* and *Wozzeck?* The answer is no, because Puccini was a culturally less lucid and psychologically less energetic artist than Strauss or Berg, and he lacked their intellectual vigor. Whatever is realized in *Tosca* pertaining to a negative conception of humanity and fate is attained through courage and anguished impulses, to which the composer, at the time, was able to give expression.

But as in *Salome* and *Wozzeck,* so in *Tosca.* All characters are obsessed or sick with melancholy, lust, rage, perversion—all, not just Scarpia: the diva, her dreaming lover, the religious, the police. And with greater imaginative force than in other decadent operas, Puccini's Roman opera parades the grim rhetoric of religious aestheticism, the inertia of religious signs in a world devoid of spirit, the sinister pomp of ceremonies and prayers chanted by the covetous, the fearful, the sadistic. The extraordinary effect of the Act I finale arises from the music's ability to amplify with religious sounds the deformed fantasies of Scarpia and his fierce political might (cannon shots!) into a depraved hyperbole. Every thought of pity, every emotion is turned into its opposite or is twisted into a nightmare: This is what happens in the dismal pantomime of Tosca's mortuary devotions over Scarpia's corpse, which is the spectral reprise of the *Te Deum* so rightly admired by Specht. Even the fragrant melancholy of the Roman dawn and of the matins is lost in the threatening, indistinct rumble of the deepest E; and here, too, we perceive a fatal sign, in the "diabolic" relation that is set up between the closing chord of the dawn, B-flat major, and the E minor of the despairing elegy (there had already been unrest in the descriptive music, in the Lydian version of E major, and in the evanescent references to Scarpia's theme).

What did Nietzsche like about the two great prophets of pessimism, Schopenhauer and Wagner? "The cross, death, the tomb." Before Puccini, before *Tosca,* no one in Italian music, no one perhaps in Italian art generally, not even d'Annunzio, had come to terms with those dark, challenging principles.

Translated by Piero Weiss

Lieutenant F. B. Pinkerton: Problems in the Genesis and Performance of Madama Butterfly

Arthur Groos

Arthur Groos, a professor of German studies at Cornell University, is co-editor of the *Cambridge Opera Journal* as well as the books *Giacomo Puccini: "La bohème"* (1986) and *Reading Opera* (1988). He has also written extensively on medieval literature and on nineteenth-century German and Italian opera. Currently he is working on books on Wolfram von Eschenbach's *Parzival* and Puccini's *Madama Butterfly*.

The continuing success of *La bohème, Tosca,* and *Madama Butterfly* on the contemporary operatic stage often obscures the fact that these mainstays of the repertory, during their genesis as well as their early stage lives, were the object of concerted argument and revision. A series of skirmishes and truces characterized the working relationship of the "Trinity" of collaborators, Giuseppe Giacosa, Luigi Illica, and Puccini himself.[1] Battle metaphors permeate the correspondence that accompanies the genesis of each opera, with the publisher Giulio Ricordi issuing summonses to decisive fights in his office:[2] "Whether it be a Roman brawl or an English boxing-match, this has to be finished once and for all!!! . . . I'll expect you at my office at 1:30 P.M."[3] Even after the apparent completion and initial success of these operas, Puccini remained a compulsive reviser, retrieving acts already sent for engraving, correcting extensively at the proof stage, and subsequently adding, removing, and altering sheets in his autograph scores as well as emending printed scores during rehearsals for productions.[4]

Publication of the orchestral score usually determined the ensuing performance history of an opera, even if the archaeological difficulties presented by the autograph and the absence or presence of other materials (such as the lack of plates and intermediate proofs, or the contradictory evidence of scores emended for performances during the composer's lifetime) make it impossible to construct "authoritative" editions. The first printed score of *Tosca* does not differ substantially from subsequent versions; *La bohème* was enriched by the bonnet scene in Act II—which was inserted between performance numbers 15 and 16 for the premiere in Palermo in 1896—and is now sung with this addition published in the first orchestral score of 1898.[5]

Madama Butterfly presents problems of an altogether different order of difficulty. There exist four different performance

1. On the genesis of *La bohème,* for example, see Arthur Groos and Roger Parker, *Giacomo Puccini: "La bohème,"* Cambridge Opera Handbooks (Cambridge, 1986), 31–54.
2. For a vivid description of the meetings in Ricordi's office, see Illica's reminiscence in the memorial for Giacosa in *La Lettura* 6 (October 1906):873f.
3. Eugenio Gara et al., eds., *Carteggi pucciniani* (Milan, 1958), 105. Future references will be by letter number, here CP 110. Giuseppe Adami, ed., *Epistolario* (1928; reprint Milan, 1982), will be cited as A, and Giacosa's correspondence in Piero Nardi, *Vita e tempo di Giuseppe Giacosa* (Verona, 1949), as N.
4. Cf. the problems of dating individual acts and describing the autograph of *La bohème,* discussed in Groos and Parker, *Giacomo Puccini: "La bohème,"* 46–48 and 102–14.
5. See Cecil Hopkinson, *A Bibliography of the Works of Giacomo Puccini* (New York, 1968), 20–23 for *Tosca,* 14–19 for *La bohème.*

versions of the opera between its premiere in 1904 and the publication of what seems to be a compromise orchestral score in 1907. The first version, created for the *prima assoluta* at the Teatro alla Scala in Milan on 17 February 1904, was withdrawn after one of the most controversial fiascos in the history of opera.[6] The Puccini team revised the opera for a second, enthusiastically received performance at the Teatro Grande in Brescia on 28 May 1904, reducing Act I, dividing Act II into two parts, and adding the tenor *romanza*, "Addio fiorito asil." A third version, mostly with further cuts, was created for Covent Garden in London on 10 July 1905. Finally, a fourth version, with many other cuts and changes—including the formal designation of the two parts of the original Act II as Acts II and III—made its debut at the Opéra Comique in Paris on 28 December 1906, by which time Ricordi—with four different piano-vocal scores to confuse his customers—had begun engraving the orchestral score that appeared a half-year later.[7]

None of these versions of *Butterfly* seems sufficiently "definitive" to exclude the others. In recent years, considerable attention has been drawn to the alternative between the first and fourth versions, for Milan and Paris respectively. Attempts to mount productions based on the "original version" for La Scala have achieved notable success in East Berlin, the Welsh National Opera, the English National Opera, Venice, Boston, and elsewhere. However, such productions often subvert their own intentions by subjectively retaining "good" elements and eliminating "bad" ones. Joachim Herz's 1978 production for the Komische Oper, for example, was a mixture of the Brescia and La Scala scores.[8] The English National Opera production of 1984 seemed to follow the La Scala score but accepted some of the composer's later cuts, attempting to differentiate between modifications "which supported Puccini's original vision, and those which did not."

---

6. See the discussions in George R. Marek, *Puccini: A Biography* (New York, 1951), 216–26; Mosco Carner, *Puccini: A Critical Biography*, 2nd ed. (London, 1974), 138–43; William Ashbrook, *The Operas of Puccini* (1969; reprint Ithaca, 1985), 106–10.
7. See Hopkinson, 24–29.
8. See Joachim Herz, "Zur Urfassung von Puccinis 'Madama Butterfly,'" in Sigrid Wiesmann, ed., *Werk und Wiedergabe: Musiktheater exemplarisch interpretiert,* Thurnauer Schriften zum Musiktheater 5 (Bayreuth, 1980), 239–61.

Unfortunately, the program booklet does not document the revelation of "Puccini's original vision."

The argument for the original Milan version in such productions is usually made at the expense of the Paris version of 1906. Recent studies assert that Albert Carré's production for the Opéra-Comique compromised the "original intentions of composer and librettists" because it was "designed to ensure easy bourgeois acceptance of an opera which had previously shown an uncomfortable picture of colonial self-interest."[9] Even if one ignores the intentional fallacy (already made suspect by the plural) and translates the radical chic into musicological terms, the charges remain serious: The Paris version reflects unusual circumstances and compromises at a particular theater and is therefore only a chronologically final version, not a definitive one.[10]

Critics of the Paris version list the cuts or "accommodations" as follows: the elimination of many details enhancing the Japanese "local color," the reduction of Kate's role, Pinkerton's insulting remarks about Japanese people and culture, and a passage in the love duet where Butterfly relates how she imagined Pinkerton to be a barbarian. The difficulty with this evidence is that these changes reflect concerns recognized by the Puccini team or modifications begun by them well before the Paris production—indeed, before the premiere at La Scala. Illica's early correspondence acknowledges the overabundance of scenic material in his first draft (CP 250), a well-known defect in acts invented by him.[11] The scene with Kate seemed inadequate as early as December 1902 (CP 292), and the team struggled with it throughout the remaining genesis of the opera (CP 295, 299, 301, 354; N 846). Pinkerton's relationship to the Japanese in general and Cio-Cio-San in partic-

9. See Julian Smith, " 'Madame Butterfly': The Paris Première of 1906," in *Werk und Wiedergabe,* 229–38, especially 231; also "A Metamorphic Tragedy," *Proceedings of the Royal Musical Association* 106 (1979–80):105–13.

10. On the parallel problem of definitive versus non-definitive revisions in Verdi, see David Lawton and David Rosen, "Verdi's Non-Definitive Revisions: The Early Operas," in *Atti del IIIo Congresso internazionale di studi verdiani 1972* (Parma, 1974), 189–237.

11. For a comparison with *La bohème,* see CP 118 and the unpublished letters quoted by George Marek (see n. 6 above), 145 and 150.

ular is more complicated and needs to be the subject of an extended discussion.

This essay will discuss that relationship with reference to the genesis of the libretto and to performance problems left unresolved by the disparate versions of *Madama Butterfly*. I will investigate Illica's preliminary draft of Act I and the first version of Pinkerton's self-characterization and description of Butterfly; the sudden revision of the libretto in 1902 and its shift in emphasis from East-West relations to character tragedy; and the addition of Pinkerton's "Addio fiorito asil" to the last act after the premiere and the question of its thematic coherence. I will then suggest some implications for selecting a performance version of the opera.

In a s m u c h as the libretto to *La bohème* had been created from both Henry Murger's novel and play of the same name, Puccini's battle-hardened collaborators—especially Luigi Illica, who was generally responsible for the shape and initial drafting of a libretto—do not seem to have been concerned about commencing *Madama Butterfly* by using a double source, the short story by John Luther Long (1898) and the one-act stage adaptation by Long and David Belasco (1900).[12] Indeed, there is evidence that the team frequently proceeded on the analogy of *La bohème*.[13] But unlike their initial consensus on sources for that opera, Illica began fashioning his libretto of *Madama*

12. Scholarship on the subject has been confused by the fact that exchanges in the correspondence refer both to a *romanzo* and a *novella* as well as the fact that Long published his short story in *Century Magazine* 55 (January 1898), 374–92, then in an often reprinted "Japanese" collection that same year (New York, 1898), 1–86, and again in a separate volume anticipating the appearance of the opera (New York, 1903). A version with three introductory chapters, referred to by Mosco Carner (see n. 6 above), 382, does not exist.

13. Illica's first progress report from March 1901 already mentions the draft of a love duet to conclude Act I "more poetic" than "the scene between Mimì and Rodolfo" (CP 249). By the following month Illica was involved in a *Bohème*-like dispute over fidelity to sources and the respect due librettists, asserting the need for conferences, "as with *Bohème!*" (CP 252). He could not anticipate that this analogy would continue to influence the tortured genesis of *Butterfly*, even in the arguments surrounding the deletion of an entire act (CP 297; N 845f.), and that the fiasco of the premiere would be due partly to the audience's and the critics' reaction to similarities between the two operas (see note to CP 349).

Butterfly from Long's story, whereas Puccini wanted a version based on Belasco's play. The divergence began by chance: Puccini had seen the play in July 1900 in London, and, although he knew no English, was captivated; he badgered Ricordi throughout the ensuing fall to obtain permission to set it (CP 236; A 69). Illica, however, began the libretto in March 1901 from a translation of the story, the only published source, since the team did not receive a manuscript of the play until June.[14] But as problems arose, Illica—who had already outlined a libretto and drafted a first act based on the story—vehemently denied the importance of the play (CP 252), while Puccini insisted on adapting the play (CP 247), even suggesting that it might provide Illica with better material for the already-completed act (CP 255), and that they travel to London to see a performance (CP 253).

Underlying this initial tug-of-war between librettist and composer is the problem that the two versions of the source differed in both scope and perspective. The short story relates a series of events from Pinkerton's arrival in Japan to Butterfly's abortive suicide; the drama concentrates on her final day of waiting and death. Expressed more generally, the story narrates a case history of East-West misunderstanding;[15] the play presents a character study of the heroine. While both versions offered viable options in terms of nineteenth-century operatic traditions, and both contributed substantially to the work (Act I is based on the story, Acts II and III on the play), they remained unpromising in one important respect: The story suggested an uncharacteristically odious role for the tenor lead, and the play provided him with almost no role at all.

The earliest version of the *Butterfly* libretto seems to be Illica's handwritten draft of Act I, composed between March and

14. The translation of the story is described as "so-so" (CP 243); by late May, Puccini had a second translation by an American woman better able to render the intentions of the author (CP 253f.). A third version by a Dr. A. Clerici was published by Giacosa in *La Lettura* 4 (February–March 1904):97–109, 193–204, to coincide with the opera's premiere. A typescript of the drama translation is in the Ricordi archives in Milan.

15. On "Oriental" operas in general, see Carner (n. 6 above), 380, and Hellmuth Christian Wolff, "Der Orient in der französischen Oper des 19. Jahrhunderts," in Heinz Becker, ed., *Die "Couleur locale" in der Oper des 19. Jahrhunderts,* Studien zur Musikgeschichte des 19. Jahrhunderts 42 (Regensburg, 1976), 371–85.

May 1901 and preserved in the Ricordi archives in Milan.[16] Although the existence of this unique document has been known for decades, it has never been the object of textual study, even though it enables us to discuss the original conception of the opera and Pinkerton's role in considerable detail. Illica's correspondence admits that there are too many incidents for a satisfactory musical setting (CP 250), but the major episodes of the finished opera are already in place, albeit often in preliminary and distended shape. In addition, there are several episodes that disappeared or were reduced not only during the genesis but also in the early stage history of the opera: Pinkerton conducts Sharpless on a tour of his house; the wedding party includes a cousin (Riso) and an alcoholic uncle, Yokousidé; there is a reunion between Butterfly and Suzuki (Cio-Cio-San's childhood servant, now Pinkerton's maid), with extensive reminiscences; Pinkerton gets Yokousidé drunk after the wedding.

Several characteristics of Pinkerton and Sharpless in Illica's draft are particularly striking. One is the comical attitude that pervades the actions of both—the most frequent stage directions for each are *laughs, laughing,* and *comically.* The consul's voice intrudes from offstage, as if preparing a slapstick entrance:

> *una voce—giù dal sentiero—irritata—stanca—a respironi—*
> Sassi a carciofo! . . . Ahi! . . . Pouah! . . .
> Uh, quali punte! . . . E ancora sù, in salita!
> *la voce: esclama a un tratto, come un gemito:*
> Scommetto, dislocato
> un piede . . .
> *dopo una pausa:*
> No, soltanto due dita!
> *vicinissima:*
> Ouf! Ouf! . . . (p. 4)

16. The 34-page draft is described briefly by Ashbrook (see n. 6 above), 111f. I am grateful to Mimma Guastoni and Teresita Beretta of the Ricordi Company for permission to quote from it (references will be to page number).

The dating is based on the following: A letter in March announces Illica's immersion in the *scena* and love duet of Act I (CP 249); in April there was a reading of portions of his draft (CP 252, N 837); on 20 May Puccini writes Giacosa that Illica has a "prologue, which is most successful" (N 836) and makes plans on the 26th (CP 254) for Illica to read it to Giacosa in Salsomaggiore. From here work on Act I passes to Giacosa, i.e., to pressuring Giacosa to work on it.

(*a voice from the path below, irritated, tiring, panting:* Rocks like thorns! ouch! Tch! Ow, what points! . . . And still up, climbing! [*the voice suddenly exclaims, half-groaning*]: I bet I've dislocated a foot [*after a pause*]: No, only two toes! [*very near*] Oof! Oof!

The humor of their ensuing conversation is more pointed than the rocks on the path. From his greeting through his farewell, "diavolo d'un Pinkerton" (you devil, Pinkerton [pp. 4 and 24]), Sharpless applauds the comedy (p. 24) that Pinkerton is staging, a comedy that the hero even sits down to watch *come persona che assiste ad uno spettacolo* (like someone watching a show [p. 13]). Far from objecting—as his more responsible and serious descendant will—to the selfish hedonism that Pinkerton espouses in his aria and description of Butterfly, the consul laughingly applauds the former and toasts the latter: "Al dì felice in che l'amico Pinkerton s'ammoglierà sul serio!" (to the happy day when our friend Pinkerton will get married in earnest! [p. 9]). Both men jokingly belittle the smaller scale of Japanese space:

> F.B.P Per carità, badate! . . . Vi affogate!
> *E gli indica comicamente una piccola pozza d'acqua:*
>   È "il lago"! Mister Sharpless, attenzione.
> MR. S: *pure comicamente:*
>   È ver, siamo al Giappone! (p. 4)

(F.B.P.: For heaven's sake, be careful! You'll drown! [*and comically points to a small puddle*] It's "the lake"! Careful, Mr. Sharpless. MR. S.: [*comically as well*] It's true, we're in Japan!)

Their response to the Japanese on a linguistic level reveals a more imperious attitude. Sharpless comments on the strange custom of naming people after flowers, insects, or things (p. 7); Pinkerton cannot accept the apparent discrepancy between his servants' names and their appearance, and so subverts the "comical" Japanese convention linking them by imposing his own comic denigration on the foreign "things":

Oh, le belle parole
sù stemperate così brutte cose!!
Ah qui il rispetto agli usi
sarebbe scherzo! . . .
Per me quelle tre cose mostruose
le chiamo: Musi! (p. 2)

(Oh, such beautiful words for such ill-suited, ugly things! Well,
here respect for custom would be a joke! . . . For myself, I'll
call those three hideous things "mugs"!)

He comments on every entrance of Japanese characters, projecting his own sense of alienation by calling them things or
animals, particularly insects. Unsettled by the size and unfa-
miliarity of his surroundings, he exclaims: "Case per pulci e
. . . un ragno l'architetto! . . . / Segreti a doppio fondo!"
(Houses for fleas and—the architect a spider! Double-bot-
tomed secrets [p. 1f.]). Sharpless joins in as the wedding party
approaches:

F.B.P. Udite? Un trillo!
    Uccello . . .
SHARPLESS (*ridendo*) o grillo!
F.B.P. (*guardando giù*)
    Oh l'effetto pigmeo!
    Rampanti sul sentiero,
    a piccoli passetti
    affatto ricoperte
    sotto le ombrelle aperte
    sembran davvero
    o funghi semoventi
    o saltellanti insetti.
(*a Goro*) quelle formiche
    là sono i parenti? (p. 10)

(F.B.P.: You hear? A trill! A bird . . . SHARPLESS. [*laughing*] or a
cricket! F.B.P.: [*looking down*]: Oh, they look like pygmies!
Swarming up the path with tiny little steps, completely covered
up beneath their open umbrellas, truly they seem either walk-

ing mushrooms or hopping insects. [*to Goro*] Those ants
there are the relatives?)

It is not surprising that the Lieutenant orders "mosche, ragni
allo zucchero, nidi al giuleppe" (candied flies and spiders, julep
nests) as customary sweets for his wedding guests (p. 17) and
dismisses the angry relatives after the Bonze's curse as a chorus
of noisy frogs (p. 28). Pinkerton is clearly disturbed by an
environment where even the cicadas seem to speak in Japanese
dialect (p. 9).

The hero's entomological projections reveal much about
Illica's sources. Already familiar with Japanese material from
his libretto for Mascagni's *Iris* (1898), he seems to have
employed Pierre Loti's *Madame Chrysanthème* (1887) as well as
Long's short story in piecing together this prologue. Inasmuch as both works are crucial to understanding the early
focus of the opera, it will be helpful to outline their relationship before proceeding. Loti's autobiographical novel follows
the outline of a travel adventure, with a voyeuristic sexual
subplot common in European narratives about the Orient in
the nineteenth century.[17] Long's story and play represent a
critical response to the sexual adventure of the novel, trans-
forming Loti's self-proclaimed "comédie japonaise" into a
tragedy. Loti specifies that the order for his hero's ship to
leave Japan comes on 17 September (Ch. 51); the only date
Long mentions is the return of Pinkerton's ship on 17 September, thus implying the fact that his tragedy of "Madame
Butterfly" takes up where the comedy of *Madame Chrysanthème* leaves off. The intertextual critique is particularly clear
at the beginning of the story and the end of the play. The
introduction to Loti's novel presents the hero Pierre and his
friend Yves, en route from Istanbul to Nagasaki, discussing a
marriage of convenience in Japan; Long's story introduces
Pinkerton and his friend Sayre, en route from the Mediterra-
nean to Nagasaki, involved in the same subject. While Pierre
returns to Chrysanthème's house at the end of the novel to
find her testing the coins he left with a hammer, and is relieved

17. See Rana Kabbani, *Europe's Myths of Orient* (Bloomington, 1986).

that his marriage ends in a joke, Pinkerton returns with the same assumptions in the play but finds a different denouement:

> I thought when I left this house, the few tears, sobs, polite regrets, would be over as I crossed the threshold. I started to come back for a minute, but I said to myself: "Don't do it; by this time she's ringing your gold pieces to make sure they're good. You know that class of Japanese girl and . . ."[18]

The intertextual criticism of Loti in Long's story contributed to the Puccini team's difficulties in deciphering its intentions (CP 253), difficulties also implied by their having to commission three translations of it.

Illica's use of both sources in his preliminary draft of Act I can be summarized as follows. Most of the plot expands on

18. David Belasco, *Six Plays* (Boston, 1928), 28.

PINKERTON (CARUSO)   SHARPLESS (SCOTTI)   TOGO (BADA)   CIO-CIO-SAN (FARRAR)

The great tenor Enrico Caruso, though he did not create the role of Pinkerton in Madama Butterfly, *sang in the Metropolitan premiere in 1907 in the presence of the composer. An amateur but gifted caricaturist, Caruso on this occasion drew a number of entertaining portraits of the interpreters and scenes from rehearsals.* (Courtesy of Michael Sisca, World Copyright) brief details from the beginning of Long's story: Pinkerton's arrangement through the marriage broker Goro for a wife and the lease of the house on Higashi Hill for 999 years, Pinkerton's insistence that Butterfly renounce her ancestors, her visit to the missionary, the wedding with the family's rejection of Butterfly as well as Pinkerton's attempt to inebriate them. Loti's novel provides the local color at the beginning of the act: Chapters 2–6 contain descriptions of the ambience, particularly the house with sliding partitions, miniature gardens, and little lakes, and the vistas of Nagasaki. Later chapters present information about the heroine's toilette (ch. 26), prayers, and ottokés (ch. 44). Above all, as we shall see, the comparisons of the Japanese with animals, insects, and things derive from Loti.

The grafting of Loti's European stance toward Japan onto Long's American story creates a double focus in the initial version of Pinkerton's aria and description of Butterfly. The adventures of Loti's Pierre comprise part of a global pattern of episodes stretching from Istanbul to China; Long's hero imposes, in a single episode, his American values on one surrogate wife. Illica's Pinkerton combines the traits of both: The summary of his introductory aria emphasizes his desire to experience "tutte le voglie" (all the desires) throughout the world while remaining "americano sempre" (American forever). At this stage, the American element predominates: Pinkerton welcomes the consul to "l' 'home' " (p. 4), offers him a choice of "Whiskey-Bourbon" or "Milk-punch," and rejects the cushions offered by the servants in favor of "Rockings-chairs," which are glossed in the stage directions as "*American seats*" (p. 5). The initial version of Pinkerton's aria continues:

> *in piedi versando il Whiskey parla:*
>   per l'istinto del Yankee vagabondo
>   d'avere casa propria in tutto il mondo
>   Gittar-capite? l'áncora
>   entro allo scoglio di qualche avventura
>   e distrarsi, e campare
>   finché nessuna raffica,

la guerra or la politica,
danneggi nave, ormeggi, alberatura;
se questo avviene . . .
all-right! . . . ancora in mare
prendendo così il mondo come viene.
però: vivere america!
(d)ovunque e sempre america!
onde—capite?—moglie giapponese
per . . . novecen novantanove nen
ridendo
 riducibile a mese
 e intanto una famiglia, un posa piè . . .
 un . . .
cerca la parola . . .
 Equitable famigliare . . . a rate . . .
 la "Mutual" dell'amore, un'affezione
 stabilita a date . . .
 Insomma—mi capite?—
 americano sempre e ove si va
 un plum pudding . . . già . . . di felicità.
 Tutti i sapori e insiem tutte le voglie. (p. 6)

(*standing, pouring the whiskey, speaks:* For the instinct of the wan-
dering Yankee to have his own house all over the world, to
drop—you know—anchor wherever adventure leads him, to
amuse himself, and stay until some squall, war, or politics
breaks his ship, mooring, mast; if this happens, "all right!"—to
sea again, taking the world as it comes. But: to live, America!
Everywhere and always America! So—you see—a Japanese wife
for nine hundred and ninety-nine *nen* [*Jap., years*] [*laughing*],
reducible to a month, and in the meantime a family, a footstool,
a [*looks for the word*] family "Equitable," by installments, the
"Mutual" of love, affection established on time. In short—you
know—American always, and wherever I go a veritable . . .
"plum pudding" of happiness. All the savors and all the desires
as well.)

Although Illica does not differentiate between British and
American borrowings, calling the hero "Sir Francis Blummy
Pinkerton" at his introduction to Butterfly's relatives and at
the wedding ceremony (pp. 20, 23), the vocabulary of this

statement is emphatically Anglo-American, laced with loan-words that express a fixed mentality: "all right," "Equitable," "Mutual," "plum pudding."[19] More precisely, the colonial vagabond who imposes his indigenous life-style wherever in the world he operates is a "Yankee,"[20] a term that appropriates a widespread stereotype of American adventurism fostered in Europe by aggressive New England merchants and reinforced by American gunboat diplomacy. This dominant image of cultural and political chauvinism is reinforced in the second half of the aria by a supporting image of sexual chauvinism. The extension from public to personal "business" applies the house lease to its inhabitant, putting human relationships on the installment plan, a tactic that makes them appear deceptively "equitable" or "mutual," rather than terminable on demand.

Whereas Pinkerton's aria reveals a jingoist adventurer, the description of Butterfly that follows presents a stereotype of Orientals derived from Loti's novel. Unlike Long's imperialistic hero, who attempts to turn Butterfly into an "American refinement of a Japanese product,"[21] Illica's Pinkerton—like Loti's Pierre—refuses to see in her more than an oriental object:

> *e, descrivendo, illustra col gesto*
> Una cosa . . . così!
> Un niente— . . . trasparente
> di gran fragilità
> e piccina, piccina, piccina,
> *illustra imitando . . .*
> dal camminare muto,
> felpa!, velluto!,
> e, seduta, un'intaglio!
> L'eterna figurina
> dal paravento,
> un guazzo per ventaglio,
> un'ornamento!

19. Even the one Japanese loan word "nen" (years) is attached to a number traditionally expressing a maximum term in Anglo-American law. The number comes from the story by Long—a Philadelphia lawyer.
20. To be more precise, his mother lives "a Newport" (p. 9). In Long's story, Pinkerton is merely "a lower-class fellow."
21. *Century Illustrated Monthly Magazine* 55 (January 1898):377.

ride, ribellandosi all'idea
   chè, donna?!! . . . No!
ride più forte
   Nè moglie! . . . Ohibò!
   Ecco . . .
cerca . . . poi conclude ancora:
   una cosa! (p. 7f.)

(*and describing her, keeps illustrating with gestures:* A thing . . . like
this! A transparent . . . nothing, infinitely fragile and tiny, tiny,
tiny, [*miming, demonstrates*] with a silent walk, felt! velvet! And
sitting, a carving! The eternal figure on a screen, the flutter of a
fan, an ornament! [*laughs, rejecting the idea*] What, a woman?!!
No! [*laughs louder*] Nor a wife! . . . Far from it! But just . . .
[*searching, then concludes again*] a thing!)

This "catalogue aria" proceeds in a circle, from a pantomime
and definition of Butterfly as a diminutive and fragile thing
through a list of ornamental objects derived from Loti,[22]
pointedly eliminating common designations for a woman
before returning inconclusively to the initial label of "thing."
   But since "Butterfly" is animated, Pinkerton's quest to define
his plaything (fueled by further doses of whiskey) shifts to
another metaphorical complex in Loti's representation of Oriental otherness—animals:

. . . *continua, quasi con entusiasmo.*
   Però, sapete che cos' ha di bello
   quest'essere così piccino e strano?
   La voce! . . . Rassomiglia a un suono . . .
cerca la parola . . . umano;
   è un istrumento in gola ad un uccello.
   E qui dove per uso le cicale

22. Even a cursory collation of metaphors from Loti provides most of Illica's list (French
citations are to the Calmann-Lévy edition [Paris, 1970]): "fragilità" ("frêle," 253),
"piccina, piccina, piccina" ("J'abuse vraiment de l'adjectif *petit* . . . En décrivant les
choses de ce pays-ci, on est tenté de l'employer dix fois par ligne," 220), "cammi-
nare muto, felpa, velluto" ("ne font pas de bruit; on n'entend, quand elles passent,
qu'un froufrou d'étoffes," 254); "figurina dal paravento" ("personnage de paravent," 19; "échappés de paravent," 90; "elle forme vignette de paravent," 136); "guazzo
per ventaglio" ("je l'avais vue, sur tous les éventails," 44), "ornamento" ("bibelot,"
25, 32, etc.).

discorrono in dialetto giapponese
è la più rara cosa del paese
questa voce . . . perfino sensuale!
Senza la voce questa moglie mia
sarebbe in verità solo un gingillo
ma quando parla e ride . . . allora è un trillo
un cinguettìo . . . che vi mette allegria! (p. 8f.)

(*continues, almost excitedly:* But do you know what's beautiful
about this strange little creature? Her voice! It seems like a . . .
[*searches for the word*] human sound; but it's the instrument in the
throat of a bird! And here, where the cicadas habitually speak in
Japanese dialect, it's the rarest thing in this country, this voice
. . . even sensual! Without this voice this wife of mine would in
truth be only a trifle, but when she speaks and laughs . . . it's a
trill, a chirp—which makes you merry!)

Whereas Loti's unflattering metaphors for the Japanese comprise a small zoo, ranging from monkeys, hedgehogs, cats,
and birds to a wide variety of insects, Pinkerton tries to differentiate: Butterfly's voice is not quite human, but it is also
distinct from the insect buzz that—according to Loti—forms
the basis of all Japanese sounds.[23] As pleasant as bird song, it
is high enough on the great chain of being to be attractive in
another "animal" sense as well—sensual. But even this differ-
entiation from things and insects is tentative, undercut when
the wedding party approaches and Pinkerton and Sharpless
laughingly exchange guesses of whether its sound is made by
birds or crickets (p. 10), and when Pinkerton jovially anticipates the bizarre wedding of "un yankee ed . . . una vesta!" (a
Yankee and a kimono [p. 12]).

One important conception underlying Illica's juxtaposition
of American and Japanese stereotypes in this first draft deserves
particular emphasis. Whereas the Americans resist assimilation and impose their own culture on alien surroundings, which
their English-laden diction in general and Pinkerton's aria in

23. Loti refers to "cet éternel chant d'insectes qui sort des arbres, des plantes, des vieux
toits, des vieux murs, de tout, et qui est la base même des bruits japonais" (279).
Most of chapter 17 is devoted to the dominant sound of cicadas (95f.).

particular emphasize, the Japanese are gradually succumbing to foreign influence, adopting Occidental customs and clothing. Not surprisingly, interest in assimilation as a manifestation of decadence, a contemporary European preoccupation and a major theme in Loti's novel,[24] dominates the discussions immediately preceding Illica's draft. Puccini was fascinated by Yamadori: "He has changed into a degenerate American millionaire. This change is completely to the advantage of the so-called 'European' element that we need" (CP 247); and Illica designed a corresponding figure for Act I, the marriage broker, who dresses like a European (CP 249), also adding Japanese officials at the wedding dressed *"in divisa, abito, cioè, stringato e caschetto russo, all'europea"* (in uniform, i.e., tight clothes and Russian cap, European style [p. 19]).[25] Such figures provide a cultural context for the more extensive and problematic assimilation of Cio-Cio-San.

The emphasis on attitudes of western colonialism and eastern decadence contributes substantially to the early conception of the opera as a tragedy of East-West relations, in which the principal characters are agents of impersonal cultural forces that determine their actions as well as those of others. Illica defended the modernity of his conception, and contemporary scholars have justifiably called attention to its radical political implications. This focus, however, was problematical from the very beginning, not just when the Paris production of 1906 ostensibly compromised it. The portrayals of Pinkerton and Butterfly already present a conflict between two systems of discourse and the two media involved in text-music relations: their literary modernity and their conventional operatic function as lovers. The chauvinist who constantly refers to the

---

24. Pierre refuses to interest himself in Japanese (103), fearing the dangers of a "décadente imitation" (298) that he perceives already in the decline of Japanese culture: "qui va bientôt finir dans le grotesque et la bouffonnerie pitoyable, au contact des nouveautés d'occident" (299).

25. Both are details from Loti. The marriage broker (Kangourou = Goro) appears "complet en drap gris, de la *Belle-Jardinière* ou du *Pont Neuf,* chapeau melon, gants de filoselle blancs" (33); the marriage takes place in the registry office, "en présence d'une réunion des petits êtres ridicules qui étaient jadis des *Samourai* en robe de soie,—et qui sont des *policemen* aujourd'hui, portant veston étriqué et casquette à la russe" (54).

Japanese as vermin is difficult to reconcile with the tenor in the love duet,[26] who concludes the act with a protestation of love, "ti voglio bene . . . sai?" (I love you, you know? [p. 34]). Nor does it seem entirely consistent to have Butterfly kiss Pinkerton's hand, imitating what she has been told is a western sign of respect offered only to saints and kings, and then immediately act *"con un po' di civetteria"* (with a little flirtatiousness [p. 29]).

Throughout the early genesis of the libretto, Puccini reserved final judgment until the balance of individual acts and the coherence of the whole could be weighed (CP 260, 269, 280). The original second and final act was expanded in February 1902, adapting events in Long's story to an alternation of scenes at Butterfly's house, the consulate in the European concession, and Butterfly's house—an extension of the East-West focus into the structure of the entire opera. Shortly after proceeding with instrumentation (A 76), Puccini abruptly requested his team to discard the consulate scene and return to a two-act structure based on Illica's prologue and "Belasco's drama with all its particulars" (CP 287). This drastic operation had far-reaching implications for the opera, demoting the East-West contrast to a secondary theme and increasing the importance of the characters. If Illica's original conception based on Loti and Long led him to emphasize Pinkerton as the agent of the conflict—"*his* is the drama" (CP 252)—the subsequent revision of the work to accord with Belasco's play led Puccini to emphasize the tragedy of Cio-Cio-San.[27] The result, understandably, is a multiplicity of discourses that makes it difficult to isolate a particular "vision" or "intention."

Let us take, for example, the revision of Pinkerton's aria

26. The different nature of the love duet suggests that it derives from different genres or media. The only analogy mentioned in the correspondence is the Act I duet from *La bohème* (CP 249), though another obvious model is the Act I duet from Verdi's *Otello*—also taking place after a fracas and also between partners of different races. Butterfly's toilette and the nighttime scene with the lovers surrounded by fireflies are reminiscent of favorite themes of Japanese prints. The short story explicitly compares Butterfly's toilette with a print by Buncho (390).
27. As Puccini later defined the opera to the conductor Mancinelli, "there's a great part for the woman, little for the tenor and baritone" (CP 321).

and description of Butterfly. The changes are not total, since
Illica attempted to salvage as much as possible from the original draft (CP 289), and Giacosa retained many motifs in the
final revision of the libretto. The beginning of the published
version of Pinkerton's aria, in particular, retains most of the
vocabulary, and even the rhyme, of Illica's draft:

> Dovunque al mondo lo Yankee vagabondo
>   si gode e traffica
>   sprezzando i rischi.
> Affonda l'áncora alla ventura
>   finchè una raffica . . .
> *Pinkerton s'interrompe per offrire da bere a Sharpless*
>   Milk-Punch, o Wiskey?
> *riprende*
>   . . . scompigli nave, ormeggi, alberatura.
>   La vita ei non appaga
>   se non fa suo tesor
>   le stelle d'ogni cielo
>   i fiori d'ogni plaga,
>   d'ogni bella gli amor.
> SHARPLESS
>   È un facile vangelo
>   che fa la vita vaga
>   ma che intristisce il cuor.
> PINKERTON (*continuando*)
>   Vinto si tuffa e la sorte riacciuffa.
>   Il suo talento
>   fa in ogni dove.
>   Così mi sposo all'uso giapponese
>   per novecento
>   novantanove
>   anni. Salvo a prosciogliermi ogni mese.
>   "America for ever!"

(Everywhere in the world the Yankee vagabond enjoys himself
and trades, scorning risks. He lets down the anchor at random
until a squall [*Pinkerton breaks off to offer Sharpless a drink.*] Milk-
punch, or whiskey? [*continuing*] upsets ship, mooring, masts.
Life doesn't satisfy him if he doesn't make his treasure the stars
of every heaven, the flowers of every region, the love of every

beauty. SHARPLESS: It's an easy gospel that makes life charming
but saddens the heart. PINKERTON [*continuing*]: Defeated, he
plunges, siezes his fate again. His talent works in every place.
So I'm marrying in the Japanese custom for nine hundred
ninety-nine years—free to release myself every month. "America forever!")[28]

Whereas Illica's draft presented us with a hero whose mai
concern was to impose American business logic on all his affair
the revised Pinkerton believes primarily in enjoying himsel
using his ingenuity to take advantage of a Japanese custom
Although he concludes with a jingoistic assertion, "Americ
for ever!" (the only English phrase in this version of the aria
Pinkerton is no aggressive Yankee, but a sexual adventure
The political chauvinist has become a male chauvinist. Th
revised emphasis of the opera on individual rather than nation
stereotypes has reversed the relative importance of the cha
acter traits derived from Loti and Long.

It has also made possible a tenor role that is both mor
attractive and more complex. The most obvious advantage o
the new focus can be seen in the poetic diction that replace
the commercial English of Illica's draft:

> . . . fa suo tesor
> le *stelle* d'ogni cielo
> i *fiori* d'ogni plaga,
> d'ogni *bella* gli amor. (my emphasis)

Stars, flowers, beauty—this is conventional lover's imagery
but its very conventionality is problematic. As the obtrusiv
use of "ogni" (every) suggests, Pinkerton's poetic fancy is di
quietingly all-embracing for the moment before his wedding
and Sharpless, no longer a laughing accomplice, interrupts
criticize precisely this passage. His objections ("facile var

28. Since most currently available versions of the libretto derive from the vocal sco
and therefore distort the original form of the text, I cite from a libretto printed f
the first performance (Milan, 1904) kindly provided by Jürgen Maehder. The quot
for the discussion of "Addio fiorito asil" are taken from the "nuova edizione" pu
lished for the second performance at Brescia, currently available in facsimile in t
Edizione del Teatro alla Scala (Milan, 1985), 11–61.

gelo," "vaga," "intristisce il cuor") complete its rhyme ("cielo," "plaga," "amor") but counter its sense, subordinating the facile quest for pleasure to concerns of the heart. We are reminded of this problem by the ensuing exchange between Sharpless and Goro, which applies the hero's poetic images to the approaching bride.[29] The consul asks, "Ed è *bella* / la sposa?" (and is the bride *beautiful?*), to which the matchmaker replies: "Una ghirlanda / di *fior* freschi. Una *stella* / dai raggi d'oro" (a garland of fresh *flowers,* a *star* with golden rays), inadvertently revealing the immediate object of Pinkerton's vagabond hedonism.

The structure of the aria further draws attention to Pinkerton's inconsistent character. The beginning and concluding sections ("Dovunque al mondo," "Vinto si tuffa") commence in a parallel manner, using an *endecasillabo* with internal rhyme and two *quinarii*. The shift in the final five lines from general to specific, from third-person to first-person narrative, applying the speaker's general beliefs to his present actions, "così mi sposo," reassuringly continues the metrical pattern, only to end abruptly in a legal escape clause and the linguistic escape to patriotic closure, "America for ever!" This jarring discrepancy between the hero's poetic pretensions and the crassness of his intentions reveals the unmediated extremes of Pinkerton's character, the source of his attraction—and his tragedy.

Pinkerton's ensuing description of Butterfly similarly adapts elements of Illica's original draft to the new concept of the opera. Instead of denigrating Oriental conventions by asking which animal or thing her name reflects, Sharpless's question, "sareste addirittura cotto?" (are you really in love), now addresses the basic issue of the hero's emotional involvement. The beginning of Pinkerton's response in particular recycles familiar words and rhymes:

Amore o grillo—donna o gingillo
dir non saprei.—Certo colei
m'ha colle ingenue—arti invescato.
Lieve qual tenue—vetro soffiato,

---

29. The ironic juxtaposition is less noticeable in the opera, since Puccini did not set the line "le stelle d'ogni cielo."

alla statura,—al portamento
sembra figura—da paravento.
Ma dal suo lucido—fondo di lacca
come con subito—moto si stacca,
qual farfalletta—svolazza e posa
con tal grazietta—silenzïosa
che di rincorrerla—furor m'assale
se pure infrangerne—dovessi l'ale.

(Love or whim, woman or plaything, I couldn't tell you. Certainly she has ensnared me with her ingenuous arts. Light as slender blown glass, in her stature, in her bearing she seems a figure from a screen. But from her shining lacquer background how—with a sudden movement—she detaches herself, like a little butterfly she flutters and rests with such silent gracefulness that a frenzy to pursue her assails me, even if I should break her wings.)

Several semantic shifts reveal the altered emphasis from insensitive westerner to irresponsible lover. In Illica's draft, "grillo" specified one of the insects with which he identified the approaching wedding party, "donna" what Cio-Cio-San was not, and "gingillo" her function as object. Now the range between "amor" (love) and "grillo" (whim) establishes the possible extent of his emotional involvement, that between "donna" (woman) and "gingillo" (plaything), his conception of her. No longer expressing occidental prejudices, Pinkerton refuses to address the extent of his feelings, shifting responsibility instead to the character traits that have ensnared him.

The most revealing image in this evasive answer is that of the butterfly. Another borrowing from Loti's novel,[30] it does not appear in Illica's draft until the concluding love duet, expressing the heroine's fear of western disregard for other forms of life.[31] Here in the revised aria, it occurs as the last in a series of metaphors illustrating Pinkerton's fascination with

30. It expresses another East-West opposition, one between Oriental respect for all life—Chrysanthème keeps a fan for shooing intruding bugs outside (92)—and the European passion for killing and collecting insects (147).
31. "E ver che v'han lontani / paesi . . . assai . . . assai . . . / lontani e . . . quasi barbari / dove la Butterfly / se cade in male mani / proprio appena afferrata / è viva ancor, vivissima, / da spillo trapassata . . . ?" [Is it true that there are countries very very far away . . . far away and . . . almost barabarian, where the Butterfly, if it falls

the heroine. Beginning with a fragile artifact, the description proceeds to the static representation of a figure and culminates in the extended flight of an animate being, in which the sudden intrusion of verbs of motion and then violence reveal the hero's emotional involvement in the heedless pursuit of his quarry. The heroine is no longer equated with an insect as the expression of general racial prejudice; rather, the butterfly symbolizes, and is synonymous with, the delicate object that Pinkerton desires to possess.

The problematic nature of this obsession is emphasized, as in the aria, by the alteration of the original monologue to a dialogue. Sharpless again interrupts, countering the hero's fixation on Butterfly's animal sensuality with a description of her visit to the consulate:

> . . . Di sua voce il mistero
> l'anima mi colpì.
> Certo quando è sincero
> l'amor parla così.
> Sarebbe gran peccato
> le lievi ali strappar
> e desolar forse un credulo cuor.
> Quella—divina
> mite—vocina
> non dovrebbe dar note di dolor.

(The mystery of her voice struck my soul. Certainly, when it's sincere, love speaks in this way. It would be a great shame to tear the delicate wings and perhaps sadden a trusting heart. That divine, mild little voice shouldn't utter notes of grief.)

Sharpless infers the sincerity of Cio-Cio-San's love from her voice, appropriates the butterfly metaphor to emphasize the

---

into evil hands, just as soon as it's grasped—and still alive, quite alive—is pierced by a pin?] To which Pinkerton responds, "*scoppiando in una risata . . . con una specie di entusiasmo:* 'Perchè non fugga più . . . / ora giù giù, ora sù, / alta pel cielo, via, / portando qua e là / la lieve sua beltà / e l'ali sue divine / per colle o per pendice / e possa alcuno alfine / dirle: Sta qui! Sei mia / ora fammi felice!' " [*bursting into a laugh . . . with a kind of excitement:* So that it won't fly away anymore . . . now down, down, now up, high into the sky, away, bringing its slight beauty here and there and its divine wings up hill and down slope—so someone can finally tell it: "Stay here! You're mine, now make me happy!"] (p. 32).

vulnerability of her heart, and concludes with a warning of potential tragedy. The hero's rejection of any potential "gran peccato" responds only to the metaphor and flights of love, avoiding the warning entirely: "Non c'è gran male / s'io vo'

After Puccini eloped with Elvira Gemignani, her infant daughter, Fosca, lived with the couple, and the composer looked upon her as his own child. Fosca's daughter, Biki (later a well-known Milanese couturière), is seen in this photograph, wearing a sailor's hat inscribed "Cio-Cio-San," a tribute both to Puccini's opera and to his passion for yachts. (Opera News/The Metropolitan Opera Guild, Inc.)

quell'ali / drizzar ai dolci voli dell'amor!" (There's no great harm if I want to direct those wings to sweet flights of love).

But the fault will not be his alone. Pinkerton's toast to his future American wife and the ensuing approach of the Japanese wedding party create an ironic disjuncture; it is seconded by a further disjuncture between Sharpless's just-voiced fears of "notes of grief" for the heroine and the offstage voice of Butterfly proclaiming herself "la fanciulla / più lieta del Giappone, anzi del mondo" (the happiest girl in Japan, indeed, in the world). This double discourse is anything but fortuitous, drawing attention to the fact that the tragedy no longer lies exclusively in a clash of cultures, but also in a contradiction between the principals' fantasies about each other and reality. Pinkerton's adventurism has brought about this mock relationship; and Butterfly's trusting heart will embellish it.

The subsequent expansion of Pinkerton's role constitutes one of those delightfully ironic reversals that make the collaboration of Illica, Giacosa, Puccini, and Ricordi such a fascinating example of *fin-de-siècle* opera production. Having been compelled by Puccini to sacrifice their original conception to Belasco's play, softening and reducing Pinkerton's role in Act I, the librettists eventually forced the composer and publisher to compromise fidelity to Belasco and surrender to the dictates of operatic necessity by expanding the tenor part in Act III. Illica had already foreseen this at the beginning of the undertaking, denigrating the "matter of the tenor" in Belasco-Long: "Let's not think of it! Pinkerton is unsympathetic! Once presented, he shouldn't be seen again!" (CP 252). Resenting the lack of attention given to his final scene, he asserted that its more imaginative conception required Pinkerton's presence in the last act, thus better fulfilling the expectations for the tenor: "That last scene makes Pinkerton necessary also in the second scene of the second part, and that is to say provides a true tenor, an exceptional type of tenor on account of his character, modernity, everything!"[32]

---

32. Ashbrook, *The Operas of Puccini*, 101, reads the letter as an indication of Illica's confusion. But the librettist, having been slighted by Ricordi, is lumping all sources together in the aggressive defense of his turf against both publisher and composer.

As the opera approached its first performance, concerns other than the libretto's fidelity to its source revived Illica's initial vision of the tenor's role. A request from Ricordi that Giacosa allow the suppression of verses in a series of tercets for Pinkerton's return to Butterfly's house ("Oh! l'amara fragranza") touched off an epistolary war in the first days of 1904. Having been taken unawares in *La bohème* by last-minute changes made without his consent,[33] Giacosa escalated the conflict, linking his objections to general principles: "This mutilation may suit the maestro, but it profoundly offends the poet" (CP 336). Unwilling to submit mangled verses to public scrutiny by "all those people who barely understand prosody," he insisted on publication of the whole libretto, charging that the role of the tenor was already reduced and unbalanced: "The part of the tenor in this interminable second act disappears entirely, with the most serious damage to the balance of scenes . . . if it does not offer a little for the part of Pinkerton, the act is monotonous and tiring." Ricordi's rejoinder reminded the distinguished poet of the traditional subordination of librettist to composer in the genesis as well as reception of an opera. Recalling that the change from two- tc three-verse stanzas— and back again—had been made to accommodate musical rhythms required by Puccini, something Giacosa had perforce approved of, the publisher also emphasized the practical risks of distracting the public and ruining "the dramatic and musical effect, because there will not lack those who observe either that the maestro has done badly in not setting verses or that the poet has written useless verses" (N 853). Turning to Giacosa's assertion of Pinkerton's insufficient prominence, Ricordi rejected the addition of a musical number on *a priori* dramatic grounds, and concluded by mocking the imaginary choice between the imminent performance at La Scala and a gratuituous *romanza:*

But how, you man of the theater, how can you think that at that moment the tenor will stop in front of the prompter's box to

---

33. Giacosa had been upset at a similar juncture in the genesis of *La bohème* by Puccini's setting of Act I. See Giuseppe Pintorno, ed., *Puccini: 276 lettere inedite* (Milan, 1974), no. 17.

think about the virtues of poor Butterfly!! . . . And as far as the wish that Puccini interrupt producing his opera at La Scala in order to write a *romanza* for the tenor, come off it!!!! (N 853f.)

Giacosa's counterargument avoids the traditional hierarchy of power evoked by Ricordi, focusing instead on a criterion that placed *fin-de-siècle* librettists and composers on a more equal footing: dramatic viability. His expertise as "man of the theater" challenged, he responded with an analogy based on a corresponding situation in *Tosca:*

> But don't try to find the dramatic reasons for me: Pinkerton, you say, doesn't sing at that moment. Does it seem appropriate to you that Cavaradossi, when he receives the announcement of his liberation, should sing those verses, "O dolci mani" etc., which you and Puccini wanted? Certainly those of Pinkerton were more appropriate. (CP 337)

But faced with the imminent premiere of the opera, Giacosa acquiesced to the publication of the libretto with "incorrect verses and an incoherent scene," reserving the right to respond to criticism with a statement distinguishing his responsibility from Puccini's: "And then I will explain how the scene originally stood, and relate my objections and the low regard in which they were held. Now go ahead and make a shambles of my opera." Those who believe that an opera is cobbled together by hack librettists and unified by the composer would do well to pause over this statement made by a leading verse dramatist of the day.

Ricordi's reply, the last of a series of four extraordinary letters in as many days, temporarily halted the discussion by transposing the focus to musical grounds. In retrospect, there is more than a little irony in the publisher's insistence on a negative view of Pinkerton, a view very dissimilar from the one he was then advertising in his house periodical, *Musica e musicisti,*[34] and indeed, one more appropriate to Illica's initial sketch:

---

34. In the issue of 15 February 1904, Ricordi published the text of "Amore o grillo," presenting it with an enticingly vague come-on as Lieutenant F. B. Pinkerton's description of Butterfly, "whom he will shortly marry—in the Japanese fashion" (109). Ricordi subsequently published a piano-vocal score of the piece in the musical

Musically speaking, you are making an enormous mistake in drawing a comparison with *Tosca*. In fact, Puccini was uncertain whether to set the verses of "O dolci mani," but a mysterious feeling led him to do it. A comparison is thus not possible: It is an outburst of the most moving tenderness. Pinkerton, on the other hand, is a feckless American . . . he is on tenterhooks, he fears Butterfly, the meeting with his wife, and beats a retreat. Puccini has composed an agitated movement for the orchestra that explains Pinkerton's state of mind. (N 855)

But if "an outburst of tenderness" could resolve the uncertainty over Cavaradossi's vocal role, could it be so out of place to consider Pinkerton singing an outburst of—remorse?

In the wake of the disastrous premiere at La Scala on 17 February 1904, the collaborators in fact added the very *romanza* so forcefully rejected by Ricordi. As soon as minor emendations had been taken care of (CP 354, 361f.; N 855f.), including the correction of the hero's name from "Sir Francis Blummy Pinkerton" to "Benjamin Franklin Pinkerton," the team turned its attention to other concerns, including the expansion of the tenor role suggested by both librettists at various stages of the opera's genesis. Although Puccini began by cursing the addition (CP 366), it was finished before rehearsals for the second performance at Brescia in late May, which demonstrated its necessity in the large-scale structure of the work: "The new piece for tenor is going well and fits in, and is needed" (A 87).

In contrast to the initial genesis of the opera, where Puccini was generally dependent on his librettists, requiring coherent sections of the text as the dramatic blueprint for musical ideas, the composer now took the lead, asking his librettists for verses in a precise meter, possibly for already conceived musical ideas (CP 366; cf. CP 269). He provided a set of mock verses with a request for "8 or 6 strong and passionate (American) verses." A request to Giacosa for revisions, including a line echoing *L'elisir d'amore* (N 856), yielded unsatisfactory results. Complaining acidly to Illica about the poet's hackneyed diction ("too

---

supplement for the issue of 15 July, praising "the gallant *boutade* of Pinkerton the lady-killer" and its "magic circle of melodic effervescence" (434).

many 'poor little ones,' 'poor childs'; only the 'gelida manina'
[cold little hand—the introductory phrase to Rodolfo's aria in
La bohème] is missing and then we're home"), he asked the
librettist instead for the appropriate *settenari* (CP 367).

The resulting *romanza,* "Addio fiorito asil,"[35] is particularly
interesting in the light of debates over the relative merit of
early versions of the opera:

> Addio fiorito asil
> di letizia e d'amor.
> Non reggo al tuo squallor!
> Fuggo, fuggo—son vil.

> (Farewell, flowered refuge of happiness and love. I can't bear
> your squalor! I flee, I flee, I'm cowardly.)

Although some critics consider this passage to be not of a
piece with the original opera, its two couplets, expressing an
opposition between the fantasy of the past and the reality of
the present, comprise a logical extension of the unmediated
disparities revealed in Pinkerton's character in Act I. Now,
however, the incompatability of desire and responsibility yields
to insight, a farewell to a happy refuge of love and flight from
the reminder of guilt. Moreover, Sharpless's comments on
the hero's views, which consistently interrupted his statements in Act I, intrude again—emphasized by a prominent
and lengthy reprise of music from that same passage—to draw
attention to the validity of his warnings:

> Vel dissi . . . vi ricorda?
> quando la man vi diede:
> Badate, ella ci crede
> e fui profeta allor.

> (I told you . . . you remember? When she gave you her hand:
> "Be careful, she believes in it," and I was a prophet then.)

---

35. The motif of the "fiorito asil" ultimately derives from Loti, whose hero plans from
the very beginning to abide "en un recoin ombreux, parmi les arbres et les fleurs
. . . et chaque matin on remplira notre logis de bouquets" (ii) until new orders make
him take leave of the "maisonnette au milieu des fleurs" (262).

His ensuing stanza, however, reminds us that the personal tragedy of Butterfly, although begun by Pinkerton, also derives from her "believing heart,"

> Sorda ai consigli, sorda
> ai dubbi—vilipesa
> nell'ostinata attesa
> tutto raccolse il cor.

(Deaf to advice, deaf to doubts, insulted, she gathered her heart in her stubborn waiting.)

and thus hastens toward its ineluctable conclusion independently of him: "Andate—il triste vero / da sola apprenderà" (Go—she'll learn the sad truth alone).

The evolution of Pinkerton in the libretto of Act I and the expansion of his vocal role in Act III reflect a complex interplay of elements in the genesis of *fin-de-siècle* opera. As we have seen, a variety of factors, ranging from divergent sources, different conceptions of fidelity to those sources, the relative importance of text and music, and questions of theatricality and dramatic viability, to concern with the equilibrium of vocal parts and audience expectations, play a role in the development of the hero. In the absence of a firm hierarchy of values, operas such as *Madama Butterfly* had to be pieced together on an *ad hoc* basis, and the result is more the product of a series of conflicts and compromises than a pre-existing and unifying aesthetic, a product that is all the richer for its ability to incorporate such a variety of discourse.

The frequent assumption that among these performance versions of the opera there must be an *Ur-Butterfly,* an intended definitive version, derives not merely from an intentional fallacy that hovers, hobgoblin-like, above traditional operatic scholarship, but also from a false analogy with the presumed finality of putatively more cohesive forms of literature—forms whose unity and autonomy are themselves being questioned in current literary theory. Even if one wished to retain the

Romantic model of the writer or composer as the creator of a self-contained and unified world, it would be difficult to extend this model to a composer as insecure about "finishing" his works as Puccini, let alone to a group of collaborators with concerns as disparate as Giulio Ricordi and his "Trinity." This trinity was certainly not triune, and any appreciation of their contribution (three of the most popular operas currently in the repertory) needs to begin with its plurality. We might follow Roland Barthes in positing for their work

> the image of a triumphant plural, unimpoverished by any constraint of representation (of imitation). In this ideal text, the networks are many and interact, without any one of them being able to surpass the rest; this text is a galaxy of signifiers, not a structure of signifieds . . . we gain access to it by several entrances, none of which can be authoritatively declared to be the main one.[36]

One obvious consequence of this viewpoint is the conclusion that the plurality of discourse in *Madama Butterfly* does not enable us to identify any of the four early performance versions of the opera as sufficiently "intentional" or even "definitive" to exclude the others. And this has implications for the current preference of the "original" La Scala over the "compromised" Paris production. The new discourse created by the reduction of the East-West conflict and the increased focus on character tragedy furthered the deletion of many details as well as the extensive revision of Pinkerton's character that I have examined here. This well-documented shift during the genesis of the opera explains most of the Paris changes more adequately than the sacrifice of a radical original vision to a potentially critical bourgeois Parisian sensitivity,[37] one that would in any case hardly have objected to the representation of colonial self-interest and images of racial stereotyping derived from *Madame Chrysanthème,* still a best-selling novel and nearing its seventieth printing in 1906. The momentum for the

36. *S/Z*, translated by Richard Miller (New York, 1974), 5f.
37. Smith, "A Metamorphic Tragedy," 111, seems to adduce this complex of factors from an allusion to Parisian taste by Giulio Ricordi and a consideration of the alterations made for the Paris premiere.

Paris changes began when Puccini diversified the focus of the libretto in November 1902—more than fifteen months before the *prima assoluta* at La Scala.

It can be misleading to base interpretations on a comparison of production scores without adequately considering the previous history of an opera, including the genesis of its libretto. The La Scala version of 1904 represents the "original intentions" of the Puccini team, if at all, only in a restricted sense: their partial consensus at the beginning of the undertaking. But that consensus, as we have seen, began in disunity and had already shifted in late 1902, requiring extensive changes that were effected immediately—and then refined by the experience of ensuing productions. The choice between the Milan and Paris scores is not really a choice between superior and inferior, intentional and accidental versions, as proponents of the initial production claim, but between earlier and later points on a larger continuum. Puccini accepted Carré's proposed Paris revisions so readily,[38] and remained enthusiastic during the rehearsals (A 93), precisely because many of the French producer's changes also realized the pluralistic discourse of composer and librettists as it had emerged during the later genesis of the work.

Compromises and *ad hoc* revisions there certainly were in the Paris production, but not all of them reflect purely local concerns. Many putatively accidental or nondefinitive changes in the Paris score could in fact be considered "authentic" in the light of the libretto's genesis. At the very least, the Paris version has as good a claim as any to be performed; and it may even prove to have a stronger claim on reexamination of the evidence—text and staging as well as music.[39] An understanding of the many considerations involved in creating an opera such as *Madama Butterfly*, including the complexities of

38. See Smith, "Madame Butterfly: The Paris Première of 1906," 230.
39. For a list of the surviving documents of Albert Carré's productions of *Madama Butterfly*, see H. Robert Cohen and Marie-Odile Gigou, *Cent ans de mise en scène lyrique en France (env. 1830–1930): Catalogue descriptif des livrets de mise en scène, des libretti annotés et des partitions annotées dans la Bibliothéque de l'Association de la Regie Théâtrale* (New York, 1986), 145f.

the libretto as well as the score, genesis as well as reception, should enhance our understanding of multiple performance options and increase the sophistication with which we evaluate their relevance.[40]

40. This chapter is a revised and slightly expanded version of an article in *Italica* 64 (1987):654–75.

Puccini's America

Mary Jane Phillips-Matz

Mary Jane Phillips-Matz is the author of a biography of Otto Kahn and of *Verdi, a Biography*, recently published by Oxford University Press.

When Buffalo Bill Cody and his troupe performed in Italy in 1890, Puccini, then on the threshold of his career, paid his admission to see the traveling show with its cowboys, armed with lassos and rifles, and Indians with their bows and arrows. In a letter to his brother Michele, who had emigrated to South America, Puccini described the "company of North Americans, with a large number of Indians and buffalos; they do splendid sharpshooting and recreate authentic scenes of the frontier." It is possible but not certain that this was Puccini's first exposure to the culture of the West, although he expressed interest in American literature, knew at least one of Poe's tales, and probably was familiar with Washington Irving and *Uncle Tom's Cabin*, both popular in Italy.

One American play that Puccini saw in London, David Belasco's *Madame Butterfly*, inspired him to go to the dressing room of the author-producer to say that he might use the drama as the basis for an opera. Thus, the collaboration between the two men began. *Madama Butterfly,* which Puccini started to compose in 1901, reached the stage of La Scala in Milan in February 1904, a date that marks one of the worst fiascos in the history of opera. The publisher Giulio Ricordi, writing in *Musica e Musicisti* (15 March 1904), described the premiere, which was greeted by "roars, howls, laughter, bellowing, and guffaws." Almost none of the music could be heard, and any applause was answered with shouts of protest and jeers.

Puccini described the experience as "a real lynching" and wrote five days after the premiere that he was "still stunned" over the outcome. But he believed in the work, as did the celebrated poet Giovanni Pascoli, who published *La farfallina volerà* (The little butterfly will fly again) in support of the composer. The triumph of *Butterfly* in Brescia in May 1904 vindicated both Puccini and his opera; but it is clear now that Puccini had suffered from a depression that marked him for years to come. It took him nearly four years to find a subject for his next opera and convince himself that it was right for him.

Moody and sometimes unsure of himself, he wrote to his librettist Illica in March 1904 of his despair: "Today is an ugly day: How disheartened I am! . . . I find it impossible that I should have to scribble more notes. And anyway, people are sick now of my sugary music." He said that he had had enough of "*Bohème, Butt.,* and Company." In 1905 he confided to Ricordi his fear of the years that were racing by but declared that he was determined to move "forward, not backward."

All of this is not to belabor the too-familiar story of *Butterfly*'s initial failure and subsequent entry into the permanent repertory, but to throw light on Puccini's frame of mind as he tried to find a new voice and free himself from the old formulas of opera, convinced as he was that the public was bored with his "musica zuccherata," as he mercilessly described his own popular works. It was these works, however, that had brought him fame and wealth and were providing a solid source of income for G. Ricordi. From two bases, Puccini moved toward his maturity: his determination to turn his back on the works that had made him famous, and his conviction that if he looked long enough, he would find the work that would lead him in another direction.

The list of literary and dramatic texts that Puccini considered between 1904 and 1907 ranges from Victor Hugo's *The Hunchback of Notre Dame* and the tales of Gorky to the lives of saints (Margherita of Cortona, for example) and Oscar Wilde's *Florentine Tragedy*. Some of these were eventually rejected by Puccini himself; some were found unsuitable by Illica, who did, though, work diligently on *Maria Antonietta* for Puccini. Giulio Ricordi vetoed the *Florentine Tragedy*. Puccini had long considered *La femme et le pantin* by Pierre Louÿs, but decided to set it aside in March 1907, fearing that it would be compared to *Carmen*. Possible collaboration with Pascoli came under review; collaboration with Gabriele d'Annunzio proved impossible and was broken off, not without some bitterness on both sides. Marquis Pietro Antinori seems to have been the first to alert the composer to the possibilities that lay in David Belasco's *The Girl of the Golden West,* which opened in Pittsburgh and was staged in New York in time for Puccini to see it there.

Puccini's first visit to North America in 1907 followed upon an earlier trip to Buenos Aires, where, in 1905, he had been greeted with wild enthusiasm by the Italian-American community. A subsequent visit to Paris in 1906 offered Puccini the chance to oversee the French premiere of *Butterfly*. In spite of the gala atmosphere and celebration of the composer, his depression persisted: "I see nothing good in the future," he wrote, adding that he asked nothing but to get back "in my shell" at Torre del Lago. It was at that moment that Heinrich Conried invited Puccini to come to the Metropolitan Opera House to supervise the new productions of *Manon Lescaut* and *Butterfly* in January and February 1907, when *Tosca* and *Bohème* were also to be revived.

Power at the Metropolitan then lay in the hands of the banker

Otto H. Kahn, who later served as Chairman of the Board. Since its first performance in 1883 the Metropolitan Opera had fought to become the city's most important producer of opera. Although it eclipsed the old Academy of Music, the "Met" was still under siege from Oscar Hammerstein's Manhattan Opera Company. With the Met's reputation as a home for Wagnerian opera, which flourished there between 1885 and 1900, the company had acquired a rather staid image. The arrival of Caruso in 1903 signalled a possible change of direction; and when it became necessary to replace Conried, Kahn urged his Board to invite Giulio Gatti-Casazza, head of the Teatro alla Scala in Milan, to take the post. The initial approach to Gatti in June 1907 was followed by a formal proposal when Kahn met Gatti in Paris. Confirmations were made, and on 12 February 1908 Kahn announced that Gatti would be the new General Manager of the Metropolitan Opera and that Arturo Toscanini would come to New York with him.

Puccini, then, was invited to the Metropolitan just as a fresh, determined, and exuberant Kahn was gaining ever more control over the theater. Kahn's goal was not just to beat Hammerstein at his game but to make the Metropolitan one of the greatest opera houses in the world. When Gatti-Casazza reached New York, however, he found the theater ill-suited to the many spectacles that it had promised its subscribers to produce. Almost none of the stage action was visible from the seats nearest the proscenium; faulty sightlines affected the upper reaches of the house as well. The stage itself was too shallow and too narrow to permit dignified productions of major operas. Gatti complained, too, about the antiquated stage machinery, as well he might have done, having just left La Scala and its monumental productions (*Aida* and *Otello,* among others). Rehearsal rooms for the singers, chorus, ballet, and orchestra were in short supply; and the dressing rooms were considered a humiliation by many important singers. There was no space in the building for the storage of sets, which were left standing on the street, covered with tarpaulins, exposed to sun, rain, and snow until they were picked up to be hauled to distant warehouses. Although Kahn promised Gatti and Toscanini a "new Metropolitan" within two or three years, they and their successors made do with the old theater until they resigned from it or died.

This was the situation that awaited Puccini in New York, for Conried had invited him to come and work, not just to sit in a box and take bows. But he was well paid for the engagement: $8,000 for about one month's effort, with all travel and lodging covered. With his wife, Elvira, Puccini set sail on the *Kaiserin Auguste Viktoria,* where he was given a cabin in the center of the ship. High seas slowed the voyage, then fog in Lower New York Bay kept the ship lying off shore until the very day of the Metropolitan Opera premiere of *Manon Lescaut* on 18 January 1907. Puccini said that he landed at six o'clock and was in the theater at eight. After the performance, he was given a huge ovation. The opera had a nearly ideal cast: the exquisite Lina Cavalieri as Manon, Caruso as Des Grieux, and Antonio Scotti as Lescaut.

Rehearsals began on the morning after *Manon Lescaut.* Writing to Sybil Seligman, Puccini reported that although *Butterfly* went well and that Geraldine Farrar had done "very, very well" (*benissimo*), the opera lacked the poetry he had put into it. "Too much of a rush during the rehearsals, and the woman [Farrar] not as she should be. And I'll give you our *divo* [Caruso], too—indolent, a lazy man with an air of self-satisfaction; his voice is always magnificent, though."

Farrar, discreet in describing the abyss that separated her from the Italian contingent at the Metropolitan, explained her own system of singing in half-voice at rehearsals and contrasted it with that of the Italian artists, who, she said, were "naturally endowed" with strong voices and showed off "their superb crescendos" while she spared herself. Puccini made free with his advice about how Butterfly should be sung—as he had every right to do. But on another occasion, when he and Tito Ricordi called on the soprano at her hotel, presumably in an attempt to get in some last-minute coaching, she took offense. She called both men the "high irritants" of the rehearsals. The popular soprano made the role her own and said that she loved it because of its "overwhelming appeal" and the dramatic possibilities afforded by this "charming and pathetic figure of the deserted Japanese bride," as she described the protagonist of the opera.

Puccini entered easily into the Italian-American community in New York, introduced to it by Gatti-Casazza and Toscanini (at a rarefied level) and Caruso and Scotti (at a point further down on the social scale). As always, Caruso amused everyone by sketching caricatures of friends and enemies and by making hand-folded and hand-pasted envelopes out of flat paper panels. The whole Italian population of New York at that time was served by a periodical called *La Follia,* published by the Sisca family; in it, Caruso's caricatures appeared regularly. With his sure pen, Caruso captured Puccini and the taut intensity of Toscanini, whom Farrar called a "musical Napoleon," as dangerous as Vesuvius in eruption.

On 18 February, when he had been in New York for almost a month, the restless Puccini wrote to Sybil Seligman that he could stand "no more of this America." He had seen all the sights, including the Brooklyn Bridge and the Statue of Liberty, had shopped and window-shopped, and had been wined and dined to the point of exhaustion. He almost certainly longed for Torre del Lago, his much-loved retreat on Lake Massaciuccoli in Tuscany. With money earned from tossing off an autograph and a few bars of "Musetta's Waltz" he bought a motorboat that he could race on the lake and cruise in the Burlamacca Canal, which connected it to the sea.

During his stay in New York City, as during the three years that had preceded it, Puccini continued searching for his ideal subject for a new opera, constantly under pressure from within himself and from Ricordi, who needed the revenues from sales and rentals of scores. At one point, the publisher even went so far as to remind Puccini of the losses the firm had suffered in promoting *Butterfly;* but Ricordi was in fact partly responsible for the hiatus in Puccini's production, as he regularly asked the composer to travel in Italy and abroad to oversee performances of his works and to bring the allure of his presence to the theaters that staged them.

For the piano score of La fanciulla del West, *the publisher Ricordi's artists in Milan adapted a photograph of the original Metropolitan production directed by Belasco, showing Enrico Caruso as Dick, slumped over the table, while Emmy Destinn, the Minnie, and Pasquale Amato, the sheriff Rance, gamble for Dick Johnson's life. (Museo Teatrale alla Scala: Foto Saporetti)*

Perhaps remembering Antinori's remark about *The Girl of the Golden West,* Puccini attended at least one performance of it, seeing Blanche Bates, "the Sarah Bernhardt of America," in the role of Minnie. In terms of its dramatic appeal, Puccini grasped the work at once, even though he did not understand English. At first sitting, however, he was not carried away by it: "Good touches in Belasco, but nothing sealed, solid, complete. I like the Western setting, but in all the works I have been to, I've only found an occasional scene here and there. Never a simple line; everything a hodge-podge, and sometimes bad taste and old stuff." (He also saw, among other plays, Belasco's *Rose of the Rancho* and *The Music Master,* and attended vaudeville at least once. Puccini was particularly interested in what was considered "exotic music," and seemed taken by ragtime, western and Black American music, and, of course, Stephen Collins Foster.)

The central attraction of *The Girl of the Golden West* was, of course, Bates as Minnie. Belasco had described the character to Bates as a surefire role with scenes that were enormously human. Minnie was intelligent, frank, and pure, without a taint of vice, cheerful and filled with sympathy for the hapless miners. She was accustomed to their adulation of her but knew exactly how to handle these rough but good-hearted men. The Italian critic Enzo Restagno was not so keen, and in a later essay on *La fanciulla del West,* remarked that "It is not easy to conceive of a character more gratuitous and unauthentic than the one that emerges from Belasco's description."

One could compile a fair-sized monograph, in fact, from the writings of many Italian, American and English critics who have criticized the characters and plot of both Belasco's play and Puccini's opera. Antonino Titone has described *La fanciulla del West* as "Puccini's great step backward . . . taken in a moment when his idea of the world (and of writing music) fell to the lowest level possible, to a conservative immobility that places him momentarily . . . in the midst of the Italian opera composers of his time." Another critic called the opera "reactionary," while Stravinsky, decades later, stated that it was a "horse opera, extraordinarily right for television, with a Marshal Dillon and professional Indians" like those hired to parade around in the hotels in Las Vegas.

Only Daniele Rubboli, in his 1990 biography *Giacomo Puccini,* takes up the sword for this work and attempts to put it in its proper contexts, those of 1848 and of 1910. Rubboli seems to understand what caught Puccini's fancy: the primitive setting, the looming forest, the raw character of the frontier, the idea of summary justice (Placerville, California was called "Hangtown" in the middle of the nineteenth century because of the extraordinary number of outlaws and innocent men who were strung up there, many in illegal lynchings).

John August Sutter, a Swiss adventurer, reached California in 1831 and pushed his way into the Sacramento River valley. Assuming Mexican citizenship in 1841, he founded Fort Sutter and bought Fort Ross from the Russians who had built it. On 24 January 1848 one of his employees found the first nugget of gold on his property. The strike at Sutter's Mill and the subsequent Gold Rush set off one of the greatest migrations in history. In 1850 the former Mexican territory became a state of the Union. Immigrants from all over the world flocked to the new state, making the population of California jump from 15,000 to 92,500 in about three years, to 380,000 by 1860, and to 864,000 by 1880.

Among these first Californians, or authentic Forty-Niners, was the father of David Belasco, a Portuguese Jew whose surname was originally Velasco. It is from him that the playwright heard the story of an outlaw being captured because his blood dripped from the floor of his hiding place in a loft onto a table below.

Within months of the first successful strike, plays with names such as *Gold Fever* and *The California Gold Mines* were being staged in New York. The very word California struck hope in the hearts of thousands of poor farmers, tradesmen, and laborers. The American novelist Bret Harte had tapped the "California vein" with *The Outcasts of Poker Flat* and other tales. Among the characters created by Harte was Miggles, the mistress of the Polka Saloon in Marysville, California. If "The Girl" has a prototype, it is Miggles.

But the figure of Minnie descends from real, historic women as well: the heroic women of the American frontier, who lived in Virginia, the Carolinas, Georgia, Tennessee, Kentucky, Indiana, Illinois, and Ohio. These women set out with their families in wagons and flatboats, changing to covered wagons farther on, journeying to whatever new land of promise lay ahead. With them went the frying pan, the bedding, and the family Bible. In the Bible, renewed faith was found every evening after supper, when the family gathered around the hearth to hear the daily reading of the Scriptures or the reciting of whole chapters of the Bible from memory, common in a land where so few could read or write or even sign their names. What is fascinating about Puccini's representation of American frontier life in *La fanciulla* is its likeness to historical reality; in contrast, Belasco, a Jew, had Minnie read pages from *Joe Miller's Joke Book* to the miners.

Minnie, like other heroines of works with Western settings, subsumes these pioneer women. The records of the county courts in, for example, Clay County, Kentucky or Burke County, North Carolina offer solid proof of pioneer women's fierce defense of their honor, homes, and families. Rubboli describes Minnie as "a feminine character of heroic, fabulous kindness who aroused Puccini's musical creativity and raised it to the heights." Yet she is not out of fable but created from reality. Thousands like her were left behind when the Forty-Niners deserted their log cabins and farm houses, their little shops and acres, to set out for California. In 1850, only eight percent of California's population was female; and in the gold mining areas, only two percent. Puccini's opera thus presents the California of 1848 in microcosm: two women in town, one the Virgin of the Saloon and the other, Nina Micheltorena, of ill repute—her surname perhaps taken from that of the hapless Mexican governor who was driven from office in 1845. Minnie represents a living reminder of the unsullied pioneer women the prospectors left at home.

Her lover, the bandit Ramerrez (alias Dick Johnson of Sacramento), is at least as believable as Verdi's Ernani or Corsaro. When sung by Franco Corelli or Mario Del Monaco, to say nothing of Caruso, Johnson seems no less "real" than Rodolfo in *Bohème* or José in *Carmen*. His chance encounter with Minnie on the road struck an honest chord in both their hearts. These two "original" Californians meet again in the post-Gold Strike state, where Jack Rance and Wells Fargo are the invaders from the east, and are "The Law," in command of posses, vigilance committees, and lynch mobs. It is small wonder that Minnie and Johnson, surrounded by newcomers, are aroused by the memory of their earlier encounter: they are kindred souls of a historic California culture that had been engulfed by the tide of adventurers.

The miners are represented in their ignorance, brutality, and homesickness. In the opera, as in the play, misery is never far away: today's strike becomes tomorrow's ruin. Loneliness, disease, and for many, death, lay at the end of the lode. If the miners in Puccini's opera seem idealized, in their own idealization of Minnie, they must be seen in terms of the culture of the time. Certainly one of the cruellest shots taken at *La fanciulla del West* was by an Italian critic who compared Minnie and the miners to Snow White and the Seven Dwarfs. The men, however, are real in their nostalgia, their despair, and their anger, as well as in their reverence for this pure woman who—like all tavernkeepers' wives and daughters—can shoot straight, play poker, and keep her accounts and her body in order.

Rance, the "invader" into the California territory, seems far more human than many operatic villains. With his "bitter and poisoned heart," he is quite at home in a mining camp not far from "Hangtown." His declaration "Cos 'è la morte? Un calcio dentro al buio e buona notte" (What is death? A kick into the darkness, then good night) suggests Verdi's Iago and his Credo. Raw coarseness is evident in his offer to Minnie of a thousand dollars for a kiss, his readiness to abandon his wife and to commit adultery. But as court records show, there were hundreds—if not thousands—like him. We can well believe him when he says that no one regretted his leaving home for California, "lured only by the fascination for gold."

In contrast, Minnie and Johnson, both more honorable, are of the old, Mexican California, with its Native American and

Spanish-American populations and its "pioneers," those who, like Minnie's parents, came long before the Gold Rush to run a tavern in Soledad. Descendants of the Scotch-Irish coming from states such as Georgia, Illinois, and Kentucky, they had ventured into this wild world at least one generation ahead of the Gold-Rush hordes. Side-by-side with those of Mexican descent, they built the territory that the prospectors invaded.

One of Otto Kahn's goals, as he took the Metropolitan Opera from the level of local company to an internationally renowned one, was the Paris engagement of 1910. In conversations with Gabriel Astruc, the impresario, he had set the conditions for

Puccini and Toscanini at the Théâtre du Châtelet in Paris, summer, 1910. The first step toward getting the Metropolitan Opera to go on tour to Paris had been taken by Otto Kahn, who was then the Chairman of the Board of Directors. In conversations with the impresario Gabriel Astruc he had set the conditions for the visit, guaranteeing the theater coverage of one-half of any possible loss on the engagement. After a public dress rehearsal on 19 May, the Metropolitan opened at the Châtelet with Aida, *conducted by Toscanini. Puccini was in the house for the last production,* Manon Lescaut, *which had its first Paris performance on 9 June and closed the enormously successful season sixteen days later.*
(Opera News/The Metropolitan Opera Guild, Inc.)

the visit, guaranteeing the Théâtre du Châtelet coverage for one half of any possible loss on the productions. Astruc, delighted, accepted.

After a public dress rehearsal on 19 May, the Metropolitan Opera opened at the Châtelet with *Aida,* conducted by Toscanini. Puccini came to Paris for the last production, *Manon Lescaut,* which had its first performance on 9 June and closed the enormously successful season sixteen days later. The total box office receipts of $172,892 proved a pleasant surprise to Kahn, Astruc, and the company.

On 9 June, the same day that Puccini and Toscanini gave *Manon Lescaut* to the Paris public, Puccini signed a contract to stage his new opera, *La fanciulla del West,* at the Metropolitan Opera during a four-week period in November and December 1910 and to be present at other performances of his works. According to the contract's terms, "Maestro Giacomo Puccini, living in Torre del Lago," agreed to give *Fanciulla* on 6 December, to arrive no less than two weeks before the premiere, to be at the "absolute disposal of the Metropolitan Opera Company," and to not attend other performances of any of his operas—concert or staged—in any other theater. The Metropolitan agreed to pay him a fee of 20,000 lire, plus round-trip fares for himself and his wife. The contract also provided for the opera company to pay for his hotel (a suite with a salon, bedroom, and bath), meals, and transportation for the entire period of his visit.

The presence of the world's most famous opera composer fit perfectly with Otto Kahn's grandiose plans for the opera house, "his" theater, which included the earlier engagement of Gatti-Casazza and Toscanini. If the signing of the contract was, for Kahn, a moment of triumph and rejoicing, it was for Puccini but one further step down a long, difficult road.

We have seen that Puccini had certain reservations about Belasco's *The Girl of the Golden West* when he first saw it in New York in 1907. But by August of that year, he wrote to Giulio Ricordi with a certainty about this work: "We've got it! The *Girl* promises to be a second *Bohème,* but stronger, more daring, and broader. I have an idea of a grandiose scenario, an open space in the great California forest, with colossal trees"—and eight or ten horses, he added. Undoubtedly his enthusiasm for Belasco's staging, especially the moving panorama at the beginning of the play that seemed to carry the audience down the path in the Cloudy Mountains to the miners' camp, but also the dimming lights as the scene shifted to Minnie's saloon, influenced his general impression of the work. Belasco's snowstorm for the scene at Minnie's cabin required thirty-two stagehands to operate wind and snow machines.

Certainly the Wilderness (as he called it) and the ancient trees awakened a response in Puccini, a self-declared enemy of civilization, who was passionately dedicated to his rough life at Torre del Lago, where he hunted and fished with Tuscans like himself on the shore of Lake Massaciuccoli. There Puccini found himself utterly happy.

> I long for the woods with its many perfumes . . . I long for the wind that blows my way from the sea, free and smelling of salt water . . . I hate pavements! I hate palaces! I hate ornate pillars! I hate styles! I love the beautiful shape of the poplar and the pine tree, the branches hanging over the shady roads . . . I love the blackbird, the warbler, the woodpecker! I hate horses, cats, city swallows and fancy dogs. I hate the train, top hats, evening clothes.

He lived, he said, "like a modern Druid with my temple, my house, my study."

The village of Torre del Lago, where families lived in rude huts, more or less as they had five hundred years earlier, provided Puccini with the perfect ambience for his work. So when he returned there after producing his works at the Metropolitan in 1907 with the idea of writing *The Girl of the Golden West,* he asked Belasco to send him a copy of the play. Arrangements were made between the two men, and Puccini began his search for a librettist. His earlier collaborators could no longer be counted upon, for Giuseppe Giacosa had died and Luigi Illica had been busy for some time with Puccini's proposed *Maria Antonietta* or *L'Austriaca,* as the projected libretto was sometimes called. Carlo Zangarini, proposed by

Ricordi, ought to have served the composer well, for he was fluent in English and seemed eager at least to create the scenario or first draft, if not the poetry as well. In January 1908 Puccini wrote that he was "convinced, absolutely convinced of my subject, a great thing."

On 2 February Puccini wrote to let Giulio Ricordi know that he had read *La fanciulla* and thought that Zangarini had done a good job. "Some points of the setting and writing will certainly have to be corrected, and I will put my remarks in the margin," he said. Notoriously hard to please, by spring Puccini had to resort to the services of an attorney to persuade Zangarini to accept a collaborator, the Leghorn-born poet Guelfo Civinini. Although the two men are credited with creating the libretto, Zangarini later stated that Puccini himself was the actual librettist. Neither Civinini nor Zangarini came close to the skill of Illica or Giacosa.

Struggling with his librettists and with composing the music, Puccini admitted in June that "*La Girl* is taking short steps but is moving ahead." A few weeks later, he confessed to Giulio Ricordi that "This *Girl* is a tremendously difficult work." Part of the difficulty lay in the substitution of the end of Belasco's play with Puccini's own "third act," which included the manhunt and Minnie's arrival, like a Brünnhilde of the Sequoias, on horseback. To make this scene as believable as the poker game of the second act proved to be a real challenge. Enzo Restagno, the Italian critic referred to earlier, states that the solution to the problems of the third act seems almost cinematic. Surely, though, part of Puccini's problems grew out of his desire to "move forward, not backward," musically and to create something rude, even shocking, that would not remind him or his public of his "sugary music."

In the late summer and fall of 1908, Puccini faced a domestic crisis that on at least one occasion almost drove him to suicide. Brought on by his wife, who out of jealousy denounced one of their young housemaids for being Puccini's "slut," this scandal reached a climax when the dismissed maid, Doria Manfredi, took poison in January 1909 and died after three days of suffering. The Manfredis then sued Elvira Puccini, won their suit, and finally settled with the composer, who paid considerable damages to get them to withdraw their charges. Puccini and Elvira separated for a time.

In October 1908 Puccini had confided to Sybil Seligman that "The *Girl* has completely dried up, and God knows when I will get the courage to work again." But at the end of December Puccini wrote to Toscanini, when he was still half mad with despair, that he was composing the opera on which he had worked for so long.

By August 1909 Puccini was back at work again. The first act of the opera was finished in January 1910 and the second act in April. He was far from happy, "fed up with Minnie and her friends." On 28 July he reported to Giulio Ricordi that the opera was finished, that he had taken out some "sweet" things in the libretto. Even so, he described the opera as being "not small" in size and scope, and in early August 1910 he declared it the "best of my operas."

Time by then was short, and plans had to be made for the return to New York. According to the terms of their reconciliation, Elvira would remain in Italy, while Tito Ricordi and Antonio Puccini, Giacomo and Elvira's son, would accompany the composer. The Metropolitan had reserved for him the most luxurious suite on the liner *George Washington*, which sailed in November. Shortly before he left, Puccini wrote to Toscanini, that he could not wait for the moment when they would work together once more, "not so much because it serves my own interests, but just to be with you, whom I love and esteem so highly." Genuinely grateful, he thanked Toscanini for everything he had done to present his operas well during their long collaboration.

When the ship docked, crowds of reporters besieged Puccini on shipboard even before he set foot on American soil. A contingent from the Metropolitan was accompanied by Belasco, who had been asked to help with the staging of the difficult new work. Tito Ricordi also assisted the composer during the next weeks; as the fourth generation to head the important publisher Casa Ricordi, he had his firm's interests at heart. Publicity was foremost in the minds of Belasco, Ricordi, the

Metropolitan, and, to perhaps a lesser degree, Puccini himself, for the world premiere of *La fanciulla del West* was to be the high point of the social and theatrical season in New York.

Puccini had received a telegram from Toscanini with information about the early rehearsals, which had gone well. Now that he was in the theater, he could report after his first days there, that the rehearsals went "splendidly." In recollections given to Arnaldo Fraccaroli, one of his biographers, Puccini described the ever present Belasco as

> a likeable sort, more like a prize-fighter than a poet, four-square and strong, with a red face and a snow-white mop of unruly hair . . . He spoke only English, and he seemed very, very happy, almost like a happy child, to see his play assume the grandiose proportions of the Metropolitan's setting of the opera; he seemed like a man under a spell as he listened to my music.

Puccini described Destinn, Caruso, Amato, Didur, and Pini-Corsi as "impassioned and precious collaborators." Caruso was, as always, genial and sure of himself, never posing and thrusting himself forward, "a good, overgrown boy and friend." Toscanini was "marvelous in his tenacity, passion, and drive for perfection."

Gatti-Casazza, ever wary, scheduled two general dress rehearsals, both of which played to the many critics who had besieged the Met and to a limited number of Metropolitan artists and subscribers. In the case of the critics, this was a measure to prevent anyone from writing in a major newspaper that "on first hearing, this work cannot be understood." Others were invited because the demand for tickets was so great that even opera house regulars had not been able to secure seats for themselves. The company, attempting to thwart scalpers, had made each buyer sign the ticket on the back at the time of purchase. The plan was to have everyone countersign before entering the theater. Rumor had it, nonetheless, that many scalped tickets were sold at outrageous prices.

ℬy the morning of 10 December 1910, the sidewalk on Broadway was crowded with curious New Yorkers who had come to get a glimpse of some celebrities. Others were hoping for black-market tickets. By three in the afternoon, the city had to send a patrol of policemen to keep order. When evening came, chaos reigned on Broadway and in the side streets, all of which were crowded with carriages and the private cars of the elite. At the door, house employees tried to limit the admissions only to bona fide ticket holders, but the system soon broke down. Inside, high excitement reigned, for it was

Minnie gallops in on horseback to save her lover, and defies Rance, who orders his posse to drag her away from Johnson. But she makes a brave show with her revolver, and, when they lay hands on her, threatens to kill both Johnson and herself. "Now this man is mine and God's!" (Opera News/The Metropolitan Opera Guild, Inc.)

truly a star-studded night. At eight o'clock the lights went down, and Toscanini entered the orchestra pit.

The American writer Ernest De Weerth was in the audience that night. Many years later he declared that Puccini and Toscanini had "made magic and carried every listener straight out of reality and into a fantasy world with the grand sweep of the music." Forgetting dignity and casting restraint aside, the audience clapped, stomped on the floor, shouted, and called for encores. Puccini claimed to have counted a total of fifty-five curtain calls, some thirty of which seemed intended chiefly for him, as he stood, surrounded by his cast and joined by Toscanini. The management and directors of the Metropolitan Opera Company gave him a fine laurel wreath of solid silver, which Destinn placed on his head. Puccini afterward swore to a friend that he had never been given such an ovation before.

All through his engagement he had kept friends in Europe informed about the progress of the opera; and after the premiere he could report on an authentic personal triumph. On one evening he was the guest of honor at a dinner held at the Vanderbilt mansion, which the composer described as "a fantastic house, furnished in fabulous luxury and in good taste." He said he seemed to have passed the evening in a dream. All his musical hopes were fulfilled as well, with the "magnificent" Caruso and Toscanini, who was "the *zenith,* kind, loveable, in short, the best."

In his letters to his wife, Puccini had described the rehearsals as "superlative" and the opera as "turning out splendidly." He faulted Destinn somewhat because she was not lively enough as Minnie, but, all in all, "not bad." He remarked on the tremendously difficult settings and score. Two days after the world premiere, he wrote to Elvira:

> The tremendous evening is over . . . Toscanini and all the others put their entire souls into it. The execution was extraordinary and the staging splendid. Belasco himself took charge of it. And the third act was magnificent, with the huge forest and all that movement in the chorus and the eight horses. Caruso splendid in appearance and voice. The audience, a bit reserved at the

beginning, later let itself be carried away. But for me, there alone, it was a dreadful agony. I was alone during the first act, which lasts one hour and five minutes, without a single bit of applause— just at the end. You can imagine how I felt.

He went on to describe the reception in the Metropolitan Opera House foyer, where he was surrounded by "all the millionaires, Astors and Goulds," and his excursion, at two in the morning, with his son Antonio, Tito Ricordi, and Toscanini, to an Italian restaurant to have dinner. The next day, Puccini stayed in bed until four in the afternoon. When he wrote once more to Sybil Seligman, he told her that *Fanciulla* was "a success, in my opinion, my best opera."

Whatever else it was, *La fanciulla del West* at the Metropolitan proved to be a huge public relations triumph for the opera company and for the composer, who had not produced a new work since *Butterfly*. Almost seven years had intervened between the two works, a long gap in production for an Italian composer who had been named the heir to Rossini, Donizetti, and Verdi. With his new opera, Puccini proved to himself, to Ricordi, and to his public not only that he could still compose and was not "dried up," to use his phrase, but that he could master a huge drama and "move forward." The new opera also made him a good deal richer than he had been in the 1904–1909 period. In addition to his fee for his work, he was paid first-night royalties, which were about sixteen hundred times the amount of the monthly pension that his mother had received for herself and her large family. The extensive newspaper coverage served both Puccini and Ricordi very well, as theaters everywhere renewed their efforts to stage his works, taking advantage of his vastly enhanced celebrity. To use a phrase that was a commonplace at the time, *La fanciulla del West* proved to be a "California gold mine" for some time after its premiere.

During the first run of *La fanciulla del West,* the audience testified to its great success. The opera appears to have captivated the New York public, which recognized some familiar music in the score and appreciated the inclusion of what was described as "Zuñi" American Indian melodies and passages from George M. Cohan's "Belle of the Barber's Ball." The tear-jerking, triumphant finale, "Addio California," with its wrenching evocation of nostalgia, triumphed not only on the first night, when the theater was hung with dozens of Italian and American flags and decked with flowers, but on the other nights of the run as well. With its swift movement and spectacle, it was a fair match for *Aida*.

The public was perhaps more ready for this work than the critics were. Early, short, silent Western or "cowboy" films had already made their way into the culture, bringing with them an iconography that Belasco and Puccini also used. Enzo Siciliano, who hit upon the comparison between *Fanciulla* and *Snow White and the Seven Dwarfs* mentioned earlier, deemed Puccini's opera the forerunner of other Western films and even of Walt Disney himself, in having created "a mediocrity without a moral." Siciliano seems to have missed the point of Puccini's accomplishment. The opera does have a moral, of course, and.it concerns the possibility of human redemption, as Minnie makes clear to the miners in her Bible reading. This scene, Puccini's own creation and inserted into the libretto by him, speaks with his own voice: it is the voice of morality, of faith.

The critics of Puccini's own time seemed unsure of his goals in this work. The critic writing for *The Nation* attacked Puccini precisely because in the opera there were none of those full and "sensual" scenes that had made *Bohème, Tosca,* and *Butterfly* famous. Yet Puccini's determination from the outset had been to turn his back on "*Bohème, Butt.,* and Company," and that, at least, he had succeeded in doing.

The critical reception of the opera in other publications reflected both appreciation and misunderstanding. Richard Aldrich of *The New York Times* wrote that Puccini had made great strides musically in the years since *La bohème,* but had perhaps undertaken a task which, even a few years earlier, would have been deemed impossible to achieve. The opera's rapid movement and shifting situations were to him a liability, as was the fact that the psychological and emotional turns of the characters rarely surfaced, perhaps because of Puccini's new emphasis on the orchestra rather than the voice. Aldrich's is a profound consideration of the work, but he clearly was not enthusiastic. Lawrence Gilman, in *Harper's Weekly*, mentioned Puccini's debts to Debussy; he reiterated the general belief, however, that Puccini had ill absorbed whatever lessons he had learned from that quarter. The Italian critic Primo Levi criticized the opera as overblown, suffering from "elephantiasis." Ravel, perhaps coming closest to Puccini's purpose, admired the score for putting the orchestra in the role of protagonist.

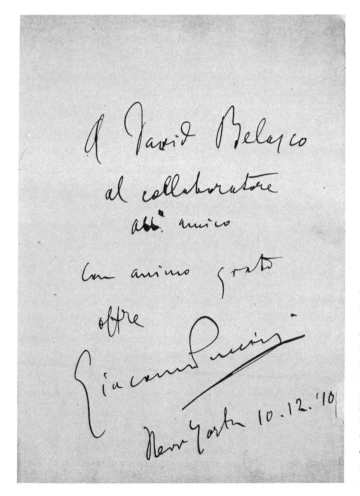

Dedication to Puccini's "collaborator" and "friend." Puccini owed debts to Belasco for his enormously successful Madame Butterfly *and for* Girl of the Golden West. *After their collaboration on* La fanciulla del West, *the composer honored his American colleague with the gift of a score of that work, which he autographed to Belasco. (Mary Jane Phillips-Matz collection)*

After the stunning publicity and the feeling of triumph in the first weeks, it soon became clear that this was not "another *Bohème*"—or *Tosca,* or *Butterfly.* Puccini may have realized from the start that *La fanciulla del West* would not be received as his earlier operas had been. Yet he continued to express gratitude for the effort put forth by Toscanini and Belasco. While he was still in New York, he bought a large, sterling silver candelabrum at Tiffany's as a gift for the Toscaninis. Writing from his cabin on the *Lusitania,* which carried him back to Europe, he confided to Carla Toscanini the "great, strong affection" he had for her and her family, recalling the joy he had felt during his visit and his love for the bright lights of New York City. "Toscanini is such a patient and loving friend!" With a whiff of sadness: "My head is full of thoughts of you two, and I envy you: I, too, would like to be like you, with your close family . . . You are good, intelligent people who tolerate me and understand me."

Home again in Torre del Lago, he wrote again in February 1911, this time to Toscanini, who continued to conduct *La fanciulla del West* during its run at the Metropolitan: from "the silence of this village, I keep thinking again and again of the days spent near you, as we were preparing *La fanciulla!* Now this part of my life, too, is over; and the very happy memory of it is not free of a bit of sorrow—those beautiful moments are too few, and they go by too quickly!"

*L*ike Rossini, Donizetti, and Verdi, Puccini almost always tried to remain with his company for the first few performances of his operas. "The fatal three," as Donizetti once said, seemed to be the minimum necessary for settling a given work onstage; it was generally accepted that if an opera could survive three nights, it had some promise. So it was that Puccini remained in the States for the Metropolitan premiere and went to Philadelphia with the company as well. In Europe, he agreed to Ricordi's request to oversee as director some of the subsequent productions, believing that if this difficult work, with its huge sets and "new" music, were to succeed, it needed his particular care.

Trusting Toscanini's judgment, as ever, Puccini wrote him from Torre del Lago to ask for advice about the casting of the next productions in Italy. The first of these was at the Teatro Costanzi in Rome. Caruso, ill, was unable to sing Johnson. About the soprano, Puccini wrote: "I simply do not know what to do," a surprising statement coming from such a consummate master of his art. The Roman premiere, in June 1911 at the Teatro Costanzi, had Pasquale Amato repeating his Metropolitan role as Rance. Amedeo Bassi, the tenor, sang Johnson, repeating a role he had sung at the Metropolitan; in Brooklyn, at the Academy; at the Chicago performances of 1910 (in 1913 he returned there in that role); and in Boston, where the soprano was the fiery Sardinian Carmen Melis. In Rome, Minnie was sung in the first performances by Eugenia Burzio, one of the great voices of her time. Nonetheless, Puccini had reservations about her, declaring at one point that she did not seem to have the voice "she once had," and, on another occasion, that she could be faulted for putting too much into her roles. Finally, he conceded her superiority in the part and was eager for her to sing Minnie years later.

Two months after the Rome opening, Puccini's opera was staged at the Teatro Grande in Brescia. Uneasy and suffering from the unbearable heat, the composer wrote to his accountant, Antonio Bettolacci:

> I am so nervous that I cannot describe it. I'll tell you when I see you; I won't write you [about it] because I don't even have faith in myself . . . Here we have an orchestra of dogs. I hope for the best—oh, this theater—and in the provinces, too—and in this season—it is absurd!"

La fanciulla del West was produced by fourteen theaters in 1911, including Covent Garden, with Destinn as Minnie, and in 1912 reached Monte Carlo, Paris, and Milan. The spectacular production at Monte Carlo brought together the young Giovanni Martinelli and the Ferrarese soprano Ernestina Poli-Randaccio. Melis was Minnie to Caruso's Johnson and Titta Ruffo's Rance under Tullio Serafin's baton at the Paris Opéra in 1912. Among other celebrated Girls were the inimitable

Gilda Dalla Rizza, Maria Jeritza, and, closer to our time, Eleanor Steber, Leontyne Price, Renata Tebaldi, and Dorothy Kirsten.

Just before World War I the opera was given in both Berlin and Vienna (1913); but *La fanciulla* was not often heard in the succeeding years, in part because of the war itself and also because of Puccini's death in 1924. It found a new audience after World War II, following a commemorative production at Viareggio, which featured Maria Caniglia as Minnie. The opera, which had never left the Italian repertory, took on a new life. The Italian critic Giorgio Gualerzi, writing in 1974, estimated that there had been perhaps as many as 220 to 230 productions of the opera, and a total of 1,300 to 1,400 performances. It was presented on the Italian radio in nine productions before 1974 and recorded by several major houses.

As Gualerzi reminds us, *La fanciulla del West* is far from the failure some biographers have made it out to be. Perhaps the chief obstacle is its costly production, including massive sets and complicated staging. Further, since the orchestra plays such a dominant role, without a strong ensemble the opera cannot be given.

In one sense, *La fanciulla* is Puccini's triumph, for he succeeded in his intention of leaving behind the fragile heroines and the "sugary music" of his early works. Quite beyond this, he found his way out of traditional operatic formulas and framework. In doing so, he was perhaps far ahead of his time. The new ground that Puccini broke with *La fanciulla del West* eventually led him to accept a greater challenge: *Turandot*.

Sources and Acknowledgments

Puccini's letters to Toscanini, Carla Toscanini, and Antonio Bettolacci are in the Music Division of The New York Public Library for the Performing Arts. I am grateful to Jean Bowen, Director of the Division, and John Shepard for their help as I transcribed and translated them. Dr. Walfredo Toscanini, Mrs. Wanda Toscanini Horowitz, and the late Wally Toscanini, Countess Castelbarco, provided information essential for an understanding of them.

Enzo Restagno's essays and Giorgio Gualerzi's performance records of *Fanciulla* are in *Giacomo Puccini, "La fanciulla del West"* (pp. 103–234), published for the Teatro Regio in Turin (Turin, 1974). Valuable chronologies can be found in Claudio Sartori, ed., *Giacomo Puccini,* in the Symposium series, edited by Guido Maria Gatti (Milan, 1959). Other sources include Amelia Bottero, *Le donne di Puccini* (Lucca, 1984); Claudio Casini, *Puccini* (Turin, 1978); Daniele Rubboli, *Giacomo Puccini: L'ultimo di una bottega di musicisti* (Lucca, 1990), and Enzo Siciliano, *Puccini* (Milan, 1976). Many previously unpublished letters are in Giuseppe Pintorno's *Puccini: 276 lettere inedite* (Milan, 1974). I am grateful to Gianandrea Gavazzeni for directing me to "Nella *Fanciulla del West* protagonista è l'orchestra?," in *Musica d'oggi* (November 1958). Father Dante Del Fiorentino, a close friend, allowed me to help him as he prepared *Immortal Bohemian* (New York, 1952) for publication and gave sound advice while I wrote two articles for *Opera News,* "Immortal Bohemian" (20 March 1950) and "Puccini and the Priest" (12 March 1951). Other sources are my article "Puccini in America," in *American Heritage* (April 1959); my essay "Panning for Gold" in the new Metropolitan Opera libretto of *La fanciulla del West;* "A Tower in the Bitter Maremma," in *Opera News* (May 1991), and "Crossing the Line," in *Opera News* (27 February 1993). My essay "Postscript: Puccini in America" appeared in Giuseppe Tarozzi, *Puccini,* translated by John Freeman (New York, 1985). Finally, I am grateful to Dr. Corrado Mingardi, Director of the Biblioteca della Cassa di Risparmio e del Monte di Credito su Pegno in Busseto (Parma), Italy, for use of that collection.

GIACOMO PUCCINI'S TRITTICO AND THE TWENTIETH CENTURY

Leonardo Pinzauti

Leonardo Pinzauti studied violin in his native Florence with Sandro Materassi and took his degree from the University of Florence under Fausto Torrefranca. He has been the music critic of *La Nazione* since 1965 and has published a number of books, including *Puccini: Una vita* (1973). He is also the editor of the *Nuova Rivista Musicale Italiana*.

*I*n examining the incubation and birth of the *Trittico,* we come upon two dates, two extremes, that possess a kind of symbolic value as far as the poetic substance of the three operas—in many ways contradictory and always fascinating—is concerned. The earlier date is the death of Giulio Ricordi, on 6 June 1912, and the other, six years later, is the death of Arrigo Boito, on 10 June 1918 (the premiere of the *Trittico* took place at the Metropolitan Opera on 14 December of that same year). The death of "Signor Giulio," whom Puccini had always regarded with filial respect and an awe approaching fear, also signaled the end of an artistic world that was driven by publishers' enthusiasms and typically nineteenth-century passions rather than by great moral and creative debate. Ricordi's death, in short, signified the loss of a last vigorous, participating witness of ottocento Italian opera, as Puccini had known it in his youth, before he encountered the famous publisher who was practically to establish him as one of the last protagonists of that tradition.

The death of Boito, on the other hand, though he had been profoundly linked with the central figure of Verdi, signified the disappearance of a more subtle personality, melancholy and controversial, who had seemed to reflect, in the dramatic vicissitudes of his endless and never-ended opera *Nerone,* a tormented destiny that soon would seem inevitable for many important figures in the world of music. Learning of Boito's death, Puccini, referred to him in a letter of 11 June 1918, as "the last of the band of our Sig. Giulio's companions," and that "last" seems to suggest the definitive sunset of an age. In fact, in that year of 1918, still ablaze with the last fires of the world war, a series of "unfinished" operas—authentic mirrors of different solitudes—was initiated. They include Boito's everlasting *Nerone* (posthumously performed on 1 May 1924), Busoni's *Doktor Faust* (21 May 1925), and Puccini's *Turandot* (25 April 1926). These operas, along with the other posthumous works, Berg's *Lulu* (2 June 1937), and Schoenberg's *Moses und Aron* (6 June 1957), are "signs" of our twentieth century, distinguished, in Massimo Mila's words, by many "Icarus flights by explorers of the infinite as brave as they were inconclusive."[1]

So the genesis of *Il trittico,* between the apparently extraneous dates of the deaths of Giulio Ricordi and Boito—with World War I also in between—is significant simply because of its chronological position, which we must keep in mind if we are to understand the sense of crisis that the three little operas represent in Puccini's later life and in the panorama of European music in the first part of this century. The *Trittico* was preceded in the Puccini canon by *La fanciulla del West* (1910), which had provoked some talk about a "second Puccini," whose American drama had announced, perhaps unconsciously, the

---

1. Massimo Mila, *Compagno Stravinski* (Turin, 1983).

transition from a confessional theater to a theater that suggested the logical absurdity of the encounter between word and music. This new kind of theater seemed destined to become a symbol and emblem, rather than a musical evocation of reality. A more or less calculated "exaggeration" became evident, tending to a sense of detachment, of alienation, between the work of art itself and the emotions of its creator. This detachment from the events narrated was to remain one of the characteristics of the musical theater of our century, in whose history the fascination of *La fanciulla del West* emerges as a moment of transition and crisis, an occasion of final adieux and premonitions of the future, as the unconscious, subterranean uneasiness of its composer was becoming manifest. And that uneasiness is found, often forged into the coherence of a masterpiece, in *Il tabarro,* in *Suor Angelica,* and in *Gianni Schicchi.*

*O*nce the euphoria of *Fanciulla*'s success, and its consequent financial rewards, had passed, Puccini was soon gripped by a familiar anxiety, the desperate search for new librettos. In the early summer of 1911, he was already worried about being "out of work," and he proved more sensitive than ever—as his international fame attracted a wide variety of offers—to the shifting moods of the public and the new cultural trends, which he could sense even when he could not easily adjust to them. As a result, the composer was more demanding and more uneasy than usual. For a while he evinced some interest in *Hanneles Himmelfahrt* by Gerhart Hauptmann; he read and was stimulated by a novel, *Two Little Wooden Shoes,* by Ouida (pen name of Louise de la Ramée). In May 1912 he received from d'Annunzio a libretto entitled *La crociata degli innocenti* (The children's crusade), which left him cold; and in the summer of 1912, his thoughts turned to Oscar Wilde's *Florentine Tragedy* (which in 1917 was set to music by Alexander Zemlinsky). Puccini then toyed briefly with the *Muette* of Anatole France but finally decided on a one-act drama by Didier Gold, *La Houppelande* (the future *Tabarro*).

In a letter of February 1913, Puccini dwells on this subject, which seems to him "highly effective," though he adds, "This red stain must be set against something opposite: a lofty piece where there is space to make music that soars." He was already thinking, evidently, of a group of one-act operas; but at the end of that year the directors of Vienna's Karltheater, Sieg-mund Eibenschütz and Heinrich Berté, suggested he write an operetta, for which they offered the considerable sum of two hundred thousand crowns. Puccini, who after Giulio Ricor-di's death was not comfortable with Giulio's son, the author-itarian and elusive Tito, wanted to assert his independence from the firm's new management, so he accepted the pro-posal, on the condition that the eventual libretto was to his liking. The project did not materialize, in fact, because the text submitted seemed to him "the usual operetta, cheap and banal." However, the Austrian offer created a breach in his relations with Casa Ricordi, and the following spring, when the Viennese showed him the outline of *La rondine* by Alfred Maria Willner (who on this occasion had collaborated with another Austrian writer, Heinz Reichert), Puccini signed a contract for the new work; he also commissioned an Italian translation from Giuseppe Adami, a young writer he had met two years before and to whom he had taken an immediate liking. The outbreak of the war was to preclude a Viennese premiere of *La rondine;* after the publisher Edoardo Sonzogno had acquired the rights, it was given in Monte Carlo on 27 March 1917. But the attention and the love Puccini lavished on this opera did not prevent him from completing, first, *Il tabarro,* then the whole *Trittico.*

References in Puccini's letters to *Il tabarro* become frequent from September 1915: "I have started translating *La Houppe-lande* into notes," he wrote to Tito Ricordi on 30 October 1915, "but for this, too, some revision is needed, to toughen the language, now too mawkish, and so I find myself a bit stalled just as the work was taking a promising turn." Again in December he assured the publisher that *La Houppelande* "is coming along very well; too bad it's in one act." And even though, in the meanwhile, he was distracted by *La rondine,* on 31 October 1916 he assured Tito: "Tabarro has reached the end and it seems good to me." (This first of the three operas was, in fact, finished "absolutely completely" on 26 Novem-

ber.) During this period Puccini was probably already thinking about the subject of the second one-act work, *Suor Angelica,*
which Giovacchino Forzano had offered him. An ambitious
Tuscan from Borgo San Lorenzo in the Mugello valley, the
young Forzano was keen to become associated with the famous
composer, but he wanted something more than the mere task
of revision he had originally been offered when Puccini had
begun to think of Gold's *Houppelande.*

Forzano himself has described in his memoirs the circumstances of the birth of Puccini's "cloister opera." If we are to
believe his account (not always reliable), it seems that when
the writer was drafting the libretto of *Suor Angelica,* he was
unaware that Puccini had a sister in a convent and therefore
would be particularly receptive to a story in which popular
notions about nuns were mingled with a "guilty love," babies,
and greedy kinfolk. In any case, Forzano was unquestionably
a born man of the theater, and the moving story he had conceived fascinated Puccini. The composer was inevitably influenced by his fondness for the "poor little nun" of his family,
Sister Giulia Enrichetta, who had prayed hard and long in
earlier years for her famous brother (then living in sin with
his future wife, Elvira Bonturi). And, perhaps, certain autobiographical influences give this second opera of the trio an
eccentric, intense emotional charge, in contrast with the modern "alienation" that characterizes *Il tabarro* and *Gianni Schicchi.*

First and foremost, *Suor Angelica* fulfilled Puccini's require-
ment, expressed in his 1913 letter, of providing something
"opposed" to *Il tabarro;* and the composer set to work with
unusual concentration, as we know from a letter Forzano wrote
to Tito in May 1917: "The work proceeds rapidly, and I am
sure that you will share my enthusiasm when you hear the
music Puccini is writing." In the meantime, the determined
Forzano had sketched out the "brief plot" of *Gianni Schicchi,*
and this had also pleased the composer so much that in the
summer of 1917 he set aside *Suor Angelica* for a while in order
to work on the new libretto. And at the most difficult times
of the war (the rout at Caporetto and the moments when he
was worried about his son Tonio, who had left for the front

as a volunteer), Puccini evidenced an extraordinary creative fervor, as if to forget, through working, all his other concerns: *Suor Angelica* was finished on 14 September 1917, and *Gianni Schicchi* on 20 April of the following year.

Even though Italy's situation was now more reassuring, the continuing conflict made it impossible until the summer of 1918 to set a date for the premiere of *Il trittico*. Puccini at first wanted to assign it to an Italian theater, but at the insistence of the shrewd Gatti-Casazza, he accepted the invitation of the Metropolitan Opera in New York. On 24 July 1918 Puccini wrote an interesting letter, significant in the history of the work's development. The letter was addressed to Clausetti, an important figure in Casa Ricordi, and referred to the composer's contract:

Dear Clausetti,
I haven't yet returned the signed contracts because I want to change a clause that is too humiliating for me, or rather, for the composer. It is this clause no. 5, which I would like to change as follows: "The firm Ricordi and Co. will have full powers to handle, accept, and reject offers of hire and to do anything else considered opportune for the common (*its own*) interests, in complete agreement with Mo. Puccini," rather than, as it now stands: "Mo. Puccini will not be entitled to make objections of any kind." And I would add: "always safeguarding the artistic and moral interest of the works." I would put this in case the Firm changed management, not wanting to see (I or my descendants) *Suor Angelica,* for example, arranged for dance music. What do you think? In any case, I am firm about changing clause no. 5.

Il tabarro, Suor Angelica, and *Gianni Schicchi* were first performed, then, at the Metropolitan Opera on 14 December 1918, under the direction of Roberto Moranzoni, a practical, experienced musician, who had been a pupil of Mascagni's in Pesaro, and who enjoyed a good professional reputation. The cast was stellar (Muzio, Farrar, De Luca). For the first time in his life, because of the uncertainties of the immediate postwar situation, Puccini was unable to be present at a premiere of his work, and he was denied one of those long Atlantic crossings that gave him such pleasure. But his regret was mitigated by the anticipation of the Italian (and European) premiere, set for 11 January 1919 at the Teatro Costanzi in Rome. There, instead of a reliable *routinier* like Moranzoni, the conductor was the illustrious Gino Marinuzzi; and again, singers of the first rank were involved. The following May, the operas were heard in Florence.

Before we take a look at the critical reception of *Il trittico,* and call to mind the cultural and moral climate of seventy-odd years ago, quite different from that of today, it is worth noting an anecdote related by the Tuscan painter Lorenzo Viani, in his *Ricordo di Giacomo Puccini.* A member of the composer's circle of young friends and admirers in Viareggio, Viani at one point gave Puccini a drawing and then later, seeing that the composer hadn't gotten around to having it framed, asked him why not. Puccini answered frankly that he wasn't able to understand how an artist could paint "that whole series of wretches," Viani's chosen subjects. "Paintings," Puccini went on, "must be pleasing, decorative, restful." This assertion shows (and there is no reason to doubt Viani's account, which is actually quite affectionate) that the musician had an antiquated concept of art, or that he felt it necessary to remain faithful, at least in theory, to models from the past; and in this he resembled other composers, from Rossini to Verdi, who often posed as conservatives, though their works contradicted them. *Il trittico* is a dramatic documentation of such a contradiction. Beginning with *La fanciulla del West* and continuing in the even more varied and problematic *Trittico,* Puccini's contemporaries sensed the existence of a new, "modern" Puccini.

Thus *Il trittico* becomes a kind of observation point of the musical twentieth century as Puccini accepts it and transforms it, not without personal anguish; the trio of operas provides a panoramic view of the tangle of artistic stimuli that he received from contemporary musicians (and they included all the major composers of the early twentieth century with the exception of Schoenberg, who had no effect on Puccini's expressive choices). Such a view only confirms the accuracy of what Puccini wrote to the Bologna critic Cesare Paglia (better known by his pen name "Gajanus"): "When you come to Viareggio, I will show you the scores of Debussy, Strauss, Dukas, and the others; you will see how they are all dog-eared from constant rereading, all analyzed and annotated by me."

Since Puccini did not have, as Strauss had, the great season of *Mitteleuropäische* symphonism behind him, or a musical culture as coherent as the German (the culture of the "revo-

After the Italian premiere of La fanciulla del West *in Rome in June 1911, Puccini returned to his house at Torre del Lago, where he spent most of the summer and autumn. It was a period of enforced idleness as he searched for a new libretto. Despite the jaunty straw hat, his expression in this photograph suggests the sober melancholy that usually affected him at such times of unemployment. (Museo Teatrale alla Scala; Foto Saporetti)*

lutionary" Strauss still left room for a natural nostalgia for the musical world of Mozart), he found himself in the first decades of this century virtually obsessed by the fear of being unable to look back, under pain of appearing "retrograde." It is as if he observed from a speeding train a landscape that aroused his curiosity, though he recognized its contradictions, with Strauss and Mascagni, Strauss and Stravinsky, all opposing one another.

But we must not be misled by the dejected tone of some of Puccini's pronouncements ("Today they head towards atonality and twist and turn as they like, and he who strays farthest is convinced he is on the right track"). For there is also some of this "twisting and turning" in Puccini himself, who came to music when there was no talk of Debussy and Stravinsky but more of Wagner, Verdi, and Bizet, and who now behaved, in everyday practice, like his younger colleagues. Puccini, like Stravinsky, composed only at the piano; and although he exclaimed "Lunacy!" upon seeing the score of *Sacre* for the first time, he later recommended it to the young Vincenzo Tommasini as an extremely interesting work. It is also certain that Stravinsky is the source of the novelties of the cornet, the siren, the claxon, and the "organ-grinder waltz" in *Il tabarro*. But the pure and simple elements of a new vocabulary do not in the least affect dramatic situations that remain substantially Puccinian; this new vocabulary cruelly shares in an unplumbed melancholy that, in effect, takes on tragically premonitory dimensions. It is no accident that the "organ-grinder waltz" could seem to Fedele D'Amico a "prophecy of *Wozzeck*" and that the sequence of chords on the "match theme" could prove capable of being inserted, as is, into a score like Bartók's *Bluebeard*.

As early as the time of the New York performances of *Il trittico,* certain critics noted in the pages of *Il tabarro* explicit similarities to Stravinsky, and in *Gianni Schicchi* certain instrumental refinements worthy of a French impressionist. Further, in contrast with the nineteenth-century concept of opera, Puccini seemed to demonstrate a new detachment toward his characters. It was said that in *Il tabarro* he had "committed the modern mistake of eliminating all sympathy for the characters," whereas in *Suor Angelica* he was accused of lapsing into an "exaggerated sentimentality." In more recent years, to support those notions of the "modernity" of the late Puccini, specific studies by Fedele D'Amico and John Waterhouse have underlined transparent ties between his last operas and the music of the young Gianfrancesco Malipiero. (Cut from the final edition, *Suor Angelica*'s "aria of the flowers" is, in D'Amico's opinion, "Malipierian.") On the other hand, some thematic notions of Alfredo Casella are drawn directly from Puccinian themes (from *Turandot,* for example).[2]

The surprise (both negative and positive) at what was considered Puccini's new, different direction that was aroused by *Il trittico*'s early performances is evident in the diverse reactions of the most prominent figures in Italian musical life. These reactions are in themselves proof that *Il trittico* was born in a moment of cultural crisis, on the eve of a genuine change of worlds. A mere cataloguing of progressives and conservatives would not suffice to explain the differences of opinion. To cite an illustrious case, Arturo Toscanini, steadfast in his Wagnerian ideals, continued to speak unfavorably of *Il tabarro* even as an old man, in conversations with musicians and critics, dismissing it as Grand Guignol. The conductor could hardly be considered a conservative (at least not in the years of his vigorous middle age), and yet he found himself in agreement with a critic like Alberto Guasco, who in Rome's *La Tribuna* had expressed reservations about the same opera, setting it up against *Suor Angelica,* which he hailed as a little masterpiece. Giannotto Bastianelli, the brilliant and acute Florentine critic who from his early youthful essays had displayed an insatiable and precocious interest in the very latest contemporary music, including works of Skryabin and Schoenberg, named as his favorite of the three works *Gianni Schicchi*. Bastianelli considered *Il tabarro* "a failure with some patches of genius," and *Suor Angelica* "a dream that does honor to Puccini and the librettist Forzano especially for the novelty of its intentions if not for the taste and musical quality of the result." He also

2. See Fedele D'Amico, *I casi della musica* (Milan, 1962) and "Una ignorata pagina malipieriana di *Suor Angelica*," in *Rassegna Musicale Curci* (April 1975), as well as John Waterhouse, "Quel che Puccini deve a Casella," in *Rassegna Musicale Curci* (December 1965).

noted (and this is a significant observation) that the "humble poetry of the convent is rendered with a softness in the music reminiscent of [the poet Giovanni] Pascoli."

In other words, at this moment of transition, as the notion of opera as a partly commercial enterprise intended to establish an immediate, direct rapport with the audience was receding in the face of new cultural attitudes that considered the operatic tradition suspect, if not downright irritating, the reactions of the *Trittico*'s first listeners revealed their own aesthetic models. *Falstaff* was the model for Bastianelli; for Toscanini, the delights of *Pelléas et Mélisande* were preeminent. These early judgments frequently had a schematic, awkward quality, and the writers often succumbed to the temptation to establish among the three works a kind of classification, ranking them according to their poetic value.

For this reason it is worth quoting an anonymous article that appeared in the *Idea Nazionale* in January 1919, whose author may well have been the notorious Fausto Torrefranca. (In 1912 Torrefranca had published an essay, *Giacomo Puccini e l'opera internazionale,* whose hostility—however scholarly—had shaken and distressed Puccini. In his last years, as a professor in Florence after World War II, Torrefranca considered his early scandalous attack on Puccini a "youthful error," though he added that his fierce criticisms at that time had forced Puccini into a kind of self-criticism, whose results—Torrefranca insisted—were evident in the operas written after 1912, especially in *Il tabarro* and *Gianni Schicchi* and later in *Turandot.*) The *Idea Nazionale* article is significant because of a kind of prescience the writer demonstrates concerning the characteristics of so-called "contemporary music," by which he means those trends of twentieth-century music that in Italy were to be established only later, in the years between the two world wars, when the Italian "1880s generation" of composers occupied the foreground.

> Puccini's three single acts can comprise a unified piece. And the unity comes, if anything, from the character of contemporary music, which Puccini has gradually approached, as his inspiration began to lose its imaginative invention, as his creative breath

thinned, while his language lost accent as it increased in emphasis. The character of contemporary music has a uniformity, an
orchestral diversity, a declamation that levels the characters,
whether they are Seine bargemen or cloistered nuns, that annuls
dialogue as comic or dramatic substance and as musical design,
that slows and blanches words into a monotonous expression of
scant humanity and of no lyrical personality. Puccini has
approached this music in refining his technique with an increasingly subtle orchestral skill, disguising with enviable good taste
the fragmentary nature of the thematic structure, coloring the
scenes with broad strokes of watercolor, with a mature art, whose
contemporariness should win him the respect and the admiration
of the young, who often do not possess, as he does, an invention,
scant and fading but still personal, and a theatrical measure that
is true artistic knowledge of effect. Puccini has been approaching
this music for some time, to the now-futile regret of those who
love the passion of *Manon Lescaut* and feel in *La bohème* a perfection of the comic-sentimental genre. He had half-detached himself from it with the unhappy *Rondine* venture, but now he has
returned to it with the three acts performed last night.

Everything leads us to believe these words are Torrefranca's, not least because of the calculated circumspection with
which the figure of Puccini is revised, with respect to the critic's essay of 1912. In any event, the diagnosis is fairly close to
reality, even if it betrays a certain resistance to confirming
Puccini's position as a protagonist. Having underlined
"orchestral skill," the good taste that dissimulates the "fragmentary nature of the thematic structure" (an undoubtedly
correct technical observation), the "good taste that dissimulates the "fragmentary nature of the thematic structure" (an
undoubtedly correct technical observation), the "broad strokes
of watercolor," but above all the "contemporariness" of his
"mature art," the writer intuitively places Puccini's *Trittico* in
an entirely twentieth-century atmosphere, quite removed from
the sensibility of listeners in the immediate postwar audience,
even the most cultivated. And in fact, if we examine the pages
of the *Trittico* today, we perceive possible defects in coherent
tension, judging not by nineteenth-century parameters but by
those of this century.

Unless we share Toscanini's reluctance to accept anything that could recall climes in contrast to those of Wagner (because even Debussy's masterpiece was for Toscanini a French translation of those Wagnerian climes, and it is therefore easy to comprehend, apart from personal motives, his aversion to Mahler, precursor of German Expressionism, which he abhorred), we find it difficult now to agree with the maestro's opinion of *Il tabarro*. On the contrary, we might consider that opera, of the three, the one that comes closest to perfection. We can accept the judgment of the composer Ildebrando Pizzetti, a sometime critic for a Florence newspaper: "Of the three the least considered by the critics," he wrote on 23 May 1919, he found in Toscanini's Grand Guignol "the most genuine Puccini, the best, the Puccini of certain parts of *Manon Lescaut* and of Acts II and III of *La bohème*." And even if more recently there has been a temptation to temper this acknowledgment of Puccini's art by a musician of the "1880s generation,"[3] we can now share Pizzetti's judgment, written in the immediate excitement of a gala performance for Puccini at the Teatro della Pergola, of the libretto of *Il tabarro:* "It was possible to create around the figures on stage a certain grayish atmosphere of frustrated ambitions, of disconsolate sadness, of commonplace sentimentality, that Puccini sensed and expressed as perhaps no other musician of his time would have been capable of doing." And this, we can say now, means musicians the likes of Strauss, Ravel, and Busoni.

In reality, the striking thing about *Il tabarro,* beyond the acknowledged orchestral skill, is the structural coherence that governs the whole opera, in an obsessive, dramatic frame. The Debussy-like 12/8 meter as the curtain rises not only is supported by happy choices of timbre but also seems to foreshadow ternary subdivisions (like fragments of rhythmic leitmotif) in all aspects of the opera—as if dialogue, quotations, and echoes of distant music, frequently "in three," are aimed at effecting an incessant—even obsessive—shuffling of characters and events. Puccini, usually aware of practical questions (such as giving an aria to both the tenor and the baritone, and

3. See Bruno Pizzetti, *Ildebrando Pizzetti: Cronologia e bibliografia* (Parma, 1980).

granting a certain prominence also to La Frugola), in fact forgets them; he allows the flow of orchestral color and the "fragmented" thematic structure to continue uninterrupted by drawn out lyrical oases, unless they produce the effect of alienation—and are therefore highly modern—like the brief aria of the song-vendor ("Primavera, primavera") and the little sketch of a duet between Frugola and Talpa as they go off arm in arm ("Ho sognato una casetta").

Thus it is understandable that at the opera's first appearance, in a culture whose median level still had not accepted the musical theater of Debussy and Strauss, *Il tabarro* provoked dissent. It was, after all, the first time a Puccini opera actually had no "arias," and Luigi's lyrical outbursts and, even more, those of Michele (the victim, really) were unable to make these characters sympathetic. *Il tabarro* is Puccini's first and only opera without heroes (not even bourgeois ones) and, especially, without heroines. And for the first time, surely unconsciously on Puccini's part, his music welcomed those "wretches" he could not tolerate in the paintings and drawings of his friend Viani.

As for *Suor Angelica,* which scales the heights of emotional tension, somewhere between rhetoric and sadism, the precise musical characterization is striking, determined as it is by a homogeneous orchestral color very different from the refined color of *Il tabarro* and surely more sinuous and saccharine. It is useful here to recall the words of the intuitive Giannotto Bastianelli, who mentioned "softness" and the poet Pascoli. Though the drama adheres to age-old paradigms of popular narrative, we can discern also a subtext of the disturbing poetry of memory, exquisitely decadent, with refinements of timbre that, to avoid falling into undue emphasis and oleographic decorativism, are kept within the difficult confines of a dimension close to chamber music. The "softness," whether comparable to Pascoli or not, in the clever exploitation of certain sentimentalities constitutes the limitation of the opera.

Compared with *Suor Angelica,* on the other hand, the score of *Schicchi* works miracles of formal excellence and theatrical skill that naturally aroused the enthusiasm of the refined and keen partisan of the "contemporary," Bastianelli. We must bear in mind that in those early postwar years *Falstaff* was a kind of banner, waved by the same avant-garde that, a few years later, would become neoclassical. Also in the air was a pervasive nationalistic pride in an "Italian" music whose most glorious traditions it was considered urgent to rediscover, notably opera buffa and the opportunities this form offered to Italian composers to continue their instrumental invention on a par with their French or German counterparts. So the enthusiastic excess of Bastianelli's review is understandable. It begins by underlining the critic's "*unconditioned* enthusiasm for this full, complete masterpiece—which reproduces, perhaps with greater tonality, the marvelous and until today unique miracle of *Falstaff.*" He then adds, symptomatically: "I believe that . . . the national significance of *Falstaff* can be repeated today with *Gianni Schicchi,* as the vibration of its spontaneous, purely Italian beauty reverberates still in my spirit, like unforgettable sunlight and blue sky." And further: "The war vanishes like a nightmare. From Tuscany we receive a new masterpiece of equilibrium and smiling wisdom. May the young receive it as the purest word of the [Italian] race."

Viewing Puccini from this nationalistic angle, Bastianelli could only be perplexed by certain practical compromises that the composer tried to mask, though with great skill; they interrupt the wondrous invention and the homogeneity of his refined and witty score, in some ways also his most modern. "Firenze è com'un albero fiorito," with the indication "like a Tuscan *stornello*"; "Addio Firenze," which is then repeated in grotesque accents, highly effective theatrically; and especially "O mio babbino caro" and "Lauretta mia" are all palpable interpolations to guarantee some of the leading interpreters the opportunity to sing at least one "aria," as the majority of the audience still demanded. The real greatness of *Gianni Schicchi* lies rather in the irresistible invention that sustains the whole orchestral texture: At times we could almost do without the narrative indications of the text and still find a continuity of tension and a variety that truly have no equal in the music of the early twentieth century. The writing itself is so detailed that it almost abolishes any sense of strophe, through the use of a restless rhythmic frame (a constant variation of binary and ternary tempos) and through frequent instructions for performance (*sostenuto, allargando molto, stringendo, rallentando, un poco affrettato,* etc.). But above all it is the color of the orchestra, detailed with the keen precision of an instrument maker, that gives each episode its dramatic significance, from the search for Buoso's will to the funereal drum that underlines the march at "Nessuno sa che Buoso ha reso il fiato"; from the description of the doctor's arrival to that extraordinary masterpiece, worthy of inclusion in any twentieth-century musical anthology, the intervention of Schicchi at "In testa la cappellina." The innovative use of color can be found everywhere, like an unconscious reassertion of the madrigal character, joining the harmonic audacities and discoveries of timbre that sharpen the use of repeated notes in the vocal parts, with the expressive use of dissonances and characterization of the instruments.

As always, all this takes place amid the shrewd employment of theatrical effects, so that *Gianni Schicchi* gives the impression not only of sealing—like the model of Verdi and *Falstaff*—the achievement of a composer, a twentieth-century composer (with linguistic similarities to Stravinsky, Ravel, Respighi, and Falla), but also of being the last and loftiest result in the history of Italian opera buffa. It is almost an isolated case in the theater of this century and, like Giulio Ricordi and Arrigo Boito—like that whole world, in short—now dead and buried.

Translated by William Weaver

$\int A$ RONDINE

William Ashbrook

William Ashbrook, born in Philadelphia in 1922, was educated at the University of Pennsylvania and Harvard. Now Distinguished Professor Emeritus of Humanities at Indiana State University, he is the author of *Donizetti and His Operas* (1982), *The Operas of Puccini* (1985), and, with Harold Powers, *Puccini's "Turandot"* in the Princeton Studies in Opera series (1991).

$\mathcal{M}$ost of Puccini's operas had troubled gestations. His problems with bringing some of them to birth are notorious. For instance, there is the case of *Manon Lescaut,* setting a record by involving seven librettists before it took reasonably final form; and then there is the case of *Turandot,* four years in the making and still incomplete at the composer's death. The genesis of *La rondine,* however, is in a class by itself. Between 1913 and 1921, that work underwent changes of genre, from operetta to sentimental comedy; it is unique among his oeuvre by being published by a house other than Ricordi; before it could be staged there were serious contractual complications to resolve; the opera evoked

charges of trading with the enemy; and Puccini, uncharacteristically, after subjecting the score to several revisions, discarded them and returned to his original intentions.

The trail that leads to *La rondine* begins in October 1913.
Then fifty-five, Puccini was a world celebrity. His most recent
opera had been *La fanciulla del West,* which had had its world
premiere at the Metropolitan Opera in New York on 10
December 1910. *La fanciulla* had been launched with much
publicity under what seemed like ideal circumstances: a cast
headed by Caruso, Emmy Destinn, and Amato; Toscanini on
the podium; the staging supervised by David Belasco, whose
play was the source of the plot; and Puccini himself present to
see that everything went as he had conceived it. When the
fanfare subsided after *Fanciulla* had been introduced to the major
opera houses, the public's curiosity about Puccini's latest score
seemed soon satisfied. In one theater after another the new
opera was allowed to lapse. Unlike *La bohème, Tosca,* and *Butterfly,* which had entered the permanent repertory in very short
order, his latest opera proved somehow disappointing. Puccini had struck off in a new direction with *Fanciulla,* disillusioning his public, who had expected tuneful pathos rather
than a redemption myth set amid the redwoods of California
and coming to a happy ending with the lovers riding off into
the sunrise. By October 1913, nearly three years after the *prima*
of his latest opera, Puccini was showing all the symptoms of
the restless anxiety that inevitably engulfed him until he had
settled upon the subject of his next opera.

For the average person in 1913, the idea that by the following summer all Europe would be convulsed by a Great War
was inconceivable. Except for Prussia's wars of 1866 and 1870
and an occasional dustup in the Balkans, or a colonial distur-
bance on some other continent, Europe seemed, superficially
at least, at peace, a condition many assumed would perpetuate
itself for the foreseeable future. Certainly to an apolitical man
like Puccini, one who regarded himself as an artist, a world
citizen, one who when he was not composing liked to hunt
with old cronies or seek consolation with compliant ladies,
the thought of worldwide hostilities would scarcely occur.
Indeed, Puccini's obliviousness to the fact that others might

not share his disregard for chauvinistic fervor would compound his problems of the next few years.

In October 1913 the composer visited Vienna, a city he enjoyed although he spoke next to no German; the purpose of the trip, in large part underwritten by Casa Ricordi, was to establish a performing tradition for *Das Mädchen aus dem West,* when *Fanciulla* received its local premiere at the Hofoper on 24 October, with Maria Jeritza and Alfred Piccaver. It was Puccini's habit to sample the theatrical wares of the cities he visited in the hope of turning up a subject that might catch his imagination. Following his wont, one night he visited the Karltheater, home of Viennese operetta, where as a celebrity he was made much of by its two managers, Siegmund Eibenschütz and Heinrich Berté.[1] In the course of the evening the prospect of Puccini's writing a work for their theater came up, along with an offer of the substantial sum of 200,000 kronen for an operetta score, consisting of a dozen or so individual musical numbers that would be separated by spoken dialogue. Because Puccini's ignorance of German did not permit him to set a text written in that language, it was hastily agreed that a scenario would be submitted to him, which then could be expanded into a full Italian text by a librettist of his choosing. The completed work would then be translated back into German so that it could receive its world premiere at the Karltheater.

As soon as gossip about Puccini's latest project began to circulate, there was much snide talk about his prostituting himself by stooping to operetta, as well as deprecating claims that he was motivated only by sheer greed and by the lure of stacks of golden kronen. It would be folly to try to assert that Puccini was impervious to wealth. The memories of his impoverished youth and of his precarious but bohemian existence as a student at the Milan Conservatory were assuaged in the years of his success by expensive automobiles, a wardrobe tailored in Saville Row, and all the other trappings that spelled

---

1. Heinrich's nephew Emil (1898–1968) would later be associated with Eibenschütz as a partner in the music publishing firm that first owned the German rights to *La rondine* and that brought out the first German score in 1920.

luxury. There is no doubt that the composer enjoyed the priv-
ileges of being a celebrity.

Puccini had said some years earlier that among his contemporaries, the only composer he truly envied was Franz Lehár,[2]
and indeed there was an inscribed photograph of the operetta
composer on the piano in Puccini's villa at Torre del Lago. In
the decade following its Viennese premiere in 1905, Lehár's
Die lustige Witwe was the only stage work with a performance
history that outdistanced that of Puccini's most popular operas.
It was not the princely royalties Lehár earned that Puccini envied
so much as his sheer popularity with that sizable segment of
the public who would not cross the street to see a regular
opera. It was this broader audience that Puccini hoped to reach.

Tempting as all these prospects might be to a man of Puccini's temperament, there was one important circumstance of
his dealing with the Karltheater, however, that set it quite
apart from his earlier negotiations for prospective operas. This
was the first time in his career that the composer entered into
even an informal agreement for a new stage work before he
knew what its subject would be. True, he had the right to
refuse a scenario that did not appeal to him, but that was a
different matter from his previous experience: He had become
convinced by the stageworthiness of the subjects of *Manon
Lescaut, La bohème, Tosca, Madama Butterfly,* and even *La fanciulla* before signing contracts for them.

Once he returned to Italy, Puccini began to have his first misgivings about the project that had glittered so enticingly in
Vienna. On 11 November 1913 he wrote to Angelo Eisner-
Eisenhof, who was acting as his agent in his negotiations with
the Karltheater: "First of all, however, I want (rather I need)
to know about the libretto, because if it should not suit me,

2. This was told to me by the late Maria Bianca Gaddi-Pepoli, whose family had close
ties with the Puccinis; her father, the marchese Ginori-Lisci, was the dedicatee of *La
bohème*. Apparently, Puccini had met Lehár on an earlier trip to Vienna, on which
occasion the two began a cordial acquaintance. It is not generally known that Lehár's
name was among those considered for the task of completing *Turandot*.

not even a million would make me set it to music."[3] The following month Puccini received a scenario from Alfred Maria
Willner and Heinz Reichert, but by 14 December he was writing again to Eisner, this time to inform him of two decisions:
one, that he rejected the first scenario, and two, that he had
decided to write not an operetta with spoken dialogue but
rather a through-composed comic opera, "like *Rosenkavalier,*
but more diverting and more organic."[4]

Puccini received an Italian translation of the second scenario
from Willner and Reichert, an act at a time, between late March
and mid-April 1914. The composer accepted this subject, but
without any great enthusiasm for it, and signed a contract
under which he received a 40,000-kronen advance. There seems
to have been little concern on the part of the participants that
the cumbersome process of translating and retranslating the
text might rob it of its essential character and leave only a
roughly equivalent tone. Surrounding the whole project was
the ripe commercial redolence of a Puccini score as a valuable
and desirable property. His less fortunate contemporaries
regarded the whole affair with eyes of envy and were quick
to criticize.

The contract that Puccini signed on 18 April 1914 committed the score's first performance to be given at the Karltheater
in German, but Puccini retained the performing rights for Italy
and South America. The eager Viennese managers, however,
had already started to market the work, as we discover from
an announcement in the 21 March 1914 issue of *Musical America* that the tenor-manager Andreas Dippel had acquired the
yet-to-be-written "operetta" for projected performances in the
United States and Canada.[5] Further advance publicity appeared
in *The New York Times* of 4 July. A misleading notice from
Berlin announced that Puccini's operetta was "created specially" for Dippel, "who himself suggested the theme," and
who had got hold of not only the right to stage the American

3. Eugenio Gara et al., eds., *Carteggi pucciniani* (Milan, 1958), Letter 636, p. 416. (Hereafter cited as CP.)
4. CP, Letter 638, p. 417.
5. The announcement is quoted in Michael Kaye, *The Unknown Puccini* (New York and
Oxford, 1987), 175.

premiere but also "the performing and publishing rights for the rest of the world."[6] This notice appeared less than a month before the outbreak of World War I, which not only wrote finis to Dippel's pretensions vis-à-vis Puccini's score but led to many future complications.

In October 1913 the kingdom of Italy was still a member of the Triple Alliance (with Germany and Austria), but instead of going along with its allies and declaring war those first days of August 1914, she proclaimed herself neutral (3 August). The disagreement between Austria and Italy hinged upon Italy's hope for concessions in the Trentino and along the Dalmatian coast to compensate for Austria's gains in the Balkans. By the time Austria was persuaded to agree to these claims, England, France, and Russia had signed a secret treaty in London on 26 April 1915, promising Italy even greater territorial acquisitions if she would enter the war upon their side. On 23 May 1915, Italy declared war against Austria-Hungary and on 28 August 1916, also against Germany. It is against the background of these events that we come to appreciate the problems for Puccini that stemmed from his contract with the managers of the Karltheater.

$\mathcal{T}$h e progress of the composition of *La rondine* can be followed in Puccini's letters. To Eisner he had reported from Torre del Lago on 28 April 1914: "I am still waiting for the first act from Adami, who promised it to me by 1 May. I am ready to start right in upon it."[7] By 26 May 1914 Puccini was experiencing misgivings, as he informed Eisner:

> I am a little anxious because the libretto of *Rondine* does not please me very much . . . We are always in that by now overworked tone of worldliness, more or less sentimental, more or less tiresome, that one finds in operettas. I would have liked something

6. Ibid.
7. CP, Letter 650, p. 423. Giuseppe Adami (1878–1946) began an association as librettist to Puccini that lasted from 1911 until the composer's death. Besides being a librettist, he was a prolific dramatist and producer of film scripts.

with a little character, something grotesque, in fact something original, and instead . . . However, I am working.[8]

On 26 July 1914, again to Eisner: "I am making progress with *La rondine,* and I am happy with my work. I hope to be finished this coming spring, no sooner certainly. But no operetta, quite the opposite!"[9]

At the end of August, Giuseppi Adami came to stay with Puccini to make some adjustments to the libretto. Although the poet gives the impression in his biography of Puccini, written some thirty years later, that it was at this meeting that the transformation from operetta to opera took place, the evidence of Puccini's letters of the time make it clear that the transformation had taken place some months earlier, in fact before he had started to compose the score.

By Christmas 1914 two acts had been finished, as Puccini informed Eisner on that date. He went on to inquire: "Tell me, given the frightful conditions produced by this horrible war, what will happen to this opera?"[10]

Puccini then put *La rondine* aside for a while. In mid-February 1915 he became embroiled in a controversy with Léon Daudet, who accused him in the pages of *L'Action Française* of deliberately not signing a formal protest by leading intellectuals from around the world against the German bombardment of Rheims. Puccini defended himself by publishing a letter explaining that he had not been asked to sign such a document, nor had he known anything about it. He had asked Tito Ricordi how best to respond to these charges, revealing, among other things:

> You know my sentiments, and you know also that, although I am a Germanophile, I have never wanted to show myself publicly as a partisan of either side, always deploring that the war

8. CP, Letter 654, p. 425. In this letter he also tells Eisner that he has seen the Italian production in Milan of Lehár's most recent operetta, *Endlich allein* (Alone at last): "Stupid libretto, in certain parts the music charming, for example in the second act, but the settings were miserable." He sums up his whole opinion of the world of operetta in a single word: "morto."

9. CP, Letter 656, p. 427.

10. CP, Letter 665, p. 430.

should spread its destruction throughout the world, and also because I want to remain within the shell of my reserve, adhering to the neutrality that our country has imposed.[11]

La rondine stayed untouched on Puccini's desk while he desperately sought a way out of his predicament, hoping above all to gain the right to give the premiere of the work where he wanted, rather than to remain tied to the Karltheater. In pursuit of these goals, Puccini made a trip in September 1915 to Interlaken, Switzerland, where he met the Viennese impresario Berté, hoping to come to an agreement amenable to both parties. Berté wanted to retain half the rights but had to return to Vienna to consult his associates before he could make a firm modification of the original contract. By the end of October 1915, Puccini had received a letter from Vienna rejecting all his proposals and insisting on retaining the right to give the premiere "after the war."[12] It was at this point that Puccini decided to start work upon what was to become *Il tabarro,* but while Adami readied that libretto, the composer turned back to *Rondine* and completed it by 22 April 1916; on that date he wrote to Adami that it was "*finitissima.*"[13]

As Tito Ricordi showed no interest in an opera for which only half the rights could be negotiated and which, even worse from his point of view, involved dealing with enemy nationals, Puccini turned elsewhere. Renzo Sonzogno, whose firm was the nearest rival to Casa Ricordi among Italian music publishers, was delighted at the idea of acquiring even part of a property from Ricordi's most lucrative composer. Apparently Sonzogno made contact with Eibenschütz and Berté and gave Puccini a week to make up his mind to the new proposals, for so the composer felt duty bound to inform Tito:

> Just now I have received serious proposals that resolve the *Rondine* problem . . . The proposal made to me relieves me of any legal responsibility, and it would resolve the political question and make me a modest sum. It hurts me that in this matter I might not reach agreement with your firm, but I can no longer

11. Undated letter quoted in CP in a footnote to Letter 668, p. 433.
12. See CP, Letter 679, p. 437, and Letter 683, pp. 438–39.
13. Giuseppe Adami, ed., *Giacomo Puccini: Epistolario* (Milan, 1928), 200.

remain up in the air and allow this work with its Viennese connection to gather mold![14]

Although Sonzogno's financial condition did not allow him to make opulent offers, he signed a contract with Puccini about the middle of December 1916, according to which the composer gained what he had wanted most. Sonzogno had a long-standing connection with the Monte Carlo Opera and its egregious impresario, Raoul Gunsbourg. A playground like Monte Carlo seemed an ideal launching site for a subject like that of *La rondine,* because the opera seasons there had an undeniable chic, offering a surprising richness of repertory performed by a cross section of well-regarded French and Ital-

14. CP, Letter 690, p. 443.

Torre del Lago, Villa Puccini, exterior. At the end of the last century, the composer began spending long periods of time in the lake Massaciuccoli area, first in humble, rented accommodation, then in 1899 he bought a simple hovel, demolished it, and built the house that was to become his favorite dwelling place. With the permission of his friend and neighbor, Count Ginori-Lisci, owner of the lake, Puccini was able to extend the property and create enough new land to allow himself a small garden. (Paolo Tosi)

ian singers. Thus it came about that the premiere of *La rondine* was announced as taking place in Monte Carlo near the end of March 1917.

As soon as the word was out, a vicious campaign against Puccini was launched by that vituperative chauvinist Léon Daudet, who took repeated delight in charging Puccini and his accomplices, meaning Gunsbourg and Sonzogno, with trafficking with the enemy. Hardly a week went by without another cannonade in the pages of *L'Action Française*. Against this hostile background the preparations for the premiere of *La rondine* moved ahead on schedule, the long-awaited event duly taking place on 27 March 1917, as a benefit for invalided soldiers. The cast was headed by Gilda Dalla Rizza (Magda), Ines Maria Ferraris (Lisette), Tito Schipa (Ruggero), Fran-

Torre del Lago, Villa Puccini, interior. Among his local friends, Puccini counted a number of painters, several of whom assisted him in decorating the villa (painting door panels and ceilings, for example). He composed at an upright piano in a ground-floor room, opening directly onto the garden. Among the photographs on the piano, the central position is given to an inscribed portrait of Franz Lehár, a composer whom Puccini admired very much. Directly behind the piano, in a former storage room transformed after Puccini's death into a shrine, the composer is buried, along with his wife and his son Antonio. (Paolo Tosi)

cesco Dominici (Prunier), and Gustave Huberdeau (Rambaldo), under the baton of Gino Marinuzzi. The audience was appreciative, summoning Puccini to take a bow from the royal box of Prince Albert of Monaco at the conclusion of each of the three acts. The reviews were favorable, and Puccini believed that the opera could prove viable as long as it was produced under favorable conditions.

That *La rondine* was more delicate than a *Trovatore,* which one impresario claimed could be a success even when performed by four "dogs," was demonstrated by the debacle of its Milanese premiere. The first two productions following its launching at Monte Carlo had given no foretaste of problems. Starting in May 1917, there had been a run of seven performances at the Colon in Buenos Aires, Magda again being sung by Dalla Rizza; the work's Italian debut, at Bologna's Teatro Comunale, conducted by Ettore Panizza, gathered an audience for eight performances, although the critics were unkind. The Milanese performances took place at the Dal Verme, the theater favored by Casa Sonzogno, but Puccini was upset during the rehearsals because the conductor, Leopoldo Mugnone, demonstrated little feeling for the score. The dress rehearsal, which was to have taken place on 4 October 1917, was postponed because of dissension in the theater.[15]

The day after the first performance, on the seventh, Puccini gave his view of it to Forzano. He thought the singers ineffective. The principal soprano (Maria Farneti) he characterized as "incommunicative on stage" and the tenor as "unmusical and careless, without a trace of bel canto." The chief culprit, however, was Mugnone, whom he found "truly a liability; no *finesse,* no *nuance,* no *souplesse,* the 3 qualities essential to *La rondine.*"[16] The critics of the majority of the Milanese newspapers ignored the polite applause of the audience and, contrary to the composer's opinion, found nice things to say about the singers and the conductor; but they lambasted the score.

15. See Puccini's letter of that date to Giovacchino Forzano, published in Arnaldo Marchetti, ed., *Puccini com'era* (Milan, 1973), 440: "There are painful problems! This evening the dress rehearsal was to have taken place. It will not, and perhaps I shall make a solemn protest."
16. Marchetti, *Puccini com'era,* 443.

"That poor excuse for music [*quella musichetta*] is neither vivacious nor of a sufficiently popular character to be described as an operetta, nor is it elevated enough to be called a lyric comedy," reported *Il Secolo*.[17]

Puccini was undeniably stung by the generally unfriendly reaction he encountered in many quarters. In the *Corriere della Sera* for 10 April 1917, he had printed a dignified letter defending himself from Léon Daudet's charges that *La rondine* was an "enemy" opera and that the Opéra-Comique had rejected the work for the reason that it would be treasonable to perform it in war-torn Paris. In his letter Puccini described how the opera had come to be written and how Sonzogno had presented him with a resolution to his difficulties with his original contract. He explained that the situation with the Opéra-Comique had been misrepresented: What was at question was the possibility of the Monte Carlo company coming to Paris for a single, special performance, but he maintained that he himself had vetoed the idea.[18] Puccini was also concerned at this time about his son Tonio, who had joined the army and would be going to the front before long. A final frustration was his being refused a visa to go to Switzerland, when the official in charge learned that he was in the habit of meeting a German lady there when he could arrange it. And with these various matters troubling him, he had to contend with the critics as well. "Critics? The worst and most useless race on earth."[19]

*I*t is on the heels of the production of *La rondine* at the Dal Verme in October 1917 that Puccini began to consider revising the work. The previous June he had written to his friend Schnabl in what may well have been a spirit of trying to convince himself that the third act, which at Bologna had not been found universally pleasing, was "*the best,*" adding that

17. Quoted in Marchetti, *Puccini com'era*, 444.
18. Puccini's letter of 10 April 1917 to the *Corriere* is reprinted in Kaye, *The Unknown Puccini*, 173–75. So far, *La rondine* has never been performed either at the Opéra or the Opéra-Comique (the latter now referred to as the Opéra-Studio).
19. So he described them to Luigi Motta on 17 October 1917, CP, Letter 713, p. 457.

"you remember it well because at Monte Carlo" the appropriate moments were found "moving and comic."[20] A year later he had changed his opinion about this act. He wrote to Sonzogno that he needed the autograph back so that he could modify it. "The third [act] is grievously problematic! It is a major stumbling-block, because the subject is the principal foe. I am expecting Adami any day now."[21] Nor was the third act all Puccini wanted to revise: He changed the range of Prunier's role to a baritone part, raised the tessitura of Lisette, strengthened the role of Rambaldo, and made Ruggero appear less a bumpkin. He was uncertain what to do with the second act, thinking that perhaps it might be advisable to change the *mise-en-scène*.

Adami had arrived by 15 July 1918, for on that date Puccini again wrote to Sonzogno:

> Adami is here. We have adjusted the first and second acts, or rather we have come to an understanding about them. When he comes back in about two weeks with ideas for the third act, it would be well if you could be here too. I would like to change the settings of the second and third acts, and I would also be of a mind to give up the hateful crinolines and update the opera in stylized modern dress.[22]

The following day Puccini wrote Sonzogno again, asking him to go to the expense of sending along Carlo Carignani, who made the piano reductions for most of Puccini's operas, to Viareggio so that he could make the new adjustments for *La rondine* on the spot. The composer insisted that this would be a useful and practical thing to do, "particularly since Adami and I are asking nothing for the work that is being done."[23]

Another addition to the score, decided on that August, was a *romanza* for the tenor in Act 1. The music for this aria, which supplanted some twenty-three bars that come at the end of

20. Simonetta Puccini, ed., *Lettere a Riccardo Schnabl* (Milan, 1982), 62.
21. CP, Letter 721, p. 462.
22. CP, Letter 722, pp. 462–63.
23. CP, Letter 723, p. 463.

the episode where Prunier tells Magda's fortune, is the same as that of a song, *Morire?*[24]

A year later, a year in which the composer was principally occupied with the launching of the *Trittico,* on 21 August 1919, Puccini wrote to Sonzogno that Adami was staying with him and working, and he reported that the problems with the third act seemed to be well resolved, especially those at the end.[25] The new arrangement for the end of the third act has been succinctly described by Cecil Hopkinson:

> First Ruggero gives Magda a ring, and Prunier and Lisette appear to try and persuade Magda to return to Paris and resume her old life there, seeing no future for her buried away in the country. Magda resists this suggestion because she is so sure of the strength of her love for Ruggero. He returns and, after making her read the letter from his mother which has just arrived, departs to write his mother to say that they are going to visit her. Prunier now returns and persuades Magda that for Ruggero's sake she must leave, writing a letter to inform him of her decision. The act ends with Magda taking off the ring, brokenhearted, and supported by Prunier.[26]

Although the situation was altered and the characters of Prunier and Lisette reintroduced, the music for the new conclusion to the third act is substantially that of the original version but redistributed and with a few brief compressions. The major musical change in this act was the recomposition and shortening by almost two-thirds of the Lisette-Prunier scene when she returns from her fiasco as a chanteuse.

This second version was patched together in two main periods of activity: July–August 1918 and August 1919. In

---

24. Kaye, *The Unknown Puccini,* 185–86. Kaye raises this question: "Was this music originally conceived for *La rondine,* or was it first composed as Puccini and Adami's contribution to the album of music sold to benefit the Italian Red Cross? At this juncture it is impossible to give an unequivocal answer." As a song it was printed in G major; as Ruggero's Act I aria it appears in the 1920 German score a semitone lower.

25. CP, Letter 760, p. 487.

26. Cecil Hopkinson, *A Bibliography of the Works of Giacomo Puccini* (New York, 1968), 38–39.

April 1920 this version was introduced at Palermo with Vittorio Gui conducting. Puccini wrote to his friend Schnabl on 20 April: "Did you like *La Rondine?* The atmosphere at Monte Carlo is better suited to this opera.[27] At Palermo under Gui it seems to have gone well in the new version."[28]

La rondine, with Adami's text translated into German by Willner and Heinz Reichert, had its long-delayed Viennese premiere at the Volksoper on 9 October 1920, but only after Puccini had tinkered once again with the score, a process that involved moving the opening back a day or so. This performance was disillusioning to Puccini: The theater was short of funds, and the scenery was skimpy. The Magda (or Madelaine), Hedwig von Debicka, lacked charm, and the Ruggero, Miguel Fleta, sang his part in Italian. The conducting was, according to the critics, dreary. No wonder Puccini wrote to his English friend Sybil Seligman:

> I am going to rewrite *La rondine* for the third time! I don't care for the second edition; I prefer the first—the edition of Monte Carlo. But the third will be the first with changes on account of the libretto; Adami has been here and has come to an agreement with the publishers and the Viennese librettists. It appears that next year they will give *La rondine* at the ex-Imperial Opera House—because this time there was a rather mediocre performance of it at the Volksoper, a theatre of only the second rank.[29]

The third version of *La rondine* was undertaken in December 1920, as Puccini informed Schnabl in a letter written on Christmas:

> Day before yesterday Adami came. We have revised the third act of *La rondine,* restoring the original edition for the first two acts, except for some little touches, and doing over the third with a prelude with a woman's voice off-stage (it is really just the opening scene of the act, but performed with the curtain low-

27. *La rondine* had been revived at Monte Carlo on 20 March 1920, when it was obviously performed in the first version, because Prunier was sung by the Russian tenor Georgevsky.
28. Puccini, *Lettere a Schnabl,* 82.
29. Vincent Seligman, *Puccini Among Friends* (New York, 1938), 320. The production "next year . . . at the ex-Imperial Opera House" never came about.

ered). Certainly with improvements and some vocal effectiveness it can be quite successful, especially as the original scene did not contribute much. Rambaldo will come on, and [after] the departure of the tenor who is angry, violent, [Magda] remains alone etc. abandoned etc. etc.[30]

The principal modifications in version III are in the third act. The music at the beginning is new only in this position, as it was previously heard in Act I in the conversation between Magda and the three girls, but here the harmony has been modified. The curtain does not rise for 114 measures, and what had been the beginning of a duet for Magda and Ruggero is now heard in the orchestra. Three new characters are introduced, three "vivaci vendeuses" who try to tempt Magda into buying fashionable accessories. Their music is a reminiscence of the Act II quartet, "Bevo al tuo fresco sorriso," which in the first two versions had accompanied Ruggero's confession that he had written his parents for permission to marry Magda. About this shift of emphasis, Alfredo Mandelli has commented:

> In the case of *La rondine* it would seem that the ambivalent ambiguity of the music winds up entering into the estranging and ironical tone of this deceptively simple opera, where tangos and foxtrots in reality are not merely tangos and foxtrots but an intermittent vein of anti-pathos that undercuts the sentimental moments.[31]

The other substantial change comes near the end of Act III. Rambaldo enters to a new theme (B-flat major, 6/8, *Andante mosso*). He tells Magda that three months have passed since he had news of her; he gives her a pin shaped like a swallow and also a well-supplied wallet. The newly composed music ends as Rambaldo exits, having seen Ruggero returning, no longer with a letter from his pious mother but with one from a busy-

30. CP, Letter 784, p. 499.
31. Alfredo Mandelli, *Tre "Rondini," un enigma e un esperimento, ovvero i "casi" de La Rondine (con un "caso" di più)*, House program of the June 1987 performances at the Teatro Comunale, Bologna, p. 47. My description of version III is much indebted to Mandelli's article.

body who has told him that when he met her, Magda was being kept by Rambaldo. With slight modifications, the music is basically that of the original version, but the tonality, the voice parts, the text, and the situation are now quite different. Ruggero reproaches her, and then he sees the wallet from Rambaldo lying on the table. At this moment, as Mandelli shrewdly observes, the love theme has become the theme of wrath.[32]

When the opera was performed at the Teatro Comunale in Bologna in June 1987, the Rambaldo-Magda episode was inserted into Act III and the balance of the score adjusted to be consistent with this plot development. The orchestral parts of version III have disappeared, perhaps destroyed when Casa Sonzogno was damaged in the bombing of Milan in 1943, but piano-vocal scores had been printed. Thus the new episode was performed (perforce) to piano accompaniment (providing a balance to the episode in Act I when Prunier begins his song to Doretta playing the piano).

*I*t has usually been assumed that the German *Urtext* for *La rondine,* the original version of the scenario accepted by Puccini, follows the same general lines as the present Italian libretto. That this is not the case is demonstrated by a long letter that Willner wrote to Puccini on 11 February 1919, two years after the opera's first performance, at Monte Carlo, and a year and a half before it was given in Vienna. Willner reacts to the composer's criticism of the plot as "insipid," which had been quoted in several Viennese papers. Because this letter sheds light on a little understood phase of the genesis of *La rondine,* it is worth quoting *in extenso.*[33]

Neither I nor my collaborator was able to exert any influence upon the development of the libretto, as the war had made it impossible to correspond either with you, worthy signor Mae-

32. Ibid., 48.
33. This letter is quoted on pp. 57–59 of the House program of the Teatro Comunale (June 1987), when *La rondine* was performed with the Act III ending from the "third" version, as arranged by Alfredo Mandelli of the Istituto di Studi Pucciniani.

stro, or with your esteemed friend signor Adami. Just a few months ago I received a piano-vocal score already printed [of the original version], and when I examined it I became aware that the elaboration of the plot carried out by Adami with your approval deviated drastically from the original that I sent you in 1914. In Adami's work all the dramatic effects have been eliminated, as the opera in its present form is purely lyrical, a circumstance that inevitably affects the scenic aspects in a drastic and very unfortunate way. In the first act the role of Lisette becomes almost incomprehensible, as no one could behave as she does in a social setting that one might describe as elegant, a maid who at every opportunity injects herself into the conversation and takes one might say a dominant part. While the original version [of the scenario] entrusted to Prunier the recipe for spending one's first night in Paris, Lisette now unduly intrudes into this. One might still get by with all this, but even worse is the weakening of the second act. While I had Rambaldo make what was clearly an exceptional appearance at the Bullier dance-hall, entering with a group of male friends who very much wanted him to do so; now he comes in alone and no one knows why this gentleman has decided to visit a common dance-hall on that particular occasion. His meeting with Madelaine is much more dramatic in the original.[34] And the way in which Prunier draws Roger away from that encounter is not very successful either. Worse still is the third act! In the original there was an atmosphere foreboding a storm that in fact took place during the highly dramatic confrontation between Roger and Madelaine; instead Adami substituted the reading of a sentimental letter from his aged mother. Such an episode would have worked very well in a novel, but on the stage the effect is lost and it leaves a flavorless taste. It is incomprehensible that Roger, when Madelaine confesses that she has been stained by the shame of being kept, can only repeat continually that this does not concern him, that this has no significance whatever. When has a man ever behaved so pusillanimously in real life? When has such a spectacle aroused interest on a stage? But even if he declares continually that he is indifferent to Madelaine's past, he suddenly lowers his head: a head that in the married state would be destined to sport a pair of horns; and he leaves the stage like a beaten dog, while Madelaine consoles herself with

---

34. In the German text the leading characters' names are changed: Magda becomes Madelaine, and Ruggero becomes Roger (pronounced as in French).

a few sentimental phrases. How virile and dramatic Roger showed himself to be in the original! How beautiful were Prunier's words to Madelaine to raise her up from her disaster.

Willner goes on to say that the rest of work shows "very good intentions," but he wanted to point our "crass" exceptions. Then he offers to participate in the revision of the libretto.

> Why don't you think about returning to the original? We [with Reichert still as collaborator] stand ready to carry out all the changes and also—when circumstances permit—not to shirk the inconvenience of a journey to be able to settle together with you whatever else.

Several things are clear from this important letter. Willner was by means averse to becoming associated once more with what might prove to be a profitable work by Puccini. Even more clearly it demonstrates that he conceived the libretto in the socially more realistic terms of the spoken dialogue of operetta, into which one could insert specific details to create an impression of a particular milieu. On the other hand, in a through-composed comic opera where everything is sung, convincing realistic details are not nearly as important as a credible premise. Characters and relationships tend to be communicated in symbolic and metaphorical terms. With opera, it is not factual truth but emotional truth that has to be convincing.

The ironic significance of Puccini's words to Eisner, "like *Rosenkavalier,* but more diverting and more organic," seems never to have been communicated to Willner. Strauss's opera, which Puccini knew as *Il cavaliere della rosa,* comes to a bittersweet conclusion, with the Marschallin's renunciation sending the youthful lovers into each other's arms. With this plot Hofmannsthal had invented a symbolic milieu in which the action seemed inevitable. Puccini and his librettists largely avoided milieux that were aristocratic or upper middle class, the sort of world approximated in *Der Rosenkavalier;* the composer's one foray in that direction, the depiction of Geronte's

Parisian salon in Act II of *Manon Lescaut,* is close to parody. The demimonde setting of *La rondine* reminds us rather of *La traviata,* but with the significant difference that Magda is not phthisic. If fatal illness exacts sympathy in Violetta's case, in Magda's, less intense feelings are aroused by a malaise that is nothing more than nostalgia for a love not bound by purse strings.

The other pair of lovers—the maid Lisette, reminiscent of Adele in *Die Fledermaus,* and the poet Prunier, suggestive of certain aspects of Offenbach's Hoffman—are basically peripheral to the main plot, unlike the central function of Octavian and Sophie, the "young lovers" in *Der Rosenkavalier.* The lopsided relationship of Lisette and Prunier holds interest, nonetheless, as it can flourish only under pretense; as soon as he tries to persuade her that she has the makings of a chanteuse, the affair is in danger, and only when she returns to her duties *chez* Magda do their "rightful" roles reestablish themselves. Puccini came to feel the plot of *La rondine* was "insipid" because although Adami's version of the argument allows for all sorts of opportunities for genre music, it lacks a convincing emotional catharsis.

Puccini was not terribly at home with plots that are supposed to end happily. Only four of his operas—*Fanciulla, Rondine, Gianni Schicchi,* and *Turandot*—do so, but each of these happy endings is to some degree compromised. True, Minnie persuades the lynch mob to spare Ramerrez, but the future into which the *ci-devant* barmaid and the ex-thief ride off seems less important than the fact that both have managed to survive. The ending of *Gianni Schicchi* demonstrates the dubious truth that unselfish thieving has its justifications in the face of greed. The happy ending of *Turandot* is perhaps the most seriously compromised as a result of Liù's suicide, leaving some people to feel that the final confrontation between Turandot and the Prince produces the sort of effect that *Butterfly* would make if it ended with a love duet for Pinkerton and Kate.

La rondine survives in the original edition of 1917, for that was Puccini's ultimate decision about the work that once referred to as "*questa porca opera Rondine,*"[35] and about which he maintained that it was "a real shame to leave in oblivion one of my most sincere compositions."[36] Puccini's frustrations with the work were more the result of the harsh treatment it received and his problems with Casa Sonzogno after his chief partisan there, Renzo Sonzogno, died on 2 April 1920. In Italy in the straitened times following World War I, the prospective expense of reengraving revision upon revision was not attractive. That Puccini believed in his work and in the efficacy of a Gilda Dalla Rizza to sustain it in the theater is shown in many of his letters to the soprano, who had become one of his favored interpreters.

Recent years have proved that Puccini's belief was not misplaced. In the climate of post–World War I, that era of cloche hats and jazz babies, the plot of *La rondine* with its aura of the *belle époque* seemed grievously out of tune with the times. At present the ambiguities of the plot with its marvelously crafted score give the opera a resonance that earlier had eluded it.

In the Act II quartet, *La rondine* can boast of an ensemble as irresistible as the *sextet* from *Lucia* or the *quartet* from *Rigoletto*. As our perspective changes and we come to understand that *La rondine* belongs to a great tradition that seems to be, alas, extinct, we can freely open up to its charm and slightly dubious morality without those feelings of enemy taint or aesthetic slumming that bothered the audiences of seventy years ago.

---

35. CP, Letter 842, to Schnabl, dated 8 October 1922, p. 529. ("This pig of an opera *Rondine.*")
36. CP, Letter 867, to Gilda Dalla Rizza, dated 15 June 1923, p. 542.

Turandot and the Theatrical Aesthetics of the Twentieth Century

Jürgen Maehder

Jürgen Maehder, born in Duisburg, Germany, in 1950, studied in Munich and in Bern, Switzerland, and received his doctorate in musicology from the University of Bern in 1977. After three years as a researcher in Rome, he returned to Bern to teach. Since 1989 he has been professor of musicology at the Freie Universität, Berlin, where he founded a Puccini Research Center. He has also taught in the United States as visiting professor and has organized and participated in many conferences, largely devoted to Puccini or his contemporary Leoncavallo. He has published many scholarly articles.

> Turandot est le modèle de la cantatrice,
> s'excédant jusqu'au silence, poussant le
> principe de l'entrée en scène jusqu'à
> l'arrêt de la mort.
>
> Cathérine Clément, "Mythe et musique
> ou L'opéra revée"[1]

1. In *Miroir du sujet* (Paris, 1975).

When Puccini started to look for a libretto for his next opera after the world premiere of the *Trittico* at the Metropolitan Opera in New York, his choice did not immediately fall on the "tragi-comic Chinese fable" *Turandot* by Count Carlo Gozzi. In the early months of 1919 the composer was considering the musical possibilities of *Sly* by Giovacchino Forzano, who had been his librettist for *Suor Angelica* and *Gianni Schicchi;* but he eventually rejected the idea, and *Sly* did not reach the stage until 1927, when Ermanno Wolf-Ferrari's opera of that name was performed at the Teatro alla Scala in Milan. However, 18 September 1919 is the date of Puccini's letter to the theater critic and playwright Renato Simoni (1875–1952), an acquaintance of many years' standing—the first sign of their friendship appears in a letter written in 1904—and this letter opens the dense correspondence between Puccini and the first librettist of his last opera:

Torre del Lago, 18 September 1919

Dear Simoni,
    You promised me that you would come to Torre del Lago some day. I set great store by it and am waiting to hear from you, we will go on the lake to hunt for some rare beast. With this implacable sun the pace is slow, but it doesn't matter: we can chat and enjoy the marsh-marine air.
P.S. As I post this, it's raining!

Those chats on the lake seem to have given birth to the first idea for a subject that Puccini described in a surprisingly detailed way in his next letter, which reads almost like a work program for the two librettists:

Rome, 18 March 1920

Dear Simoni,
    I have read *Turandot* and I don't think we should look further than this subject. Yesterday I spoke to a foreign lady who told me that this work was staged in Germany by Max Reinhardt in a very strange and original way. She will write for photographs of this "mise en scène" so we will be able to see it for ourselves.

But my advice would be to stick to this subject. We will have to simplify it as far as the number of acts is concerned and rework it to make it fluent and effective, and above all we must heighten Turandot's amorous passion, which has suffocated for so long beneath the ashes of her great pride. Reinhardt made Turandot a tiny little woman surrounded by tall men deliberately chosen for their height; large chairs, large furnishings, and this little viper of a woman with the strange heart of an hysteric . . . In short, I find Turandot the most normal and human play in Gozzi's entire output.

To sum up: a Turandot perceived by the modern brain, yours, Adami's, and mine.

I went to see Valenti, but nothing has appeared in the *Corriere* about the revival of *Il trittico* here. It was a huge success. And it was so important to me that they should know about it in Milan. Instead [illegible] never mind!

P.S. Still suffering from this bronchial cold.

In this letter the future collaboration between Renato Simoni and the playwright and librettist Giuseppe Adami (1878–1946) seems already to have been established—a collaboration that for Puccini was to seem like a second version of the famous partnership between Luigi Illica and Giuseppe Giacosa, to which he, his collaborators, and his publisher Giulio Ricordi all owed their happiest memories even if their work together did not always proceed smoothly. Simoni and Adami, both from Verona, seemed almost destined to collaborate on a Venetian subject. Both had made their theatrical debuts with plays in Venetian dialect. After his first plays, *La vedova* (1902) and *Tramonto* (1902), Simoni wrote a *Carlo Gozzi* (1903), making the author of *Turandot* the protagonist of a plot that is superficially grotesque but pervaded by the sadness of an eighteenth-century Venice in economic and moral decline. Adami made his debut with the dialect play *I fioi di Goldoni* (1903), the two playwrights thus covered the dualism between the two most important writers that had characterized Venetian theater in the eighteenth century.

From Puccini's letters to Simoni (only partially published in the *Carteggi pucciniani* [1958] but more fully in the programme for La Scala's *Turandot* in 1983) it is clear that it was

Simoni who proposed the subject, while Adami—associated with Casa Ricordi for many years through his librettos for *Il tabarro, La via della finestra* (music by Riccardo Zandonai, 1919), and *Anima allegra* (music by Franco Vittadini, 1921)—had the job of drafting an outline of the action. Although the demarcation of tasks does not seem as clear-cut as in the collaboration between Illica and Giacosa, who from the time of *La bohème* had considered the construction of the plot and the invention of psychologically convincing dialogue as Illica's tasks and the versification and "polishing" Giacosa's, we can take most of the versification to be the work of Simoni, who therefore assumed the Giacosa role in his collaboration with Adami.

Simoni's intense activity as theater critic of *Corriere della Sera* from 1914 until his death in 1951 and as one of the most famous stage directors of the thirties has obscured interesting aspects of his work for the musical theater. Simoni's theatrical output falls into three clearly distinct phases. His plays, which make up the first phase, all date from a relatively brief period between 1902 and 1910, so they precede his work for *Corriere della Sera*. The transfer to musical theater was made with fairly light works: In 1908 Simoni wrote the satirical review *Turlupineide,* which was an enormous success, and in 1910 he supplied the libretto for the operetta *La secchia rapita,* with music composed by J. Burgmein—the pseudonym of the publisher Giulio Ricordi. So Simoni, in the role of librettist, was linked to Casa Ricordi from the very beginning. His first libretto for a real opera was destined to be for a grand international premiere: *Madame Sans-Gêne,* based on Sardou's play and composed by Umberto Giordano, was performed in 1915 at the Metropolitan Opera in New York under Toscanini's direction, in an obvious attempt to launch a second Casa Ricordi composer in America after the great success enjoyed by Puccini in 1910 with *La fanciulla del West*. Simoni's work as a stage director, begun in the last period of his life, from 1936, brought him back to the plays of eighteenth-century Venice; he was famous above all for his open-air stagings of Goldoni in Venetian piazzas.

If the choice of a subject taken from Gozzi's "theatrical fables" for the libretto of Puccini's opera may seem natural for two writers so steeped in Venetian culture, it certainly did not reflect the dramaturgical practices of Italian opera at that time. Since the first successes by Pietro Mascagni (*Cavalleria rusticana,* 1890), Ruggero Leoncavallo (*Pagliacci,* 1890), and Puccini (*Manon Lescaut,* 1893), the dramatic code of so-called verismo was fixed: An almost unilinear musical structure that accompanied the action by way of psychological comment corresponded to the direct expression of the characters' emotions. The characters were psychologically differentiated, the temporal structure of the action followed the natural flow of time as closely as possible, and all the scenic apparatus was aimed at the maximum identification of the audience with the characters onstage and with their actions and reactions. There were many examples of this kind of theater—which Puccini managed to develop, diminishing the directness of its scenic effects and the immediacy of its hold on the audience—even after the caesura of World War I; but a libretto as early as that for *La fanciulla del West* also reveals the cracks in a musical dramaturgy that no longer corresponded directly to contemporary straight theater.

Although the libretto for *La bohème* could be considered an adaptation of a novel within the framework of contemporary straight theater in Italy—and it was not in fact dissimilar to the play most typical of the nineties, *Come le foglie* (1898) by Giacosa, who had also collaborated on *La bohème*—the aesthetic unity between theater and opera had already started to dissolve in the last decade of the nineteenth century. In Italy, while the metrical innovations of the poetry being written by Carducci and d'Annunzio offered new possibilities to librettists, the development of poetic language towards the ever-more-exotic vocabulary of the poetry of decadence made it more difficult to find the right linguistic medium for librettese. From abroad, after the first performances of Gustave Charpentier's *Louise* (1900), Claude Debussy's *Pelléas et Mélisande* (1902), and Richard Strauss's *Salome* (1905), the new genres of the prose libretto *(Louise)* and the "literary opera" (*Literaturoper,* i.e., an existing play directly set to music without the intervention of a librettist) spread rapidly to Italy as well.

While Pietro Mascagni adopted a similar procedure to that

of the German and French literary opera for his *Guglielmo Ratcliff* (1895), a direct musical setting of Andrea Maffei's translation of Heinrich Heine's drama, many Italian composers who acted as their own librettists still favored traditional versification—in many cases more traditional than that of professional librettists. Ruggero Leoncavallo's attempts in his first operas to achieve a unity between poet and composer, undoubtedly under the direct influence of the Wagnerian doctrine that this was necessary for the aesthetic unity of the *Gesamtkunstwerk,* yielded felicitous results in the librettos for *Pagliacci* and for his *La bohème* (1897), less felicitous in the case of the forcedly literary libretto for *I Medici,* his "grand opéra," which failed spectacularly in 1893. The fact that Puccini's generation could not yet free itself from the need for verse in an opera libretto bears witness to its importance in the Italian tradition. It fell to the next generation, as illustrated, for example, by the libretto for Franco Alfano's *La leggenda di Sakùntala* (1921), written by the composer himself, to adopt the most recent European practices in this field.

The prospect of a tradition of literary operas was opened up for Italian opera by the composers of Puccini's generation who started to set Gabriele d'Annunzio's dramas to music. The first attempt in this direction was made by Alberto Franchetti, a friend of Puccini's since the time of *Manon Lescaut* and with whom Puccini shared a number of interests—including the Touring Club Italiano, of which Franchetti was president. After collaborating on several operas with Luigi Illica—*Cristoforo Colombo* (1892), written for the anniversary celebrations of the discovery of America, and *Germania* (1902), written to compensate the composer for ceding the libretto of *Tosca*—Franchetti argued with Illica about the *Tosca* libretto, originally promised to him and only given to Puccini afterward because of the intrigues of Giulio Ricordi, Puccini, and Illica himself. Franchetti then set about composing music for the drama *La figlia di Iorio* (1904); the resulting opera had an unsuccessful premiere at the Teatro alla Scala in 1906. We know that at this time Puccini had also entered into negotiations with d'Annunzio; of the three subjects he considered, however, *Parisina* passed to Mascagni, while *La rosa di Cipro* and *La crociata degli innocenti* never became finished librettos.

The years immediately following the disastrous premiere of *Madama Butterfly* at La Scala (1904) marked the deepest crisis in Puccini's career. Even though later performances of the opera proved it to be a lasting success, from the premiere of the second version in Brescia in May 1904 to the Paris premiere in 1906, the composer remained dissatisfied with the dramaturgical foundations of his operas. In the years between 1905 and 1909 his three most important projects for future operas foundered because of insurmountable problems with the librettos. *Maria Antonietta,* to which Luigi Illica returned repeatedly without managing to provide Puccini with a usable libretto, was reduced from a grand historical pageant of the French Revolution to the personal, almost intimate drama of the unfortunate queen; *Margherita da Cortona,* a libretto full of thirteenth-century local color proposed by the writer Valentino Soldani (1874–1935), and the drama *Parisina,* suggested to him by d'Annunzio, were rejected because their poetic language was not suited to Puccini's scenic imagination, and he took exception to the application of fake local color in both cases. But he too was tempted by the idea of setting an existing drama to music, probably because of his knowledge of Richard Strauss's *Salome,* and he had a fleeting bout of enthusiasm in 1906 for Oscar Wilde's *A Florentine Tragedy,* a play later set to music by Alexander Zemlinsky.

In terms of an ideal vision of opera as a fusion of words and music, ingredients of equal artistic importance, the choice of David Belasco's *The Girl of the Golden West* as the basis for the libretto of *La fanciulla* was undoubtedly a makeshift solution; Puccini simply repeated the choice that, with *Madama Butterfly,* had led him towards a new conception of theater while distancing him from the operatic tradition in which his musical means of expression were firmly rooted. It is surely significant that the same procedure—the choice of an author who had already been tested in a previous collaboration—was repeated after *Il trittico,* when Puccini first considered Forzano's proposal and then accepted the idea that involved the other coauthor, Giuseppe Adami.

We know from Puccini's letters that the idea of a "triptych," a series of three operas in different styles and with different characters to be performed in the same evening, had arisen as early as 1904 when the composer communicated this idea to Illica, who would have had to prepare the librettos based on three stories by Maxim Gorky. With this idea, Puccini renounced the conception of musical dramaturgy that had traditionally characterized Italian opera; he developed the vision of a multiform dramaturgy that, instead of portraying a continuum of psychologically coherent action, put various historically distinct genres of musical theater side by side, thus making a widely divergent series of impressions on the audience within the same evening.

With this change in his basic theatrical conception, Puccini shifted the major focus of interest away from the drama's content and onto the form in which it was presented; instead of aiming at psychological identification with the protagonists of the drama, this dramaturgy favored the intellectual fascination of the way in which the composer handled the diverse genres. And if we read the libretto of *Turandot* as a sophisticated game with different theatrical genres, we immediately realize that the basic idea of *Il trittico* was projected onto the simultaneity provided by a single drama. The key idea of the libretto that Simoni and Adami had to extract from Gozzi's fable is to be found not in the bringing together of different genres in three separate operas, but in the interweaving of tragic, comic, and romantic elements—an interweaving that is prefigured by the tragic, grotesque, and romantic elements in Gozzi.

In the years between *La fanciulla del West* and *Il trittico*—between 1910 and the end of World War I—the dramaturgical landscape of Italian opera had changed considerably. Following Franchetti's example, Pietro Mascagni (*Parisina*, 1913), Riccardo Zandonai (*Francesca da Rimini*, 1914), Ildebrando Pizzetti (*Fedra*, 1915), and Italo Montemezzi (*La nave*, 1918) had created operas based on dramas by d'Annunzio. And when Puccini wrote to Adami on 19 December 1919—"Poor Illica!

Another one gone"—he not only paid homage to the most faithful collaborator of the early years of his career but also noted the end of an entire period of Italian libretto writing, one that straddled the two centuries.

The choice of a fable by Carlo Gozzi, and in general the decision to choose a fantastical subject for his next opera, represented a conscious decision on Puccini's part to embark on a new type of theatricality; it is no accident that the composer, in numerous letters to Adami and Simoni, talks of the subject in terms of its "novelty" and "originality." Although he was correct as far as Italian theatrical tradition is concerned, the situation was different in other European theater in the immediate postwar period.

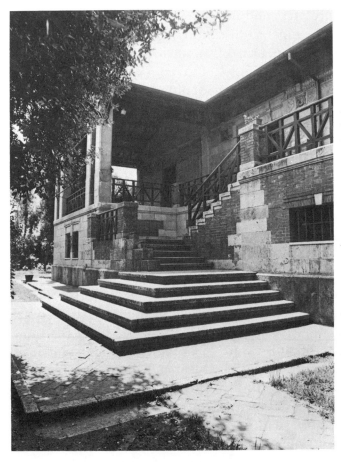

Viareggio, Villa Puccini. A few years before his death, Puccini had to move from his Torre del Lago home when a neighboring landowner allowed a noisy and smelly peat-processing plant to be installed on his property. At the far northern end of the resort town of Viareggio, Puccini had built a low, rather dark house, surrounded by trees. He spent the last years of his life there (when he was not traveling), and it was there that he composed most of Turandot. *It was from this house that he set out for his last, futile journey to Brussels, where he died. (Paolo Tosi)*

We know that the good fortune enjoyed by Gozzi's fables was, especially during the nineteenth century, a phenomenon linked exclusively to the German theater. The translation that Friedrich Schiller used for a staging in 1802 at the Weimar Hoftheater, and for which Goethe provided enigmas that were changed at every performance, generated a whole series of operas on the subject of *Turandot* (recently investigated by Kii-Ming Lo for her thesis at Heidelberg). In Italy there was a sole example: the opera *Turanda* by Antonio Bazzini, who was later to be Puccini's teacher of composition at the Milan Conservatory. His librettist, A. Gazzoletti, moved the setting from China to Persia, evidently because the authors did not know how to create the required Chinese atmosphere. The opera was judged to be undramatic by Giulio Ricordi and was forgotten after its unsuccessful premiere and never revived. The operas written in German in the nineteenth century met with the same fate; the *Turandot*s by Franz Danzi (Karlsruhe, 1816), Carl Gottlieb Reissiger (Dresden, 1835), J. Hoven (Vienna, 1838), and Theobald Rehbaum (Berlin, 1888) did not manage to establish a tradition of treating the cruel princess as one of the century's operatic heroines.

The international revival of interest in *Turandot* was linked to the activities of two people working in Berlin whose international fame contributed to the rapid diffusion of the subject: the Italo-German composer Ferruccio Busoni and the director Max Reinhardt. At a Berlin concert in 1905 Busoni conducted the world premiere of his *Turandot-Suite,* which was conceived independently of any theatrical project; the work's great success was repeated everywhere it was played, and the performance Gustav Mahler gave of it in his New York concerts in 1910 made a particularly strong impression. It is quite probable that Max Reinhardt, working in Berlin at the same time as Busoni, became aware of Gozzi's play and its intrinsic theatrical possibilities through Busoni's composition, but we have no documents to confirm this. In any case, when Reinhardt conceived his staging of Gozzi's fable in Karl Vollmoeller's German translation, he chose Busoni's *Turandot-Suite* as incidental music. The score was slightly expanded for the occasion, and Busoni reused two numbers from the *Suite* as movements of his *Elegie* for piano (1907–1908). Reinhardt's production was an enormous success, and although it was never revived—in spite of the director's intention to do so—its influence is evident even in the letter quoted above from Puccini, who had heard about the staging and had a fairly clear impression of it.

After the beginning of the first world war Busoni took refuge in Switzerland, taking the unfinished score of his opera *Arlecchino* with him. During his stay in Zurich Busoni signed a contract with the Stadttheater to give the premiere of his opera; to fill out the evening he composed the score of *Turandot* in a few months, reusing themes and whole numbers from the *Suite* and from the music for Reinhardt's production. The two operas had their joint premiere on 11 May 1917; the critics were rather hostile, probably because they could not understand the specific aesthetic principles behind Busoni's musical theater. In many respects Busoni's *Turandot* is like an adaptation of Gozzi's fable in the manner of the eighteenth-century Viennese *Singspiel,* of which Mozart's *Magic Flute* is the supreme example. Busoni's discretely neoclassical music often seems like an accompaniment to the dramatic structures of a *Magic Flute* transported to China; the composer appears to have been particularly attracted by the subdivision of the characters on different levels and in different styles: Turandot and Calaf are on the highest level, just as Pamina and Tamino were, while the three *commedia dell'arte* characters represent the lowest one.

Although research on Puccini's opera has not yet managed to establish whether the composer knew Busoni's opera when he started to compose his own *Turandot,* it seems quite probable that Puccini, while not having seen the production in Zurich, did know the repertory of the Stadttheater. The year 1917 saw him quite often in the canton of Ticino for clandestine meetings with his lover Baroness Josephine von Stängel; so often, in fact, that the Italian consul in Lugano refused to grant him a visa for Switzerland in October 1917 on the pretext that his frequent visits had aroused the suspicion that he was acting as a spy. But even if Puccini had come to know Busoni's score immediately after the war, the difference of style between his music and Busoni's would have prevented any direct influence.

It appears that while Puccini was waiting at Torre del Lago for his librettists to send him the remaining acts—at this point he had only received the first one—the success of Max Reinhardt's production inspired another version of Gozzi's *Turandot,* a version that was to turn out as fatal for its creator as Puccini's was for him: *Turandot,* the last staging by Yevgeni Bogrationovich Vakhtangov at the "Studio" of the Artists' Theater in Moscow. Vakhtangov (1883–1922), a pupil of Stanislavsky and Meyerhold, had founded the Studio in order to stage productions that realized his own artistic ideas, which had begun to diverge significantly from those of his teachers. His staging of *Turandot,* as famous for its use of new improvisation techniques as for its fresh approach to Gozzi, had its premiere in his absence on 28 February 1922; he was to die of cancer on 29 May of the same year without having seen a complete performance of his last production.

Vakhtangov's direction, which certainly had no influence on Puccini's composition but which shows some surprising similarities to his new operatic vision, was founded on the idea of "theater within the theater": The actors represented members of an Italian theater company who were performing Gozzi's *Turandot* in an improvised form. The double level in Vakhtangov's production seems like an echo of the role Puccini gave to the "masks," the three ministers who in Gozzi's fable are the traditional comic characters of Venetian comedy.

Even if it cannot be completely ruled out that Simoni—as the theater critic of the leading Italian newspaper—might have heard about the production in Moscow, another influence on Puccini seems much more probable: the most recent operas by Richard Strauss. We know that Puccini went to Vienna and Munich to see new works for the theater and that he attended performances of *Ariadne auf Naxos, Die Frau ohne Schatten,* and Pfitzner's *Palestrina.* Even though the judgments that Puccini gave in his letters were decidedly negative—and the account he gave Josephine von Stängel of the first version of *Ariadne* on 24 March 1915 is even more negative—it is not impossible that Puccini, while not liking the music, took some theatrical ideas from the fruits of the collaboration between Hugo von Hofmannsthal and Strauss.

It certainly seems likely that the fundamental configuration of the characters in *Turandot,* with the "noble" couple and the three ministers who act as a contrast, has its basis in the superposition of two genres of musical theater—by the ingenious device of the contemporaneous performance of an opera seria and an opera buffa—which is the dramatic pivot of *Ariadne*. It is probably impossible to decide whether the vocal character of the tenor who plays a very old man was invented by Puccini, who with the Emperor Altoum created a type of role unknown until then in Italian opera, or whether we can discern the model in the patriarch Abdisu in the second act of Pfitzner's *Palestrina*. In any case, Strauss's two operas must have exercised considerable influence on the composer's scenic imagination; in the final phase of his work, only five weeks before his death, Puccini remembered details of the staging of *Ariadne* in Vienna and instructed his collaborators to invent something similar:

> And for the trio outside the action a balustrade with marble struts could be fixed up, with a gap towards the center
>
> [here Puccini makes a scrawl to illustrate his point]

and this could stay in place for the second scene with the big staircase—Make the masks play or sit or stretch out or straddle this balustrade—I am not explaining this well—I know that in Strauss's Ariadne in Vienna they did something like this with the Italian masks—but the masks came up on two ladders from the orchestra pit—Perhaps this could not be done at La Scala—so have the masks enter by coming down a ladder at the sides. I think we need a great idea for the staging of this trio—we really need Reinhardt and he would find it for us. Discuss it among yourselves—and if you can see *Caramba* ask him for advice—[2]

2. Puccini, letter to Giuseppe Adami; facsimile in Giuseppe Adami, ed., *Giacomo Puccini: Epistolario* (Milan, 1928), facing p. 249.

As far as its scenic vision and its conception of musical dramaturgy are concerned, Puccini's *Turandot* was born from the fusion of diverse European traditions. It is a fully mature opera not only in terms of Puccini's own output but also as the last descendant of the Italian operatic tradition of the nineteenth century, and it reflects in both its dramaturgy and its music the ideas that were currently sweeping across Europe.

THE NONOPERATIC WORKS OF GIACOMO PUCCINI

Michael Kaye

Michael Kaye, a graduate of the New England Conservatory, often serves on the staffs of opera companies in Europe and in the United States (most recently the Metropolitan Opera in New York). He has edited numerous operas and prepared a new critical edition of *The Tales of Hoffmann.* He is the author of *The Unknown Puccini* (New York and Oxford, 1987), for which he was awarded the Luigi Illica prize. His editions of Puccini's songs have been recorded by Placido Domingo. He is currently editing and translating a volume of hitherto unpublished Puccini letters.

The term "nonoperatic" is often used to classify a variety of music not intended for the stage by composers primarily known for writing operas. In the case of Giacomo Puccini, this description is somewhat inaccurate, because portions of most of Puccini's "nonoperatic" works were eventually incorporated in his operas. Notwithstanding, I will enumerate these compositions in chronological order and describe the ways Puccini used them in his operas.[1]

1. My research has been facilitated by the studies published by Alberto Cavalli: "Inediti giovanili di Giacomo Puccini," in *Giacomo Puccini*

On 4 October 1883, the musical appendix of Edoardo Sonzogno's weekly illustrated newspaper, *La Musica Popolare,*
presented Giacomo Puccini's first published composition, a
song for voice and piano entitled *Storiella d'amore.*

> Today's issue of *La Musica Popolare* contains a work by the young
> maestro Giacomo Puccini, one of the most distinguished stu-
> dents to graduate this year from the Milan Conservatory, who is
> already favorably known in the world of music for one of his
> noteworthy instrumental works [i.e., the *Capriccio sinfonico*], per-
> formed with great success at the close of this past academic year
> at our best institute of music . . . Giovanni [*sic*] Puccini studied
> music first with Angeloni, in Puccini's native city, and then with
> Bazzini and Ponchielli, in Milan; he has written a Mass for four-
> part chorus and orchestra, which was greeted with approbation
> at the Lucca Cathedral, and various smaller chamber composi-
> tions. Art can expect much from his talent.

The article concluded with the comment that in Lucca the
word "composer" is synonymous with "Puccini." In fact, five
generations of Puccinis were musical.

From 1739 until Giacomo left Lucca to study at the Milan
Conservatory and pursue his passion for opera, the position
of Lucca's official musician was always occupied by a member
of the Puccini family. The first Giacomo (1712–1781) was a
contemporary of Gluck, and his son, Antonio Puccini (1747–
1832), was a contemporary of Mozart. Antonio's son, Domenico (1775–1815), was a contemporary of Beethoven
and a student of Paisiello. Domenico's son, Michele (1813–
1864), was born in the same year as Verdi and studied with
Donizetti and Mercadante. The second Giacomo followed in
their footsteps, but he enjoyed a brilliant international career
as Italy's preeminent opera composer.

nel centenario della nascita 2/4 (September 1958), and "I frammenti pucciniani di Celle,"
in *Critica pucciniana* (Lucca: 1976); Cecil Hopkinson: *A Bibliography of the Works of
Giacomo Puccini: 1858–1924* (New York, 1968); Giorgio Magri: "Una ricetta di Puccini," also in *Critica pucciniana; Puccini e le sue rime* (Milan, 1974); and Mario Morini:
"Il Puccini minore," in *Discoteca Alta Fedeltà* 16/147 (1975). Facsimiles of several of
the manuscripts of Puccini's so-called minor works have been published in *Mostra
pucciniana* (Sept.–Nov. 1974); *Giacomo Puccini nel centenario della nascita;* and in my
book *The Unknown Puccini* (New York and Oxford, 1987).

When Michele Puccini died on 23 January 1864, Giacomo was five years old. The city council not only granted the widow Puccini a pension, it also appointed Giacomo's uncle, Fortunato Magi, as organist and choirmaster with the stipulation that he "should and must" hand over the position to Giacomo as soon as he was qualified. Puccini studied with Magi for two years, then continued his musical education with Carlo Angeloni at Lucca's Istituto Musicale Pacini (now known as the Istituto Musicale Pareggiato "L. Boccherini").

When Puccini was ten years old he was a choirboy at San Martino and San Michele. At age fourteen, he played the organ at the local churches, often improvising some of the music for the services. He began composing between the ages of sixteen and seventeen, but he disliked the organ and did not aspire to a career in liturgical music. When he was eighteen, he walked twenty miles from Lucca to Pisa to attend a performance of Verdi's *Aida;* and with that, his life's ambition was clear to him.

Puccini was an individualist. By the time he was twenty-two, he was no longer content to remain in Lucca. Having received his diploma from the Pacini Institute, he was determined to study in Milan. Financial assistance from a wealthy great-uncle, Dr. Nicolao Cerù, and a scholarship from Queen Margherita di Savoia enabled him to attend the Milan Conservatory (Conservatorio Reale, now known as the Conservatorio di Musica Giuseppe Verdi), where he studied composition with Antonio Bazzini and Amilcare Ponchielli.

*M*anuscripts of Puccini's student works are preserved in public and private collections. They include notebooks, exercises in harmonization of figured basses, fragments of dance suites (including an *Allemanda* in G minor, a *Grave* in E-flat major, a *Corrente* in G minor, and a *Gavotta* in G major—which Puccini later used in Act II of *Tosca* at Scarpia's words "Tarda è la notte" [The night is late]), as well as several short organ compositions written in Lucca for liturgical use.[2]

---

2. Some of these works for organ were composed for Puccini's student Carlo Della Nina, and the manuscripts are in the possession of Della Nina's heirs.

The song for voice and piano entitled *A te* probably dates from Puccini's student years at the Pacini Institute.[3] Very little is known about its origins, and the authorship of the text is uncertain. Initially, *A te* evokes the classical simplicity of an aria by Gluck. An interesting example of Puccini's later musical language occurs at the final statement of "E dammi un bacio e il mondo intier, e mi farai tosto obbliar!" (And give me a kiss, and you will at once make me forget the whole world!), which reappears as Tosca's "Gli occhi ti chiuderò con mille baci e mille ti dirò nomi d'amor" (I shall close your eyes with a thousand kisses, and I will call you a thousand love names) in Act III of *Tosca*.

In the summer of 1876, Puccini composed the *Preludio sinfonico* in E minor. The frontispiece of the manuscript reads: "Preludio a orchestra di Giacomo Puccini—1876," and the last page is signed and dated "Lucca a dì 5 Agosto 1876."[4]

*I*n 1878, Puccini composed two important liturgical compositions for the church of San Paolino in Lucca. The first was the *Mottetto per S. Paolino,*[5] a large work for baritone soloist, chorus, and orchestra performed in June of that year. The second was a *Credo* for tenor and bass soloists, chorus, and orchestra, the manuscript of which is dated "a dì 8 luglio 1878." They were both successfully performed at the church of San Paolino on 12 July 1878. In 1880, Puccini incorporated the *Credo* in his longest liturgical work, the *Messa a 4 Voci* (widely known as the *Messa di Gloria*).[6]

Sometime between 1874 and 1880, Puccini was commissioned by his friend Adelson Betti to set the Passiontide processional hymn *Vexilla Regis prodeunt,* by Venantius Honorius Fortunatus, to music for the little church in Bagni di

---

3. The undated manuscript was among those given by the composer to that institute (hereafter referred to as I:Li) in 1901. All of Puccini's songs for voice and piano ("arie da camera e da chiesa") have been recorded by Placido Domingo (tenor), with Justino Díaz (bass-baritone) and Julius Rudel (piano and organ) on CBS Masterworks/ Sony Classical (*The Unknown Puccini;* CD: MK 44981 and cassette: MT 44981).
4. The manuscript was reputedly part of a private collection in Milan owned by Natale Gallini.
5. According to Magri, the manuscript was privately owned by Paola Ojetti of Lucca.
6. The manuscript of the *Credo* is preserved in I:Li.

Lucca. Betti was an apothecary as well as the organist and choirmaster of the church in Bagni. When Puccini was a student at the Pacini Institute, he often went to the fashionable summer resort of Bagni di Lucca to play the piano at the local casino, for which he received a salary equivalent to about one dollar per night. He usually arrived early to take supper with the Betti family and play his latest compositions and excerpts from operas he admired. As payment for the *Vexilla,* Puccini received ten lire cash (about eighty cents!) and one of the special cakes for which Bagni di Lucca was famous.

Puccini only set the first two stanzas of *Vexilla Regis prodeunt.* The signed title page of the undated manuscript states: "Vexilla / a 2 Voci / G. Puccini."[7] It was probably sung in Bagni di Lucca by a small two-part men's chorus with organ accompaniment.

*I*n 1880, Puccini composed a Mass for Lucca's church of San Paolino and scored it for tenor and bass soloists, chorus, and orchestra. With the exception of the Credo, which he had already written in 1878, the music was newly created for this occasion.

The mass begins with an orchestral introduction and consists of the Kyrie in A-flat major ("Kyrie eleison" in A-flat major, "Christe eleison" in F minor, and "Kyrie eleison" in A-flat major, repeated); Gloria in C major (divided into several sections: "Gloria in excelsis Deo"—a choral fugue in C major—"Et in terra pax" and "Laudamus Te," "Gratias" in G-flat major for tenor solo, reprise of the "Gloria in excelsis Deo" for the "Domine Deus," "Qui tollis peccata mundi" in F minor, "Quoniam" in C major, "Cum sancto Spiritu"— another fugue in C major—and a final reprise of the Gloria); Credo in C minor (comprised of the "Credo in unum Deo" and "Patrem omnipotentem," "Qui propter," "Et incarnatus" in G major for tenor and chorus, "Crucifixus" in G minor for bass solo, "Et resurrexit" in G major, "Et unam Sanctam" in

---

7. The manuscript is preserved in the Music Division of the Library of Congress, Washington, D.C.

C major—including a reprise of the first theme of the Credo, and the "Et vitam" as a fugue in C major); Sanctus (consisting of the "Sanctus" in G major, "Pleni sunt coeli" and "Benedictus" in E-flat major for bass solo, and the "Hosanna" in E-flat major); and the Agnus Dei (with sections alternating between C major and A minor for tenor and bass soloists and chorus, concluding with the "Dona nobis pacem" in C major).

Puccini used portions of the Kyrie for the prayer and Tigrana's entrance in Act I of his second opera, *Edgar* (repeated in Act II, at Tigrana's words "Quel che sognavi un dì" [All that you dreamed one day]). The opening theme of the Gloria foreshadows the beginning of the *Inno a Diana* (1897). The Agnus Dei was transformed into the madrigal "Sulla vetta tu del monte" (Over the summit of the mountain) in Act II of *Manon Lescaut*. The title *Messa di Gloria,* sometimes associated with this work, is apocryphal.[8]

Milan was the operatic center of Italy. Some of the repertory Puccini heard in Milan in 1881 included *Mignon, Der Freischütz, Simon Boccanegra* (in the revised version), Emilio Usiglio's *Le nozze in prigione, Carmen, Don Giovanni, Mefistofele, Gli ugonotti, La stella del nord, I puritani, Belisario, Faust, La forza del destino, La favorita, Semiramide, Guglielmo Tell,* and *Il Guarany.*

In 1881, Puccini composed a *Scherzo* in A minor for string quartet, which he later used in an expanded orchestration in the first scene of the ballet in his first opera, *Le villi.*[9] For his final examinations in the summer of 1882, Puccini composed the *Preludio sinfonico* in A major. This work for orchestra is often confused with a *Preludio sinfonico* in E minor, written in 1876; however, the title page of the autograph full score of the A-major *Preludio sinfonico* is dated "Milano giugno 1882." At the end of the manuscript, Puccini signed his name and added

8. The title originated in 1952, with the first (unauthorized) publication of the music by Mills Music, New York City. Puccini's Mass has also been published by Ricordi as the *Messa a 4 Voci.*
9. The original title of which was *Le willis.*

"Luglio 1882 Milano."[10] He made further use of some of this music in *Le villi, Edgar,* and in the song *Avanti "Urania"!* In a letter written to Dr. Cerù on 6 December 1882, Puccini depicts the cold Milan winter of his impoverished student days, which he later translated into such vivid music in Act I of *La bohème:*

> My studies are going well and I am working hard. The cold up here is extraordinary and worse than in past years; therefore I must ask you for a favor, which I hope you will find justified. I have to study and, as you know, I usually study late in the evening all through the night, and since my room is really very cold I could use some fire. I have no money because, as you know, that which you send me is for the basic necessities, so I would need some money to buy one of those coal burners that produce much heat.
>
> The expense for the stove is not much, but what worries me is that the coal costs a lot and by the end of the month amounts to a considerable sum.[11]

Like Rodolfo, perhaps Puccini used some of the manuscripts of his scholastic compositions to fuel the fire in the small apartment he shared with Pietro Mascagni.

Unpublished compositions dating from this period include fragments of a work for piano marked "Finale"; a Trio for two violins and piano[12]; and the songs *Salve regina* and *Ad una morta!* with texts by Antonio Ghislanzoni. Puccini's extant manuscripts of these songs are undated, but the texts were published in 1882 in a collection of Ghislanzoni's poetry entitled *Melodie per canto.*[13]

Puccini used the music of *Salve regina* (originally for soprano

---

10. Manuscript: Conservatorio di Musica Giuseppe Verdi, Milan (hereafter referred to as I:Mc) (full score); I:Li (parts); Publisher: Elkan-Vogel, Bryn Mawr; ed. Pietro Spada.
11. Arnaldo Marchetti, ed., *Puccini com'era* (Milan, 1973), 8.
12. Manuscript: I:Li.
13. The author and poet Antonio Ghislanzoni (1824–1893) was a prominent Milanese exponent of *scapigliatura,* a literary movement in Italy dating from the 1860s. Perhaps best remembered as the versifier of Verdi's *Aida,* Ghislanzoni was also an exseminarist, a student of medicine, a contrabass player, and a well-known baritone. He directed Ricordi's *La Gazzetta Musicale* (1866) and founded several newspapers. He was also a raconteur, journalist, and critic.

and organ or harmonium) in *Le villi* for the orchestral introduction to No. 5 and as the basis for the prayer "Angiol di
Dio, che i vanni rivolgi al ciel stasera" (O, angel of God, who
dost spread thy wings tonight unto heaven).[14] He composed
Ad una morta! for baritone and piano and planned to orches-
trate it, but apparently abandoned the idea.[15] Instead, he put
this music to other uses: portions of it appear in the revised
two-act version of *Le villi:* in Roberto's *romanza* "Torna ai
felici dì" (Return to the happy days) at the words "Ridean i
fior, fioria per me l'amor" (The flowers laughed, for me love
flowered); and as the theme that introduces Anna's "Tu dell'
infanzia mia le gioie dividesti" (You shared the joys of my
childhood). Other sections of *Ad una morta!* were incorporated
in his graduation piece, the *Capriccio sinfonico* (1883), and in
Manon Lescaut (1893).

The year 1883 marked the end of Puccini's studies at the
Milan Conservatory. His obligations for his composition classes
included three fugal studies in counterpoint—*Fuga* (in A major),
Fuga (in D major, dated 5 April 1883), and *Fuga* (in G major);
some fugues for voices (S.A.T.B.); two fugues based on brief
themes provided by his professors—*Fuga a 4 Voci* (in D minor)[16]
and *Fuga* (in G minor);[17] a string quartet in D major, only
fragments of which survive;[18] the dramatic scene and aria for

14. With the exception of the word "Salve," the text is not related to the office hymn
    that begins "Salve Regina."
15. According to the extant autograph manuscripts, Puccini never composed a defini-
    tive version of *Ad una morta!* In 1989, this writer made a performing edition of the
    song that was recorded by Placido Domingo and Julius Rudel.
16. The five-page autograph manuscript at I:Mc is signed at the end by Puccini's teach-
    ers, Antonio Bazzini and Amilcare Ponchielli, and judges A. Panzini, Michele Sala-
    dino, and Cesare Dominiceti. The tempo indication is "Moderato"; there are eighty-
    three measures with the indication "Ricevuto alle ore 5⁰⁰ Pom[eridiane]."
17. The four-page autograph manuscript at I:Mc is signed at the end by Puccini's teach-
    ers, Antonio Bazzini and Amilcare Ponchielli, and judges A. Panzini, Michele Sala-
    dino, and Cesare Dominiceti. The tempo indication is "Piutosto lento" and the
    fugue is complete (sixty-six measures, two of which are crossed out). Seven pages
    of composition sketches, marked "Piutosto *lento* quasi Andante," are also preserved
    in I:Mc.
18. According to a letter to his mother written in March 1883, Puccini lamented that
    "mi par mill'anni di essere a casa, che devo fare un quartetto ad archi per Bazzini."
    The Museum of Pucciniana in Celle possesses an unpublished manuscript of a four-
    hand piano arrangement of the last movement of this quartet made by Puccini's
    brother, Michele. The manuscript is headed "Giacomo Puccini. Scherzo per archi
    [Allegro vivo in D minor], Riduzione per pianoforte a 4 mani di Michele Puccini.
    Lucca Ottobre-Novembre [18]83."

tenor and piano, *Mentìa l'avviso;* the *Capriccio sinfonico,* a large-scale work for orchestra; and his first published composition, a charming song entitled *Storiella d'amore.*

Dante Del Fiorentino, a priest who knew Puccini in Lucca before immigrating to the United States, wrote an "intimate memoir" of the composer in which he reported that Puccini considered Ponchielli so absentminded that Puccini brought him the same homework he prepared for Bazzini: "I even submitted to him the same fugue three or four times over with only the smallest changes."[19]

The young Puccini demonstrated his brilliant ability to write for the voice in the dramatic recitative and aria *Mentìa l'avviso,* for tenor and piano, composed on 10 June 1883 in fulfillment of the requirements for graduation. The text is taken from the libretto of Felice Romani's melodrama *La solitaria delle Asturie, ossia La Spagna ricuperata.*[20] The autograph manuscript bears the signatures of Puccini's teachers Antonio Bazzini, Amilcare Ponchielli, and other professors. On the last page, Puccini wrote, "Pietà un dolor di denti noioso che mi ha tormentato dalle 7 alle 2." (Have mercy! I have been bothered by a wearisome toothache 7 to 2).

Puccini used the second *Lento* theme of *Mentìa l'avviso* as the basis of the famous tenor aria "Donna non vidi mai" (I never before beheld such a lady), sung by Renato Des Grieux in Act I of *Manon Lescaut* (1893). Earlier in the act, the same theme is played to symbolize Des Grieux's fascination with Manon. The piano part of *Mentìa l'avviso* is appropriately operatic, resembling a piano reduction of an orchestral accompaniment more than music written for the keyboard. There is no evidence that Puccini ever orchestrated *Mentìa l'avviso,* or that it was published in his lifetime.

19. See Dante Del Fiorentino, *Immortal Bohemian: An Intimate Memoir of Giacomo Puccini* (New York, 1952), 45.
20. In Puccini's manuscripts, "Parole di Felice Romani" is the only reference to the text. One of the most important librettists of the nineteenth century, Felice Romani (1788–1865) abandoned a career in law to write for the lyric stage. He wrote more than one hundred libretti—some of which were composed by Mayr, Rossini, Meyerbeer, Donizetti, Bellini, and Verdi. *La solitaria delle Asturie, ossia La Spagna ricuperata* was first set to music by Carlo Coccia (1838), then by Mercadante (1840), Vincenzo Mela (1840), Luigi Ricci (1845), and Giuseppe Sordelli, Jr. (1846).

On 20 June 1883, Puccini wrote to his mother: "I am working finally to complete my piece, which now is at a satisfactory stage. After my examinations I shall concern myself with my future and I shall go to Ricordi, but I don't hope for much."[21] Four days later, he completed his final examinations, whereupon he graduated with highest honors. On 10 July, rehearsals began for the premiere of the *Capriccio sinfonico*. After the second rehearsal, Puccini sent the following report to his mother:

> Today I had the second rehearsal. My composition will be successful; the performance probably will not be perfect, but (modesty aside) the material is very good. Dominiceti and Bazzini have paid me many compliments, and so has the orchestra. Ponchielli, my beloved teacher with a heart of gold, is really very happy. Tomorrow at two o'clock we have the public rehearsal and the performance is on the following day. Some people have already judged me as the best of all; perhaps the critics will rebuke them. I am completely broke. I send you a kiss. If you could wire me a little money—Thank you.[22]

The *Capriccio sinfonico* was first performed on 14 July 1883 by a largely student orchestra led by a guest conductor, the composer Franco Faccio (1840–91). Additional performances were given on 15 and 16 July. The following year, it was played in Turin (on 6 July and 26 October 1884), when Faccio included the work in concerts performed in conjunction with the Italian General Exposition. It was published that year in Milan by a firm owned by Francesco Lucca (later acquired by Ricordi), in a four-hand piano arrangement by G. Frugatta. The first edition was dedicated "To His Highness Prince Carlo Poniatowski."[23] Lasting about sixteen minutes, the *Capriccio sinfonico* begins with an *Andante moderato,* some of which was certainly influenced by Wagner. Puccini later reused parts of the introduction for the funeral procession in Act III of *Edgar,* and in Act I of *Le villi.* A sudden shift to *Allegro vivace* features

---

21. Marchetti, *Puccini com'era,* Letter 10.
22. Marchetti, *Puccini com'era,* Letter 16.
23. "A.S.A. Il Principe Carlo Poniatowski"; Plate No. 38150.

a brilliant motif played by the bassoons, celli, and contra-basses, which is quickly taken up by the entire orchestra. Those familiar with *La bohème* will recognize it as the theme of the orchestral introduction to the opera.

The development section of the *Capriccio sinfonico* includes several skillfully orchestrated interwoven melodies and waltzes. Puccini concludes the piece with some expressive music he composed for *Ad una morta!* and would later utilize in *Le villi* and in *Manon Lescaut.*

On 1 April 1883, Sonzogno's *Il Teatro Illustrato* announced its first competition for young unknown Italian composers to write a one-act opera (the prize was 2,000 lire). Eligible entries were to be submitted by 31 December 1883. During his final months at the Milan Conservatory, Puccini decided to enter the contest. Ponchielli introduced Puccini to Ferdinando Fontana and initiated their collaboration on *Le villi,* which was composed during the summer and fall of 1883 and submitted to the Sonzogno competition at the last possible moment (on 31 December). Although Puccini was well-known to the judges, he did not even receive an honorable mention when the results were announced.[24] This is all the more curious considering that three months earlier *Storiella d'amore* was featured as Puccini's first published composition in Sonzogno's weekly illustrated newspaper *La Musica Popolare;* and on 26 July 1883, the following review of the *Capriccio sinfonico* appeared in the same publication:

> In Puccini, more than a young student who has fulfilled his requirements for graduation, one admires a secure musician who displays his own identity and writes as though inspired by imagination, without showing allegiance to a contemporary idol.
>
> [Armando] Seppilli and Puccini are two young men for whom everything promises a fine career.

Of the Ghislanzoni poems Puccini set to music, the one entitled *Noi leggevamo un giorno per diletto* became his first published composition. This song was completed before 4 Octo-

---

24. The judges of the competition were Ponchielli, Cesare Dominiceti, Franco Faccio, and Amintore Galli.

ber 1883, for on that date, as noted above, it was included in the musical appendix to *La Musica Popolare* (as *Storiella d'amore*).[25] When Puccini became a protégé of Giulio Ricordi, the Casa Musicale Sonzogno did not publish any of Puccini's other works until *La rondine*.

The text of *Storiella d'amore* is an amusing setting of Dante's account of the illicit love between Paolo da Verrucchio and Francesca da Rimini, who fell in love while reading together from the French prose romance *Lancelot of the Lake*. In the music, Puccini displays many characteristics of his distinctive melodic style and harmonic language. The *Lento* theme at the words "Eco alla voce mia" (Echo to my voice) provided Puccini with material for the trio for soprano, tenor, and baritone in Act III of *Edgar*. The first phrase of *Storiella d'amore* foreshadows Mimì's "Sola mi fo il pranzo da me stessa, non vado sempre a messa" (Alone, I prepare dinner for myself; I don't always go to Mass) in Act I of *La bohème*.

*I*t is very likely that on 1 March 1888, Puccini composed the beautiful salon song *Sole e amore*. It was published for the first time in Genoa that year in the musical supplement to a magazine entitled *Paganini*.[26] Puccini, who always enjoyed writing verses and foolish doggerel for his friends, probably wrote the lyrics himself.[27]

> Il sole allegramente batte ai tuoi vetri;
> Amor pian pian batte al tuo cuore
> E l'uno e l'altro chiama.
>
> Il sole dice: "O dormente, mostrati che sei bella!"
> Dice l'amor: "Sorella, col tuo primo pensier
> Pensa a chi t'ama, pensa a chi t'ama! Pensa!
>   Al *Paganini,* G. Puccini

25. Ghislanzoni's name was omitted from Sonzogno's publication, but it appears on one of Puccini's autograph sketches for the song headed "Noi leggevamo insieme / parole di A. Ghislanzoni."
26. *Paganini* was issued for five seasons, from 1887 to 1892.
27. Puccini may have paraphrased some of the well-known sonnet "Mattinata," by Giosuè Carducci.

(The sun joyfully taps at your windows;
Love very softly taps at your heart,
And both of them are calling you.

The sun says: "Oh sleeper, show yourself
    for you are beautiful!"
Love says: "Sister, with your first thought,
Think of the one who loves you." Think!
                    To the *Paganini,* G. Puccini)

Originally, the last line of sung text was "Il 1° di marzo dell'ottanotto"; but in the first edition it was changed to the sung dedication "Al *Paganini,* G. Puccini." While he was composing *La bohème,* Puccini utilized *Sole e amore* as the basis of the famous quartet "Addio dolce svegliare alla mattina!" (Goodbye, sweet wakening in the morning!), which concludes the third act. He referred to *Sole e amore* as "questo germe primo di *Bohème*" (this first embryo of *Bohème*).

In the spring of 1888, Puccini began to consider his third opera, which was to be *Manon Lescaut.* The composition of it occupied him for almost five years, with significant revisions made thereafter. (As late as August 1922, he revised the work for a production at La Scala conducted by Arturo Toscanini.) From the first note to the last, in *Manon Lescaut* Puccini displays a genuinely inspired succession of youthful yet sophisticated melodies, some of which originated with self-borrowings of seemingly incongruous material. The source for the Act II madrigal was originally the Agnus Dei of the *Messa a 4 Voci.* Other parts of the opera were based on the string quartets *Crisantemi* and *Tre minuetti.*

On 30 March 1890, Ricordi's *Gazzetta Musicale di Milano* announced the publication of Puccini's elegy for string quartet composed that January, titled *Crisantemi* (Chrysanthemums). According to a letter written to his brother, Michele, on 6 February, Puccini composed *Crisantemi* in one night and dedicated it to the memory of Prince Amadeo di Savoia, Duca d'Aosta and King of Spain, who died on 18 January. It was performed with "great success" by the Campanari Quartet at the Milan Conservatory and in Brescia.[28]

The *Tre minuetti* for string quartet probably also date from 1890. They were all published by Pigna in Milan.[29] The first is dedicated to Vittoria Augusta di Borbone, Princess of Capua; the dedicatee of the second is the violinist Augusto Michelangeli; and the third is dedicated to Puccini's lifelong friend Carlo Carignani, who prepared the published versions of the piano reductions of Puccini's operas. Parts of the first minuet were used in *Manon Lescaut* in the scene of the presentation of gifts to Manon in Act II and in her pastoral air "L'ora, o Tirsi, è vaga e bella" (The hour, O Tirsus, is pleasant and beautiful). With a slight rhythmic variation, the initial theme of the second minuet was transformed into the *Allegro brillante* orchestral introduction to the same opera. A charming cadence from the third minuet was also used in Act II of *Manon Lescaut,* while some of the most poignant moments in Acts III and IV are based on themes from *Crisantemi.*

GRAND OPERA SENSATION . . .

Was Puccini's posthumous opera, *Turandot,* a plagiarism, copied note by note from an opera by two young women of Germany, who published the score of their work in Hamburg in 1896?

This amazing allegation, reported in the international press during the summer of 1928, apparently originated in Tel Aviv, and involved the sisters Frieda and Goldina Rubinsohn, who

28. See Eugenio Gara et al., eds., *Carteggi pucciniani* (Milan, 1958), Letter 36. The Ricordi edition of *Crisantemi* bears the plate number 54282 and the dedication "Alla memoria di Amedeo di Savoia, Duca d'Aosta."
29. Pigna plate numbers c. 1892: [No. 1:] 333; [No. 2:] 334; [No. 3:] 335. Minuets No. 1 and No. 3 were published by Heugel in 1898 as "Deux Menuets", and by Ricordi in 1902 as "Due Minuetti." Pigna also published the three minuets in a four-hand piano arrangement made by Guglielmo Andreoli (published separately with the plate numbers 506, 507, and 508, and together as 509). In 1898, Heugel published a solo piano arrangement of No. 1 (plate number 19370) and No. 3 (plate number 19380) by Alberto d'Erasmo. Andreoli's four-hand arrangement was announced in *Le Ménestrel* of 2 October 1898.

earned their living in Palestine teaching piano. When they examined a copy of Puccini's score, they claimed that Puccini's work was an exact transcription of their own opera.[30] According to the *Corriere della Sera*, the work of the Rubinsohn sisters was an *opera-ballo* in a prologue and three acts, with a libretto by Sophie Behrenz (based on Schiller, after Gozzi). In a report from Jerusalem published in Vienna's *Neue Freie Presse*, a correspondent recounted that in 1896, a certain Signorina Prevosti interpolated an aria from the Rubinsohns' *Turandot* in the lesson scene of the *Barber of Seville* whenever she sang the role of Rosina in German theaters!

Amusing though this may be, Ernest Newman placed things in a more realistic perspective for readers of *The Sunday Times* when he wrote that "the year 1896 was the period of Elgar's *Light of Life,* of Strauss's *Also sprach Zarathustra,* of Debussy's *L'après-midi d'un faune,* of Mascagni's *Guglielmo Ratcliff* and *Iris,* of Giordano's *Andrea Chénier,* of Puccini's *La bohème.* Stravinsky, in 1896, was a boy of fourteen; Ravel at that time had not even got as far as the *Pavane pour une infante défunte.* Yet in 1896 these two astounding young German ladies were handling with the utmost certainty and point a method of harmony of which no one else in Europe of that day had the slightest inkling, a method that called for some twenty years of intensive cultivation by dozens of gifted composers before Puccini." The idiom of Puccini's *Turandot* is the natural, logical completion of the idiom that was becoming richer and richer from *Manon Lescaut* to *La bohème,* to *Tosca,* to *Madama Butterfly,* to *La fanciulla del West,* to *La rondine* and the *Trittico.*

For Puccini, 1896 marked the premiere of *La bohème* at the Teatro Regio in Torino. By October of that year, melodies

---

30. The story originated in *Comœdia* (15 August 1928, a Parisian dramatic and literary daily newspaper. *The London Sunday News* confirmed the report and stated that the American consul in Jerusalem, Oscar M. Heiser, had called together "all of the musical people of Jerusalem, before whom the two pieces were played, and they were astounded to learn that they were identical. Mr. Heiser advised the Misses Rubinsohn to go to the United States (where *Turandot* was first produced [*sic*])." Lacking the funds to undertake such a long journey, the sisters forwarded a statement to the Committee of Intellectual Co-operation at Geneva, from which they received the advice to go to Italy and take the matter up with the heirs of the composer. In *The Sunday Times* of 26 August 1928, Ernest Newman informed his readers that nothing more had been heard of this strange story.

Puccini later developed in *Tosca* and *Madama Butterfly* were already stirring in his musical imagination. They are manifest in *Avanti "Urania"!*, a song for voice and piano to a text by Renato Fucini, composed on 4 October 1896, and in the *Inno a Diana*, written the following year.[31]

Puccini wrote *Avanti "Urania"!* for Marchese Carlo Benedetto Ginori-Lisci, a wealthy industrialist descended from the famous porcelain and ceramics artist Carlo Lorenzo Ginori. Marchese Ginori-Lisci shared Puccini's passion for music, hunting, and automobiles. He allowed the composer to use his private hunting estates and gave him the land at Torre del Lago for Villa Puccini, the composer's favorite home. As a token of his esteem for the Marquis and his family, Puccini made Ginori-Lisci the dedicatee of *La bohème* and his wife, Anna, the dedicatee of the first edition of *Avanti "Urania"!*

Avanti "Urania"! celebrated Ginori-Lisci's acquisition of the ex–*Queen Mary*, a Scottish-built 179-ton iron screw-steamer launched under the Italian flag as the *Urania*. The first phrase of the song hints at themes Puccini developed in *Tosca* (in Tosca's Act I aria "Non la sospiri la nostra casetta" (Don't you sigh for our little house) and the melody played by the first bassoon in Act III at the words "Tieni a mente . . . al primo colpo . . . giù . . ." [Remember . . . at the first shot . . . down . . .]) and in *Madama Butterfly* (for the music associated with Butterfly's entrance and the love duet). In *Avanti "Urania"!*, the melody at the words "si librano a guardar" and "mi guardano passar" is reminiscent of a phrase from the A–major *Preludio sinfonico*. The final exclamation "Forward *Urania!*" anticipates Butterfly's exaltation "ei torna e m'ama!" (He is coming back and he loves me!).

On 12 December 1897, Puccini composed a song for voice and piano in praise of Diana, the Roman goddess of light, forests, and the chase. He dedicated this song, *Inno a Diana*, with a

---

31. Renato Fucini (1843–1921) was one of Puccini's hunting companions. He sometimes wrote under the anagrammatic pseudonym of Neri Tanfuccio.

The first page of Puccini's autograph manuscript of Inno a Diana *includes frequent dynamic markings, tempo indications, and shorthand annotations showing changes that Puccini made to the structure of the composition. It was not unusual for the engravers at Ricordi to throw up their hands in dismay at the difficulties in deciphering Puccini's often hard-to-read musical calligraphy.* (The Pierpont Morgan Library, New York. KOCH 6)

text by Carlo Abeniacar,[32] to all Italian hunters and authorized its publication two years later in a magazine titled *Sant' Uberto* (their patron saint).

It begins in a spirited marchlike tempo, the theme of which resembles the enthusiastic opening measures of the Gloria of the *Messa a 4 Voci*. At the words "Tu li guida alle imprese più audaci" (Guide them to the most daring undertakings), the music anticipates the moment in Act I of *Tosca* where the diva sings to Cavaradosi of their "nido a noi sacro, ignoto al mondo inter, pien d'amore e di mister" (sacred nest, unknown to the whole world, full of love and mystery)—perhaps a musical allusion to one of the hunting retreats Puccini adored.

Between May and September 1899, a series of scientific conferences and social events were scheduled in conjunction with the Esposizione Elettrica, Serica e Artistica, and the World Congress of Telegraphers held in Como, Italy. For this occasion, which also marked the centenary of Alessandro Volta's invention of the battery, Puccini supplied a *marcetta brillante* for piano entitled *Scossa elettrica* (Electric shock). The exposition featured productions of *Otello, Cavalleria rusticana,* and the ballet *Excelsior* (music by Romualdo Marenco), and Como's Teatro Sociale was completely renovated and illuminated with electricity.

Scossa elettrica was engraved by Ricordi and published in a special *numero unico* in homage to Alessandro Volta, entitled *I Telegrafisti a Volta*. A notice on the first page of music indicates that the music is the property of the committee of telegraphers that organized the events honoring Volta ("proprietà del Comitato dei Telegrafisti per le onoranze a volta").[33] The manuscript is signed, but not dated. At the Como Exposition it was probably performed in an arrangement for concert band.[34]

---

32. Carlo Abeniacar was an aficionado of hunting, a humorist, author, poet, painter, sculptor, and photojournalist.
33. Como: Tipografia Pietro Cairoli, 1899. The work was reprinted in March 1927 with the same notice in *Voltiana* 2/6, "pubblicazione a cura dell'Ufficio Stampa del Comitato Voltiano con sede in Como," which was then headed by Guglielmo Marconi.
34. The extant manuscript, in the collection of Richard Macnutt, Tunbridge Wells, is only for piano.

In 1899, Puccini also composed the lullaby for voice and piano entitled *E l'uccellino*. He wrote it at Torre del Lago, and Ricordi published it that year. The first edition bears the dedication "Al bimbino Memmo Lippi," the infant son of one of Puccini's closest Lucca friends, Dr. Guglielmo Lippi, who died of a typhus infection a few days after his marriage to the Countess Nelda Prosperi. Their baby, born in 1898, was nicknamed Memmo. (Also known as Memmino, he later adopted his stepfather's name of Francesconi and became the director of a mental institution in Lucca. In 1944, he was deported and killed by the Nazis.) The text of *E l'uccellino* is by Renato Fucini. *E l'uccellino* has proved to be a popular song that is often heard in recitals and on recordings.

On 3 October 1902, Puccini finished composing an impressionistic vignette for voice and piano entitled *Terra e mare,* which he contributed to Edoardo de Fonseca's "Albo Annuale d'Arti e Lettere" (Annual Album of Arts and Letters), *Novissima*.[35] It is a setting of a poem of the same name by Enrico Panzacchi, a leading Bolognese critic and ardent Wagnerian. The autograph manuscript of *Terra e mare* is signed and dated "Torre del Lago / 3 October 1902"; the text is the sixteenth entry in section fifteen of Panzacchi's *Ultime rime*.

On 15 April 1903, Puccini signed a contract to provide Alfred Michaelis, the head of the Gramophone Company (Italy), with "a song for one voice for exclusive reproduction on the Gramophone or other talking machines." For this commission Puccini received one thousand discs of his choice. The song was due within two months, but it was not ready until 1904. With great reluctance, Puccini wrote *Canto d'anime,* for voice and piano, to a text by Luigi Illica.[36] The sheet music was published late in 1904 by the Gramophone Company. Puccini hoped it would be recorded by Enrico Caruso, but it

35. Founded in 1901, *Novissima* featured artwork, poetry, writings, polychromes, and music from the brushes and pens of "Italy's most original contemporary artists, composers and leading literary figures." The theme of *Novissima* 1902 was the sea. Edoardo de Fonseca was a journalist, art critic, author, and playwright.
36. Luigi Illica (1857–1919) was a poet, journalist, author, and dramatist who began his career writing under the pseudonym of Luigi della Scorziana. His flair for polemics cost him part of his left ear in a duel. In addition to the libretti of *La bohème* (1896), *Tosca* (1900), and *Madama Butterfly* (1904), all written in collaboration with Giuseppe Giacosa, Illica supplied the texts for over thirty operas.

was first recorded in 1907 on the Gramophone and Type-writer label by the dramatic soprano Ida Giacomelli.

In *Canto d'anime*, the music at the words "Nelle notti del cuore un ideale" is particularly evocative of portions of *Madama Butterfly*. Listening to *Canto d'anime*, one is reminded of the patriotic energy of *Columbia, Gem of the Ocean*. It could easily be considered a prototype for Rinuccio's "Firenze è come un albero fiorito" (Florence is like a tree in blossom) in *Gianni Schicchi* (1918).

Early in January of 1905, Puccini planned to travel to Cairo to supervise the first performances of *Madama Butterfly* given in Africa, but the illness of one of the principal singers caused the journey to be canceled. Instead, he became involved in a project commemorating the fourth anniversary of the death of Giuseppe Verdi by composing a very brief *Requiem*—sixty-seven measures in all—for three-part chorus, solo viola, and organ (or harmonium). The manuscript of the *Requiem* in memory of Verdi is dated 19 January 1905.[37] It was first performed on 27 January by musicians from La Scala for a small audience in the chapel of the Casa di Riposo where Giuseppe and Giuseppina Verdi are entombed.

By this time, Puccini had achieved the status of an international celebrity. He traveled everywhere he could to supervise productions of his operas. Shortly after his arrival in New York in January 1907, where the Metropolitan Opera was about to present a series of performances of his most successful works, he told reporters:

> I try to follow out my own feelings. My temperament is essentially dramatic. I don't believe I could write anything but operas. I love the dramatic—the theatric, even. It is what I can do my best work with. I could not write music for the concert hall. I don't understand that sort of thing. The real modern Italians express themselves. They couldn't follow out their ideas in elaborate polyphony, for that is not the way they think. They are

---

37. Manuscripts of the *Requiem* are preserved in the Ricordi archives and at the Museo Teatrale of the Teatro alla Scala. It has been recorded by the Cappella Musicale S. Cecilia, with Elisa Ardinghi (viola) and Marco Tomei (organ) in the series entitled "I Puccini, Musicisti di Lucca" (Edizioni Bongiovanni GB 2037-2).

emotional. . . . If subjects don't suit me, or I can't get what I want out of them, I lay them aside.[38]

In the fall of 1908, Puccini was attempting to sell the house he owned in Abetone. On 29 November, he composed the brief song *Casa mia, casa mia* at the request of Edoardo de Fonseca, who was then publishing a magazine entitled *La Casa*. On 16 December, an article about Puccini's residences at Torre del Lago, Chiatri, and Abetone was published in Rome in *La Casa*, along with a facsimile of the manuscript of *Casa mia, casa mia*. The text of this very brief song is based on that of *Home, Sweet Home:*

> Casa mia, casa mia
> Per piccina che tu sia,
> Tu mi sembri una badia,
>
> Casa mia, casa mia
> Per piccina che tu sia,
> Tu mi sembri una badia,
> Casa mia, casa mia, casa mia.[39]
>
> (My home, my home
> However small you may be,
> You seem like an abbey to me.)

In exchange for *Casa mia, casa mia,* de Fonseca offered to find a buyer for Puccini's house in the hills of Abetone.

Near the end of Puccini's career, he and his librettist Giuseppe Adami contributed a song for voice and piano entitled *Morire?* to an album of music dedicated to Queen Elena di Savoia, sold to benefit the wartime relief efforts of the Italian Red Cross. This album was designated simply "Per la Croce Rossa Italiana" (published without any date, but certainly ca. 1917–18).[40] Puccini used *Morire?* transposed one half tone lower, with a new text and an altered ending for the accom-

---

38. Quoted in English (probably a translation) in "Puccini Suggests an American Opera," *Musical America* (26 January 1907).
39. In Italian, the text is a variation of the saying "Casa mia, casa mia, benche piccola tu sia, tu mi pari una badia."
40. The album also included compositions by Boito, Franchetti, Giordano, Leoncavallo, Mascagni, and Zandonai.

paniment, in the second version of *La rondine* (first performed in Palermo and Vienna in 1920).[41] In its operatic form, the music of *Morire?* serves as an entrance aria for Ruggero, but Puccini deleted this *romanza* from the third version of the score (which has yet to be performed). *Morire?* is one of Puccini's most haunting compositions, in which occasional ambiguous harmonies underscore the enigmatic text.

In April 1918, the municipal authorities of Rome commissioned Fausto Salvatori to write an ode commemorating the Italian victories in the final months of World War I.[42] Puccini was invited to set the hymn to music. The first performance was scheduled for 21 April 1919, during the anniversary celebrations of the birth of the Eternal City. On 24 March 1919, Puccini wrote to Guido Vandini, "It's crazy of me to write the *Inno a Roma*"; but four days later it was finished. Puccini called it "una bella porcheria" (a real piece of trash), but he was optimistic that it would become popular. He sent a presentation copy of the manuscript to the mayor of Rome and one another to Alessandro Vessella, who scored it for his famous concert band.

The premiere of the *Inno a Roma* was to have taken place at Villa Umberto at 5:30 P.M. on 21 April, with four thousand performers—including five hundred soldiers, the nursery school teachers, the students of the *scuole normali,* the children of grades four through six, the chorus of the Costanzi Theater, Vessella's band and all the military musicians of Rome, along with the brass band of the Royal Carabinieri. Fearing that without large forces the hymn would not turn out well, Puccini objected

41. Giuseppe Adami (1878–1946) was a drama critic and playwright. In 1912, he attempted to develop a libretto for Puccini entitled *Anima allegra*. Puccini declined to use it, but invited him to collaborate on the Italian libretto of *La rondine* (composed in the period 1914–17 and revised from 1918 to 1922). Adami was also the librettist of Puccini's *Il tabarro* (composed 1915–16, but not performed until 1918) and *Turandot* (in collaboration with Renato Simoni, composed 1920–24, performed posthumously in 1926). Adami wrote many other libretti for operas, operettas, and ballets; he also wrote and produced films. After Puccini's death, Adami edited an important collection of Puccini's correspondence and became one of his first biographers.

42. Fausto Salvatori (1870–1929) was a Roman author, poet, librettist, and playwright. He also wrote for films and made an adaptation of Shakespeare's *A Midsummer Night's Dream*.

to the idea of also singing the hymn later that evening at the Costanzi Theater before a gala performance of *Aida*.

On the afternoon of the premiere, all of the orchestras of the Roman theaters went on strike, and *Aida* was canceled. By five o'clock a huge crowd and dignitaries had gathered in the Piazza di Siena. Just as the first notes of the hymn were played, a storm dispersed the crowd, estimated to be in the tens of thousands. The rain persisted and the performance was suspended. The first performance of the *Inno a Roma* was rescheduled for 1 June 1919 at the National Stadium during the Royal Gymnastic Competition, where it was greeted with approbation. In 1923, the *Inno a Roma* was published by the Casa Musicale Sonzogno and dedicated to Princess Jolanda di Savoia. When the fascists took power, Puccini's hymn acquired an unwarranted identification with Mussolini.[43]

$\mathcal{T}$he authorship of several of Puccini's nonoperatic works has been either misattributed to another composer or inaccurately catalogued in lists of Puccini's works. In addition, the manuscripts of a few of his compositions are now deemed missing. Specifically (in chronological order): in 1877, Puccini composed a hymn for chorus entitled *I figli d'Italia bella* for a contest for native composers sponsored by the municipality of Lucca. The manuscript is missing and is presumed to be lost; the text, by an unknown poet, begins: "Dei tuoi figli, Italia bella, uno il volto e uno il core."

In 1879, the Banda Comunale Lucchese (Lucca Civic Concert Band), directed by Enrico Toschi, performed an unidentified waltz by Puccini.

The manuscript of a *romanza* titled *Melanconia* (sometimes catalogued as *Melancholia* or *Malinconia*), dated 19 June 1881 and thought to be preserved at the Milan Conservatory, is

---

43. After Mussolini's regime, the *Inno a Roma* was remembered by some as the *Inno al Duce*. It is catalogued as such in several American discographies. Recordings of the *Inno a Roma* were made by baritones Apollo Granforte (1929) and Josef Hermann (in German, 1941), tenor Beniamino Gigli (1937), a children's chorus, the Italian Marine Band, and the chorus and orchestra of La Scala.

missing. The text is by Ghislanzoni; it begins: "Allor ch'io
sarò morto." The song title *Spirto gentil,* included in some lists
of Puccini's works, is actually part of the first line of *Ad una
morta.* I have been unable to locate the manuscript of a *romanza*
for tenor and piano entitled *Ah! se potesse,* which, according
to Mario Morini, was composed on 15 July 1882.

Shortly after he wrote *Sole e amore,* Puccini composed a set
of vocal exercises, or *Solfeggi.* According to Karl Gustav Fellerer, the manuscript of these pedagogical pieces is dated 20
March 1888. The manuscript is presumed to be lost.[44]

It has been conjectured by many of Puccini's biographers
that the composer supplied a *Movimento di valzer* for the
launching of an Italian battleship at Sestri Ponente in Genoa,
and that he reputedly transformed the piece into Musetta's
waltz. It has also been asserted that a work for chorus and
orchestra entitled *Cantata a Giove* (1897?) served as the source
for the offstage cantata in Act II of *Tosca.*

The song *Ditele,* often attributed to Puccini, was actually
composed by the Russian Princess Yelizaveta Vasilevna
Kochubei. There is also some doubt concerning the authentic-
ity of two piano compositions attributed to Puccini: *Piccolo
tango* and *Foglio d'album,* published in New York City in 1942
by Edward B. Marks.[45] Several commentators have suggested that Puccini wrote these pieces in America during one
of his visits to the Metropolitan Opera.

And finally, it is possible that Puccini presented the manu-
script of a song for voice and piano to the dramatic soprano
Rosa Ponselle when she visited him at his villa in Torre del
Lago.

44. See Karl Gustav Fellerer, "Unbekannter Puccini," in the *Allgemeine Musikzeitung,*
    1937.
45. Plate numbers 11781 and 11782, respectively. Both of these compositions have been
    recorded by Tan Crone in "Puccini Songs and Other Pieces" on the Etcetera label
    (XCT 1050).

Early Puccini Performance: A Condition of Transition

David   Hamilton

David Hamilton edited *The Metropolitan Opera Encyclopedia* (1987) and is the author of *The Listener's Guide to Great Instrumentalists* (1982). He has written music criticism for *The Nation, Opera Quarterly, Opus, Opera News, High Fidelity, The New Yorker,* and *The New York Times.* A member of the board of New World Records, he has produced numerous historic vocal recordings.

In the history of operatic performance, as of operatic composition, Puccini sits astride a secular shift. Subject matter founded in the passions and politics of highborn personages was giving way to a more naturalistic theater of "ordinary" people, and, at the same time, the musical center of gravity was moving away from the voice, as the orchestra came to share equally in presenting the musical discourse rather than primarily underpinning it. For singers, larger orchestras and more complex textures demanded more carrying power; less symmetrical musical structures made memorization more difficult, rehearsal more necessary; and the new subject matter was less amenable to formal, stylized stage deportment, more dependent on naturalism, personal intensity, and charm.

Inevitably, many singers who took part in Puccini premieres and early performances had been trained for pre-veristic opera; their teachers had specialized in Donizetti and Verdi, and so had they. Some proved adaptable to the new style, others did not. In an era when appearing in successful new operas was the surest way to fame, young singers concentrated on acquiring the skills that would make them effective in the latest works. Thus the popularity of the operas of Mascagni, Leoncavallo, Puccini, Giordano, Zandonai, and the like soon stimulated a generation of singers trained to meet their demands—singers who, when they dealt with earlier repertory, often did so less well than—or at least quite differently from—their predecessors. The coincidence between Puccini's rise and the early stages of serious operatic recording has bequeathed us copious evidence of this transformation, compensating for the surprising dearth of discs by the actual "creators" of his works. Many of the singers involved in Puccini premieres were active recording artists, yet from the original casts of *Manon Lescaut, La bohème,* and *Tosca,* only Cesira Ferrani (Manon and Mimì) set down music from these works in the studio. Later, when recording was widespread, no "creators' records" were made from *La fanciulla del West*[1] or *La rondine,* and only Florence Easton's "O mio babbino caro" survives to recall the premiere of *Il trittico* (perversely, Claudia

---

1. Since the principals of its premiere at the Met (Destinn, Caruso, and Amato) were all under contract to Victor, the lack of recordings from *Fanciulla* has long been puzzling. Robert Tuggle calls attention to a notice in the 17 December 1910 issue of *Musical America* that may provide an explanation: "Tito Ricordi . . . has refused to permit American talking-machine companies or music roll houses to reproduce mechanically any of the music of *The Girl of the Golden West.* Selections from *Tosca, Bohème,* and *Madame Butterfly* have a large sale in player-piano rolls and talking-machine records. Some of the interest being taken in *The Girl* by the public is shown by the fact that out of 1,000 scores sent to this country, not one was unsold at the end of the first week." Tuggle suggests that Ricordi feared recordings might undermine the sale of printed music. (Quoted in Robert Tuggle, *The Golden Age of Opera* [New York, 1983], 71.) Music from *Fanciulla* was recorded in Europe as early as 1911, but the first American recording appears to have been Edward Johnson's 1920 Victor of "Ch'ella mi creda."

Muzio, Giorgetta on that occasion, recorded only music from the two operas she *didn't* sing!).

A traditional exercise would be to scrutinize the recordings of Ferrani and other "Puccini creators" to discover what in their singing attracted the composer—traditional but frustrating, given the sparseness of the evidence and the central fact that theatrical personality, obviously so significant to Puccini, is not necessarily well transmitted by records. Consider Rosina Storchio, the first Butterfly, of whose records (none of them devoted to Puccini) Michael Scott notes that "she was only in her early thirties, but the voice, especially in the middle register, is already threadbare. Her remarkable personality made such an effect in the theater, but little of it gets through to the records."[2] Or Maria Jeritza, another favorite, whom Puccini described to Sybil Seligman as "one of the most original artists I have ever known."[3] On records, her singing is healthy enough, but lacks color and nuance; in the theater, it was obviously "nuanced" by her glamour and personal presence and dramatic imagination.

As an alternative, this essay considers two discrete groups of recorded material for the information, both direct and indirect, they yield to the historian, especially about the transitional aspects of early Puccini performance. The first is the unique set of recordings from *Tosca* made during performances at the Metropolitan Opera in 1902 and 1903; the second, a selection of early versions of "Che gelida manina" preserving features of interpretation that subsequently died out.

The Met *Tosca* recordings—the only known live-performance recordings of Puccini's operas from the composer's lifetime—were made on wax cylinders by Lionel Mapleson, the Met's librarian, during the opera's second and third seasons at that theater.[4] The seven surviving recordings (see Table

---

2. Michael Scott, *The Record of Singing to 1914* (London, 1977), 153.
3. Quoted in Mosco Carner, *Puccini: A Critical Biography* (New York, 1968), 189n.
4. Mapleson apparently recorded part of the second-act finale of *La Bohème* on 13 February 1903 (the cast included Marcella Sembrich, Fritzi Scheff, Carlo Dani, Giuseppe Campanari, Charles Gilibert, and Marcel Journet, with Luigi Mancinelli on the podium) on a cylinder that has evidently not survived. In 1985, the entire extant *corpus* of Mapleson recordings was reissued in a ten-LP set (R&H-100) by the Rodgers and

1) total about fourteen minutes; the two selections from 1902 are duplicated among the cylinders from 3 January 1903. Fragmentary, dim, and distorted, they demand close, patient listening (headphones give clearer results than speakers), but the evidence they contain of tempos and other performance practices is uniquely unmediated by the assorted temporal, spatial, instrumental, and psychological constraints imposed on contemporary studio recordings.

They are also about as close as we can get to the opera's early performances under the composer's aegis. Hariclea Darclée, Tosca of the Rome and La Scala premieres, recorded "Vissi d'arte" for Fonotipia in 1905, but the record was never published (all that survives of her are a few Romanian folk songs made in the late 1920s), while none of Scarpia's music was included among the fairly numerous recordings of Eugenio Giraldoni, Scarpia on those same occasions. The voice of their colleague in Rome, Emilio de Marchi, is known only from these and other Mapleson cylinders. Luigi Mancinelli led *Tosca*'s London premiere (12 July 1900), which Puccini attended. Antonio Scotti, the Met Scarpia, was also a veteran of that London performance, in which his colleagues were Milka Ternina (another singer audible—though barely—only on Maplesons) and Fernando de Lucia. Puccini would hear Emma Eames as Tosca, teamed with de Marchi and Scotti, in Paris in the fall of 1904.[5]

The principals of the Met *Toscas,* born between 1861 and 1866, were all trained for pre-veristic opera and had indeed all embarked on their careers by 1890, when *Cavalleria rusticana* exploded onto the stage. Ternina (1863–1941) had a Central European background: born in Croatia, trained in Zagreb and Vienna, dramatic soprano of the Munich Court Opera during the 1890s. Aside from Tosca and single stabs at Santuzza and Valentine (*Huguenots*), her Met roles were German, predom-

---

Hammerstein Archives of Recorded Sound in the New York Public Library at Lincoln Center, which now houses nearly all of them; the *Tosca* recordings will be found on Side 7 of this set. Previous editions of most of them—less well engineered, less well documented—had appeared from the International Record Collectors' Club on 78-rpm records (catalogue numbers 179, 216, 3057) and LPs (L-7004, L-7032), and on other LPs, including Herrold H-5000 and Unique Opera Records UORC-323.

5. Eugenio Gara et al., eds., *Carteggi pucciniani* (Milan: 1958), 284.

inantly the Wagnerian heroines. Eames (1865–1952), an American born in Shanghai, studied in Paris with Mathilde Marchesi and made her debuts at the Opéra (1889) and the Met (1891) as Gounod's Juliette, at Covent Garden (1891) as his Marguerite. In New York she eventually added Italian spinto roles (the *Trovatore* Leonora, Aida, Santuzza) and the Wagnerian *jugendlich-dramatisch* category (Elsa, Sieglinde, Eva) to her French parts.

The careers of the two Italians, de Marchi (1861–1917) and Scotti (1866–1936), ran similar courses en route to the Met: After singing classic Donizetti and Verdi roles on the Italo-Hispanic circuit, they both took part in the Italian premiere of

Table 1.   THE MAPLESON *TOSCA* RECORDINGS

3 January, 1 February, or 17 February 1902

1) Act I, *Te Deum:* "[con] spasimo d'amor" . . . to end of act
Antonio Scotti, Metropolitan Opera Chorus and Orchestra, conducted by Philippe Flon

1 February 1902

2) Act III, Finale: "Come è bello mio Mario!" . . . "Colla mia!"
Milka Ternina, Jacques Bars (Spoletta), Lodovico Viviani (Sciarrone), Metropolitan Opera Chorus and Orchestra, Philippe Flon

3 January 1903

3) Act I, *Te Deum:* "[prezio]sa. Ah! di quegli occhi" . . . to end of act
Antonio Scotti, Metropolitan Opera Chorus and Orchestra, conducted by Luigi Mancinelli

4) Act II, Torture Scene: "Ah! mostro, lo strazi" . . . "Ma fatelo tacere!"; "[Nel pozzo] nel giardino" . . . "Basta, Roberti!"
Emma Eames, Emilio de Marchi, Antonio Scotti, Metropolitan Opera Orchestra, Luigi Mancinelli

5) Act II: "Vittoria! Vittoria!" . . . "Volete che cerchiamo insieme il mo[do di salvarlo?]"
Emma Eames, Emilio de Marchi, Antonio Scotti, Metropolitan Opera Orchestra, Luigi Mancinelli

6) Act II, Tosca's Prayer: "[Sem]pre con fè sincera" . . . to end of aria
Emma Eames, Metropolitan Opera Orchestra, Luigi Mancinelli

7) Act III, Finale: "Come è bello mio Mario!" . . . to end of opera
Emma Eames, Jacques Bars (Spoletta), Bernard Bégné (Sciarrone), Metropolitan Opera Chorus and Orchestra, Luigi Mancinelli

Wagner's *Die Meistersinger* (La Scala, 1898, under Toscanini). De Marchi's Met roles included Turiddu, Canio, and Rodolfo as well as Verdi parts; he remained only two seasons and was succeeded by Caruso. Scotti chose to concentrate his career after the turn of the century at Covent Garden and the Met, where he dominated the role of Scarpia to a degree unmatched by any other principal singer in any role there: Of the company's first 233 performances of *Tosca* (from 1901 to 1931), Scotti sang all but 16. Though the bloom of his voice faded (he made no recordings after 1912), his histrionic skills evidently carried him for years as Falstaff, several Puccini characters (Lescaut, Marcello, and Sharpless as well as Scarpia), and Chim-Fen, the villain of Leoni's *L'Oracolo,* a role tailored for him.

In his only studio recording from *Tosca* ("Già mi dicon venal," a passage not included in Mapleson's recordings; Victor 88122, 1908), Scotti sings firmly and rather plainly, concentrating on vocal poise and tonal solidity, with surprisingly little verbal inflection; though the tempo is not slow, the effect

The international popularity of Puccini's music was, to some extent, linked with the diffusion of the gramophone. Caruso, who began his recording career in 1902 and continued to make records almost until the time of his death, in 1922, made many Puccini recordings. Among his best selling disks were the two arias from Tosca, *which he recorded several times. (Courtesy of Michael Sisca, World Copyright)*

is stodgy, far from erotic.[6] Juxtaposing this with the cylinders underlines how misleading studio recordings can be, for the Scarpia of the performance is anything but stodgy. In the torture scene he frequently shouts lines: "Mai Tosca alla scena più tragica fu!" is certainly delivered "con entusiasmo," but quite freely; at "Aprite le porte che n'oda i lamenti!" the injunction "gridando, quasi senza intonazione" is taken literally; "Ma fatelo tacere!" is indeed a "grida terribile."

Yet in the page or so after "La povera mia cena fu interrotta," before the cylinder breaks off, we hear the elegant bel canto stylist, with mellow tone, suave legato, and a sweet head note on E ("*Via,* mia bella signora") to underline his trenchant irony. Earlier, in the *Te Deum* cylinders, Scotti produces the poised tone of the studio recording, but is propelled by an urgency totally lacking there. (The 1903 *Te Deum* begins just before "Ah! di quegli occhi vittoriosi," and though Scotti doesn't carry the previous phrase through as notated, he sings the new phrase *piano,* as does neither Amato nor—more surprisingly—Battistini in their studio recordings.) Unlike Giraldoni, five years younger, who abandoned whatever he had learned of the old singing style, Scotti incorporated it into his verismo characterizations, at the same time exploring new modes in which to express his theatrical instincts.

About de Marchi we learn less. His offstage role in the torture scene is pretty well limited to screams of anguish; "Vi sfida" rings out clearly. Unexpectedly, each cry of "Vittoria!" is sung on a single pitch, instead of starting with the written lower upbeat. That aside, the phrase is delivered as excitingly as it ever has been. (Throughout these recordings, in accordance with a longtime, widespread convention, vocal entries such as this, notated to overlap the end of an orchestral buildup, are sung after the orchestra has finished; modern performances sometimes follow the notation literally.) In the subsequent trio (taken by Mancinelli closer to quarter note = 160

6. Scotti makes a transposition during the selection, dropping a semitone at "debbo" in the phrase "Se la giurata fede debbo tradir." According to William Ashbrook, this transposition was authorized by Puccini: see *The Operas of Puccini* (Ithaca, N.Y., 1985), 89, fn. 54.

than Puccini's 144), de Marchi sings with fire if not always precise pitch and manages to keep together with the orchestra, with which he shares the "tune." His colleagues aren't so lucky: Eames inserts her "pietà! taci!" randomly, and Scotti loses his place completely towards the end, carrying on *parlando* through the subsequent chromatic scales in octaves.

Famously aloof and reserved, Eames was evidently a personality, as well as a singer, of the "old school," yet these cylinders bring us a passionate and convincing Tosca. The tone is straight and white compared to what her successors would cultivate and without the distinct chest register that became a trademark of many later Toscas. There is little evidence of difficulty at the top of the voice that contemporaries reported as a consequence of her undertaking the role. The top notes in the torture scene (after rehearsal number 36: "Ah! Più non posso . . .") have impact, and in the parallel passage after the "Vittoria" trio (rehearsal number 44), she even fills in the high B flat that Puccini didn't write between C and A flat (conceivably, he thought the soprano could use a rest!). Amidst all of Scotti's hurly-burly, she holds her own, and the tension between her unfailingly chaste, aristocratic tone and the surrounding violence is dramatically telling. (Of course, in 1903, the violence was the novel element in the situation; to us listening today, the purity of her sound is unexpected.)

The "Vissi d'arte" excerpt is equally effective, though Eames reveals a tendency to "swim" around the beat that seems unintentional, particularly in the triplets at "Nell'ora dell dolore . . ." Puccini marked the beginning of the aria "Andante lento appassionato" (quarter note = 40), and an "a tempo" in the orchestral score at "Sempre con fe sincera" (rehearsal number 52) appears to confirm a single tempo for the whole piece. But the aria is invariably—and plausibly—performed with two tempos: a slow beginning (often even slower than 40, as in Eames's 1908 studio recording with orchestra [Victor 88010] or, more recently, the Callas/de Sabata complete set), and something rather faster beginning with "Sempre con fe sincera." In the 1903 recording this latter tempo moves at around 58 (it's still faster in the studio version) and—again like most performances—slows down for precisely the phrase Puccini marks "con anima" ("diedi fiori agl'altar").

Direct comparison of Eames in the final scene with the Met's other non-Italian Tosca might be illuminating, but Ternina's Mapleson cylinders (there are also a couple from *Tristan* with Jean de Reszke) are largely undecipherable. In the *Tosca* finale, her *quasi-parlando* mutterings after the firing squad's volley are inaudible; she rises above the surface noise with a vivid scream as she discovers Mario dead but thereafter is covered again, only emerging into the clear to deliver "Finire così? finire così!" very much *a piacere,* with tearful emphasis. The recording breaks off as she is about to launch "O Scarpia, avanti a Dio!" This is frustrating, given Puccini's high opinion of Ternina's Tosca; as he wrote to Angelo Eisner in February 1901 after hearing reports of her New York creation of the role: "Tosca is an opera that requires an ultradramatic woman . . . Ternina in London in August and now in New York has made it a true creation! That is a Tosca!"[7]

In the 1903 recording of this scene, Eames is more audible, and her mutterings are clearly on pitch, more sung than spoken. She launches "Presto, su!" before the orchestra has reached the fermata of the preceding measure; again she expresses clear pitches and adjusts easily after having moved up the chord to C too soon. Thereafter she falls behind the orchestra and, like Ternina (and many sopranos since, though not Callas under de Sabata), sings all of "Finire così? finire così!" during the orchestra's rest. More curiously, when Spoletta is quite late with his "Tosca, pagherai ben cara la sua vita" in both recordings of the finale, both conductors, instead of holding the D-major chord until he finishes, plunge forward in strict time through the trumpet riffs ascending in thirds, reaching the climactic pause before Tosca has had a chance to reply ("Colla mia!"), after which she still has to sing her final line.

"Vissi d'arte" aside, tempos in the Mapleson *Tosca* recordings are generally very close to Puccini's metronome mark-

7. "*Tosca* è un opera che richiede una donna ultra drammatica . . . La Ternina in agosto a Londra e adesso a New York ne la fatto una vera creazione! Quella è una Tosca! . . ." *Carteggi pucciniani,* 205–206.

ings; Flon takes the final bars of Act I and the firing-squad march in Act III a bit faster than Mancinelli. Less comfortable to modern ears is imprecise ensemble; in the 1903 *Te Deum,* the imposing "cannon" reports aren't always on the beat, and neither is Scotti. In an age when pianists routinely played the left hand before the right, people simply didn't expect perfect unanimity; "together" was a fuzzier concept than it would become later in the twentieth century. (A principal impetus for the sharpening, I believe, was the increasing prevalence of texturally complex and, later, metrically irregular music, which is harder for listeners to construe if played imprecisely—or, in the case of irregular meters, if played with too flexible tempos. Thus Strauss, Stravinsky, and Bartók—as Beethoven, Wagner, and Verdi before them—have affected the performance of the music of their predecessors.)

Obviously, early studio recordings also have things to tell us about performance practices—and not merely the recordings of the most famous or "best" singers. For evidence of "common practice" the work of second-string performers can be more informative than the occasionally quirky usages of imaginative or innovative individualists. For example, in his 1917 recording of "Che gelida manina," Fernando De Lucia (1860–1925), a celebrated mannerist, adds a lavish measure of graces to the score, while not singing all those Puccini has notated. That this was no mere whim of a perverse throwback is demonstrated by a random selection of De Lucia's younger colleagues great and small, born from 1865 to 1880 (and listed in order of birth year): Edoardo Garbin, Romeo Berti, Florencio Constantino, Alessandro Bonci, Enrico Caruso, Amedeo Bassi, Elvino Ventura, Giovanni Zenatello, Giuseppe Anselmi, Giorgio Malesci, and Aristodemo Giorgini.

None of them is as extravagant as De Lucia (who alters the melodic line of his opening phrase to move with the orchestral melody), but all of them (and, for that matter, the even younger John McCormack in his Odeon recording) add—and often also subtract—appoggiaturas and mordents along the way. The sparest in this aria is the oldest, Garbin, creator of Fenton in *Falstaff* and subsequently very active in the verismo/Puccini repertory; however, other records show him pursuing such elegances in more unlikely places, such as the Brindisi from *Cavalleria*. For that matter, these early tenors have not yet reached a consensus that Puccini's suggested alternative is the only way to sing a high C (whether real or transposed); some try fitting in all of the original phrase "la *dolce* speran*za*," while poor McCormack, perhaps improvising an underlay in the studio, miscalculates and ends up with "speranza" on the downbeat.

The above suggests that this generation of singers still regarded such inflections as an interpretive resource, for both expressive and musical purposes; not a violation of the score's integrity, they were, rather, extensions of less notationally specific means of nuance and emphasis, such as dynamic and verbal accenting, phrasing, and tone color and rhythm. In other words, these recordings suggest that the border between interpretation and license was once much fuzzier, less exclusively tied to notation than it has become. Certainly, this inflectional tradition died out: Surveying subsequent generations, we find Giovanni Martinelli (recorded in 1913), Beniamino Gigli (1931), Jussi Bjoerling (1936), Richard Tucker (1947), Luciano Pavarotti (1972), and Placido Domingo (1973) singing only the ornaments notated in the score (and all of them). There's one exception: The mordent in the climactic phrase ("la spe*ranza*"), familiar from Caruso's recording, remains common; Bjoerling, Tucker, and Domingo employ it, Gigli and Pavarotti give at least a little push there, while only Martinelli hits the note squeaky clean.

It is also clear from this latter comparison that, along with such minor alterations in the vocal line's pitches, much else has disappeared from Puccini singing since the works were new; many of the less notationally rigorous means of nuance and emphasis are no longer considered desirable, even acceptable—and, indeed, some of them inevitably strike modern listeners, accustomed to reasonably steady tempos, as totally disruptive. (Performers cannot ignore audience expectations; what was "transparent" to one generation can become irritating to another—and, conceivably, may become transparent again.) But the modern performances certainly sound bland, even impersonal, after listening to the early ones.

The evidence gleaned from these recordings tends to confirm what other research suggests, that such practice was the norm in the pre-verismo repertory and for a time was carried over into the new style. While increasing textual absolutism and conductorial authority played a role in its demise, so, too, did the changes in vocal technique engendered by the new musical style: voices became fatter and less flexible, technique concentrated on power rather than nuance. Living when he did, Puccini was able to enjoy the virtues of the old school as well as the potential of the new. Surely, like most of us, he always had in his ears the kind of singing he grew up with, the style of the teachers of his prime interpreters-to-be. Did he imagine that its virtues would eventually vanish so completely? Very possibly, he assumed they would live on, side by side with the technique and talent necessary to express fully his novel contributions. It certainly didn't work out that way.

PUCCINI:
A BIBLIOGRAPHICAL
SKETCH

Nigel Jamieson

Nigel Jamieson was born in Scotland and educated at Glasgow University. He has lived in Italy since 1984, writing on opera for the *Times* (London) and translating opera librettos for Casa Ricordi.

The centenary of Puccini's birth saw the publication of two books that must still head any bibliography of the composer: Eugenio Gara's *Carteggi pucciniani* (Milan, 1958) and Mosco Carner's *Puccini: A Critical Biography* (London, 1958; enlarged edition 1974). Other important collections of correspondence are not nearly as compendious as Gara's, and Carner stands out amongst Puccini biographers for his balanced treatment of carefully sifted material.

Carteggi pucciniani consists of over nine hundred items to, from, or about Puccini; the first is a letter to his mother describing the conservatory entrance exam ("una sciocchezza"), and the last is a telegram from his publisher to his librettist announcing the heart attack that killed him. In between, we witness the vicissitudes of his life and career at first hand: "Whatever triumphs art may bring me, the loss of my dear mother means that I will never be really happy." "Doctor Cerù has ordered me to pay back the money he spent to keep me in Milan while I was studying, with interest to date!" "[*Tosca* in Paris] was a *véritable* triumph!—real, in the Italian sense, with roars and *bis,* in spite of the snobbish critics who wanted the obscurantism of the 'young school' instead of our clarity." To Rosina Storchio, on the day of *Madama Butterfly*'s disastrous premiere: "My good wishes are unnecessary! . . . the public will certainly be overpowered by your great art! And I hope, through you, to race to victory! Until this evening, then, with a calm mind . . ." And to Toscanini, for his conducting of *Manon Lescaut* in 1923: "You have given me the greatest satisfaction of my life . . . you managed to capture all my passionate young spirit of thirty years ago!"

Some vivid glimpses of the composer's character are also provided by the letters of his long-suffering collaborators, such as this exchange in 1893—Illica: "Puccini is already tired of *La bohème* . . . [he is] a clock that winds up and runs down quickly." Ricordi: "I'm not surprised, because I expected it . . . the subject was chosen by Puccini and I didn't fail to point out the huge scenic and musical problems it presented . . . [but he] was carried away and absolutely had to have *that* subject . . . And now that he is faced with the first problems—pardon the expression—he does it in his pants."

Gara's footnotes provide biographical information about the names mentioned in the correspondence, explanations of obscure references, and a generous selection of press reviews of first performances. The most serious gap—caused by the suppression of plentiful material—concerns 1909, the year of Doria Manfredi's suicide, which is represented by just seven letters and a cryptic reference to "unpleasantness in the family." In general Gara tends to overlook the less flattering aspects of his subject's life, such as his womanizing and his behavior during the First World War.

But when one turns from the *Carteggi* to Giuseppe Adami's *Giacomo Puccini: Epistolario* (Milan, 1928), the first major collection of letters to be published, one immediately feels grateful to Gara for his care and precision—Adami muddles dates and has Puccini meet Prévost (instead of Proust!) in Paris. Many of the important letters are reprinted in *Carteggi*. The most interesting correspondence concerns the composer's inability to finish *Turandot:* "I see darkness. I have already made a complete fool of myself over this duet . . . We must find a solution because I am now in real trouble." He had by then been worrying about the duet for almost three years.

Puccini's friendship with Sybil Seligman from 1905 until the end of his life was in large measure conducted by letter, to the eternal gratitude of his biographers. This correspondence forms the basis of her son Vincent Seligman's *Puccini Among Friends* (London, 1938), which chronicles in particular his quest for libretti and his views on performers. Caruso, he confided to Sybil, "won't learn anything, he's lazy and he's too pleased with himself—all the same his voice is magnificent." "Jeritza is really an original artiste—perhaps the most original artiste that I have ever known." And although he sometimes worshipped Toscanini, he did not trust him with *Il trittico*—"I won't have this *God*. He's no use to me . . . when an orchestral conductor thinks poorly of the operas he has to conduct, he can't interpret them properly."

Sybil Seligman was one of Puccini's most trusted friends, and these are amongst the most affectionate letters he wrote; his streak of self-pity is also well documented. Vincent Seligman's linking text gives a partial and partisan account of events.

Puccini com'era, edited by Arnaldo Marchetti (Milan, 1973), is principally a self-portrait in letters of Puccini as brother and brother-in-law—the bulk of this correspondence is addressed to his sister Ramelde and her husband Raffaello Franceschini, and there are more letters to his brother Michele (and from his first librettist Ferdinando Fontana) than are published elsewhere. Although operatic matters are mentioned, it is Puccini's other obsessions that are to the fore—ten pages are devoted to Raffaello's bicycle!

In 1899 Puccini became friendly with Riccardo Schnabl, who appears to have been a gentleman of leisure with a passion for travel and music. Schnabl sent the composer operatic news from abroad and was himself responsible for staging *Il trittico* in Hamburg in 1921. Their correspondence, mostly from the

Puccini's last years were marked by many disappointments. Embittered by what he considered the treachery of the Italian musical establishment (including his publisher Tito Ricordi), by rivalry with younger composers, and by personal troubles, he also suffered failing health. This rare photograph, taken a few months before his death, shows him as a haggard old man, though he was only sixty-five at the time. (Music Division. The New York Public Library for the Performing Arts. Astor, Lenox and Tilden Foundations)

last years, is collected in *Giacomo Puccini: Lettere a Riccardo Schnabl* (Milan, 1982), edited and scrupulously annotated by Simonetta Puccini, and contains clear statements of Puccini's views on subjects ranging from his native land ("my country disgusts me") to the performance of his operas: "That conductor slackens the tempi and enervates everything—with Wagner it is possible to slacken off but not with me."

The correspondence in Giuseppe Pintorno's *Puccini: 276 lettere inedite* (Milan, 1974) is of comparatively minor interest; it includes a number of the composer's poems.

Mosco Carner's *Puccini: A Critical Biography* comprises three separate but closely interrelated parts: a biography, a highly personal essay on the roots and branches of the composer's art, and a musico-dramatic analysis of the operas. The first part assembles the jigsaw of Puccini's life and work in a way that not only produces an exceptionally vivid picture but that also makes the pieces interlock tightly and inevitably—we feel that the operas could only have been written by the man we see here. Carner's approach combines frank admiration for much of his subject's music, copious quotation from primary sources, and a rigorous adherence to verifiable facts.

Part Two is much more controversial, especially when Carner ties Puccini to the psychoanalyst's couch—his central hypothesis is that in writing his operas Puccini was both driven and imprisoned by "a neurotic fixation which may be defined as an unresolved bondage to the mother-image." This ingenious theory fits the facts very neatly, although in expounding it Carner displays almost as much ambivalence to his subject as he tells us Puccini felt toward his heroines / victims: "Puccini's musical characters are . . . in the last analysis [*sic*] symbols of his own unconscious drives and tensions. They speak less for themselves than for their creator." This reductive near-dismissal hardly seems reconcilable with the assertion, a few pages later, that "*Gianni Schicchi* and *Turandot* . . . can almost be mentioned in the same breath as Verdi's *Otello* and *Falstaff*."

The only writer before Carner to attempt a balanced, properly documented biography was George Marek (*Puccini*, New York, 1951), whose pioneering research first produced the main lines of the story as we know it today. His book is still interesting for the many letters he quotes, especially between Puccini and Elvira, although his own prose veers between sententiousness and fireside familiarity.

Before Marek, Puccini's life was hazily and patchily presented—his first biographers were also his personal friends and seem to have regarded it as their task to immortalize their happiest memories rather than to establish the facts. As Claudio Sartori observes in his own *Puccini* (Milan, 1958): "His friends were too fond of their good old Puccini and, through an excess of love, often distorted situations and suppressed events."

Arnaldo Fraccaroli was a journalist to whom Puccini gave an account of his life, so that *Giacomo Puccini: Si confida e racconta* (Milan, 1957) is a kind of autobiography. But in spite of its firsthand flavor, it often leaves the reader with the feeling of being twice removed from what actually happened—the narrative has been filtered first by the self-indulgent Puccini and then by his devoted amanuensis, although even Fraccaroli distances himself from such reminiscences as: "Those were the days! . . . Unforgettable time of *La bohème,* when all of life seemed to smile around me, and the world was all beautiful, and men were all good . . ." And to cite just one example that can be checked against documentary evidence, the magnanimity of Puccini's views on Leoncavallo as expressed here is very far from what we know he thought of "Leonbestia."

The most extreme exponent of rose-tinted biography is Giuseppe Adami, who makes even more extensive use of imaginary (or is it supposed to be remembered?) dialogue than Fraccaroli. Perhaps Adami is also the most honest, since he actually calls one of his books *Il romanzo della vita di Giacomo Puccini* (Milan, 1942)—in this "novel of the life," even the details of the author's first dealings with Puccini differ from those to be found in Adami's own *Puccini* (Milan, 1935), and the "dialogue" is altered accordingly. Other examples of this extensive genre are Guido Marotti and Ferruccio Pagni's *Giacomo Puccini intimo* (Florence, 1926) and Carlo Paladini's *Giacomo Puccini* (Florence, 1961). These problematical works have all been comprehensively mined by later biographers for any information that can be plausibly corroborated.

Claudio Sartori's *Puccini,* mentioned above, was the first serious biographical study to appear in Italian, and provides a well-documented warts-and-all portrait. A large portion of the book, however, amounts to a rather rambling reflective essay on the composer's life and work, and the non-Italian reader is bound to be struck by two recurrent features that Sartori's writing shares with his native successors in this field—the attribution of many facets of Puccini's character to the mere fact that he was from Tuscany and an obsession with his (sometimes petty-) bourgeois mentality. The literature thus identifies Tuscans as cynical, realistic, parsimonious, ambitious, and family-loving; they are inclined to buy a patch of their *patria,* they swear a lot, and they find Sicily uncongenial. And in Sartori's discussion of *La bohème,* his highest praise for the third act takes this curious form: "It is a drama that breaks free from every bourgeois sentiment, it is a victory over himself [by the bourgeois Puccini] that shapes a character [Rodolfo]."

Postcentenary Italian writers seem to feel the need to redress a balance—their predecessors tended to make such assertions as "Puccini was a true bohemian" and "Puccini lived for art," so they exorcise their embarrassment at this naiveté by stressing what they see as his shallow bourgeois nature. Claudio Casini is the Adami of the hard-boiled school: his *Puccini* (1978, Turin) is full of such remarks as "Puccini's behaviour may not have been irreprehensible, but he was becoming less and less petty-bourgeois" and even claims that "The unprecedented success of *Aida* [the work that inspired Puccini to become an opera composer] depended on the fact that it was an opera aimed at the petty bourgeoisie." When he is not the victim of his unresolved bondage to a single idea, Casini provides a detailed account of his analysand's life and a very full bibliography, including articles in Italian periodicals.

Nori Andreini Galli's *Puccini e la sua terra* (Lucca, 1974) is a straightforward, nonmusical biography, copiously illustrated with photographs of Lucca and the area around Torre del Lago whose fanciful captions attempt to relate them to Puccini's life and work.

In the field of musical analysis, there are also notable differences of approach between English-language and Italian commentators: the former assume that their task is to be performed by empirical deduction, the latter are more drawn towards metaphysical speculation. Carner, with the help of a few seminal music examples, identifies important themes and considers their deployment, characterizes orchestration by deft description of some telling incidents, and in general draws together the musical threads that tie the dramatic knot in Puccini's unmistakable way. His depiction of the literary background to the operas and the transformation of source into libretto is also masterly.

This method is broadly shared by William Ashbrook in *The Operas of Puccini* (New York, 1968); Ashbrook's close study of the autograph scores yields rewarding insights—the changes Puccini made to the autographs and the differences between these and the printed scores give us a direct view of the composer at work. Most are minor adjustments to sharpen a scene or clarify a phrase, but an alteration to *Tosca* is the most striking example: The heroine herself was originally intended to sing the much-lambasted fortissimo reprise of the tune of "E luceven le stelle" at the end of the opera.

Charles Osborne's *The Complete Operas of Puccini* (London, 1981) contains interesting material about libretto sources, but his treatment of the music tends to be unbalanced by his attention to marginal issues and by his numerous disparaging asides.

Two volumes in the Cambridge Opera Handbooks series have so far been devoted to Puccini: Carner's *Tosca* (1985) and *La bohème* (1986), by Arthur Groos and Roger Parker. These studies consider the operas in far more detail than is possible in the synoptic works mentioned above; they pay particular attention to the literature that fertilized Puccini's imagination and the relationship between musical structure and dramatic effect.

Puccini's Turandot (Princeton, 1991), by William Ashbrook and Harold Powers, is subtitled *The End of the Great Tradition*, but this is only the first of the many aspects of their subject that the authors adroitly examine in great detail. They consider the process by which ". . . *Turandot* evolved retroactively into a fitting Finale for the Great Tradition, into a number opera in the grand manner . . ." and also the reasons why the Great Tradition died when it did. There are full accounts of the opera's sources, its genesis, its musical structure and very particular *tinta,* and of the drafts and sketches Puccini left at his death.

Ashbrook and Powers also confront the work's huge flaw: ". . . at first blush the closing passages of the opera seem unmotivated, perhaps even shocking, as though Butterfly's suicide had been vulgarly and anticlimactically followed by a final love duet for Pinkerton and Kate." But having admitted that for Puccini the *clou* of the whole opera was the transformation of icy princess into passionate woman, they unexpectedly conclude that *Turandot* is his masterpiece. A masterpiece can be unfinished, but surely not if the most important part of it is missing—and it is impossible to believe that Puccini himself would be satisfied with the work in any of its existing forms.

Claudio Sartori, vanguard of the Italian critical team, eschews both music examples and cold linear analysis: In his long treatment of *La bohème,* he develops the theory that everything in Puccini's operas is unreal and dreamlike, in keeping with the composer's "conception of opera as a product of magic." In his *Puccini: Una vita* (Florence, 1974), Leonardo Pinzauti avers that this opera's perfection is partly due to "the constant presence of a sentimental force that operates outside the drama proper, with a cohesion that is purely musical. Even Mimì and Rodolfo's love is as if related by 'others' rather than being experienced . . . by the characters themselves." And Claudio Casini, after considering the musical dramaturgy of the same work, reaches the conclusion that the opera "is not so much concerned with the characters as with the dynamics of their states of mind and the influence exercized on them by events."

An extreme exception to the national rule is Gianfranco Musco's *Musica e teatro in Giacomo Puccini* (volume 1; Cortona, 1989), which provides an exhaustive bar-by-bar description of the operas up to *Bohème. Puccini: Tutte le opere* (Pisa, 1989), by Laura Padellaro and Michele dall'Ongaro, is a general guide drawing on the work of numerous commentators.

Giacomo Puccini e l'opera internazionale (Turin, 1912), by Fausto Torrefranca, takes the form of a savage polemic which some believe influenced critical opinion in Italy for several decades, perhaps even to the present day. Its thesis is that "the current state of Italian opera defames our culture abroad," and Puccini is chosen as exemplary victim because he personifies "all the decadence of current Italian music, all its cynical commercialism, all its pitiful impotence and its celebration of international fashion."

Alfredo Bonaccorsi traces the history of the Puccini dynasty in *Giacomo Puccini e i suoi antenati musicali* (Milan, 1950) and describes the Lucca musical traditions in which Giacomo's ancestors worked.

The richest iconographical collection is Leopoldo Marchetti's *Puccini nelle immagini* (Milan, 1949), which ranges from a portrait of Puccini's great-great-grandfather Giacomo—founder of the family's musical tradition—to a facsimile of the last words scrawled by the dying Giacomo, "the end of the line."

In *Puccini e le sue rime* (Milan, 1974) Giorgio Magri brings together a number of Puccini's poems, using them as pegs on which to hang biographical incidents.

The composer's songs are collected in *The Unknown Puccini* (New York and Oxford, 1987), by Michael Kaye, who provides clear accounts of the circumstances of their birth (no simple matter in the case of the *Inno a Roma*).

Cecil Hopkinson's *A Bibliography of the Works of Giacomo Puccini 1858–1924* (New York, 1968) lists the versions of the scores that have been printed, with details of the changes that differentiate them.

Casa Ricordi was Puccini's publisher for all the operas except *La rondine,* which went to Casa Sonzogno, so editions published by other houses are copies of the Ricordi scores. Critical editions of *La bohème* and *Tosca* have recently been prepared by, respectively, Francesco Degrada and Roger Parker, and will be published by Ricordi in both vocal and full score. Other critical editions are currently projected, but the difficulties of arriving at a definitive edition of Puccini's operas are immense because he changed them so often, and there are gaps of information between the autograph scores and the various printed versions—the stage at which many important alterations were made.

None of the English works mentioned has been translated into Italian, and vice versa, with the exception of Carner (Milan, 1961) and the *Epistolario* (as *The Letters of Giacomo Puccini* [London, 1931]).

A SELECT *B*IBLIOGRAPHY OF *A*RTICLES AND *D*ISSERTATIONS *A*BOUT *P*UCCINI AND *H*IS *O*PERAS

Deborah Burton

Deborah Burton was educated at Mannes College of Music, the Accademia Chigiana (Siena), and Yale. She is currently a doctoral candidate at the University of Michigan (her thesis is on *Tosca*).

Articles

GENERAL

Carner, Mosco. "The Exotic Element in Puccini." *The Musical Quarterly* (January 1936). In Italian in *Symposium: Giacomo Puccini,* 173–99. Milan: Ricordi, 1959. The author identifies authentic tunes used in *Madama Butterfly, Turandot,* and *La fanciulla del West,* and remarks on Puccini's unusual harmonies, instrumentation, meter changes, and polyrhythms that derive from "exotic" influences.

Gallini, Natale. "Gli anni giovanili di Giacomo Puccini." In *L'Approdo Musicale,* 28–52. Rome: ERI, 1959. The author creates an excellent composite picture of the composer, through the time of *Le villi* and *Edgar,* utilizing school documents and letters by Puccini, his mother, Ponchielli, and Fontana. Also described are a manuscript of a youthful orchestral prelude (1876) and a copy of Berlioz's treatise on instrumentation and orchestration, which Puccini owned and read.

Leibowitz, René. "L'Arte di Giacomo Puccini." In *L'Approdo Musicale,* 3–27. Rome: ERI, 1959. Puccini's art is the synthesis, Leibowitz asserts, of the lyric traditions of Verdi and Wagner, enriched with his own great originality. This argument is supported with well-chosen examples from *Manon Lescaut, Tosca, La bohème,* and *Gianni Schicchi.*

Magri, Giorgio. "Una ricetta di Puccini: . . . 'rifritture da lavori precedenti'." In *Critica pucciniana,* edited by Comitato Nazionale per le onoranze a Giacomo Puccini nel cinquantenario della morte, 69–93. Lucca: Nuova Grafica Lucchese, 1976. Magri discusses Puccini's reuse of his own material in *Le villi, Edgar, Manon Lescaut, La bohème, Tosca,* and part of the first version of *Madama Butterfly.*

Rinaldi, Mario. "La strumentazione nelle opere di Giacomo Puccini." In *Giacomo Puccini nel centenario della nascita,* 54–76. Lucca: Industria Grafica Lorenzetti e Natali, 1958. This article deals with Puccini's instrumentation in all of the operas.

Operas

Atlas, Allan W. "Newly Discovered Sketches for Puccini's *Turandot* at the Pierpont Morgan Library." *Cambridge Opera Journal* 3/2:173–93. Three previously unknown sketches from *Turandot* are described here with hypotheses as to their possible use.

Budden, Julian. "The Genesis and Literary Source of Giacomo Puccini's First Opera." *Cambridge Opera Journal* 1/1 (March 1989):79–85. The author corrects the misconception that the source for *Le villi* was the same as that for the ballet *Giselle,* and he reveals that the true source was a short story by Alphonse Karr published in 1852, entitled *Les Wilis.* He also refutes the myth that Puccini was inspired to compose operas only after seeing Verdi's *Aida.*

Carner, Mosco. "Le Villi." *Quaderni Pucciniani* 2 (1985):15–29. This curious but informative article was written within a year before the author died, and it remained half in English, half in Italian. Carner describes the genesis of *Le villi;* the subject (which he states is the same as the ballet *Giselle*); and the influences of Wagner, Verdi, and Catalani on Puccini at that time.

Döhring, Sieghart. "Musikalischer Realismus in Puccinis *Tosca.*" *Analectica Musicologica* 22 (1984):249–96. The author examines Puccini's use of motivic material, which he classifies into three types, and discusses elements of form, melody, and local color in *Tosca,* as well as the sense of suspense in the third act, when the audience knows more than the characters do.

Gavazzeni, Gianandrea. "La *Tosca* come campione esecutivo pucciniano." In *Critica pucciniana,* edited by Comitato Nazionale per le onoranze a Giacomo Puccini nel cinquantenario della morte, 52–62. Lucca: Nuova Grafica Lucchese, 1976. This consummate musician uses *Tosca* to illustrate his observations on performing practices in Puccini's operas, by correcting some traditionally accepted distortions of the score.

Girardi, Michele. "La rappresentazione musicale dell'atmosfera settecentesca nel second'atto di *Manon Lescaut.*" In *Esotismo e colore locale nell'opera di Puccini,* edited by Jürgen Maehder, 65–82. Pisa: Giardini, 1985. The author illustrates how Puccini evokes eighteenth-century France in the music for Manon's toilette scene, the madrigal, the minuet, and the pastoral song.

———. "Studien zum Fragmentcharakter von Giacomo Puccinis *Turandot.*" *Analecta musicologica* 22 (1984):298–379. Reprinted in Italian as "Studi sul carattere di frammento della *Turandot* di Giacomo Puccini." *Quaderni Pucciniani* 2 (1985):79–163. Condensed and in English as "Puccini's *Turandot:* A Fragment—Studies in Franco Alfano's Completion of the Score." In *Turandot: Giacomo Puccini.* English National Opera Guide 27; edited by Nicholas John, 35–53. London: ENO, 1984. In this extensive article, Maehder quotes the relevant correspondence, compares the opera to the Gozzi original, describes the sketches in detail, and gives a history of the opera's completion, including the influence of Toscanini who had heard Puccini play the whole opera through. Included are appendices in which the three versions of the libretto are set side by side, the deployment of Puccini's sketches is charted, and Alfano's two versions are compared.

Groos, Arthur, "Madame Butterfly: The Story." *Cambridge Opera Journal* 3/2 (July 1991):125–58. Through fascinating detective work, Groos has unearthed the true story upon which John Luther Long's short story, David Belasco's play, and Puccini's opera were based, and he identifies the real participants. Groos's research involved reviewing a previously neglected eyewitness account by Long's missionary sister and digging into U.S. Navy files.

———. "Return of the Native: Japan in *Madame Butterfly* / *Madame Butterfly* in Japan." *Cambridge Opera Journal* 1/2 (July 1989):167–94. Applying a cross-cultural approach, the author discusses the phenomenon of "japonisme" in Europe, the return of this material to Japan, and some of the unintended clashes of cultures, including racial stereotyping. The interesting history of *Madama Butterfly* in Japan includes, for example, the opera's first performance in 1914 (which was only one scene long and followed by popular songs), and its appearance as the first foreign subject treated by the ancient Bunraken puppet theater.

Maehder, Jürgen. "Paris-Bilder. Zur Transformation von Henry Mür-
gers Roman in den *Bohème*-Opern Puccinis und Leoncavallos." *Jahrbuch der Opernforschung* 2 (1986):109–76. In Italian, as "Immagini di
Parigi: La trasformazione del romanzo *Scènes de la vie de bohème* di
Henry Murger nelle opere di Puccini e Leoncavallo." *Rivista Musicale
Italiana* 24 (1990):402–55. In compiling this in-depth article, which details
the geneses of both Puccini's and Leoncavallo's versions of *La bohème,*
Maehder examined letters from Puccini, Giacosa, and Ricordi to Illica,
which are unpublished to date, and two manuscripts of the libretto in
Giulio Ricordi's hand that Puccini used in working on Acts I and III.
He describes the procedures adopted by Leoncavallo and the Ricordi-
Illica team to transform Murger's novel. Interesting details that are
mentioned include the fact that Murger used his own addresses for places
in his novel, and that there was even a real painting entitled "Passage
through the Red Sea." The appendices include a list of quotations Murger cited, the disposition of Murger's chapters in both operas, Leoncavallo's first jottings for his libretto, and a transcription of the libretto
manuscript in Ricordi's hand.

———. "Roma anno 1800. Riflessioni sulla struttura drammatico-musi-
cale dell'opera storica in Puccini." House program. *49o Maggio Musicale Fiorentino* (1986):1037–55. This article reveals the identity of the
person upon whom Sardou based the character of Angelotti (a Roman
doctor named Liborio Angelucci) in his play *La Tosca,* while providing
a historic overview of the period. In addition, the lengthy letters between
Giulio Ricordi and Puccini regarding the former's doubts about the last
act of the opera are reproduced in their entirety.

Maguire, Janet. "Puccini's Version of the Duet and Final Scene of *Turandot.*" *The Musical Quarterly* 74 (1990):319–59. The author is a composer who, after a long study of Puccini's sketches for *Turandot,* some
of which had been neglected by Alfano, demonstrates how they could
have been intended. Maquire has written a new ending for the opera.

Mandelli, Alfredo. "Puccini 'western': crisi o evoluzione nella *Fanciulla
del West?*" House program, Gran Teatro La Fenice (March–April
1981):341–58. Mandelli reviews the genesis of the opera, other subjects
Puccini considered, Puccini's voyage to America, the rehearsals, and
the early performance history, and then touches upon some musical
points, such as the use of whole-tone scales.

———."Puccini e il 'caso Rodine'." In *Conferenze degli "Amici della Scala"
1968–1970,* 65–85. Aquapendente: La Commerciale, 1972. In this first
of several articles about *La rondine,* Mandelli details the history of the
opera and points out several unusual compositional features, such as the
use of contemporary dance forms (tango, polka, waltz, fox trot) and an
ironic quote from Strauss's *Salome.* (See also by the same author: "Il
'Caso-Rondine'." Concert program, Teatro Comunale Treviso [9
October–22 December 1974]:18–33; and, for more detailed comparisons of the three versions of the opera: "Le *Rondini* son tre, l'enigma è

uno,' ovvero: Le versioni e i 'casi' della *Rondine.*" Concert program, Gran Teatro La Fenice [1983]:418–29.)

Morini, Mario. "*Tosca* all'anagrafe della storia." House program, Teatro alla Scala (March 1963). Reprinted in House program, Teatro La Fenice (1978–79):129–37, and in *49o Maggio Musicale Fiorentino* (1986):57ff. This article gives a thorough history of the opera's genesis, including quotes from documents that show that Franchetti gave up the rights to *La Tosca* voluntarily at least three months before they were offered to Puccini.

Parker, Roger. "Analysis: Act I in Perspective." In *Giacomo Puccini: Tosca,* edited by Mosco Carner, 117–42. Cambridge: Cambridge University Press, 1985. This rich essay contains sections on words and music (in which verse forms of *Tosca* and *Aida* are compared), tonal and dramatic interaction, and motivic work (wherein the author compiles a list of musical motives without tags).

Torchi, Luigi. "*Tosca:* Melodramma in tre atti di Giacomo Puccini." *Nuova Rivista Musicale* 7 (1900):78–114. Written by the director of the *Rivista Musicale Italiana* within a year of *Tosca's* premiere, this essay is usually portrayed as wholly critical of the opera. But interspersed among the condemnations of Puccini's compositional technique (unstable harmonies, lack of passion, and too much unity) one can find praise of his melodies and even a disclaimer that analysts can be wrong.

For Further Reading

GENERAL

Carner, Mosco. "Debussy and Puccini." *The Musical Times* 108 (1967):502–505. Musical examples from both composers are compared here, and points of mutual contact between the composers and their styles are highlighted.

———. "Esotismo e colore locale nell'opera di Puccini." In *Esotismo e colore locale nell'opera di Puccini,* edited by Jürgen Maehder, 13–35. Pisa: Giardini, 1985. The author describes ways in which the composer used exotic material, including contrasting Western and pentatonic scales in the service of dramatic significance, and using local color as the generative spark for the opera's music.

Gavazzeni, Gianandrea. "Introduzione alla critica di Puccini." *La Rassegna Musicale* (January 1950):13–22. Reprinted in *Symposium: Giacomo Puccini,* 129–41. Milan: Ricordi, 1959. A history of early Puccini criticism.

Meyrowitz, Jan. "Puccini: musica a doppio fondo." *Nuova Rivista Musicale Italiana* 1 (1976):3–19. The author discusses the popularity and the social compassion of Puccini's operas, his personal harmonic style, and points out the use of quasi-*idées fixes* in many of his operas.

Sartori, Claudio. "I sospetti di Puccini." *Nuova Rivista Musicale Italiana* 2 (1977):232–41. Some of Puccini's letters from 1919–20, which do not appear in the *Carteggi Pucciniani,* are reproduced here; they were omitted from the collection apparently because they deal with sensitive financial matters between Puccini and the Casa Ricordi.

Vlad, Roman. "Attualità di Puccini." In *Critica pucciniana,* edited by Comitato Nazionale per le onoranze a Giacomo Puccini nel cinquantenario della morte, 152–89. Lucca: Nuova Grafica Lucchese, 1976. Vlad elucidates how Puccini's early works were infused with Wagnerism, and how, in turn, Puccini influenced many twentieth-century composers, including Schoenberg, Berg, Stravinsky, Ravel, and Dallapiccola.

OPERAS

Carner, Mosco. "The Genesis of the Opera." In *Turandot.* English National Opera Guide 27:7–18. London: John Calder, 1984. Carner writes about other settings of the Turandot legend and the sources of Gozzi's tale, and he outlines the clash between Toscanini and Mussolini, which came to a head at *Turandot's* premiere. The author also offers psychological motivations for why Puccini "could not" finish the opera, although it is now known that the opera had been played through completely by Puccini for Toscanini and others.

————. "The Score." In *Turandot.* English National Opera Guide 27:19–34. London: John Calder, 1984. This informative article focuses on Puccini's use of original Chinese tunes (which are identified), the whole tone scale, bitonality, and polyrhythms. The author also details some aspects of musical characterization, and the musico–dramatic structure of Act I.

Cesari, T. O. "*Tosca* di Giacomo Puccini." In *Rivista d'Italia* (Fasc. 1–1900). Rome: Società Editrice Dante Alighieri, 1900. A contemporary Wagnerian critic writes an extended review of *Tosca* only hours after the première, placing Puccini and his work in an overview of cultural history and mentioning his use of dissonance and other compositional techniques.

Christen, Norbert. "Vom Grand-Guignol zur Commedia dell'Arte." House program, Bayerische Staatsoper (17 December 1982):5–15. After relating the genesis of *Il trittico,* the author compares *Il tabarro* and *Gianni Schicchi* to their original sources.

Damerini, Adelmo. "Suor Angelica in una rara bozza di stampa." In *Giacomo Puccini nel centenario della nascita,* 84–99. Lucca: Industria Grafica Lorenzetti e Natali, 1958. This article describes and reproduces a proofsheet of *Suor Angelica* which was removed from use by Casa Ricordi and retained by the singer Salomea Krusceniski. The proof differs with the published version in some of the lyrics and performing indications.

D'Amico, Fedele. "Una ignorata pagina malipierana di *Suor Angelica*." *Rassegna Musicale Curci* 1 (April 1975):5–14. A "flower aria," which resembles the first of the *Sette canzoni* by Gian Francesco Malipiero, was eliminated from *Suor Angelica* after the first edition. Originally Puccini objected to this cut but was later reconciled to it, as the documentation in this article shows. The aria is reproduced here.

Girardi, Michele. "*Turandot*: Il futuro interrotto del melodramma italiano." *Rivista Italiana di Musicologia* 17 (1982):155–81. Puccini's letters regarding *Turandot* are quoted here, accompanying a discussion of his use of Chinese themes, his association of musical intervals with certain characters, and his manipulation of a basic motive or theme throughout the work.

Leibowitz, René. "Un opéra contestataire: *Tosca*." In *Les fantômes de l'opéra*, 261–74. Paris: Éditions Gallimard, 1972. Leibowitz points out the progressive aspects of the score, such as the sometimes suspension of tonality and use of the total chromatic, and then relates them to the drama.

Leukel, Jürgen. "Puccini et Bizet." *Revue Musicale de Suisse Romande* 35/2 (May–June 1982):61–66. Puccini saw *Carmen* in Milan in 1880 and, the author contends, Bizet's realistic masterpiece influenced *Le villi, Edgar, Manon Lescaut,* and a subject on which Puccini began to work, *La femme et le pantin.*

———. "Sulla rappresentazione dell'extramusicale nelle opere di Puccini." In *Esotismo e colore locale nell'opera di Puccini*, edited by Jürgen Maehder, 241–45. Pisa: Giardini, 1985. This article deals with Puccini's musical representation of objects or ideas; examples from *La bohème, Tosca, La fanciulla del West, Suor Angelica, Il tabarro, Gianni Schicchi,* and *Turandot* are included.

Mandelli, Alfredo. "La *Pavane* e *Senza Mamma*: Incontro quasi 'a tesi' tra Puccini e Ravel." *Quaderni Pucciniani* 1 (1982):119–32. The author observes the relationships between Puccini's compositional techniques and those of Ravel, Debussy, Wagner, and Mascagni (in his *Iris*).

Morini, Mario. "Nuovi documenti sulla nascita di *Manon Lescaut*." House program, Teatro Comunale dell' Opera di Genova (1983):89–98. The author has researched contemporary documents, and he quotes Leoncavallo, Illica, and Marco Praga.

Pinzauti, Leonardo. "Il *Trittico* di Giacomo Puccini." House program. *460 Maggio Musicale Fiorentino,* Teatro Comunale di Firenze (1983):581–97. The author relates the history of Puccini's choice of librettos for *Il trittico,* the first performance in New York, and the contemporary critical climate.

Santi, Piero. "Nei cieli bigi . . ." *Nuova Rivista Musicale Italiana* 2 (1967):350–58. Santi argues that in *La bohème* Puccini added a new dimension to opera composition by treating time, like the modern novel, in a discontinuous, relative, and multi-directional way. He also likens the relationship of words and music in Puccini's operas to the relation-

ship of the Bohemian lovers—they come together and separate now
and then.

Dissertations

Bögel, Hartwig. *Puccinis Orchestrierung.* Ph.D. diss., Universität Tübingen, 1978.

Burton, Deborah. *An Analysis of Puccini's "Tosca": A Heuristic Approach to the Unifying Elements of the Opera.* Ph.D. diss., University of Michigan, in progress.

D'Ecclesiis, Gennaro. *The Aria Techniques of Giacomo Puccini: A Study in Musico-Dramtic Style.* Ph.D. diss., New York University, 1961.

De Sanctis, Dona. *Literary Realism and Verismo Opera.* Ph.D. diss., City University of New York, 1983.

Fairtile, Linda. *Giacomo Puccini's Operatic Revisions as Manifestations of His Compositional Priorities.* Ph.D. diss., New York University, in progress.

Ferrara, Franca. *Il linguaggio melodico di Puccini nella drammaturgia di "Bohème," "Tosca" e "Madama Butterfly."* Ph.D. diss., Università degli Studi di Bologna, 1989–90.

Greenwald, Helen M. *Dramatic Exposition and Musical Structure in Puccini's Operas.* Ph.D. diss., City University of New York, 1991.

Hiss, Charles. *Abbé Prevost's "Manon Lescaut" as Novel, Libretto, and Opera.* Ph.D. diss., University of Illinois, 1967.

Lo, Kii-Ming. *"Turandot" auf der Opernbühne.* Ph.D. diss., Universität Heidelberg, 1988.

Peretti, Mario. *"Madama Butterfly" I-IV tra variante e ricomposizione: appunti e rilievi per una realizzazione scenica e musicale.* Ph.D. diss., Facoltà di Lettere e Filosofia dell' Università di Venezia, 1983.

Rosenthal, Miriam. *Giacomo Puccinis "La Fanciulla del West": eine neue Opernkonzeption im Oeuvre des Komponisten.* Ph.D. diss., Universität Bayreuth, in progress.

Scherr, Suzanne. *Puccini's "Manon Lescaut": Compositional Process, Stylistic Revision, and Editorial Problems.* Ph.D. diss., University of Chicago, 1993.

Schuller, Kenneth Gustave. *Verismo Opera and the Verists.* Supplementary volume: *Annotated Vocal Score of Puccini's "Tosca."* Ph.D. diss., Washington, University, 1960.

Valente, Richard. *The Verismo of Giacomo Puccini: From Scapigliatura to Expressionism.* Ph.D. diss., Université de Fribourg, 1971.

Wright, Peter. *The Musico-Dramatic Techniques of the Italian Verists.* Ph.D. diss., Eastman School of Music, 1965.

Zappa, Paul Joseph. *The Revisions of Three Operas by Giacomo Puccini: "Manon Lescaut," "La Bohème," "Madame Butterfly."* Ph.D. diss., University of Cincinnati, 1963.

A Chronology of Puccini's Life and Works

Maria Grazia Bajoni

Maria Grazia Bajoni is engaged in research at the Istituto di Filologia Classica at the Catholic University of Milan. She has translated a number of works from Latin, but is also concerned with Puccini studies. She assisted in preparing the "Puccini a Milano" exhibit at La Scala and read a paper at the Puccini conference sponsored by the theater in 1990 to celebrate the centenary of *Edgar*. She is a member of the Istituto di studi pucciniani.

1858

22 Dec. | In the night between 22 and 23 December, Giacomo Puccini is born in Lucca on Via di Poggio 30, to Michele and Albina Magi. The birth certificate says 22 December, but Puccini preferred to give his date of birth as the 23rd. He is named Giacomo Antonio Domenico Michele Secondo Maria. The family occupies the apartment on the second floor of the house and is already large: before Giacomo there were his sisters Otilia, Tomaide, Temi (or Zemi), Nitteti, and Iginia; Ramelde, Macrina, and his younger brother Michele (junior) were to follow. (CARNER, 31–41)

1864

23 Jan. Michele Puccini dies in Lucca. His successor in his musical posts is Fortunato Magi, Albina's brother and Giacomo Puccini's first teacher; his contract stipulated that he "conserve and release to Signor Giacomo, son of the aforesaid late Signor Maestro, the post of *maestro di cappella* and organist . . . as soon as the aforementioned Signor Giacomo Puccini is capable of assuming such an office."   (CARNER, 42)

19 Apr. Albina Magi, three months a widow, gives birth to another son, Michele.   (CARNER, 41)

1867–1873

Completes his classical secondary school studies in Lucca.

1874

Begins regular studies at the Istituto Pacini in Lucca, with Carlo Angeloni as teacher.   (CARNER, 43)

1875

Composes pieces for organ; *A te* for voice and piano.

(KAYE, 3)

1876

Composes *Preludio sinfonico* for orchestra.   (CARNER, 681)

1877

With a cantata for solo voices and orchestra, *I Figli d'Italia bella,* participates unsuccessfully in the contest for the anthem of the Lucca Esposizione d'Arte sacra.   (CARNER, 681)

1878

Composes *Vexilla regis* for male chorus and organ (or harmonium). Text by Venantius Honorius Clementianus Fortunatus.   (KAYE, 13)

12 July For the feast day of San Paolino, Lucca's patron saint, presents a *Credo* for solo voices, chorus, and orchestra, and a *Mottetto* for four voices. A success with the public. Begins earning money as organist in the churches of Mutigliano and of San Pietro Somaldi and in the Oratorio of the Benedictine sisters of S.S. Giuseppe and Gerolamo.   (CARNER, 681)

1880

12 July In the church of San Paolino in Lucca, his *Mass* for four voices with orchestra, including the *Credo* and the *Mottetto* of 1878, is performed.   (CARNER, 681)

Oct.–Nov.   Having obtained a study grant of 100 lire a month from Queen Margherita for the academic year 1880–81, goes to Milan, where he is admitted to the Conservatory, as a student of Antonio Bazzini. Among his schoolmates is Pietro Mascagni. In the following two years, pursues his studies thanks to a financial subsidy from his great-uncle, Doctor Nicolao Cerù. (MARCHETTI, 1)

1881

Composes *Melanconia,* also known as *Allor ch'io sarò morto,* for voice and piano, or for voice and orchestra, text by Antonio Ghislanzoni; *Scherzo* for string quartet.
(KAYE, 217; CARNER, 681)

1882

Composes *Ad una morta,* aria for baritone and piano and for baritone and orchestra, text by A. Ghislanzoni; the hymn *Salve Regina* for soprano and organ (or harmonium), text by A. Ghislanzoni; *Trio* for two violins and piano; *Ah! se potesse* for tenor and piano. (KAYE, 27, 217, 218)

1883

Composes *Adagietto* for orchestra; *Mentìa l'avviso,* recitative and aria for tenor and piano, text by Felice Romani; *Fuga* in A major, *Fuga* in C minor, *Fuga* in G major, all for string quartet; *Quartetto* for strings in D major; *Storiella d'amore* for voice and piano, text by A. Ghislanzoni. (KAYE, 33, 45)

14 July   His *Capriccio sinfonico,* for orchestra, dedicated to Prince Carlo Poniatowski, is performed at the Conservatory of Milan as his graduation piece. (MARCHETTI, 16)

16 July   Obtains his diploma from the Royal Conservatory. Franco Faccio, conductor at La Scala, manifests the intention to include the *Capriccio sinfonico* in the theater's concert season.

summer   Puccini visits Ponchielli in the country at Maggianico and also stays at Caprino Bergamasco. Meets Ferdinando Fontana, poet, journalist, librettist, bohemian, who prepares for him the libretto of *Le willis,* a one-act opera-ballet to be entered in a competition sponsored by Casa Sonzogno in April.

early Sept.   Returns to Lucca to compose; doesn't have time to have a fair copy made, and his illegible scribbling apparently prevents the work from winning.
(MARCHETTI, 22; CARNER, 69)

1884

spring Plays score of *Le willis* for an influential group of music lovers in the salon of Marco Sala.

31 May First performance of *Le willis* at Teatro Dal Verme in Milan, staged with the help of a subscription promoted by Arrigo Boito and Marco Sala. It is a splendid success with both public and critics. Giulio Ricordi buys the opera and commissions a full-length work from Puccini.   (GMM, 8 June 1884)

June In Lucca.

6 July In Turin, where the *Capriccio sinfonico* is performed with the Scala orchestra conducted by F. Faccio.   (MARCHETTI, 71)

17 July Albina Magi Puccini dies in Lucca. Shortly afterwards Giacomo meets Elvira Bonturi Gemignani, a married woman with whom he elopes (they finally marry in 1904).
    (CARNER, 77)

26 Dec. *Le villi,* expanded into two acts, the title changed, with a dedication to A. Boito, is performed at the Teatro Regio in Torino.   (GARA, 16)

1885

24 Jan. Premiere of *Le villi* at La Scala.   (MARCHETTI, 93)

Apr. In Lucca.   (GARA, 17)

June In Lucca.   (MARCHETTI, 95; GARA, 18)

July In Lucca.   (MARCHETTI, 103)

Nov., Dec. In Lucca. Works on the composition of *Edgar,* a lyric drama in four acts with libretto by F. Fontana, freely adapted from *La coupe et les lèvres* by A. de Musset.   (GARA, 20–21)

1886

Feb., Mar. In Lucca.   (MARCHETTI, 107)

22 Dec. In Monza the only child of Giacomo Puccini and Elvira Bonturi, Antonio, is born in their rented house at Borgo Milano 8.   (CARNER, 28)

1887

5 Feb. In Trieste for the Teatro Comunale premiere of *Le villi.*
    (MARCHETTI, 113)

Mar. In Milan.   (MARCHETTI, 114)

Apr. In Lucca.   (MARCHETTI, 114)

June In Milan.   (MARCHETTI, 118)

July–Oct. In Caprino Bergamasco.   (MARCHETTI, 119, 121, 123)

Dec. In Milan. Works on *Edgar.*   (MARCHETTI, 124–26)

1888

15 Jan.	Attends the premiere of *Le villi* at the Teatro S. Carlo in Naples. (MARCHETTI, 127)
Jan.–Apr.	In Milan. (GARA, 28; MARCHETTI, 130) Composes *Sole e amore,* aubade for voice and piano, text anonymous (maybe by Puccini); and *Solfeggi,* for voice and piano. (KAYE, 55, 223)
summer	Goes to Pizzameglio near Chiasso. (MARCHETTI, 131)

1889

21 Apr.	At La Scala in Milan, premiere of *Edgar,* dedicated to J. Burgmein (Giulio Ricordi).
7 May	Writes to Giulio Ricordi: ". . . I'm thinking of Tosca! I beg you to do what's necessary to obtain the rights from Sardou . . . in this Tosca I see my kind of opera, not of excessive dimensions, not a decorative spectacle, or one that succumbs to the usual musical overabundance." (GARA, 31)
Sept.	In Vacallo. (GARA, 32; PINTORNO, 1)
Dec.	In Milan. (GARA, 33)

1890

5 Jan.	From Milan he writes to his brother Michele, who has emigrated to Buenos Aires. "I am working on *Manon.*" The adaption into libretto of the novel by Abbé Prévost involves Giuseppe Giacosa, Luigi Illica, Ruggero Leoncavallo, Marco Praga, Domenico Oliva, Giacomo Puccini, and Giulio Ricordi. (GARA, 34)
winter– summer	In Milan. Composes *Crisantemi,* elegy for string quartet in memory of Amedeo di Savoia, duke of Aosta; two minuets for string quartet. (CARNER, 682)
Nov.	In Vacallo. (PINTORNO, 2)
Dec.	In Milan. (GARA, 49)

1891

12 Mar.	Michele Puccini, younger brother of Giacomo, dies in Rio de Janeiro, after a brief, adventurous exile. Puccini is in Milan. (MARCHETTI, 143–45)
June	Goes to Torre del Lago for the first time.
Sept.	In Torre del Lago. (GARA, 53–55)
Dec.	In Milan. (GARA, 58)

1892

Jan.	In Milan.	(GARA, 58–62)
19 Mar.	In Madrid to attend the premiere of *Edgar* at Teatro Real.	
		(GARA, 67)
Aug.	In Vacallo.	(PINTORNO, 4)
29 Nov.	In Hamburg he attends *Le villi* at the opera.	(GARA, 78)

1893

Jan.   In Turin for *Manon Lescaut* rehearsals, meets Toscanini.

1 Feb.   At Turin's Teatro Regio for the premiere of *Manon Lescaut*, lyric drama in four acts with an anonymous libretto. The public is enthusiastic. The most authoritative critics speak of great artistic value, powerful musical conception, passion and melody, of a sense of theatricality.   (MARCHETTI, 154)

Mar.   In a Milan café he meets Leoncavallo and announces to him that he is working on an opera based on Murger's novel *Scènes de la vie de Bohème.* Leoncavallo asserts his prior right to the subject, on which he has been working, apparently without Puccini's knowledge. End of friendship. (GARA, 81)

May   In Milan.   (MARCHETTI, 155–56)

July–Aug.   At Torre del Lago.   (MARCHETTI, 157; GARA, 87–90)

Oct.   At Torre del Lago.   (MARCHETTI, 158)

4 Nov.   Attends the Bologna premiere of *Manon Lescaut;* eighteen performances.   (MARCHETTI, 162)

7 Nov.   *Manon Lescaut* is premiered in Hamburg. (MARCHETTI, 159)

9 Nov.   Attends the Rome premiere of *Manon Lescaut.*

        (MARCHETTI, 162)

Dec.   In Milan.   (MARCHETTI, 164–66)

Begins work on *La bohème* with librettists Giuseppe Giacosa and Luigi Illica.

1894

21 Jan.   Attends the first performance of *Manon Lescaut* at the San Carlo in Naples.   (MARCHETTI, 171)

7 Feb.   First performance of *Manon Lescaut* at La Scala in Milan.

        (MARCHETTI, 172)

12 Apr.   Goes to Budapest.   (MARCHETTI, 174)

14 May   In London; attends the premiere of *Manon Lescaut* at Covent Garden.   (MARCHETTI, 175)

June   Goes to Sicily, accompanied by some friends from Lucca, to meet Giovanni Verga and discuss the possibility of adapting *La lupa,* Verga's short story and his dramatization of it, for an opera libretto; also goes to Malta.

        (GARA, 105; PINTORNO, 141)

13 July	In a letter written from Torre del Lago to Giulio Ricordi, expresses doubts and reservations about setting *La lupa* to music. (GARA, 106)
18 July	From Torre del Lago, writes to Carlo Clausetti regarding a possible collaboration with d'Annunzio: "You explain my genre to him. Poetry, poetry, ardent affections, flesh, scorching, almost surprising drama, fireworks finale." (GARA, 107)

1895

winter–spring	In Milan. (MARCHETTI, 181–85)
May–June	In Milan. (GARA, 122–23)
summer–fall	In Pescia at the Villa Castellaccio; works on *Bohème*. (GARA, 124–41, 143) In his correspondence of this year there are frequent mentions of *Tosca*.

1896

1 Feb.	At Turin's Teatro Regio, first performance of *La bohème*, lyric drama in four acts, dedicated to the Marchese Carlo Ginori Lisci. Mixed reception; no consensus in the press; twenty-four sold-out performances. (GARA, 156)
23 Feb.	At Rome's Teatro Argentina *La bohème* is given; Puccini is present.
9 Apr.	In Palermo. (GARA, 162)
May	In Florence. (PINTORNO, 25)
June	*La bohème* is given in Buenos Aires. (CARNER, 166)
summer–fall	In Torre del Lago. (GARA, 163–65, 167–68, 170–71)
22 Aug.	From Torre del Lago he writes to Illica: "*Tosca* begun." (GARA, 168) Composes *Avanti "Urania"!,* for voice and piano, text by Renato Fucini, dedicated to the Marchesa Anna Ginori-Lisci. (KAYE, 61)

1897

Feb.	In Milan. (GARA, 175; MARCHETTI, 212)
Mar.	At Torre del Lago. (PINTORNO, 28–29)
22 Apr.	*La bohème* is performed in English with the title *The Bohemians* at the Comedy Theatre, Manchester; Puccini present. (MARCHETTI, 213)
May	In Milan. (MARCHETTI, 214; PINTORNO, 30)
2 Oct.	*La bohème* is staged at Covent Garden, London, in English. (CARNER, 147)

5 Oct.	La bohème is staged at the An der Wien, Vienna.
	(PINTORNO, 34)
Nov.	Puccini is in Rome. (PINTORNO, 35)
	Composes *Inno a Diana,* for voice and piano, text by Carlo Abeniacar. (KAYE, 69)

1898

Jan.	In Milan; works on *Tosca.* (GARA, 178)
Feb.	In Paris. (GARA, 179)
Mar.	In Milan. (GARA, 180–81)
Apr.–May	In Paris. (GARA, 182–91)
13 Jun.	Attends the Paris Opéra premiere of *La bohème.* The critics are reluctant to declare it a success, but the audience is enthusiastic. During his Parisian stay Puccini approaches Sardou to discuss the *Tosca* libretto. (GARA, 187, 189–90)
summer	Works on *Tosca* in the villa at Monsagrati.
	(GARA, 193, 194, 195)
Nov.	At Torre del Lago. (GARA, 197, 198, 199)
Dec.	In Milan. (MARCHETTI, 227, 228)

1899

11 Jan.	In Paris for the reprise of *La bohème* at the Opéra-Comique; negotiates with Sardou. (PINTORNO, 49, 50; GARA, 200)
Feb.	In Milan. (PINTORNO, 52; MARCHETTI 231, 232)
25 Mar.	Puccini's first letter from Torre del Lago to Riccardo Schnabl-Rossi, Umbrian nobleman who will be Puccini's friend and confidant for twenty-five years. (PUCCINI S, 1)
July	In Milan. (GARA, 204)
30 Oct.	Writes to his painter friend Luigi de Servi giving indications for the decoration of the new house at Torre del Lago. Correspondence with painter friends Ferruccio Pagni, Francesco Fanelli, Plinio Nomellini, and Luigi de Servi, shows his great interest in this new residence.
	(MARCHETTI, 233; SIMONETTA PUCCINI, in QUADERNI PUCCINIANI I, 17–19)
fall	At Torre del Lago.
Dec.	In Rome. (MARCHETTI, 235)
	Composes *E l'uccellino,* lullaby for voice and piano, text by R. Fucini, dedicated "To the baby Memmo Lippi."
	(KAYE, 79)

1900

14 Jan.	At Teatro Costanzi, Rome, first performance of *Tosca,* lyric opera in three acts, libretto by Giacosa and Illica. Present are

Queen Margherita, Prime Minister Pelloux, Minister of Education Baccelli, and other political and cultural figures; among the musicians: Mascagni, Cilea, Franchetti, Sgambati, Marchetti, Costa. Also present are correspondents from the leading European and American newspapers. The critics express reservations about the opera.   (GARA, 220)

Feb.   At Torre del Lago and at Turin.
                        (MARCHETTI, 236, 237; PINTORNO, 59, 60, 61, 62)

17 Mar.   *Tosca* is staged at La Scala, Milan, and is a great success: twelve performances.   (GARA, 224)

15 May   From Milan, writes to Illica making clear the unfeasibility of a collaboration with d'Annunzio.   (GARA, 226)

12 July   First performance of *Tosca* in Italian at Covent Garden, London. Puccini is present. During his London visit, attends David Belasco's play *Madame Butterfly,* an adaption of the short story by John Luther Long, who, in his turn, was inspired by Pierre Loti's novel *Madame Chrysanthème.*
                        (CARNER, 182)

summer   At Torre del Lago.   (GARA 235, 236; PINTORNO 70–73)
Oct.   In Brussels.   (GARA, 237)
Dec.   In Milan. After *Tosca,* considers new subjects for operas, which, however, come to nothing. Among these: *La faute de l'abbé Mouret* by Emile Zola; *Notre Dame de Paris* and *Les miserables* by Victor Hugo; *From a House of the Dead* by Fyodor Dostoyevski; and *Tartarin de Tarascon* by Alphonse Daudet. A *Maria Antonietta* is also mentioned.
                        (MARCHETTI, 242; CARNER, 177–79; GARA, 136)

1901

27 Jan.   Giuseppe Verdi dies in Milan. With Mascagni, Leoncavallo, and other musicians, Puccini participates in the funeral.
                        (PINTORNO, 74)

1 Feb.   Is present at the commemorative concert for Verdi at La Scala, conducted by Toscanini.   (CARNER, 186)

spring   In Milan and Torre del Lago.   (GARA, 245–48, 251)
7 Apr.   From Milan, writes to Illica: "*Butterfly* deal closed. Final agreement has arrived from America."   (GARA, 251)

May   Goes to Florence.   (GARA, 253)
summer–fall   In Tuscany.   (GARA, 256–62)
Dec.   At Torre del Lago and in Milan.
                        (GARA, 263; MARCHETTI, 251–53)

1902

Jan.–Mar.   In Milan and Torre del Lago.   (GARA 264–274)
Passes almost the entire year at Torre del Lago. This year,
like the preceding one, is marked by hard work on *Butterfly*.
This is evidenced in the intense correspondence with the
librettists Giacosa and Illica. Composes *Terra e mare* for voice
and piano, text by Enrico Panzacchi.
(GARA, 276–78, 280–90, 232?; KAYE, 85)

1903

Jan.   In Milan.   (GARA, 296–302)
Feb.   In the night between 25 and 26 February, while returning
from Florence by car to Torre del Lago, in the vicinity of
Vignola di San Macario near Lucca, is victim of an accident;
injuries keep him immobilized for months, making work
impossible. Undergoes long period of physical and moral
suffering and depression. A form of diabetes is discovered,
which delays his complete recovery. Remains in Tuscany.
(GARA, 303)

Apr.   Breaks off relationship with a certain Corinna from Turin;
no other information about her.   (MARCHETTI, 272)
summer   In Boscolungo Abetone; works on *Butterfly*.
(MARCHETTI, 274–78; GARA, 321–22)
13 Oct.   In Paris for the first performance of *Tosca* at the Opéra-
Comique.   (PINTORNO, 93)
Nov.   At Torre del Lago and Milan.   (PUCCINI S, 2, 3)
29 Dec.   From Torre del Lago writes to Clausetti: "I announce that I
finished *Butterfly* yesterday."   (GARA, 335)

1904

3 Jan.   In the church of Torre del Lago he marries Elvira Bonturi
Gemignani.   (MARCHETTI, 287)
17 Feb.   At La Scala in Milan the first performance of *Madama Butterfly*, Japanese tragedy in two acts, libretto by Giacosa and
Illica, dedicated to Her Majesty Queen Elena. Badly received
by both public and critics. The authors—Puccini, Giacosa,
and Illica—with the consent of the publisher, withdraw the
work and repay the theater's advance. In a note written just
after the failure of the opera, Puccini says: "The public was
very hostile to *Butterfly*, but my conscience as an artist is
untroubled." Consolation arrives from Giovanni Pascoli, a
poem entitled *La farfallina volerà*, in which the poet expresses
certainty of the opera's imminent success.
(GARA, 364; CARNER, 203)

spring	In Milan and Torre del Lago.	(GARA, 368–79)
28 May	At Brescia's Teatro Grande, *Madama Butterfly* in a new three-act version is enthusiastically received.	(GARA, 380–81)
June	In Milan and at Acqui Terme.	
	(GARA, 384–87; MARCHETTI, 298–303)	
2 July	*Madama Butterfly* is staged in Buenos Aires with great success.	
summer	At Boscolungo Abetone and at Torre del Lago.	
	(GARA 388–93)	
Oct.	In London Francesco Paolo Tosti introduces him to Sybil Seligman, a clever, refined socialite who, after a brief affair, remains a devoted friend to the composer and his family for life.	(PINTORNO, 98)
Dec.	Goes to Capalbio.	(PINTORNO, 101)
	Composes *Canto d'anime* for voice and piano, text by Illica.	
	(KAYE, 93)	

1905

27 Jan.	In Milan, at the Verdi Casa di Riposo, attends the performance of his *Requiem* for three voices, organ (or harmonium), and viola, composed in memory of Verdi at the suggestion of the Casa's board.	(CARNER, 186)
June–July	With his wife, goes to Argentina to attend the Puccini Season organized by the newspaper *La Prensa* at the Teatro Colón of Buenos Aires. Performed are *Manon Lescaut, La bohème, Tosca, Madama Butterfly,* and *Edgar,* revised on this occasion for the third time.	(GARA, 425–26; PINTORNO, 107–12)
Sept.	At Torre del Lago.	(GARA, 428–29)
27 Oct.	Attends the revised *Butterfly* at Covent Garden.	
	(GARA, 430–32; PINTORNO, 113)	
29 Oct.	At the Teatro Comunale in Bologna, attends *Butterfly,* conducted by Toscanini.	(GARA, 433–34)
fall	Considers new subjects to which he can set music, particularly *Maria Antonietta.*	(GARA, 437–40, 446, 450)

1906

Jan.	In Milan, then Naples.	(GARA, 451–63)
Feb.–Mar.	In Tuscany.	(PUCCINI S, 4)
Apr.	In Milan.	(GARA, 472)
May	In Budapest for a Puccini week; *La bohème, Tosca,* and *Madama Butterfly* are sung in Hungarian respectively on 9, 10, and 12 May. In London at end of month.	(MARCHETTI, 321–23)
13 July	From Paris, writes to Alfredo Vandini: "I have made the final arrangements for *Butterfly* at the Opéra-Comique."	
	(GARA, 479; PINTORNO, 130)	

13 Aug.	From Boscolungo Abetone, informs Giulio Ricordi that "the agreement with d'Annunzio has for now gone up in smoke." (GARA, 484)
16 Aug.	From Boscolungo Abetone (Serra Bassa), writes to Gabriele d'Annunzio: "I don't want a *realism* of the kind you would find hard to accept, but a 'quid medium' that captivates the listeners through dolorous and amorous action, which logically lives and throbs in a halo of the poetry of life rather than of dreams." The poet was proposing to Puccini stories like *La rosa di cipro* and *La Parisina*. (GARA, 481)
2 Sept.	Giacosa dies at Coileretto Parella.
fall	Puccini seems determined to set to music *La femme et le pantin* by Pierre Louys, then Wilde's *Florentine Tragedy*. (GARA, 490, 494)
Oct.	At end of month, goes to Paris. (MARCHETTI, 329)
28 Dec.	In Paris for *Butterfly* at the Opéra-Comique. (PUCCINI S, 6; PINTORNO, 137)

1907

	At the beginning of the year, sails with Elvira from Cherbourg to America. (MARCHETTI, 333)
18 Jan.	The Puccinis are in New York for the premiere of *Manon Lescaut* at the Metropolitan. During this stay in New York, attends Belasco's drama *The Girl of the Golden West*. (GARA, 499, 500)
19 Mar.	From Torre del Lago, writes to Clausetti: "I'm still distressed about the libretto. I will no longer do *La femme et le pantin*. An idea has come up: Some time ago I had thought of doing three different sketches (three acts) from Gorky." (GARA, 501)
Apr.	In Torre del Lago. (GARA, 502)
May	In Milan. (GARA, 506–16)
10 July	From Torre del Lago, writes to Clausetti: "Now my ideas are focused on two things: an American girl of the West, very colorful and vital; the other about the revolution with M. Antoinette." (GARA, 517)
Aug.	From Boscolungo, writes to Giulio Ricordi: "That's it! *Girl* promises to become a second *Bohème*, but stronger, more daring and fuller. I picture a grandiose setting, an open space in the Californian forest with colossal trees, but eight or ten horse-extras are necessary." Librettist is Carlo Zangarini. (GARA, 521)
Sept.	In Chiatri. (GARA, 523, 526; PINTORNO, 148)

29 Oct.	In Vienna for *Madama Butterfly* performance on the 31st at the Teatro Imperiale. (PINTORNO, 149)
Nov.–Dec.	In Torre del Lago. (GARA, 529–33)

1908

Jan.	In Milan. (GARA, 534, 537; PINTORNO, 150)
Feb.	For *Butterfly*, being staged in Alexandria, the Maestro spends the month in Egypt with his wife. (GARA, 540–41; MARCHETTI, 344–45)
Mar.	In Torre del Lago and in Rome. (GARA, 543, 544)
Apr.	Guelfo Civinini joins Zangarini in the writing of the libretto for *Fanciulla del West*. (GARA, 545)
May	In Milan. (MARCHETTI, 348)
June–July	In Chiatri. (GARA, 546–48)
fall	In Torre del Lago, he composes a song, *Una riga di musica,* to the words "Casa mia, casa mia." (KAYE, 111)

1909

28 Jan.	Doria Manfredi, a young servant in the Puccini home at Torre del Lago, victim of Elvira's jealous libel involving Puccini, kills herself in her mother's home. Puccini suffers months of tragic anguish because of the ensuing family breach. (MARCHETTI, 351–59)
Feb.	In Rome and Milan. (MARCHETTI, 355)
spring	In Torre del Lago. (GARA, 551–57; PINTORNO, 158)
June	In London and Paris. (GARA, 553; MARCHETTI, 364)
summer	In Torre del Lago. (GARA, 554–55)
Oct.	In Brussels. (MARCHETTI, 367–68)
Nov.	In Torre del Lago. (PUCCINI S, 7)
Dec.	In Torre del Lago and Milan. (MARCHETTI, 370–72)

1910

	In the first months of the year, in Milan and Torre del Lago.
May	In London. (PINTORNO, 163)
June	In Paris, where *Manon Lescaut,* conducted by Toscanini, is given at the Théâtre Le Chatelet. (GARA, 561–63)
28 July	From Torre del Lago, informs Giulio Ricordi that he has finished *La fanciulla del West*. (GARA, 567)
Sept.	With wife and son Antonio, takes a vacation in Switzerland. (MARCHETTI, 380)
Oct.	In Milan. (MARCHETTI, 382–83)
Nov.	Departs for America with his son Antonio. (MARCHETTI, 384)

10 Dec.	At the Metropolitan Opera, New York, the premiere of *La fanciulla del West,* opera in three acts, libretto by Civinini and Zangarini, dedicated to Queen Alexandra of England. Present are the composer and his son. The initial great public success is followed by more cautious judgments from the critics. The opera is given nine performances and remains in the repertory of the Metropolitan for three consecutive years. (GARA, 571)

1911

winter–spring	In Milan and Torre del Lago. (GARA, 574–81)
May	In London. (MARCHETTI, 396)
12 Jun.	*Fanciulla del West*'s Rome premiere, Teatro Costanzi. (PUCCINI S, 9)
14 Jun.	In London. (PINTORNO, 178)
Aug.	Goes to Stelvio. (MARCHETTI, 398)
19 Aug.	Goes to Brescia. (MARCHETTI, 399)
Sept.	In Torre del Lago. (PUCCINI S, 12)

Throughout the year, looking for new librettos; considers *Zoccoletti (Two Little Wooden Shoes),* a novel by Ouida (the pseudonym of Louise de la Ramée), and *Hanneles Himmelfahrt* by Gerhart Hauptmann. In Viareggio he meets the German baroness Josephine von Stängel, with whom he begins an affair that lasts until 1917.

(GARA, 584–85; PUCCINI S, 17)

1912

In the first months of the year, in Tuscany and Milan.

(GARA, 593–95)

29 Feb.	In Budapest for the premiere of *La fanciulla del West,* then in Milan. (MARCHETTI, 403; PINTORNO, 181–83, 185)
2 Apr.	In Monte Carlo, where the Teatro del Casinò performs *Fanciulla del West.* (MARCHETTI, 408; GARA, 596)
8 Apr.	Puccini's sister, Ramelde Puccini Franceschini, dies in Bologna. (MARCHETTI, 409)
16 May	In Paris for *La fanciulla del West* at the Opéra. (MARCHETTI, 413)
6 June	Giulio Ricordi dies. (GARA, 612)
June	In Munich. In search of new subjects, renews contact with d'Annunzio. (MARCHETTI, 414; GARA, 597)
27 Aug.	From Karlsbaden, writes to d'Annunzio: "I persist in wanting from you what I'm looking for and what I lack. Perhaps you are not very aware of my hypersensitive nature under this boorish exterior that makes me seem at times com-

pletely different from what I am; and it is with closer acquaintance and collaboration that one comes to understand what there really is in my timid self . . . I desire so much to work and no one so far has given me what I really want! You, I am sure, can work the miracle; but you must come to me complete, vibrant, original." (GARA, 601)

Sept.–Oct.	In Tuscany, Viareggio, Rome, Torre del Lago, and Boscolungo Pistoiese. (GARA, 602–7)
Nov.	In Marseilles and Paris. (GARA, 608–9; MARCHETTI, 418)
29 Dec.	La Scala premiere of *Fanciulla del West* in Milan. (GARA, 671)

1913

Jan.	d'Annunzio is writing the libretto of *La crociata degli innocenti* (The Children's Crusade), which Puccini is to set music. The subject does not convince him; reconsiders *Zoccoletti*. (GARA, 613–18)
9 Feb.	From Milan he writes to Illica regarding *La Houppelande* by Didier Gold: "It is totally an 'apache' subject, almost Grand Guignol; no, without the almost; but that doesn't matter. I like it and it seems to me very effective. But we must contrast this purple patch with something that is its opposite: what I'm looking for is this: something elevated, with room to make music that soars." (GARA, 619)
28 Mar.	*Fanciulla del West* is performed in Berlin, with Puccini present. (GARA, 621)
Apr.	In Milan and Torre del Lago. (PUCCINI S, 15)
May	In Paris. (GARA, 624–27)
June	From Munich, writes to d'Annunzio: "I'm thinking of great poetic things and tenderness" and "give me a scene of great love." (GARA, 628–29)
5 Oct.	In Leipzig for *Tosca*. (GARA, 631)
24 Oct.	Attends the premiere of *Fanciulla del West* at the Hofoper in Vienna. Following this success, is given the star of the Order of Franz Joseph. (GARA, 632–33)
6 Nov.	From Torre del Lago he writes to the baron Angelo Eisner in Vienna to clarify the request from Heinrich Berté and Siegmund Eibenschütz—directors and impresarios of the Karltheater—for an operetta at a fee of two hundred thousand Austrian crowns. (GARA, 638)
Dec.	In Milan. (GARA, 637–40)
14 Dec.	Writes to Angelo Eisner: "The subject you have sent is absolutely not for me. It's the usual tired, banal operetta . . . an operetta I will never do: comic opera, yes: see *Rosenkavalier*, but more amusing and more organic." (GARA, 638)

1914

Jan.–Feb.	In Milan. (GARA, 641–43)
Mar.	In Milan and Torre del Lago. To Schnabl, expresses his intention to devote himself again to *Zoccoletti,* from Ouida's novel. (PUCCINI S, 16)
Apr.	In Torre del Lago. Negotiations for film adaptation of his operas come to nothing. Receives the contract from Eibenschütz and Berté for the new opera, to be called *La rondine,* with a libretto by Alfred Maria Willner and Heinz Reichert. Plot is reminiscent of *La traviata* and *Die Fledermaus.* (GARA, 647–51; PUCCINI S, 18)
26 May	Writes from Milan to Angelo Eisner: "I'm somewhat distressed because I'm not over fond of the *Rondine* libretto." (GARA, 654)
summer	At Viareggio, works on *Rondine* with Giuseppe Adami, who adapts into Italian the Viennese libretto; Adami drafts sixteen acts before completing the three approved by the Maestro. (GARA, 656–59; PUCCINI S, 19)
Oct.–Nov.	At Torre del Lago. (GARA, 663–64)
25 Dec.	Announces to Eisner that "*La Rondine* is well along; two acts are finished." (GARA, 665)

1915

Jan.–Feb.	In Milan. (GARA, 667–72; MARCHETTI, 425–28; PUCCINI S, 20)
Mar.–May	In Torre del Lago. (GARA 673–75; MARCHETTI, 432–34)
summer	In Torre del Lago. (GARA, 676–77)
2 Sept.	Returns from Switzerland, where he has met Berté for the *Rondine* contract. (GARA, 679)
30 Oct.	From Torre del Lago, writes to Tito Ricordi: "I've had a letter from Berté, who, together with other accomplices, rejects my proposals and postpones until . . . after the war, as after spring, the arrival of la *Rondine.* I . . . have begun to translate the *Houppelande* into notes, but even for this a revision is needed, to make the language, which is now too syrupy, more coarse." Works on *Tabarro* with Adami, who completes the adaptation of Didier Gold's drama begun by Ferdinando Martini. (GARA, 683)
fall	In Torre del Lago. (PUCCINI S, 21–22)
Dec.	In Maremma. (PUCCINI S, 24)

1916

Feb.	In Rome.	(PINTORNO, 197)
Holy Saturday	Writes to Adami: "*La rondine* is absolutely finished! The last scene seems very fine to me. I'm scoring *Tabarro*."	
		(ADAMI, 130)
	The *Zoccoletti* project is abandoned. He spends almost the entire year at Torre del Lago.	(GARA, 686–700)
July	In Torre del Lago.	(PUCCINI S, 25)
31 Oct.	From Torre del Lago, writes to his friend Alfredo Vandini: "I have worked and set free *La rondine*, which will be Sonzogno's."	(GARA, 695)
26 Nov.	From Torre del Lago, informs Tito Ricordi that he has "finished *Houppelande* once and for all."	(GARA, 697)

1917

Jan.	In Milan.	(GARA, 702–705)
Feb.	In Torre del Lago and at Viareggio. (MARCHETTI, 438–39)	
3 Mar.	Giovacchino Forzano writes Tito Ricordi from Viareggio that he has sent Puccini the libretto of *Suor Angelica* and that he has finished a brief synopsis of *Gianni Schicchi*.	
		(GARA, 706)
27 Mar.	In Monte Carlo for premiere of *La rondine,* comedy in three acts, libretto by A. Adami, Alfred M. Willner, and Heinz Reichert—at the Opera.	(PUCCINI S, 29–31)
3 Apr.	Alberto I, prince of Monaco names him Grand Officer of the Ordre de Saint-Charles.	(GARA, 708)
Apr.–May	In Milan. (GARA, 707–8; MARCHETTI, 441; PINTORNO, 203)	
2 June	First Italian performance of *La rondine* at Teatro Comunale, Bologna.	(PUCCINI S, 35)
summer–fall	In Tuscany and Milan.	(GARA, 712–15)
14 Sept.	Finishes *Suor Angelica* (date noted on autographed score).	
7 Oct.	*La rondine* staged at the Teatro dal Verme, Milan.	
		(MARCHETTI, 447)
Nov.	In Viareggio. Works on *Gianni Schicchi;* composes *Morire?,* for tenor and piano, text by Adami, dedicated to Elena di Savoia, Queen of Italy. It was part of an album sold to raise funds for the Italian Red Cross.	
		(PUCCINI S, 38, 39; GARA, 713; KAYE, 119)

1918

10 Jan.	*La rondine* is staged at Teatro Costanzi, Rome.	
		(PUCCINI S, 40)
Mar.	In Viareggio.	(PINTORNO, 214)

July	Begins making revisions of *La rondine*. Adami retouches the libretto. Puccini's three versions of the opera vary chiefly in the third act, which differed very much from the first edition.
summer	In Viareggio, and, with the painter Galileo Chini, discusses the staging of *Trittico*. (GARA, 727, 728)
fall	At Torre del Lago. (GARA, 732–36)
Nov.	In Viareggio. (PUCCINI S, 45)
Dec.	In Rome for the preparation of *Trittico*. (GARA, 738–40)
14 Dec.	At the Metropolitan Opera House, New York, premiere of the three one-act operas collectively called *Il trittico: Il tabarro*, libretto by Adami; *Suor Angelica* and *Gianni Schicchi*, librettos by Forzano. The opinions of the critics are discordant, but the work is a great success with the public. Because of precarious postwar travel conditions, Puccini does not attend. (GARA, 738)

1919

Jan.	Italian premiere of *Il trittico*, conducted by Gino Marinuzzi, at the Teatro Costanzi, Rome, in the presence of the royal family and the duchess of Aosta. Puccini is also present. (PUCCINI S, 46)
Feb.–Apr.	At Torre del Lago.
26 Mar.	Writes to his wife: "I have finished *Inno a Roma* (a real piece of crap)." It is an occasional composition, for chorus and orchestra, text by Fausto Salvatori, dedicated to the princess Jolanda di Savoia. (GARA, 751; KAYE, 127)
20 June	Attends *Il trittico* at Covent Garden, London. (GARA, 754–56)
July–Aug.	At Torre del Lago. Further revision of *La rondine*. Adami works with him. (GARA, 760)
fall	In Tuscany. (PINTORNO, 223–26)
16 Dec.	Illica dies at Colombarone.

1920

| Feb. | At Torre della Tagliata (Orbetello).   (GARA, 765; MARCHETTI, 453–54) |
| 18 Mar. | In the Maestro's correspondence, first mention of *Turandot*, of which he writes from Rome to Renato Simoni: "I have read *Turandot*; it seems to me wise to stick to this subject. Yesterday I spoke with a foreign lady who told me about this work as it was staged in Germany by Max Reinhardt . . . Turandot was a tiny, tiny woman; surrounded by very tall men, especially chosen; big chairs, big furnishings, and this little viperish woman, and with a strange hysterical heart."   (GARA, 766) |

Apr.	Present in Venice at second performance of *Il trittico*. (Puccini S, 51)
18 June	*Trittico* is staged at London's Covent Garden; Puccini present. (Gara, 767; Puccini S, 52; Pintorno, 229–31)
28 July	Develops in detail the scenario of *Turandot*. From Torre del Lago, writes to Simoni: "Our princess (on whom my mind focuses more and more) will be happy to see us united to vivisect her soul." (Gara, 770)
Aug.	At Bagni di Lucca and Torre del Lago. (Puccini S, 54–57)
Sept.	At Torre del Lago. (Puccini S, 58–61)
9 Oct.	In Vienna, present at premiere of *La rondine* at the Volksoper. (Puccini S, 61)
20 Oct.	Attends premiere of *Il trittico* at the Staatsoper of Vienna. (Puccini S, 61)
4 Dec.	At Torre della Tagliata; writes to Simoni: "My anxiety—I'd almost say suffering—at my idleness and my frenzy to be at work—that is, for the tyrannical princess—are growing day by day . . . I jot down themes and conceive processions, I whisper hidden choruses, invent unearthly harmonies . . . but for goodness sake, hurry, hurry; I'd like all the work finished, choice, polished; already I can savor the goodness and the beauty of the verses, and also of the images and above all the clear and moving humanity that is in this story full of poetry and of special perfume." (Gara, 779)
Dec.	At Torre della Tagliata (Orbetello). (Puccini S, 65–66)

1921

Jan.–Feb.	In Milan. (Gara, 786–91; Marchetti, 455–58; Puccini S, 70–74)
Mar.	In Milan. (Puccini S, 76)
19 Mar.	*Il Trittico* is staged at the Monte Carlo opera. (Puccini S, 76)
22 Mar.	From Monte Carlo, writes to Simoni: "I believe (maybe) that I will never be so attached to a work as I am to *Turandot*." (Gara, 806)
May–June	At Torre del Lago. (Gara, 796–804)
4 July	Goes to Rome. (Gara, 806)
23 July	From Torre del Lago, writes to Simoni: "I pray you, beg you, to see and speak with Signor Toeplitz, head of the Banca Commerciale, so that he will intervene with the direction of the peat company, so that I am not deprived of my hunting rights which I have had for the last 15 years . . . Otherwise I must decamp forever from Torre del Lago." (Gara, 809)
1 Aug.	From Torre del Lago, writes to R. Schnabl: "I have finished Act One of *Turandot*." (Puccini S, 84)

16–26 Aug.	In Munich.	(GARA 814–15; PUCCINI S, 85)
Oct.	In Bologna.	(GARA, 888)
Dec.	Moves to Viareggio to the house he has had constructed on Viale Buonarrotti 76. Spends a period at Torre della Tagliata.	(PUCCINI S, 90)

1922

Jan.	In Milan.	(PUCCINI S, 92–93)
13 Jan.	To Raoul Gunsbourg, director of the Opera of Monte Carlo, expresses the intention to stage once again the "poor little *Rondine*" in its third version.	(GARA, 824)
28 Jan.	*Il trittico* performed at the Teatro Costanzi in Rome.	(PUCCINI S, 93)
29 Jan.	*Il trittico* performed at La Scala in Milan.	(PUCCINI S, 93)
Feb.	In Rome.	(PUCCINI S, 95)
Mar.	In Rome and Viareggio.	(GARA, 818; PUCCINI S, 96–98)
2 Apr.	From Viareggio, writes Schnabl: "I'm working on *Turandot* so that, if God spares my life, it will turn out to be a notable thing—nay, an extraordinary thing."	(PUCCINI S, 99)
May–June	In Viareggio.	
summer	In Viareggio.	(PUCCINI S, 100–105)
20 Aug.	With his son Antonio and his friends the Magrinis, departs for a motor trip across Europe. The itinerary is the following: Cutigliano, Verona, Bolzano, Innsbruck, Munich, Oberammergau, Nuremberg, Frankfurt, and along the Rhine to Cologne. Then all of Holland up to the North Sea, then Amsterdam, Rotterdam, the Hague, etc.	(PUCCINI S, 106–7; PINTORNO, 241–42)
28 Aug.	In Ingolstadt, at a luncheon, nearly chokes to death on a goose bone.	(GARA, 838)
fall	In Viareggio.	(PUCCINI S, 108–15)
2 Oct.	In the Augustinian nuns' convent at Vicopelago, near Lucca, his sister, Iginia, Sister Giulia Enrichetta, dies.	(PUCCINI S, 109–10; MARCHETTI, 463; PINTORNO, 243)
Nov.	In Rome.	(GARA, 850)
Dec.	In Milan.	(GARA, 852)
26 Dec.	At La Scala in Milan, Toscanini conducts "a great *Manon*."	(PUCCINI S, 118)

1923

Jan.–Feb.	In Milan and Viareggio. Goes to Venice.	(PUCCINI S, 119; PINTORNO, 244)
Apr.	In Viareggio.	(GARA, 859–60)

May	Goes to Vienna to be present at some of his operas: *Tosca, Madama Butterfly, La bohème,* and *Manon Lescaut.* This last is postponed until the autumn season; the others are performed respectively on 15 and 20 May and 6 June at the Staatsoper. (GARA, 861–65; PUCCINI S, 120)
summer	In Viareggio. (PUCCINI S, 121–25)
15 Oct.	In Vienna for *Manon Lescaut* at the Staatsoper. (GARA, 871–72)
Nov.	To his friend Angiolino Magrini, confides that he is in poor health. (GARA, 873)
22 Dec.	From Viareggio, writes to Schnabl: "I work, orchestrate, and compose; however I lack the grand finale of the third act, which I have had redone for the fourth time"; and to Simoni: "Steal an hour or two from your great activity and dedicate them to this poor old maestro who urgently needs to finish this magnum opus." (PUCCINI S, 126; GARA, 877)

1924

Jan.	In Milan. (GARA, 880)
Feb.	In Viareggio. (GARA, 881–86)
25 Mar.	From Viareggio, writes to Simoni: "I have worked relentlessly for four months and I'm almost at the end: all I lack is the final duet . . . I seem to have 'travailed' well; maybe I'm mistaken, what with the trends that nowadays they are venturing, along treacherous paths of sounds and discordances where sentiment, that sentiment that produces joy and tears, is abolished or kept distant. I have placed, in this opera, all my soul." Suffers a severe sore throat but the doctors find nothing serious. (GARA, 887)
May	Is named Senator of Italy. (GARA, 889)
1 June	Goes to Salsomaggiore for a thermal cure, which proves unhelpful. (PUCCINI S, 131–32)
summer	In Viareggio. (PUCCINI S, 134–35)
Aug.	Desires to dispel the lingering tension with Toscanini after the conductor's ban on spectators at the dress rehearsal of Boito's *Nerone* (at the end of April) was not lifted for Puccini. His sore throat worsens; considers consulting specialists in Switzerland and in Germany. (GARA, 894, 895; PUCCINI S, 136)
7 Sept.	From Viareggio, writes to Adami: "Toscanini has just left here. We're in perfect, heartfelt accord and finally I can breathe easy." (ADAMI, 233)
Oct.	With Brunelleschi and Chini the Maestro perfects the *mise en scène* of *Turandot.* The thought of the final duet troubles

him. The pain in his throat becomes intolerable; accompanied by his son, consults three eminent specialists. Torrigiani, Toti, and Gradenigo find a carcinoma on the pharynx and advise a radium cure, which in Europe is carried out in Berlin and Brussels.   (GARA, 902)

3 Nov.   Informs Schnabl of his imminent departure: "They're sending me to Brussels!!! It's serious! You can imagine my morale. I'm going with Tonio. Elvira is too frail to undertake a long trip. What misery. And *Turandot?* Oh, it pains me not to have finished this opera. Will I recover? Can I finish it in time?"   (PUCCINI S, 138)

4 Nov.   Departs for Brussels with his son. Brings with him the rough draft of the *Turandot* finale.   (PUCCINI S, 138)

5 Nov.   In Brussels, admitted to the Institut de la Couronne, Professor Ledoux's clinic, where tumors are experimentally treated with X-rays.   (PUCCINI S, 138)

12 Nov.   Begins treatment with external applications of radium. During this first phase of treatment, is permitted to leave the clinic for short periods. Goes with his son to a performance of *Butterfly* at the Théâtre de la Monnaie.
                                            (GARA, 907; PINTORNO, 249)

24 Nov.   Undergoes surgery and internal applications of radium.
                                                              (GARA, 913)

28 Nov.   Toward evening has a heart attack.   (GARA, 915)

29 Nov.   The Maestro dies in the morning.   (MARCHETTI, 471)

1 Dec.   A religious ceremony takes place in Brussels in the church of Sainte Marie.   (CARNER, 331)

3 Dec.   Cardinal Tosi celebrates the official funeral in Milan Cathedral. In the church, Toscanini conducts the Scala orchestra in a performance of the *Funeral March* from *Edgar*. An enormous crowd attends. Puccini is temporarily buried in the Toscanini family tomb in the Cimiterio Monumentale, Milan.   (CARNER, 332)

1925

At Toscanini's suggestion, Franco Alfano is engaged to complete the *Turandot* score.   (CARNER, 332–33)

1926

25 Apr.   First performance, at La Scala, of *Turandot,* three-act opera, libretto by Simoni and Adami. Performed without Alfano's ending (heard, however, in subsequent performances).
                                                            (CARNER, 333)

29 Nov. Puccini's remains are transported to Torre del Lago and entombed in the chapel he had his son construct inside the villa. (CARNER, 107)

Note: Some of Puccini's nonoperatic compositions remain uncertain as to chronology and sometimes attribution. For the relative critical debate, see Michael Kaye's contribution to this volume.

Translated by William McKnight

References

ADAMI Giuseppe Adami, ed., *Giacomo Puccini: Epistolario* (Milan, 1928).

CARNER Mosco Carner, *Giacomo Puccini: Biografia critica* (Milan, 1961).

GARA Eugenio Gara et al., eds., *Carteggi pucciniani* (Milan, 1958).

KAYE Michael Kaye, *The Unknown Puccini* (New York and Oxford, 1987).

MARCHETTI Arnaldo Marchetti, ed., *Puccini com'era* (Milan, 1973).

PINTORNO Giuseppe Pintorno, ed., *Puccini: 276 lettere inedite* (Milan, 1974).

PUCCINI S Simonetta Puccini, ed., *Giacomo Puccini: Lettere a Riccardo Schnabl* (Milan, 1981).

QUADERNI PUCCIANI I *Quaderni Pucciniani I* (Lucca: Istituto di Studi Pucciniani, 1982).

QUADERNI PUCCIANI II *Quaderni Pucciniani II* (Lucca: Istituto di Studi Pucciniani, 1985).

GMM *Gazzetta Musicale di Milano* (Milan, 1842–1902).

APPENDIX A

DRAMATIS PERSONAE

Simonetta Puccini and William Weaver, with Michael Elphinstone and William McKnight

William McKnight graduated from New York University, where he majored in Italian. He also pursued studies in Bologna.

ABENIACAR, CARLO. Author, photojournalist, possible hunting companion of Puccini, for whom he wrote the text of the song *Inno a Diana,* dedicated "to Italian hunters."

ADAM, ADOLPHE-CHARLES (1803–56). French composer and student of Boieldieu, by whom he was strongly influenced. His forty-one *opéra-comiques,* which prepared the way for Offenbach, are characterized by a fluidity of ideas and lightness of style. His most famous work remains the ballet *Giselle* (1841), the subject of which is similar to that of Puccini's *Le villi.*

ADAMI, GIUSEPPE (1878–1946). Italian playwright, critic, and writer. Librettist of *La rondine, Il tabarro,* and—in collaboration with Renato Simoni (*q.v.*)—*Turandot.* Also wrote the text of the song *Morire?* (1917). After Puccini's death, Adami published an important collection of the composer's letters (*Epistolario,* 1928) and two biographies: *Puccini* (1935) and *Il romanzo della vita di Giacomo Puccini* (1942).

AMATO, PASQUALE (1878–1942). Italian baritone. Debut in Naples, 1900, as Lescaut in *Manon Lescaut.* Created the part of Rance in *La fanciulla del West,* New York (1910), and many roles under Toscanini (*q.v.*), including Golaud in the Italian premiere of Debussy's *Pelléas et Mélisande*. After his debut with the Metropolitan Opera (Germont) in 1908, he remained with the company until 1921, creating Damrosch's Cyrano (1913) and Napoleon in Giordano's *Madame Sans-Gêne* (1915). His repertory also included Puccini's *Tosca, Bohème,* and *Le villi* (in its Metropolitan premiere, 1908).

ANGELONI, CARLO (1834–1901). Italian composer and music teacher from Lucca, where he studied with Michele Puccini (the composer's father) and later taught *armonia teorico-pratica* at the Istituto Pacini until 1872, when he replaced Fortunato Magi (*q.v.*) as *professore di composizione e contrappunto.* Puccini's first important teacher of composition, introducing his student to Verdi scores—*Rigoletto, La traviata,* and *Il trovatore.*

ANTINORI, COUNT PIETRO. Italian nobleman. The first to recommend Belasco's play *The Girl of the Golden West* to Puccini.

ARRIVABENE, COUNT OPPRANDINO (1805–87). Italian nobleman, writer, patriot, and close friend of Verdi's.

BADA, ANGELO (1875–1941). Italian tenor. Debut in 1898. Sang small roles at La Scala and Covent Garden before becoming *primo tenore comprimario* at the Metropolitan Opera, a position he held from 1908 until 1938. In that theater, sang in the premieres of three of Puccini's operas, as Trin in *La fanciulla del West,* 1910, and as Tinca and Gherardo in *Il trittico* (*Il tabarro* and *Gianni Schicchi* respectively), 1918.

BARACCHI, ARISTIDE (1885–1964). Italian baritone *comprimario.* Created the Mandarin in *Turandot.* Repertory included Schaunard and other Puccini roles.

BAZZINI, ANTONIO (1818–97). Italian violin virtuoso, composer, and teacher. Strongly encouraged by Paganini, spent early part of career touring Europe as a soloist. Lived for several years in Germany and France, establishing close friendships with Schumann and Mendelssohn. After returning to Italy, dedicated himself to composition, particularly of instrumental music. Wrote one opera, *Turanda* (1867), based, like Puccini's *Turandot,* on the fable by Gozzi (*q.v.*). For almost two years (December 1880 to June 1882) he was Puccini's professor of composition at the Regio Conservatorio, Milan; when he became director of that institute in July 1882, his teaching duties were taken over by Ponchielli (*q.v.*).

BELASCO, DAVID (1854–1931). American playwright, impresario, and director, particularly famous for his stage effects. Author and producer of the original play *The Girl of the Golden West* and of *Madame Butterfly,* based on a short story by John Luther Long (*q.v.*). Collaborated in staging the world premiere of *La fanciulla del West* at the Metropolitan Opera.

BERNHARDT, SARAH (1844–1923). French actress. Creator of the role of Floria Tosca in the original play *La Tosca* (1887) by Sardou (*q.v.*), who dedicated the work to her.

BERTÉ, HEINRICH (1858–1924). Austro-Hungarian composer of ballets and operettas, including the extremely successful Schubert pastiche *Dreimae-derlhaus,* known in English as *Lilac Time* or *Blossom Time.* With Eibenschitz directed the Karltheater in Vienna, for which Puccini was originally commissioned to write the work that became *La rondine.*

BIAGINI, CARLO. A Puccini cousin who befriended and gave hospitality to Giacomo in Milan during the latter's conservatory years.

BOITO, ARRIGO (1842–1918). Italian poet, librettist, critic, opera composer, translator, and member of the Milanese *scapigliatura.* Author of numerous librettos, including the texts for his own operas, *Mefistofele* and *Nerone,* as well as *La Gioconda* for Puccini's teacher Ponchielli, and *Otello* and *Falstaff* for Verdi, whose close friend he became during the older man's last two decades. Impressed by a private hearing of Puccini's *Le villi,* he helped arrange its first public performance, Puccini's professional debut. Puccini's later music found him less enthusiastic.

BOLZONI, GIOVANNI (1841–1919). Italian conductor, violinist, composer, and teacher. On Verdi's recommendation he was named conductor of the Teatro Regio in Turin (1884), where he remained until 1889. He conducted the premiere there of *Le villi* in its two-act version. At the Turin Conservatory one of his pupils was Edgard Varèse.

BORONAT, ELENA. Italian soprano, sister of the more famous Olimpia. First interpreter of Anna in the two-act version of *Le villi* (Turin, 1884).

BRUNELLESCHI, UMBERTO (1879–1949). Italian painter and caricaturist. Studied in Florence, but settled in Paris, where he began his theater activity as a scene painter in 1912. Friend of Modigliani, Soutine, Picasso, and d'Annunzio. Did a lively caricature portrait of Puccini for the humorous review *L'Assiette au Beurre* (under the pseudonym Aroun-al-rashid). Designed the costumes for *Turandot* (sketches preserved in the Museo della Scala, Milan). Died in Paris.

CAMPANINI, CLEOFONTE (1860–1919). Italian conductor and violinist. Expelled from the Parma Conservatory for lack of discipline, studied privately; acted as assistant to Faccio, Usiglio, and Mancinelli. Won success in 1882 at the Regio, Turin, with *Carmen.* In 1884 he was conductor at the Turin Exhibition. Conducted the premieres, at La Scala, of Cilea's *Adriana Lecouvreur,* Giordano's *Siberia,* and the disastrous *Madama Butterfly* of 1904.

CAPONETTI, ROSINA. Soprano. Created the role of Anna in *Le willis,* Milan, 1884.

CAPPELLETTI, MEDARSE. Italian writer and journalist, from Lucca. In 1882 he had apparently agreed to provide the student Puccini with a short libretto, which would have enabled the composer to enter the Bonetti Competition organized by the Milan Conservatory.

CARIGNANI, CARLO (1857–1919). Italian composer, conductor, and voice teacher. Lifelong friend of Puccini's. Conducted premiere of the revised, three-act version of *Edgar* (Ferrara, 1892). Prepared the piano-vocal scores of all of Puccini's operas, except *Le villi* and *Turandot,* for the publishing houses of Ricordi and Sonzogno (*La rondine*).

CARRÉ, ALBERT (1852–1938). French impresario. Director of the Opéra-Comique, Paris, 1898–1912, where he produced premieres of Charpentier's *Louise* and Debussy's *Pelléas.* He also presented the French premiere of *Madama Butterfly* (1906), in a specially revised version, with his wife, the soprano Marguérite Carré (1880–1947) in the title role. He also wrote several librettos, the best known for Messager's *La Basoche.*

CARUSO, ENRICO (1872–1921). Italian tenor of undying fame. After making his debut in *Cavalleria rusticana* (Naples, 1895), had early successes in St. Petersburg, Buenos Aires, and Milan (La Scala) before moving to New York, where he sang with the Metropolitan Opera from 1903 to 1920. While admiring his voice, Puccini was sometimes irked by Caruso. Still, he wrote for him the part of Dick Johnson (*Fanciulla*), which Caruso created with success at the Met. Caruso was also a favorite Des Grieux, Rodolfo, and Pinkerton.

CASELLA, ALFREDO (1883–1947). Italian composer, conductor, and pianist. Studied in Paris (under Gabriel Fauré), then enjoyed international success as pianist and conductor. As a composer he can be classified an antiromantic and cosmopolitan. In addition to his activity as teacher, composer, and soloist, also edited music for pianoforte, wrote essays on various aspects of music history and theory, and was active in setting up several Italian musical organizations and festivals. Inevitably, he was unsympathetic to Puccini's music, which belonged—he felt—to a world that had run its course.

CATALANI, ALFREDO (1854–1893). Italian composer. A native of Lucca, he studied there with Puccini's uncle Fortunato Magi, then in Paris, and at the Milan Conservatory (with Bazzini). His graduation piece, the one-act *La falce* (libretto by Boito), launched him well in 1875, but his career was uneven. He taught composition at the Regio Conservatorio from 1890 until his death. He had many admirers, Toscanini in particular, and his last opera, *La Wally* (1892), has maintained a precarious foothold in the Italian repertory. Other works include *Elda* (1880), *Dejanice* (1883), *Edmea* (1886), and *Loreley* (1890). He lived in Milan during the period in which

Puccini studied and composed his first operas there, but their relationship was a rather cool one.

CATANEO, AURELIA CARUSON (1864–91). Italian soprano. Debut in Salerno, 1881 (*La traviata*). Gradually developed into a dramatic soprano and triumphed as the first Italian Isolde (Bologna, 1888). Created the role of Fidelia (*Edgar*) in 1889. She died in childbirth at the height of a brilliant career.

CAVALIERI, LINA (1874–1944). Italian soprano, who made her debut in 1900 at the Teatro San Carlos, Lisbon, in *Pagliacci,* then, shortly afterward, sang in *La bohème* at the San Carlo, Naples. Famed more for her beauty and acting ability than for any vocal prowess, she was a much-admired Manon Lescaut and Tosca.

CERÙ, NICOLAO (1817–94). Puccini's so-called great-uncle (really, nephew of his paternal grandmother), a well-known doctor and philanthropist in Lucca. He gave generous financial assistance to Giacomo during his student years at the Milan Conservatory and, later, also helped Giacomo's younger brother Michele (*q.v.*).

CHINI, GALILEO (1873–1956). Italian painter, ceramist, designer. Chiefly a decorator of churches, ships, and palaces, including the Royal Palace, Bangkok, which he worked between 1911 and 1914. Later taught at the Accademia delle Belle Arti in Florence. At La Scala, designed the sets for the world premiere of *Turandot* and the house premiere of *Gianni Schicchi*.

CIVININI, GUELFO (1873–1954) Italian journalist (from Livorno), foreign correspondent for various important newspapers including *La Riforma, La Patria, Il Giornale d'Italia,* and *Il Corrierre della Sera.* Also poet, novelist, and travel writer. Collaborated on the libretto of *Fanciulla,* reducing and revising the version first prepared by Carlo Zangarini (*q.v.*).

CONRIED, HEINRICH (1848–1909). Austrian-born impresario. Managed several New York theaters, and in 1903 leased the Metropolitan Opera House for five years. He introduced many important singers, including Enrico Caruso and Geraldine Farrar, who starred in a special production of *Madama Butterfly* supervised by the composer, whom Conried had brought to America for a gala Puccini season.

CORSI, EMILIA (1870–1927). Italian soprano, born in Lisbon. Created Musetta in the *Bohème* of Leoncavallo, but also sang Puccini's Mimì and, particularly, his Manon, with which she achieved an immense success in Palermo in 1898. Retired around 1910.

CREMONINI, GIUSEPPE (born GIUSEPPE BIANCHI) (1866–1903). Italian tenor. Debut in Genoa, 1889, in *Linda di Chamounix*. Created the role of Des Grieux in *Manon Lescaut,* Turin, 1893.

CRIMI, GIULIO (1885–1939). Italian tenor. Made debut in *La Wally,* Treviso, 1912. Sang with the Chicago Opera from 1916 to 1918 and then from 1922 to 1924, and was engaged by the Metropolitan Opera, New York, from 1918 to 1922, where he was principal tenor in the world premiere of *Il trittico,* singing the roles of Luigi in *Il tabarro* and Rinuccio in *Gianni Schicchi.* Other Puccini roles included Rodolfo and Mario Cavaradossi (which he sang in the United States premiere of *Tosca* at the Met in 1901). Pupils included Tito Gobbi.

DALLA RIZZA, GILDA (1892–1975). Italian soprano. Debut in Bologna, 1910 (Charlotte, *Werther*). Her moving performance of Minnie in Florence (1913), brought her to Puccini's attention, and he wrote the role of Magda (*La rondine*) for her. She created it at Monte Carlo in 1917, then sang in the Italian premiere of *Il trittico* in Rome, 1919 (Suor Angelica and Lauretta). Her repertory also included Puccini's Manon, as well as Tosca and Butterfly. After her performance in *La fanciulla del West,* Monte Carlo, 1921, Puccini said, "At last I've seen my fanciulla." Puccini wrote the part of Liù (*Turandot*) with Dalla Rizza in mind, but she did not participate in the posthumous premiere. Greatly admired by Toscanini.

D'ANDRADE, ANTONIO (1854–1942). Portuguese tenor. Came to Italy in 1881 to study with Miraglia and Ronconi. Debut in Varese, 1882, in Donizetti's *La Favorita.* First Roberto in *Le willis,* Milan, 1884. After singing in all major European houses, he was forced by deafness to retire prematurely. He spent his last years in Lisbon.

D'ANNUNZIO, GABRIELE (1863–1938). Italian poet, novelist, playwright, and political figure. When Puccini, in mid-career, was conducting one of his regular searches for a libretto, Tito Ricordi (*q.v.*) brought him together with d'Annunzio, then at the height of his notoriety. The poet made several suggestions, which Puccini rejected. Mascagni set one of them (*Parisina*). Other d'Annunzio dramas were set by Zandonai, Franchetti, Pizzetti, and Montemezzi.

DARCLÉE, HARICLEA (born HARICLY HARTULARY) (1860–1939). Romanian soprano. Studied in Paris with Jean-Baptiste Faure, making her debut in *Faust* (1888) as Marguérite. In 1890 she had huge success at La Scala in Massenet's *Le Cid,* after which she was immediately engaged by all leading Italian theaters. Created roles of Wally, Iris (Mascagni), and Tosca (Rome, 1900), but also sang coloratura roles, i.e. Gilda and Ophelia (*Hamlet*), and heavier Verdian roles (e.g. Aida). Her voice began to decline as early as 1905.

DE LUCA, GIUSEPPE (1876–1950). Italian baritone. Debut in Piacenza, 1897 (Valentin). In 1902 he created Michonnet in *Adriana Lecouvreur.* The following year, at La Scala, sang in world premiere of Giordano's *Siberia.* Was the first Sharpless in Puccini's *Madama Butterfly,* both in Milan, 1904, and in Brescia, 1904 (revised version). Later created the title role of Gianni Schicchi (*Il trittico*), in New York, 1918. His Puccini roles also included Marcello. Starting in 1915, sang at the Metropolitan for more than twenty seasons. He gave his farewell recital in 1947, fifty years after his debut.

DE MARCHI, EMILIO (1856 or 1861–1917). Italian tenor. His vocal gifts were discovered while he was serving as a lieutenant of the Bersaglieri. Debut in 1886 in *La traviata* at the Teatro Dal Verme in Milan. Was soon engaged by major opera houses, including Palermo, Rome, Bologna, Madrid, Barcelona, and Buenos Aires (where he sang from 1890 until 1900). Sang the role of Roberto in *Le villi* (Naples, 1888). Created the role of Cavaradossi in *Tosca* (Rome, 1900). He sang the role in leading opera houses all over the world, rivaled only by Caruso in the part. Some fragments of his interpretation were recorded on Mapleson cylinders. Retired in 1909 because of a throat illness.

DE NEGRI, GIOVANNI BATTISTA (1850–1923). Italian tenor. One of the most highly esteemed dramatic tenors of the closing decades of the nineteenth century. Was a famous interpreter of Verdi's *Otello* (considered by some as superior even to the creator Tamagno [*q.v.*] in this role), Wagner's *Tannhäuser,* and Saint-Saëns's *Samson.* Created Mascagni's Ratcliff, La Scala (1895). Was engaged to sing the title role in Puccini's *Edgar* for the 1890 spring season at La Scala, but production was cancelled when he became ill. (De Negri did eventually sing Edgar for performances staged at Brescia, August, 1892.)

DE SERVI, LUIGI (1863–1945). Italian painter. Native of Lucca and childhood friend of Puccini's. After a stay in Argentina, De Servi lived for many years in Genoa. He was one of the artists who decorated Puccini's Torre del Lago villa. He also painted several portraits of the master.

DESTINN, EMMY (born EMA KITTL) (1878–1930). Czechoslovakian soprano admired as singer and actress. Made debut as Santuzza in *Cavalleria rusticana* in Dresden and at the Krolloper in Berlin, 1898. She sang at Covent Garden from 1904–19, where she was London's first Cio-Cio-San, and at the Met from 1908–16 and 1919–21, where she created the role of Minnie in *Fanciulla del West* (1910). Great interpreter of Puccinian roles, particularly Cio-cio-san, but repertoire ranged from Mozart to Wagner to Richard Strauss.

DIDUR, ADAMO (1874–1946). Polish bass. Debut in Rio (1894). During his stay at the Warsaw Opera he sang Colline (*Bohème*). He then moved to La Scala (1904–1906), and to Covent Garden. Between 1908 and 1933 he sang chiefly at the Met, where he created Ashby in the premiere of *Fanciulla* and Il Talpa in *Il tabarro*. He returned to Poland in 1939, briefly directed the Lwów Opera, and taught voice.

DOMINICETI, CESARE (1821–88). Italian composer and teacher. He was professor of composition at the Regio Conservatory, Milan, during Puccini's student years; together with Faccio, Ponchielli, and Galli (*q.v.*) served on the commission which selected the winning opera in the first Son-zogno Competition (1883). An important figure in the Italian musical world, his best known work was *Il lago delle fate* (1878).

DOMINICI, FRANCESCO (1885–1968). Italian tenor. Debut in *Figlia del reggimento* (Bergamo, 1915). Created the role of Prunier (*La rondine*) at Monte Carlo in 1917 (a role he repeated in the Italian premiere of the opera, Bologna, 1917) and that of Altoum in the posthumous 1926 premiere of *Turandot*. His other Scala roles included Shuisky in *Boris Godunov*, David in *Meistersinger von Nürnberg,* and Cajus in the Toscanini *Falstaff.*

D'ORMEVILLE, CARLO (1840–1924). Italian dramatist, librettist, impresario, agent, music critic, and Director of Scenery at La Scala. Founded several publications in Rome and Milan (including *La Gazzetta dei Teatri*). In 1871 he staged the premiere of *Aida* in Cairo. Wrote about eighty librettos, among them those for Marchetti's *Ruy Blas,* Ponchielli's *Lina,* and Catalani's *Loreley.*

DUROT, EUGENIO (?–1908). French tenor, specializing in dramatic roles (he was a renowned Otello.) At La Scala, 1883–84. He sang the title role of Edgar in the second production of Puccini's opera (Lucca, 1891) and in the revised, three-act version (Ferrara, 18 August 1892).

EASTON, FLORENCE (1884–1955). English operatic and lieder soprano. Debut, Moody-Manners Company in 1903 (Shepherd, *Tannhäuser*). Spent periods in United States and Berlin (Royal Opera, 1907–13). She sang at the Metropolitan Opera from 1917–29 and 1935–36, where she created Lauretta in *Gianni Schicchi.* Also sang Turandot and Tosca, as well as Wagnerian roles and Carmen.

EIBENSCHÜTZ, ZSIGÀ (SIEGMUND; sometimes erroneously identified as OTTO) (1856–1922). Director, with Harry Berté (*q.v.*), of Vienna's Karltheater, for which Puccini was originally contracted to write an operetta that eventually turned into the opera *La rondine.* For various reasons the work had its premiere in Monte Carlo and not Vienna.

EISNER-EISENHOF, BARON ANGELO. Viennese nobleman, member of important Viennese theatrical and artistic circles. Made Puccini's acquaintance in 1892 when the composer was in Hamburg for a production of *Le villi* and eventually came to act as Puccini's "honorary agent" in Vienna. Active in the original negotiations with the Karltheater for the work that subsequently became *La rondine.*

FACCIO, FRANCO (born FRANCESCO) (1840–91). Italian conductor and composer. Close friend of Boito's (*q.v.*) from Conservatory days. His first opera, *I profughi fiamminghi* (libretto by Ghislanzoni) was given at La Scala in 1863; his *Amleto* (libretto by Boito) in Genoa, 1865. Considered a partisan of Wagner and thus (by Verdi) an enemy of Verdi. But after his appointment as chief conductor at La Scala in 1871 (where he conducted the Italian premiere of *Aida* and the premieres of the revised *Simon Boccanegra* (1881) and of *Otello* (1887), he gradually—like Boito—gained the older composer's friendship. Played an important role in the performance and diffusion of Puccini's earliest Milanese compositions, conducting the first performances of Puccini's school-leaving piece, *Capriccio sinfonico* (July 1883, July and October 1884), the first Scala performance of *Le villi* (January 1885), and the world premiere of *Edgar* (Scala, April 1889). Died in a mental asylum, Monza.

FANELLI, FRANCESCO (CECCO) (1863–1924). Italian painter. Lived at Torre del Lago and was in the local circle of Puccini's friends. Decorated "La Piaggetta," villa of Marchese Ginori.

FARRAR, GERALDINE (1882–1967). American soprano. Debut in Berlin, Royal Opera Company, 1901. Metropolitan debut in 1906 as Juliette. Remained with the company until her retirement in 1922. Her repertory included twenty-nine roles. She sang in the North American premiere of *Butterfly* (February 1907) and created Suor Angelica in the world premiere of *Il trittico* (Met, 1918). She sang several other Puccini roles, including Mimì and Manon. Though her voice was not exceptional, she was enormously popular because of her acting ability and charm. She made a number of films.

FERRANI, CESIRA (born CESIRA ZANAZZIO) (1863–1943). Italian soprano. Studied with the Verdian interpreter Antonietta Fricci (Frietsche). Like Farrar, Ferrani was more a great interpreter than a great singer. She created, with success, the roles of Manon Lescaut (Turin, 1893) and Mimì in *Bohème* (Turin, 1896). She was the first Italian Mélisande (chosen by Toscanini), and also sang lighter Wagnerian roles (Eva and Elsa). In 1909, after a disastrous performance of *Pelléas* in Rome, Ferrani retired to Turin and established a salon, which became the center of intellectual life in that city.

FERRARIS, INES MARIA (1886?–?). Italian soprano. Debut in Bologna, 1908, as Philine (*Mignon*). Created the soubrette role of Lisette in *La rondine* (Monte Carlo, 1917).

FILIPPI, FILIPPO (1830–87). Italian music critic. Wrote regularly for *La Gazzetta Musicale di Milano*, 1858–62, and for *La Perseveranza*, 1859–67. A leading Italian Wagnerian and therefore considered suspect by Verdi. Went to Cairo in 1871 for the premiere of *Aida* and wrote a colorful series of articles, later published in book form. Recognized Puccini's talents in the early *Capriccio sinfonico* and wrote favorably about both versions of *Le villi* while denying Puccini's Wagnerism. An important contributor to the composer's initial success.

FILIPPI-BRESCIANI, ENRICO. Italian tenor. Sang Roberto in the premiere of the second version of *Le villi* (Turin, 1884).

FLETA, MIGUEL. (1893–1938). Spanish tenor. Debut in Trieste, 1919, as Paolo (*Francesca da Rimini*). Possessor of beautiful voice and excellent technique, was particularly admired in *Carmen, Tosca, Pagliacci,* and *Rigoletto.* Created Calaf in *Turandot* (Scala, 1926). Repertory also included Cavaradossi and Rodolfo. Also created Romeo in the Zandonai opera *Giulietta e Romeo* (1922).

FONTANA, FERDINANDO (1850–1919). Italian poet, journalist, librettist, scholar, and member of the later *scapigliatura* movement in Milan. Met Puccini in July 1884 and, thanks to the mediation of Puccini's teacher Ponchielli, supplied librettos for *Le villi* and *Edgar.* Wrote Puccini's first biography (an article in 1884 in the *Gazzetta Musicale di Milano.* Wrote librettos of Franchetti's *Asrael* (1883) and *Il signor di Pourceaugnac* (1897). A prolific writer, his output also includes plays in Milanese dialect, an anthology of Milanese poetry, and several books on travel, including *New York* (1883), *In tedescheria* (1893), and *In viaggio per la Cina* (1900).

FORNIA, RITA (born REGINA NEWMAN) (1878–1922). American contralto or mezzo-soprano. Created La Badessa in *Suor Angelica* (Met, 1908). Debut in Hamburg, 1901, as Eudoxia in Halévy's *La juive.* At the Met, during her brief career, she sang Euridice (as a soprano) in a successful concert version of Monteverdi's *Orfeo,* conducted by Boris Pasternak.

FORZANO, GIOVACCHINO (1884–1970). Italian playwright, journalist, stage director at La Scala, and librettist. During the Fascist regime he acted as Mussolini's co-author for three plays. He directed several films (some musical) and provided the librettos for *Suor Angelica* and *Gianni Schicchi* (1918). He proposed other subjects to Puccini, but nothing came of the suggestions. Instead he wrote librettos for Franchetti (*Notte di legenda,* 1915; *Glauco,* 1922), Giordano (*Il re,* 1929), Leoncavallo (*Edipo re,* 1920), Mascagni (*Lodoletta,* 1917; *Il piccolo Marat,* 1921), and Wolf-Ferrari (*Sly, Ovvero la leggenda del dormiente risvegliato,* 1927), which Puccini had for a time considered setting to music.

FRACCAROLI, ARNALDO (1883–1956). Prolific Italian journalist and writer, especially for the theater. Longtime friend of Puccini's, though the friendship was marked by some dissension. Author of a biography published in 1925, shortly after the death of the composer, who supposedly supplied much of the information.

FRANCESCHINI, RAFFAELLO (1854–1942). Puccini's brother-in-law (husband of Ramelde Puccini [*q.v.*]) and hunting companion.

FRANCHETTI, ALBERTO (1860–1942). Italian composer and nobleman. Studied first in Turin and Venice, then in Monaco and Germany (Dresden); his personal wealth freed him from the stress experienced by some of his fellow composers. Made his professional debut with a highly acclaimed Symphony in E minor (1884). His first operas, *Asrael* (1888), *Cristoforo Colombo* (1892), and *Il signor di Pourceaugnac* (1897), encountered only ephemeral success, but his *Germania* (1902) enjoyed a certain international fame. He originally acquired the rights to Sardou's *La Tosca* but ceded the work to Puccini, at Giulio Ricordi's persuasion. Franchetti shared Puccini's passion for motor cars.

FUCINI, RENATO (1843–1921). Italian writer and critic, a specialist in Tuscan life. Provided the text for two Puccini songs: *Avanti "Urania"!* and *E l'uccellino*.

GABRIELESCO, GREGORIO. Romanian tenor. Created the role of Edgar (1889), instead of Tamagno, whom Puccini had intended for it. This was his only season at La Scala (he also appeared in operas by Callignani and Franchetti, and as Enzo in *La Gioconda,* a role he sang with success elsewhere).

GALLI, AMINTORE (1845–1919). Italian music critic, composer, and for many years artistic director of the music publishing firm of Sonzogno. Music critic of *Il Secolo* and Puccini's professor of history and philosophy of music at the Milan conservatory. Instrumental in the launching of Mascagni and other Sonzogno composers.

GALLINI, NATALE (1891–1943). Italian musicologist, dealer, and noted collector of musical manuscripts and documents; his collection, which was divided and sold after his death, included several valuable Puccinian autograph scores, among them the *Preludio sinfonico* in E minor (1876) and the "Madrid" prelude (1892) for Act I of *Edgar*.

GATTI-CASAZZA, GIULIO (1869–1940). Director of La Scala in Milan, 1898–1908. He was engaged by the Metropolitan, New York, in 1908, as co-director with Andreas Dippel, and then from 1910 to 1935 as director by himself. Toscanini came with him to the Met and remained until 1915, the most brilliant period in the history of the house. Gatti-Casazza was largely responsible for securing the world premieres of *La fanciulla del West* and *Il trittico* for the Met.

GEMIGNANI, FOSCA (1880–1968). Daughter of Narciso Gemignani and Elvira Puccini (*q.v.*). Accompanied her mother when she left Gemignani to live with Puccini. Was first married to tenor and impresario Totò Leonardi, by whom she had three children, Franca, Antonio, and Elvira (known as Bicchi or Biki). Her second husband was the industrialist and senator Mario Crespi.

GEMIGNANI, NARCISO (1856–1903). Italian merchant, in Lucca. First husband of Elvira Bonturi Puccini, father of Fosca and Renato. Amateur baritone.

GENTLE, ALICE (1885–1958). American mezzo-soprano. Debut Manhattan Opera House, 1909. Created Frugola in *Il tabarro* (Met, 1918).

GHISLANZONI, ANTONIO (1824–93). Italian dramatist, journalist, librettist, musician, man of letters and—for a brief period in his youth—baritone. Member of Milanese *scapigliatura*. Between 1866 and 1872, editor of *La Gazzetta Musicale di Milano*. He turned the French prose sketch for the libretto of *Aida* into Italian verses. Collaborated with Verdi on the revision of *Forza del destino*. Large literary output: about eighty-five librettos, including texts for *Edmea* (Catalani), and *I lituani* (Ponchielli). Three of the four poems by Ghislanzoni were set by Puccini in the Milan Conservatory years: *Melanconia* (now missing, 1881?), *Salve Regina* (1882?) and *Storiella d'amore* (1883). His novel, *Gli artisti da teatro,* despite its melodramatic story, offers valuable glimpses of operatic life in the mid 19th-century.

GIACONIA, GIUSEPPINA. Italian mezzo-soprano. Created Suzuki in *Madama Butterfly* at La Scala (1904) and repeated the role in the Brescia production later that same year. Her only other appearance at La Scala, also in 1904, was as Maddalena in *Rigoletto*.

GIACOSA, GIUSEPPE (1847–1906). Italian dramatist, poet, and man of letters. Major works include *La partita a scacchi* (1871), *Tristi amori* (1887), *La signora di Challant* (1891), and *Come le foglie* (1900). Together with Luigi Illica (*q.v.*), provided Puccini with librettos for *La bohème, Tosca,* and *Madama Butterfly*. While Illica generally elaborated the scenario and invented picturesque incidents, Giacosa dealt with versification of the libretto and assumed literary responsibility. He was a close friend of Boito's and Verga's. Wrote plays for Bernhardt and Duse.

GILLY, DINH (1877–1940). French (born Algiers) baritone. Debut in Paris, 1899, as a priest in Reyer's *Sigurd*. Created role of Sonora in *Fanciulla del West* (1910) at the Met, where he sang regularly (1909–14). He also sang at Covent Garden, where he was London's first Jack Rance in *Fanciulla*. He settled in England, where he was still singing as late as 1925 on British radio.

GINORI-LISCI, MARCHESE CARLO (1851–1905). Italian nobleman and industrialist. Friend, neighbor, and hunting companion of Puccini, who dedicated *La bohème* to him. Puccini also wrote the song *Avanti "Urania"!* to celebrate the marchese's acquisition of a ship; the song is dedicated to the Marchesa Anna Ginori-Lisci, wife of the Marchese Carlo.

GIRALDONI, EUGENIO (1871–1924). Italian baritone. His father was also a well-known baritone, and his mother (and teacher) was the dramatic soprano Carolina Ferni. Debut as Escamillo in *Carmen* (Barcelona, 1891). Created Scarpia (Rome, 1900) and sang the role also at the Scala premiere. At the Metropolitan Opera, 1904–1905. Popular in verismo roles (Giordano, Franchetti), he had a large repertory that included even Boris Godunov.

GNACCARINI, AGOSTINO. Italian baritone. Sang Guglielmo Wolf in the Turin premiere of *Le villi* (second version of the opera) in 1884. His repertory also included Meyerbeer, Wagner (Telramund and Wotan in *Walküre*); he was chiefly active at the Regio, Turin.

GOLD, DIDIER. French writer. Puccini saw his one-act play *La Houppe-lande* (The Cloak) at the Théâtre Marigny, Paris, in spring of 1912, and later had Adami turn it into a libretto, *Il tabarro,* as part of *Il trittico*.

GORGA, EVAN (1866–1958). Italian tenor, created Rodolfo in *Bohème* (Turin, 1896). Puccini had to lower some passages in the original score to compensate for Gorga's vocal deficiencies. Gorga's only other appearance at the Regio was as Faust, replacing De Bassini in Boito's opera *Mefistofele* that same season.

GOZZI, CARLO (1720–1806). Italian playwright. Today remembered for his ten "fiabe drammatiche" or dramatic fables, most of which occasioned heated literary disputes with rival fellow-Venetian Carlo Goldoni. The fourth of these fables, the five-act tragicomedy *Turandotte* (1762), was the literary source of Puccini's last opera; it was adapted for the German stage by Schiller, whose version was translated back into Italian by Andrea Maffei. Puccini examined Maffei's translation before deciding to set the subject to music.

GUI, VITTORIO (1885–1975). Important Italian conductor and composer. Conducted the revised *Rondine* in Palermo (1920). He was widely admired as a Rossini specialist and conducted at Glyndebourne as well as in all major European theaters.

GUNSBOURG, RAOUL (1859–1955). Romanian-born French composer and impresario. Appointed Director of the Monte Carlo Opera in 1890, he held the position for fifty years and made the small house a brilliant opera and ballet center. Produced world premieres of works by Massenet, Fauré, Ravel, and Honegger, as well as Puccini's *Rondine* in 1917. Devised the first staged version of Berlioz's *La Damnation de Faust*.

HEINE, HEINRICH (1797–1856). German poet, dramatist, and narrator, popular among members of the Milanese *scapigliatura*. Close friend of Meyerbeer's, and music critic of *Allgemeine Zeitung* from 1840 to 1847. Musical works derived from the writings of Heine include Mascagni's *Guglielmo Ratcliff* (*Wilhelm Ratcliff,* 1823) and Wagner's *Der fliegende Hol-länder* (*Memoiren des Herrn von Schabelwopski,* 1831).

HOWARD, KATHLEEN (1880–1956). American mezzo-soprano. Debut (Metropolitan Opera) in 1907 as Azucena. Created Zita in *Gianni Schicchi*

(1918). Memoirs, *Confessions of an Opera Singer,* published in New York, 1918.

HUBERDEAU, GUSTAVE (1874–1945). French baritone. Debut, Opéra-Comique, 1898. Created Rambaldo in *La rondine* (1917). Sang at Manhattan Opera, Philadelphia Opera, and Chicago Opera.

ILLICA, LUIGI (1857–1919). Italian playwright and librettist. For a time involved with the Milanese *scapigliatura* movement and collaborated with Fontana (*q.v.*) on a drama, *I Narbonnerie La Tour* (1883). Journalist for *Corriere della Sera.* Author of numerous plays, several in Milanese dialect; some have been revived recently with success. In collaboration with Giacosa (*q.v.*) he wrote three librettos for Puccini: *Bohème, Tosca,* and *Butterfly.* By himself, Illica provided texts for many other composers, including Catalani (*La Wally*), Franchetti (*Cristoforo Colombo, Germania*), Giordano (*Andrea Chénier, Siberia*), Mascagni (*Iris, Le Maschere, Isabeau*), and Zandonai (*Conchita*). Illica was particularly concerned with local color and historical accuracy; his stage directions tended to be verbose and digressive. Was also the author of the text of Puccini's song *Canto d'anime (pagina d'album),* 1904.

JERITZA, MARIA (1887–1982). Czech-born American soprano. Debut Olomouc as Elsa (*Lohengrin*) in 1910. Created Richard Strauss's Ariadne in Stuttgart (1912). Member of the Vienna State Opera from 1911–32 and 1949–52. There she created Marietta in *Die tote Stadt* and the Empress in *Frau ohne Schatten.* A celebrated Tosca (she made a habit of singing "Vissi d'arte" lying prone at Scarpia's feet). She moved to the Met in 1921 and sang until 1932, reappearing in 1951. First American Turandot, also a memorable Minnie in *Fanciulla* (she sang in the first Vienna staging, 1913). Much admired by Puccini.

KARR, ALPHONSE. French writer admired by the Milanese *scapigliatura* writers. His *Les Wilis* (1852), based on a German legend narrated by Heine (*q.v.*) in *Ueber Deutschland,* provided Fontana with the subject for the libretto of Puccini's opera.

KRUSCENISKI, SALOMEA (1872–1952). Ukrainian-born Italian soprano. Debut in L'vov (1892). In 1895 she studied in Italy, making her debut as Ponchielli's Marion Delorme in Cremona, where she then sang Manon Lescaut (1895–96 season). After several seasons in Russia, she returned to Italy, which remained her home. She sang Cio-Cio-San in the successful first performance of the revised *Butterfly* in Brescia, 1904. Her varied repertory also included Wagner and Richard Strauss (she was the first Italian Elektra), and Puccini's *Tosca.* Retired in 1925, having married in 1910 the lawyer Cesare Riccioni who later became Mayor of Viareggio; lived there until the outbreak of the second World War, when she returned to Russia.

Lehár, Franz (1870–1948). Hungarian-Austrian composer. After graduating from Prague Conservatory, he conducted military bands, then settled in Vienna, where the most famous of his many successful operettas, *Die lustige Witwe* (*The Merry Widow*), was first heard in 1905. He and Puccini were reciprocal admirers, and Puccini kept a signed photograph of Lehár on his piano at Torre del Lago.

Leoncavallo, Ruggero (1858–1919). Italian librettist and composer. Studied at the Conservatory of Naples, then earned a humble living as a composer and café pianist for a time in Paris, until 1892, when his *Pagliacci* was enthusiastically acclaimed; his later operas, by comparison, were relatively unsuccessful and some were complete failures. Was at one time friend of Puccini's and was involved in the initial preparation of the libretto for *Manon Lescaut*. But relations were broken off in March 1893, when, after a public controversy involving the right to use Murger's *Scenes de la vie de Bohème* as the basis for an opera, each composer resolved to compose his own *La bohème*. Leoncavallo's version (1897), despite some felicities, was overshadowed by the triumphant Puccini version, which premiered fifteen months earlier. Other major opera is *Zazà* (1900). He aimed at ambitious works, conceiving a vast trilogy about the Renaissance, to rival the *Ring*. He also wrote some operettas.

Long, John Luther (1861–1927). American writer. His short story, *Madame Butterfly,* was published in the *Century Magazine* in 1898 and later collected in a volume with other stories. A practicing Philadelphia lawyer. His story, adapted by David Belasco, became a hit play, starring Blanche Bates. Giacosa and Illica, working from both story and drama text, adapted Long's idea as a libretto for Puccini.

Lucca, Giovannina (1810–94). First with her husband Francesco Lucca (1802–72), then on her own for many years after his death, she directed the successful music publishing firm that bore his name, Ricordi's most serious rival at the time. She secured the Italian performing rights not only of Wagner and Meyerbeer but also of popular French composers like Halévy and Gounod. She appreciated the young Puccini's talent when he was still at the Conservatory and published his *Capriccio sinfonico* in a piano four-hands version in 1884. Her firm was bought out by Giulio Ricordi in 1888.

Lukacevska, Giovanna. Sang the Madrigal-singer in *Manon Lescaut* in January 1894, and the following season, in February 1895, she sang the title role in the same opera. Alternating between soprano and mezzo-soprano roles, she sang Suzuki in the Brescia performance of the revised *Butterfly,* on 28 May 1904.

Magi, Fortunato (1839–82). Italian music teacher and composer. Puccini's uncle (brother of the composer's mother Albina Magi) and student of the composer's father Michele. In 1857 Magi became teacher of organ at the Istituto Pacini in Lucca and, on Michele Puccini's death, was named teacher of composition and counterpoint. In 1872 he was briefly the Istituto's director. He then held positions in Ferrara and La Spezia, and in 1877 became director of the Istituto Musicale Benedetto Marcello, Venice. After succumbing to a mental disorder, he died in 1882. His pupils included Catalani (in Lucca) and Franchetti (in Venice). He also tried to teach his nephew Giacomo, but the relationship was not a success, and the boy moved on to another, more congenial instructor, Angeloni (*q.v.*).

MAGINI-COLETTI, ANTONIO (1855–1912). Italian baritone. Debut in Rome, 1882 (Valentin). Created the role of Frank in *Edgar* (Milan, 1889). Engaged by the Metropolitan Opera in 1891, making his debut as Nevers (*Les Huguénots*). He also sang Marcello and Scarpia; and his repertory included Wagner, Massenet, Verdi, and many verismo works.

MALIPIERO, GIAN FRANCESCO (1882–1973). Italian composer, music editor, and teacher. Studied in Vienna, Venice, and Bologna. His music, essentially "anti-romantic," is inspired also by Gregorian chant and Italian sixteenth-century monody while adapting itself to formal and expressive innovations of the twentieth century. In the course of his long career, Malipiero taught history of music at the University of Padua, and was director of the Conservatory Benedetto Marcello in Venice. Particularly interested in Italian music from the sixteenth to the eighteenth centuries, he edited the complete works of Monteverdi, and was director of the Istituto di Studi Vivaldiani. Like Casella (*q.v.*), a member of the eighties generation, he was basically unsympathetic to Puccini's music.

MANCINELLI, LUIGI (1848–1921). Italian conductor, composer, and violoncellist. Particularly esteemed as a conductor, Mancinelli made his debut with Verdi's *Aida* in Perugia (1874), thereafter attaining great success throughout Europe and South America. In 1881 he was nominated Director of the Teatro Comunale, Bologna. Wrote several operas whose success was short-lived; most popular compositions were orchestral works including *Scene veneziane* (1888) and *Ouverture romantica* (1908), which reveal his talent as an orchestrator. Like Faccio (*q.v.*), played an important role in the diffusion of Puccini's first operas; conducted *Le villi* in Bologna (1885), and an important production of *Edgar* in Madrid (1892).

MANFREDI, DORIA (1885–1909). Maidservant in the Puccini household at Torre del Lago. A suicide, after Elvira Puccini's public accusations of adultery with the composer. Her innocence was established by an autopsy, but the tragedy caused a great rift and temporary separation. After her death, the Manfredi family took Elvira Puccini (*q.v.*) to court, accusing her of instigating Doria's suicide. The charge was later dropped. Some writers have seen the character of Liù (*Turandot*) as an idealization of Doria.

MAPELLI, LUIGI (1855–1913). Italian composer. Studied with Disma Fumagalli and Franco Faccio at the Regio Conservatorio, Milan. Was winner, together with Guglielmo Zuelli (*q.v.*), of the first Concorso Sonzogno (1883), which Puccini had entered with *Le willis;* the libretto of Mapelli's winning opera, *Anna e Gualberto,* was also written by Fontana.

MARINI, PIO. Italian bass. Created the role of Gualtiero in *Edgar* (La Scala, 1889).

MARINUZZI, GINO (1882–1945). Italian conductor and composer. Conducted in all major European and South American theaters. Played an important role in "discovering" operas by Donizetti and Bellini, but was also renowned for his interpretations of Wagner and Strauss. Most successful compositions include the *Suite siciliana* (1909) and the opera *Palla de' Mozzi* (1932). From 1915–19 he was director of Liceo Musicale, Bologna, and was artistic director of the Chicago Opera from 1919–21. Conducted premiere of *La rondine* (Monte Carlo, 1917), and the Italian premiere of *Il trittico.*

MAROTTI, GUIDO (1890–1988). Italian journalist; co-author with the painter Ferruccio Pagni (*q.v.*) of *Giacomo Puccini intimo* (1925), recollections of Puccini at Torre del Lago.

MARTINI, FERDINANDO (1841–1928). Italian journalist, critic, poet, politician, cabinet minister. A Tuscan, he was a friend of Puccini's (also of Boito's) and was approached to provide the text for *Il tabarro,* but quickly abandoned the project, to be succeeded by Adami.

MASCAGNI, PIETRO (1863–1945). Italian composer. After initially studying composition with Alfredo Soffredini (*q.v.*) in his native Leghorn, entered the Regio Conservatorio, Milan, to study with Ponchielli; in Milan he established close friendship with Puccini, the two young composers sharing lodgings for a short period. He played the double-bass in the orchestra for the premiere of *Le villi.* Left conservatory before completing studies, becoming conductor of small, itinerant light-opera company. In 1889 he won the Sonzogno competition with his one-act opera *Cavalleria rusticana,* whose premiere (1890) was triumphant, an enduring success; his later operas, which include *L'amico Fritz* (1891), *Guglielmo Ratcliff* (1895), *Iris* (1898), *Isabeau* (1911), *Parisina* (1913), and *Il piccolo Marat* (1921), never repeated the success of *Cavalleria.* In later years, relations with Puccini were chilly, largely because of professional jealousy.

MASSENET, JULES (1842–1912). French composer. Winner of the prestigious *Prix de Rome* in 1863. Wrote over thirty operas, including *Le roi de Lahore* (1877), *Manon* (1884), *Le Cid* (1885), *Werther* (1892), *Thaïs* (1895), and *Le jongleur de Notre-Dame* (1902). His *Manon* (1884) was almost certainly known to Puccini, who took care not to repeat too closely the situations of the French libretto.

MAZZARA, MICHELE. Italian bass. First Colline in *Bohème,* Turin, 1896. That same season he sang Hagen in the Toscanini *Die Walküre.*

MONTESANTO, MICHELE (1887–1954). Italian bass. Debut as Escamillo (Conegliano Veneto, 1909); that same year sang in the successful Palermo *Bohème.* Created Michele in *Tabarro,* New York (1918). Sang in all major opera houses of the world.

MORANZONI, ROBERTO (1880–1959). Italian conductor. In his first season at the Metropolitan, he conducted world premiere of *Trittico* (1918), assisting Puccini with some ensemble problems. Director-conductor, Boston Grand Opera (1910–17).

MORO, ACHILLE. Italian baritone. Created Lescaut in *Manon Lescaut,* Turin (1893). Sang Amonasro and Pogner also at the Regio in the nineties.

MUGNONE, LEOPOLDO (1858–1941). Italian conductor and composer. Began his conducting career relatively early, at the same time establishing himself as composer with two successful operettas. Conducted the premiere of *Cavalleria rusticana* at the Teatro Costanzi in Rome (1890); ten years later, in the same theater, he conducted the premiere of *Tosca.* Also conducted world premiere of *Falstaff* (1893). Was at first highly esteemed by Puccini (he conducted an extremely successful production of *La bohème* in Palermo, 1896), but later fell out of favor with the composer. Was conductor of the Buenos Aires production of *Edgar* (1905), and of the Milan premiere of *La rondine* (1917), a performance which did not please Puccini. Was an admired Wagnerian.

MURGER, HENRY (1822–61). French novelist of German extraction. His autobiographical *Scènes de la vie de Bohème* appeared serially in *Le Corsaire* between 1845 and 1848. When they were published in book form in 1851 they met with immediate success and were soon afterwards transformed into a five-act play by Théodore Barrière; Puccini's *La bohème* is based both on Mürger's novel and the play adapted from it.

MUSSET, ALFRED DE (1810–57). French poet and playwright. His play *La coupe et les lèvres* served as the basis for the libretto of *Edgar.*

MUZIO, CLAUDIA (1889–1936). Italian soprano. Debut in Arezzo, 1910, as Massenet's *Manon* (she later sang Puccini's heroine). At La Scala she sang Tosca and Mimì with success (partnered by Caruso). Metropolitan Opera debut in 1916 as Tosca. Created Giorgetta there in the world premiere of *Tabarro* (1918).

NAPPI, GIOVANNI BATTISTA (1857–1932). Italian music critic, Filippi's successor on *La Perseveranza.* Early supporter of Puccini.

NESSI, GIUSEPPE (1887–1961). Italian tenor. Made his debut as Alfredo (*La traviata*) in Saluzzo, 1910. Upon Serafin's advice, dedicated himself to character roles, becoming renowned for his interpretations of Spoletta and

Goro. From 1921 until 1959 he was primo *tenore comprimario* at La Scala, where he created the role of Pong in *Turandot* (1926). In his last years he sang Goro (*Butterfly*) and Altoum (*Turandot*) in the Callas recording.

NOMELLINI, PLINIO (1866–1943). Italian painter and friend of Puccini's. Was born in Leghorn, worked for a time in Genoa, then lived at Torre del Lago and at Lido di Camaiore, near Viareggio, before retiring to Florence. Painted some frescoes (later covered) for the composer's villa at Torre del Lago.

NOVELLI, GIULIA (1860–1932). Italian mezzo-soprano or contralto, said to have had one of the most beautiful voices after Marietta Alboni. Repertoire included *Aida* (Amneris), *La Gioconda, Don Carlos, Amleto, Il trovatore, Carmen,* and *La favorita;* created the roles of Loretta and Anaconda in Franchetti's *Asrael* and *Cristoforo Colombo* respectively. Was originally chosen to interpret Tigrana in the Scala premiere of *Edgar* (April 1889). Because of illness, was replaced by Romilda Pantaleoni (*q.v.*).

OLIVA, DOMENICO (1860–1917). Italian writer, journalist, theater critic, poet, lawyer, and politician. Asked by Marco Praga (*q.v.*) to collaborate on the versification of the libretto for *Manon Lescaut.*

PAGNI, FERRUCCIO (1866–1935). Italian painter. A native of Leghorn, he settled at Torre del Lago, where he became Puccini's closest friend and hunting companion. In 1904 he emigrated to South America, where he founded an academy of fine arts at Rosario. He later returned to Torre del Lago. Most of his paintings feature the landscape and scenery of the Torre del Lago area. Was one of the decorators of Puccini's villa at Torre del Lago.

PANIZZA, ARTURO. Argentinian conductor of Italian descent, father of the more famous Ettore (Héctor) (*q.v.*). Conducted world premiere of *Le willis* (Milan, Dal Verme, 1884), Puccini's operatic debut.

PANIZZA, ETTORE (1875–1967). Argentinian composer and conductor of Italian descent. Encouraged by Giulio Ricordi and by Toscanini, he enjoyed a considerable international success, culminating in a long period at the Met. Admired by Puccini, who chose him to conduct an important *Butterfly* in Genoa (shortly after the Scala fiasco and the Brescia resurrection). Conducted the first Scala performances of *Trittico.* Also conducted regularly in South America and wrote (in Spanish) a volume of memoirs.

PANTALEONI, ROMILDA (1847–1917). Italian soprano and leading figure in the musical life of Milan in the 1870s and 1880s. Debut at the Teatro Carcano in Milan, 1868, as Margherita in *Faust* (also sang the role in Boito's version of the story). Lover of conductor Franco Faccio, who persuaded Verdi to assign her the role of Desdemona in the premiere of *Otello* (dissatisfied, Verdi did not have her engaged for subsequent productions). Sang the role of Anna in *Le villi,* when the opera was given its La

Scala premiere (January 1885), and, after a five-year period of rest, she returned to the stage, appearing as Tigrana in the world premiere of *Edgar* (La Scala, 1889), replacing mezzo-soprano Giulia Novelli (according to Michael Kaye, Verdi persuaded Pantaleoni to accept the part of Tigrana). Was first interpreter (and dedicatee) of Ponchielli's *Marion Delorme* (1885). After Faccio's death in 1891, she retired.

PANZACCHI, ENRICO (1840–1904). Italian poet and critic. Friend of Boito's and Giacosa's, ardent Wagnerian. Puccini's song *Terra e mare* is a setting of a Panzacchi poem.

PASINI, CAMILLA (1875–1935). Italian soprano. First Musetta in *Bohème* (Turin, 1896). Later sang Mimì and Puccini's Manon. Many verismo roles, including Fedora, Santuzza, and Wally.

PASQUA, GIUSEPPINA (1855–1930). Italian mezzo-soprano. Debut as a soprano, in her native Perugia, as Oscar (*Ballo in maschera*), 1871. The following year she sang Amelia in the same opera. Sang Eboli in revised version of *Don Carlos,* La Scala, 1884, and created the role of Quickly in Verdi's *Falstaff.* Interpreted Tigrana in the important Madrid production of *Edgar* (1892).

PELTZ, ERMINIO. Italian baritone. Created the role of Guglielmo Wulf in *Le willis* in Milan, 1884.

PERINI, FLORA (1887–?). Italian contralto. Debut as Anaconda in Franchetti's *Cristoforo Colombo* in Milan, 1908. Sang at the Met during the First World War, appearing in the world premiere of Granados's *Goyescas* in January 1916. She created the role of the Princess in *Suor Angelica* (1918) and appeared as Pantalis (Boito's *Mefistofele*) in 1920. That same year she sang with Caruso in Havana.

PICCAVER, ALFRED (1883–1958). English tenor. Spent childhood in USA, where he began his musical studies, continued then in Europe. Debut in Prague, 1907, as Gounod's Roméo. In 1912 he began a long association with the Vienna Opera, where he appeared in the local premieres of *Fanciulla del West* (with Jeritza as Minnie) and *Tabarro*. Much admired by Puccini. Repertory included Des Grieux, Rodolfo, and Cavaradossi. Recorded several Puccini arias.

PINI-CORSI, ANTONIO (1858–1918). Italian baritone. Debut in Cremona, 1878, as Don Magnifico (*La Cenerentola*). A popular buffo singer, he also sang serious roles and created Ford in Verdi's *Falstaff* (Scala, 1893) and Schaunard in *Bohème* (Turin, 1896).

PIZZETTI, ILDEBRANDO (1880–1968). Italian composer and critic. Studied in Parma, making his debut there as a composer in 1905 with *musiche di scena* for *La nave* by d'Annunzio. While Respighi and Casella (*q.v.*) were trying to revive the art of Italian instrumental music, Pizzetti set out to transform Italian opera through a return to Florentine monody, early polyphony, and above all, Gregorian chant. Wrote many operas, ballets, orchestral and chamber works. Was director of the conservatories of Florence and Milan. Generally hostile to Puccini, who cordially disliked his work.

PLATANIA, PIETRO (1828–1907). Italian composer. Was director of the Conservatory of Palermo, of the Chapel of the Milan Cathedral, and of the Conservatory of Naples. Wrote several operas (characterized by a severe, academic style), including *Matilde Bentivoglio* (1852) and *Spartaco* (1891). Also composed sacred and symphonic music. Was a member of the Sonzogno jury that did not award prize to *Le villi,* and later, of the jury that chose *Cavalleria.*

POLONINI, ALESSANDRO. Italian bass. Created Geronte in *Manon Lescaut* in Turin (1893), and Benoit in *Bohème* three years later. He also sang Beckmesser at the Regio in 1892 (Cesira Ferrani, the first Mimì, was Eva).

POMÉ, ALESSANDRO (1853–1934). Italian conductor and composer. Conducted premiere of *Manon Lescaut* in Turin, 1893. Long associated with the Regio of Turin. In his last years he published autobiographical articles in *La Stampa.*

PONCHIELLI, AMILCARE (1834–86). Italian composer and teacher. Puccini's teacher at the Milan conservatory from June 1882 to July 1883 (Giacomo's final year of studies), and instrumental in persuading Ferdinando Fontana (*q.v.*) to provide Puccini's first libretto. In addition to two ballets and a small quantity of instrumental music, he wrote several operas, including *I promessi sposi* (1872), *I lituani* (1874), *La Gioconda* (1876), *Lina* (1877), *Il figliuol prodigo* (1880), and *Marion Delorme* (1885), of which only *La Gioconda* is frequently heard today.

PONIATOWSKI, PRINCE CARLO. Dedicatee of the piano (four-hands) arrangement of Puccini's orchestral *Capriccio sinfonico,* 1883, transcribed by Giuseppe Frugatta and published by Giovannina Lucca (*q.v.*) in 1884.

PRAGA, MARCO (1862–1929). Italian playwright, novelist, and critic. Son of the poet Emilio Praga, member of the *scapigliatura* movement. Was one of the several collaborators on the *Manon Lescaut* libretto and was a go-between in the attempt to initiate a collaboration between Puccini and d'Annunzio in 1906.

PRÉVOST D'EXILES, (ABBÉ) ANTOINE-FRANÇOIS (1697–1763). French Benedictine priest and author. The seventh and final volume of his *Mémoires et aventures d'un homme de qualité* (entitled *L'histoire du Chevalier des Grieux et de Manon Lescaut*) was used as an opera subject by Auber, Massenet, Puccini, and more recently, Henze.

PUCCINI, ALBINA (1830–84). Wife of Michele Puccini and mother of Giacomo. Widowed in 1864, kept her large family together with great strength and courage, and through enormous sacrifice managed to educate all of her children.

PUCCINI, ANTONIO (1886–1946). Only child of Giacomo Puccini and Elvira Bonturi. Received early education in Milan, then studied engineering in Germany. Had one child, Simonetta.

PUCCINI, ELVIRA (née BONTURI,) (1860–1930). Wife of Giacomo Puccini and mother of his only child, Antonio. In an earlier marriage was wife of Narciso Gemignani (*q.v.*), wholesale liquor merchant from Lucca, by whom she had two children (Fosca [*q.v.*] and Renato Gemignani); after leaving her husband in 1886, she went to live with Puccini, taking with her the older child, Fosca, then six years old. After first husband's death in 1903, she became Puccini's legitimate spouse.

PUCCINI, IGINIA (1856–1922). Daughter of Michele and Albina Puccini. Entered order of Augustinian nuns at early age, taking the name Sister Giulia Enrichetta. The composer was very close to this sister and often visited her at the convent of Vicopelgo, near Lucca. Traditionally, the convent inspired much of *Suor Angelica*.

PUCCINI, MICHELE (father) (1813–64). Composer and musician. Fourth generation of an established family of musicians from Lucca. Studied first in Bologna under Giuseppe Pilotti (where he was nominated Accademico Filarmonico), and then in Naples with Saverio Mercadante and Gaetano Donizetti. Was highly esteemed in Lucca, both as an organist and as the composer of sacred music and two operas (*Antonio Foscarini* and *Giambattista Cattani*). In 1850 he married Albina Magi, by whom he had eight children, including Giacomo, born in 1858.

PUCCINI, MICHELE (brother) (1864–91). Last child of Michele and Albina Puccini. Born three months after the death of his father, he was raised by his mother and sisters. Like his brother Giacomo, he studied music initially in Lucca and then at the Regio Conservatorio, Milan. In 1890 he emigrated to South America, settling first in Buenos Aires, then at Jujuy, from whence he was forced to flee as a result of his relationship with a married woman. Died soon after from yellow fever, in Rio de Janeiro.

PUCCINI, NITTETI (1854–1928). Daughter of Michele and Albina Puccini. From her marriage to Pisan lawyer Alberto Marsili, had two children, Carlo and Alba.

PUCCINI, OTILIA (1851–1923). Eldest child of Michele and Albina Puccini. Studied pianoforte with her father. Married doctor Massimo del Carlo, and had one son, Carlo.

PUCCINI, RAMELDE (1859–1912). Daughter of Michele and Albina Puccini. Married Raffaello Franceschini (*q.v.*) from Lucca, who worked as a tax collector at Pescia, near Lucca. Had three daughters, Alba, Nina, and Nelda.

PUCCINI, TOMAIDE (1852–1917). Daughter of Michele and Albina Puccini. Married Enrico Gherardi, widower with two children. Like her husband, she was a primary-school teacher.

PUCCINI FAMILY. *See also* Simonetta Puccini, pp. 3–48.

QUARANTA, FRANCESCO (1813–87). Italian (Neapolitan) composer, largely of popular songs. Was to have written an opera on Fontana's *Le willis* libretto, which he apparently rejected (or was dissuaded from using by the poet). It was duly given to Puccini.

RAISA, ROSA (1893–1963). American soprano of Polish birth. Studied in Naples with Barbara Marchisio. Debut in Rome, 1912. Though she sang widely in Europe, she was associated chiefly with the Chicago Opera. In 1924, Toscanini engaged her to create Asteria in Boito's posthumous *Nerone;* two years later she was the first Turandot. She also sang Mimì and, more frequently, Tosca. She retired in 1937.

REICHERT, HEINZ (born HEINRICH BLUMENREICH) (1877–1940). Austrian writer. Together with various other authors, among them Alfred Willner (*q.v.*), he produced librettos for operettas (for example *Frasquita* and *Der Zarewitsch* by Franz Lehár). Collaborated with Willner on the original libretto, in German, for *La rondine* (*Die Schwalbe*).

RICORDI, GIULIO (1840–1912). Italian music publisher, writer, painter, and, under the pseudonym J. Burgmein, composer. Succeeded his father Tito (1811–88) as director of the publishing house founded by grandfather Giovanni (1785–1853). Maintained a good rapport with Verdi (was originally a staunch anti-Wagnerian) and immediately recognized and encouraged Puccini's talent. In his dealings with Puccini he demonstrated an almost paternal interest; this affection was reciprocated, and Puccini dedicated the piano-vocal score of the four-act *Edgar* to J. Burgmein. Personally involved in the shaping of the libretto for *Manon Lescaut.* Casa Ricordi published all of Puccini's operas except *La rondine,* which was published by Sonzogno, largely because of Puccini's dissatisfaction with Tito II.

RICORDI, TITO II (1865–1933). Italian music publisher and opera producer, son of Giulio Ricordi. Initially studied engineering, but after his father's death he took over direction of the Casa Ricordi. He lacked Giulio's tact and business sense (he even quarrelled with Puccini over the publication of *La rondine*), and the direction of the firm eventually passed to people from outside the immediate family.

RIMINI, GIACOMO (1888–1952). Italian baritone. Made his debut in *Werther*, in Desenzano (Verona), 1910. After some provincial appearances (including *La fanciulla del West*), he was highly acclaimed in Rome for his interpretation of Scarpia (1915). He created Ping in *Turandot* in Milan, 1926 (his wife, Rosa Raisa [*q.v.*], sang the title role); he was also a highly esteemed Gianni Schicchi. Was a much-praised Falstaff under Toscanini at the Dal Verme, Milan (he was protagonist of the first complete recording of the opera). With Raisa, he sang for many seasons in Chicago, where, after their retirement, they ran a successful school of voice training.

ROMANI, FELICE (1788–1865). Italian writer and librettist—one of the most important Italian librettists of the early nineteenth century. Abandoned a career in law to write, and produced well over a hundred librettos. These include *Aureliano in Palmira*, *Il turco in Italia*, and *Bianca e Faliero* for Rossini; *Il pirata*, *La straniera*, *I Capuleti e i Montecchi*, *La sonnambula*, and *Norma* for Bellini; *Anna Bolena*, *L'elisir d'amore*, *Parisina*, and *Lucrezia Borgia* for Donizetti; and *Un giorno di regno* for Verdi. The text of Puccini's student composition *Mentìa l'avviso* (1883) was taken from Romani's libretto for *La solitaria delle Asturie, ossia La Spagna ricuperata*, which was first set to music by Carlo Coccia in 1838.

RUSS, GIANNINA (1878–1951). Italian soprano. Debut in Bologna, 1903, as Mimì (the following year she sang Musetta in Palermo). Vast repertory, ranging from Mozart to Rossini to Wagner. She sang Tigrana in an *Edgar* in Buenos Aires in 1905 during a special Puccini Festival at which the composer was present.

SALA, MARCO (1842–1901). Journalist and musical dilettante. Friend of Boito's, Ricordi's, and others in Milanese artistic circles. In his house a hearing of Puccini's *Le willis* was arranged after the score had been rejected by the judges of the Sonzogno competition. Sala and his brother were among those whose contributions helped defray expenses of the work's first staged performance at the Dal Verme.

SALVATORI, FAUSTO (1870–1929). Italian poet, author, dramatist, scenarist. Author of the text of the *Inno a Roma*, which Puccini set in 1919.

SANTARELLI, AMADEA. Italian soprano. Began career as mezzo-soprano. Early roles included Tigrana in the second (three-act) version of *Edgar*, in Ferrara (1892), and Amneris, Mexico City (1894). Later she became famous in veristic soprano roles.

SARDOU, VICTORIEN (1831–1908). Prolific French playwright. His drama *La Tosca* (1887), conceived as a vehicle for Sarah Bernhardt (*q.v.*), became the basis for the libretto of Puccini's opera. Sardou plays inspired operas by Bizet (*Grisélidis*), Giordano (*Fedora* and *Madame Sans Gêne*), and others.

SCHIPA, TITO (1888–1965). Italian tenor. Made his debut in 1910 in Vercelli, interpreting the role of Alfredo in *La traviata*. Created Ruggero in *La rondine,* Monte Carlo (1917). His graceful but not large voice made him outstanding in a lighter repertory (especially in French works), but he sang Rodolfo, Cavaradossi, and Pinkerton and recorded numerous Puccini arias. He continued singing in public until a short time before his death.

SCHNABL-ROSSI, RICCARDO (1872–1955). Italian landowner of Austrian origin. An ardent music-lover, Schnabl became acquainted with Puccini in the 1890s, and they remained close friends until the composer's death. Schnabl often acted as Puccini's confidant, traveling companion, and—in matters requiring a knowledge of German—his mediator, virtually his agent. The composer's letters to his friend have been published in a critical edition by Simonetta Puccini (Milan, 1981).

SCOTTI, ANTONIO (1866–1936). Italian baritone. Debut in Naples (1889), in *La vestale.* An elegant actor, he sang such roles as Don Giovanni, Posa, and Falstaff in the earlier part of his career; later he specialized in character roles. His Puccini repertory included Marcello, Lescaut, Sharpless, and—particularly popular—the wicked Baron Scarpia.

SELIGMAN, SYBIL. English music-lover and hostess. After a brief love affair with Puccini, she became his close and trusted friend, and was a friend as well to Elvira and Tonio Puccini. She suggested various English-language texts to the composer as possible librettos and kept him informed of musical life in London, where she moved in exalted social and intellectual circles. Many of Puccini's letters to her were published (with some abridgment) by her son Vincent in the volume *Puccini Among Friends* (London, 1938).

SIMONI, RENATO (1875–1952). Italian theater critic, playwright, later film and theater director. In addition to his collaboration with Adami on the libretto for *Turandot,* he wrote librettos for Giulio Ricordi, alias J. Burgmein (*La secchia rapita,* 1910), and Giordano (*Madame Sans-Gêne,* 1915).

SOFFREDINI, ALFREDO (1845–1923). Italian composer, critic, musicologist, and educator. Teacher of the young Mascagni. Later he worked for Casa Ricordi both as critic for the *Gazzetta Musicale di Milano* and in preparing the piano-voice reductions of operatic scores.

SONZOGNO, EDOARDO (1836–1920). Italian publisher. The firm, founded by Edoardo's grandfather, published various periodicals and a successful series of cheap classics and popular works. In 1874 Sonzogno also went into music publishing and quickly became a serious rival of Ricordi's. Sonzogno acquired the Italian rights to *Carmen* and the operas of Thomas. The celebrated Sonzogno Competition for a one-act opera was first held in 1883; Puccini's entry, *Le willis,* was unsuccessful. The winner of the second competition (1889) was Mascagni with *Cavalleria rusticana.* Sonzogno published many verismo composers (Giordano, Cilea, Leoncavallo) and, when Puccini briefly quarreled with Ricordi, *La rondine.* Puccini's *Inno a Roma* (1909) was also published by Sonzogno.

SPECHT, RICHARD (1870–1932). Austrian music critic and writer. Studied with Zemlinsky and Schreker. Wrote many introductions to published works of music (including most of Mahler's symphonies). His *Puccini* (1931) was the first serious study of the composer.

STORCHIO, ROSINA (1876–1945). Italian soprano. Made her debut as Micaela (*Carmen*) at the Teatro Dal Verme, Milan, 1892. Joined La Scala company in 1895 and in that theater created many veristic roles. Was the first Butterfly at the disastrous 1904 premiere. In 1917 she sang in the Paris premiere of the opera. She sang both Mimì and Musetta, and she also was in the cast of the premiere of the Leoncavallo *La bohème.*

TAMAGNO, FRANCESCO (1850–1905). Italian tenor. Member of the chorus at the Regio, Turin. He made his debut there in 1873, replacing an indisposed colleague in a secondary role. At La Scala from 1877, where he sang in the premiere of the revised version of Verdi's *Simon Boccanegra* and created his *Otello.* Much to Puccini's disappointment, Tamagno did not create Edgar at La Scala in April of 1889; only after unrelenting persuasion from both Puccini and Giulio Ricordi did he finally agree to sing the role for a production of the opera in Madrid, 1892.

TETRAZZINI, EVA (1862–1938). Italian soprano, older sister of the more famous Luisa Tetrazzini, and wife of the conductor Cleofonte Campanini (*q.v.*). Was Fidelia in the Madrid *Edgar,* 1892. The following year she sang the title role in the first *Manon Lescaut* in Naples, and repeated the role in local premieres in Florence, Seville, Madrid, and Lisbon. Repertory also included *Tosca* (which she introduced to Spain in 1900).

TOSCANINI, ARTURO (1867–1957). Italian conductor. Conducted world premieres of *Bohème* (Turin, 1896), *Fanciulla del West* (Metropolitan, 1910), and *Turandot* (Milan, 1926). Despite some disagreements, he maintained a warm friendship with Puccini, who sometimes accepted the conductor's advice on musical matters (for example modifications to the orchestration of *Manon Lescaut* for performances given at La Scala, November 1922). Toscanini conducted the Scala orchestra and chorus (in the requiem scene from *Edgar*) at Puccini's funeral service in Milan, 1924.

TOSTI, SIR FRANCESCO PAOLO (1846–1916). Italian (later British subject) song composer and teacher. Gave voice lessons to Italy's Queen Margherita and to members of the British royal family. His salon songs (some to d'Annunzio texts) were immensely popular, and Tosti's warm personality enhanced his reputation. He was a good friend of Sybil Seligman's (q.v.) and of Puccini's, who confided in him during the tragic Doria Manfredi episode.

VANDINI, ALFREDO. Italian government official. Native of Lucca, childhood friend of Puccini's. After Vandini settled in Rome, Puccini often called upon him for small favors and advice. Many of the composer's letters to Vandini survive and have been published, testifying to this warm, unruffled friendship.

VENTURINI, EMILIO (1878–1952). Italian tenor. Created Pang in *Turandot* (1926). Admired as a character actor, he also sang Spoletta (*Tosca*) and Pinkerton (*Butterfly*) in Chicago.

VOENNA, ROSINA. Italian soprano. Tigrana in Turin *Edgar* (1892). Also at the Regio sang Rachel in *La Juive* and Amelia in *Duca d'Alba* (1885–86 season). In 1888 she sang the title role in Goldmark's *Die Königen von Saba*.

WALTER, CARLO. Italian bass. Scala debut in 1923 as Sparafucile under Toscanini. Created role of Timur in *Turandot*, Scala, 1926. Also sang Don Basilio (*Il barbiere di Siviglia*) and Arkel (*Pelléas et Mélisande*), the latter again under Toscanini's direction.

WILLNER, ALFRED MARIA (1859–1929). Austrian composer and librettist. With Heinz Reichert (q.v.) he wrote the original version of the story that became *La rondine*.

WILMANT, TIESTE. Italian baritone. Created Marcello in *La bohème* in Turin, 1896. Was Gunther in the Toscanini *Götterdämmerung* in Turin that same year. In the 1881–82 season at the Regio he had sung Barnaba (*Gioconda*), Enrico (*Lucia*), and a role in Gounod's *Le Tribut de Zamore*. At La Scala, he was Puccini's Lescaut (1894) and Toscanini's Alberich (1899).

ZAMBONI, MARIA (1895–1976). Italian soprano. Debut in Piacenza, 1921, as Margherita (*Faust*). Created Liù (*Turandot*), Milan (1926). Was a highly esteemed Mimì under Toscanini at La Scala.

ZANAZZO, LUIGI (1860–1911). Italian poet and playwright, specializing in Roman dialect. Contributed the text of the shepherd boy's song for the opening of Act III of *Tosca*. Librarian of the Ministero dell'Instruzione Pubblica.

ZANGARINI, CARLO (1874–1943). Italian poet, author, and journalist from Bologna. One of the librettists of *Fanciulla del West*. Also wrote or versified librettos for other composers, including Wolf-Ferrari (*I gioielli della Madonna*) and Zandonai (*Conchita*). After 1934 he was Professor of Dramatic and Poetic Literature at the Liceo Musicale Martini, Bologna.

ZENATELLO, GIOVANNI (1876–1949). Italian tenor (originally baritone). Made his debut in Belluno as Silvio (*Pagliacci*). Created Pinkerton in

Madama Butterfly (Scala, 1904). After 1916 he sang mostly in America, where he retired in 1928 and opened a singing school with his wife, Maria Gay. A famous Des Grieux in Puccini's *Manon Lescaut*.

ZILLI, EMMA (1864–1901). Italian soprano. Tigrana in both the Lucca (1891) and Brescia (1892) productions of *Edgar*. Frequently heard as Puccini's Manon Lescaut. Much admired by the composer, who described her as "an exciting singing-actress." Created Alice Ford in Verdi's *Falstaff* (Scala, 1893).

ZUELLI, GUGLIELMO (1859–1941). Italian composer. Together with Luigi Mapelli (*q.v.*), was winner of the first Sonzogno Competition, 1883. In later life he admitted that his winning opera, *La fata del Nord,* was greatly inferior to Puccini's *Le willis,* which had failed to gain even an honorable mention in the competition. Later he became a noted conductor and teacher. Most famous composition is the orchestral *Festa delle sirene,* taken from the symphonic poem *Un saluto al mare* (1908).

Appendix B
First Performances
of Puccini Operas

Puccini frequently revised his operas, often slightly, sometimes drastically, as they were given in different theaters at different times in the course of his career. Here, only the major reworkings are indicated. For obvious reasons, only the posthumous *Turandot* was not subjected to Puccini's revising pen after its premiere.

Le willis

Libretto by Ferdinando Fontana
Teatro dal Verme, Milan, 31 May 1884
Arturo Panizza, conductor

Guglielmo Wulf	*Erminio Peltz*
Anna	*Rosina Caponetti*
Roberto	*Antonio d'Andrade*

Le villi (revised version)

Teatro Regio, Turin, 26 December 1884
Giovanni Bolzoni, conductor

Guglielmo Wulf	*Agostino Gnaccarini*
Anna	*Elena Boronat*
Roberto	*Enrico Filippi-Bresciani*

Edgar

Libretto by Ferdinando Fontana
Teatro alla Scala, Milan, 21 April 1889
Franco Faccio, conductor

Edgar	*Gregorio Gabrielesco*
Gualtiero	*Pio Marini*
Frank	*Antonio Magini-Coletti*
Fidelia	*Aurelia Cataneo*
Tigrana	*Romilda Pantaleoni*

Edgar (revised version)

Teatro Comunale, Ferrara, 28 January 1892
Carlo Carignani, conductor

Edgar	*Oreste Emiliani*
Gualtiero	?
Frank	*Innocente D'Anna*
Fidelia	*Tilde Maragliano*
Tigrana	*Amadea Santarelli*

Manon Lescaut

Libretto by Ruggero Leoncavallo, Domenico Oliva, Giulio Ricordi, Luigi
Illica, Giuseppe Giacosa, and Marco Praga
Teatro Regio, Turin, 1 February 1893
Alessandro Pomé, conductor

Manon Lescaut	*Cesira Ferrani*
Lescaut	*Achille Moro*
Chevalier Des Grieux	*Giuseppe Cremonini*
Géronte di Ravoir	*Alessandro Polonini*
Edmondo	*Roberto Ramini*
A dancing master	*Roberto Ramini*
A lamplighter	*Roberto Ramini*

La bohème

Libretto by Giuseppe Giacosa and Luigi Illica
Teatro Regio, Turin, 1 February 1896
Arturo Toscanini, conductor

Rodolfo	*Evan Gorga*
Marcello	*Tieste Wilmant*
Colline	*Michele Mazzara*
Schaunard	*Antonio Pini-Corsi*
Benoît	*Alessandro Polonini*
Alcindoro	*Alessandro Polonini*
Mimì	*Cesira Ferrani*
Musetta	*Camilla Pasini*

Tosca

Libretto by Giuseppe Giacosa and Luigi Illica
Teatro Costanzi, Rome, 14 January 1900
Leopoldo Mugnone, conductor

Tosca	*Hariclea Darclée*
Cavaradossi	*Emilio de Marchi*
Scarpia	*Eugenio Giraldoni*
Angelotti	*Ruggero Galli*
Sacristan	*Ettore Borelli*
Spoletta	*Enrico Giordani*
Sciarrone	*Giuseppe Gironi*

Madama Butterfly

Libretto by Giuseppe Giacosa and Luigi Illica
Teatro alla Scala, Milan, 17 February 1904
Cleofonte Campanini, conductor

Cio-Cio-San	*Rosina Storchio*
Suzuki	*Giuseppina Giaconia*
Pinkerton	*Giovanni Zenatello*
Sharpless	*Giuseppe De Luca*
Goro	*Gaetano Pini-Corsi*

Madama Butterfly (revised version)

Teatro Grande, Brescia, 28 May 1904
Cleofonte Campanini, conductor

Cio-Cio-San	*Salomea Krusceniski*
Suzuki	*Giovanna Lucacevska*
Pinkerton	*Giovanni Zenatello*
Sharpless	*Virgilio Bellatti*
Goro	*Gaetano Pini-Corsi*

La fanciulla del West

Libretto by Guelfo Civinini and Carlo Zangarini
Metropolitan Opera House, New York, 10 December 1910
Arturo Toscanini, conductor

Minnie	*Emmy Destinn*
Jack Rance	*Pasquale Amato*
Dick Johnson	*Enrico Caruso*
Nick	*Albert Reiss*

Ashby	*Adamo Didur*
Sonora	*Dinh Gilly*
Trin	*Angelo Bada*
Sid	*Giulio Rossi*
Handsome	*Vincenzo Reschiglian*
Harry	*Pietro Audisio*
Joe	*Glenn Hall*
Happy	*Antonio Pini-Corsi*
Larkens	*Bernard Bégné*
Billy Jackrabbit	*Georges Bourgeois*
Wowkle	*Marie Mattfield*
Jake Wallace	*Andrés de Segurola*
José Castro	*Edoardo Missiano*
A postilion	*Lamberto Belleri*

La rondine

Libretto by Giuseppe Adami
Théâtre du Casino, Monte Carlo, 27 March 1917
Gino Marinuzzi, conductor

Magda de Civry	*Gilda Dalla Rizza*
Lisette	*Ines Maria Ferraris*
Ruggero	*Tito Schipa*
Prunier	*Francesco Dominici*
Rambaldo	*Gustave Huberdeau*
Gobin	*Jean-Francisque Delmas*
Bianca	*André Moreau*

Il trittico

Metropolitan Opera House, New York, 14 December 1918
Roberto Moranzoni, conductor

IL TABARRO

Libretto by Giuseppe Adami

Michele	*Luigi Montesanto*
Luigi	*Giulio Crimi*
Il Tinca	*Angelo Bada*
Il Talpa	*Adamo Didur*
Giorgetta	*Claudia Muzio*
La Frugola	*Alice Gentle*
Song Vendor	*Pietro Audisio*
Lovers	*Marie Tiffany*
	Albert Reiss

SUOR ANGELICA

Libretto by Giovacchino Forzano

Sister Angelica	*Geraldine Farrar*
The Princess	*Flora Perini*
The Abbess	*Rita Fornia*
The Monitress	*Marie Sundelius*
The Novice Mistress	*Cecil Arden*
Sister Genovieffa	*Mary Ellis*
Sister Osmina	*Marguerite Belleri*
Sister Dolcina	*Marie Mattfield*
A Novice	*Phyllis White*

GIANNI SCHICCHI

Libretto by Giovacchino Forzano

Gianni Schicchi	*Giuseppe De Luca*
Lauretta	*Florence Easton*
Zita	*Kathleen Howard*
Rinuccio	*Giulio Crimi*
Gherardo	*Angelo Bada*
Nella	*Marie Tiffany*
Betto	*Paolo Ananian*
Simone	*Adamo Didur*
Marco	*Louis D'Angelo*
Ciesca	*Marie Sundelius*
Spinelloccio	*Pompilio Malatesta*
Amantio	*Andrés de Segurola*
Pinellino	*Vincenzo Reschiglian*
Guccio	*Carl Schlegel*

Turandot

Libretto by Giuseppe Adami and Renato Simoni
Teatro alla Scala, Milan, 25 April 1926
Arturo Toscanini, conductor

Turandot	*Rosa Raisa*
Altoum	*Francesco Dominici*
Timur	*Carlo Walter*
Calaf	*Miguel Fleta*
Ping	*Giacomo Rimini*
Pang	*Emilio Venturini*
Pong	*Giuseppe Nessi*
Mandarin	*Aristide Baracchi*
Liù	*Maria Zamboni*

A PPENDIX C
P LOT S UMMARIES

Le villi ★

Guglielmo Wulf	*Baritone*
Anna, his daughter	*Soprano*
Roberto	*Tenor*
Villagers	
The Villi (*spirits*)	

ACT I

It is springtime, in a clearing in the Black Forest. In front of the house of Guglielmo Wulf, foresters are holding a banquet to celebrate the engagement of his daughter Anna to Roberto. Roberto must leave for a short time, however, in order to journey to Mainz and claim a large inheritance bequeathed to him by a recently deceased relative. Prior to his departure, Anna places a small bouquet of forget-me-nots on Roberto's luggage to remind him of her devotion. Roberto tries to console Anna and answers her fears of losing him with an oath of undying love and fidelity. Anna responds with her own pledge of eternal love, and all join in a prayer for Roberto's safety on his long journey.

Two intermezzi follow. The first of these, entitled "The Abandonment," is introduced by a poem, which tells that Roberto has been seduced by a "temptress" in Mainz and that he has become so enraptured that he has completely

★ *Le villi* began as a one-act opera. In order to include certain dramatic and narrative elements omitted in the original libretto, Puccini added two intermezzi and expanded the drama into its present two-act version.

forgotten Anna. The intermezzo ends with a vision of Anna's funeral cortege.

The second intermezzo is also preceded by a poem. It describes the Villis—spirits of abandoned girls—who wreak vengeance on their faithless lovers by forcing them to dance to their deaths. We are also told that Roberto is returning home after being abandoned by his seductress. This intermezzo, "The Witches' Sabbath," concludes with a ballet danced by the Villis.

ACT II

Mourning the unavenged death of his daughter, Guglielmo enters his house and hears the menacing voices of the Villis. Roberto returns, racked by guilt and remorse and hoping for Anna's forgiveness. Her spirit appears but rejects his pleas and tells him instead of her suffering and longing during his absence. At last she extends her arms to embrace him. Not realizing that she, too, has become a Villi, Roberto moves toward her. Immediately the rest of the Villis descend on the pair and Roberto is forced into his dance of death. He falls dead at Anna's feet as the Villis rejoice.

Edgar ★

Edgar	*Tenor*
Gualtiero	*Bass*
Frank, his son	*Baritone*
Fidelia, his daughter	*Soprano*
Tigrana, his adopted daughter	*Mezzo-soprano*

ACT I

*I*t is dawn in the square of a Flemish village. The Angelus sounds, and the peasants make their way to the fields. Edgar, who has fallen asleep at the local tavern, is awakened by Fidelia, who leaves him with a branch of almond blossoms as a token of her affection. Tigrana, a Moorish orphan raised by Fidelia's father, appears and waits for Edgar. As they meet she mocks his feelings for the innocent Fidelia and suggests that he is more disposed to her own sensuous eroticism. Edgar protests and retreats to his house while Tigrana scornfully laughs at his weak self-deception.

Fidelia's brother Frank, infatuated with Tigrana, approaches and chides her for her failure to meet him the previous night, as planned. Indifferent to Frank's passion, Tigrana cruelly taunts him as he curses the power she holds over him.

★ *Edgar* first appeared in a four-act version. Puccini reduced it to three acts by reworking certain sections of the libretto and significantly reducing the part of Tigrana.

The villagers file out after Sunday Mass and are met by a defiant Tigrana, who sings a tune with pointedly "earthy" lyrics. The crowd is furious and is further angered when Edgar rises to her defense. He becomes enraged at the situation and, in a fit of passion, sets fire to his house and announces his intentions to leave the village with Tigrana. Frank reappears, and a duel ensues despite the pleas for calm by Fidelia and her father, Gualtiero. Frank is wounded; Edgar and Tigrana make their escape, cursed by the villagers.

ACT II

It is night on the terrace of an elegant palace. Edgar has grown tired of Tigrana's charms and is filled with remorse at his abandonment of Fidelia. Tigrana appears, but Edgar rejects her. A group of soldiers passes and, to his great surprise, Edgar recognizes Frank, their leader. The former rivals make their peace; and in a burst of patriotic fervor, Edgar joins the troop. Tigrana tries to persuade Edgar to stay. But he insists, and Tigrana swears revenge on her faithless lover.

ACT III

Near the fortress of Courtray, Frank and a monk, his face hidden by a cowl, take part in a funeral procession. The crowd chants a Requiem for Edgar, whose heroic death in battle Frank narrates. In rebuttal, the monk reminds everyone of Edgar's past sins, but Fidelia rises to her lost lover's defense. Tigrana approaches the casket to pray. Frank and the monk offer her a reward of jewels if she will speak out against Edgar. She does, and the crowd, outraged at the thought of Edgar's crimes, tears open the coffin to find only an empty suit of armor inside. The crowd is struck with terror; then the monk steps forward and reveals himself as Edgar. He rages at Tigrana and drives her from the scene. Fidelia rushes forward to embrace him but Tigrana suddenly reappears and stabs her. Overcome with grief, Edgar falls next to the lifeless body of Fidelia as soldiers seize Tigrana and take her away to be executed.

Manon Lescaut

Manon Lescaut	*Soprano*
Lescaut, her brother and Sergeant of the King's guards	*Baritone*
Chevalier Des Grieux	*Tenor*
Geronte di Ravoir, Treasurer-General	*Bass*
Edmondo, a student	*Tenor*
The Innkeeper	*Bass*
A singer	*Mezzo-soprano*

A dancing master	*Tenor*
A lamplighter	*Tenor*
Sergeant of the Royal archers	*Bass*
A Captain in the navy	*Bass*
The hair dresser	*Mime*

Students, Townspeople, Singers, Dancers, Sailors, Soldiers, Ladies and Gentlemen, Police, Guards.

ACT I

*I*n the village square of Amiens, Edmondo entertains a group of fellow students with a mock-pastoral. At Des Grieux's appearance, the talk turns to love and to his weakness for women. The students' revels are cut short by the arrival of the coach from Arras containing Lescaut, Manon, and Geronte. Seeing Manon alight from the carriage, Des Grieux is immediately captivated by her beauty and takes advantage of her brother's momentary absence to engage her in conversation. He learns her name and that she is bound for convent life. Lescaut calls his sister. But before joining him she arranges a rendezvous with Des Grieux. Manon's traveling companion, the elderly Geronte, also has designs on Manon and asks the innkeeper to provide him with a coach with which to spirit Manon away. Edmondo overhears Geronte's plotting and warns Des Grieux, who in turn informs Manon. The two young lovers take advantage of the situation and make their escape in the coach Geronte has unwarily provided. Geronte is furious, but Lescaut assures him that Manon will soon tire of her penniless lover and be only too happy to accept an offer from a wealthy suitor.

ACT II

Despite the elegant surroundings of Geronte's Parisian mansion, Manon is overcome with nostalgia for the modest life she once shared with Des Grieux. Lescaut arrives and senses Manon's mood. After a madrigal performance by some hired musicians, he leaves in search of Des Grieux, while Manon submits to a dancing lesson. Geronte enters with friends and joins her in a dance as the onlookers shower them with compliments. The visitors depart; Manon is left alone. Des Grieux enters and an impassioned scene of confrontation and reconciliation follows. They embrace as Geronte appears unexpectedly. Manon taunts the old man, who leaves outraged. Manon decides to flee with Des Grieux but has second thoughts about abandoning her jewels. Lescaut bursts in and tells them Geronte has ordered Manon's arrest as a thief and prostitute. But the warning comes too late. Gendarmes arrive and seize Manon.

ACT III

After an opening intermezzo, the curtain rises on a square at Le Havre next to the jail where Manon awaits deportation. It is dawn, and Lescaut and Des Grieux are plotting Manon's escape. Lescaut goes off to make preparations and Des Grieux manages to talk with Manon through the window of her cell. An alarm is sounded. Lescaut returns to tell Des Grieux that their plot has failed. The Sergeant begins the roll-call of the deportees, and as Manon appears, Des Grieux rushes to her side and begs the captain to be allowed to follow his love, working for his passage. The captain, moved by Des Grieux's emotion, consents.

ACT IV

"An interminable desert on the frontier of New Orleans." Manon and Des Grieux, exhausted, enter. Despite Des Grieux's attempts at encouragement, Manon faints. She regains consciousness and complains of thirst. When Des Grieux has gone off to search for water, Manon expresses her fear of dying alone in these desolate surroundings. Returning empty-handed, Des Grieux finds Manon delirious. With her last breath Manon assures Des Grieux of her undying love. Des Grieux embraces Manon's lifeless body.

La bohème

Rodolfo, a poet	*Tenor*
Marcello, a painter	*Baritone*
Colline, a philosopher	*Bass*
Schaunard, a musician	*Baritone*
Benoît, a landlord	*Bass*
Alcindoro, a councilor of state	*Bass*
Parpignol, a toy vendor	*Tenor*
Customs Sergeant	*Bass*
Mimì	*Soprano*
Musetta	*Soprano*

Students, Working Girls, Bourgeois, Shopkeepers,
Vendors, Soldiers, Waiters, Gamins, etc.

The time is about 1830.
The place is the Latin Quarter, Paris.

ACT I

Rodolfo, a poet, and his friend Marcello, a painter, are trying to work in their Paris garret. It is Christmas Eve, and they are cold and hungry—and without money. Colline, another bohemian, comes in, equally discouraged. But then Schaunard, the fourth and luckiest of the group, enters with money and provisions. The friends decide to celebrate by dining out. After a successful skirmish with their landlord, Benoît, they set out for the Café Momus. Only Rodolfo stays behind to finish an article he must write. When he is alone there is a knock at the door. To his surprise, he finds a beautiful young girl on the landing. It is his neighbor, Mimì, who has knocked to ask for a light. Her candle has gone out. Rodolfo relights it for her, but it goes out again, and in the confusion, she loses her key. In the darkness she and Rodolfo search for it. Their hands touch. Rodolfo and Mimì exchange confidences and, finally, declarations of love. Then they go off to join his friends.

ACT II

Christmas Eve in the Latin Quarter. The group of friends is separated in the bustling of merrymakers and vendors of every kind. Rodolfo and Mimì go into a milliner's, and he buys her a pink bonnet. Later all are reunited at the Café Momus, where they order a sumptuous supper. As they are enjoying themselves, Musetta—Marcello's beautiful but fickle beloved—enters with Alcindoro, an elderly and strait-laced admirer. Seeing Marcello, Musetta contrives to get rid of her escort. Soon she and Marcello are again in each other's arms. The friends all go off, leaving their bill to the hapless Alcindoro.

ACT III

A cold February dawn. Outside a tavern near one of the gates of Paris, Mimì appears and sends for Marcello, who is working in the tavern with Musetta. When he comes out, Mimì tells how Rodolfo's insane jealousy is forcing them apart. Their conversation is cut short when Rodolfo, who was sleeping in the tavern, wakes and comes out. Mimì hides behind a tree. Taxed by Marcello with his fickleness, Rodolfo reveals that he is really concerned for Mimì's health and thinks that another person, less poor than he, could take better care of her. Mimì's presence is discovered, and though she first bids Rodolfo good-by, in the end they agree to stay together at least until spring comes. As Musetta and Marcello quarrel in the background and finally separate, Rodolfo and Mimì go off reconciled, arm in arm.

ACT IV

The garret, months later. Rodolfo and Marcello are again trying to work, but this time each is distracted and tormented by the memory of his lost love. Schaunard and Colline come in, and the four friends clown, making light of their poverty, until Musetta interrupts them, bursting in with the news that Mimì is outside, too ill to climb the last stairs. Rodolfo helps her into the room, where she is settled on the bed. Musetta sacrifices her earrings and Colline his coat to buy medicine and a muff for the dying girl. Marcello goes for a doctor. Left alone, the two lovers renew their vows of love and recall their first meeting. Soon the others return. As Musetta prays, Mimì quietly dies, with Rodolfo calling her name in despair.

Tosca

Floria Tosca, a famous singer	*Soprano*
Mario Cavaradossi, a painter	*Tenor*
Baron Scarpia, Chief of Police	*Baritone*
Cesare Angelotti, a political prisoner	*Bass*
The Sacristan	*Baritone*
Spoletta, a police agent	*Tenor*
Sciarrone, a gendarme	*Bass*
A Jailer	*Bass*
A Shepherd	*Boy soprano*

A Cardinal, a Judge, Roberti the Executioner, a Scribe,
an Officer, Soldiers, Police, Ladies, Nobles,
Bourgeois, Populace, etc.

The time is June 1800.
The place is Rome.

ACT I

The interior of the Church of Sant'Andrea della Valle. A political prisoner, Angelotti, enters furtively, having just escaped from the Castel Sant' Angelo through the help of his sister, the Marchesa Attavanti, who has left him some clothes in the church and the key to the Attavanti Chapel, where he can hide and disguise himself. When Angelotti is hidden, the painter Mario Cavaradossi comes in to resume work on a painting of Mary Magdalen. The comic sacristan points out a resemblance between the Magdalen in the painting and a strange lady who has been coming often to the church recently (this is the Marchesa). Cavaradossi ponders the curious harmony of this stranger's beauty with that of his beloved Tosca. Then Angelotti reappears and recognizes Mario, an old friend and political ally. Cavaradossi promises to help, but their talk is interrupted by the arrival of Tosca. Angelotti hides, and Mario has to deal with Tosca's jealous suspicions. Finally they are allayed, and the lovers agree to meet again that evening. Once Tosca has left, Angelotti comes out of the chapel again, and—since time is pressing—Mario takes the fugitive away, to conceal him at his villa outside the city.

The sacristan comes in to announce Napoleon's defeat, but Mario has gone. There is a sudden eruption of choristers and acolytes, excitedly preparing the *Te Deum* that is to celebrate the victory of the royalists, but the arrival of Scarpia silences them. Angelotti has been traced to the church. Mario's empty lunch basket is found in the Attavanti Chapel. This discovery throws suspicion on the painter. When Tosca comes back and is disturbed not to find Mario, Scarpia cleverly uses the Marchesa Attavanti's fan—also discovered in the church—to play on the singer's jealousy and to trap her into a false move. In fact, she rushes out to go to the villa, and Scarpia sends his henchman, Spoletta, after her. During the *Te Deum,* Scarpia expresses his desire to have Mario executed and, at the same time, to possess the beautiful Tosca.

ACT II

Scarpia's apartments in the Palazzo Farnese. In another part of the building the Queen of Naples is holding her celebration. Spoletta arrives with the news that Angelotti could not be found in Cavaradossi's villa. The painter himself is brought in to be questioned, but he refuses to say anything. Tosca—summoned by a note from Scarpia—also arrives, and Mario, in a whisper, exhorts her to reveal nothing (having been to the villa, she now knows all). Scarpia has Cavaradossi tortured, and though the painter still keeps silent, Tosca, horrified at his sufferings, discloses Angelotti's hiding place. Cavaradossi reproaches her bitterly, but his anger turns to joy when Sciarrone—another of Scarpia's agents—rushes in with the news that the Battle of Marengo has really been won by Napoleon, not by the royalists, as first reported. Cavaradossi's gloating and taunting infuriate Scarpia, who has him taken off to Castel Sant'Angelo, to be executed at dawn. Tosca pleads for mercy in vain, and Spoletta returns to say that Angelotti, rather than submit to capture, killed himself. Once he is alone with Tosca, Scarpia offers her a revolting bargain: her love in exchange for Mario's life. She is forced to agree, on condition that she and Mario be allowed to flee the country immediately afterward. Scarpia then explains that there will be a mock execution. As he is writing out the safe-conduct for Tosca and Mario, Tosca spies a sharp knife on the table. She conceals it behind her back, and when Scarpia comes to claim his part of the bargain, she plunges the knife into his back, killing him.

ACT III

A parapet on top of the Castel Sant'Angelo, just before dawn. A shepherd is heard singing. Mario is brought in and left alone, to think of Tosca and his life, which must now end. But Tosca arrives, gives him the good news of his planned escape, and confesses that she has murdered Scarpia for his sake. They sing of their love and their future. The execution takes place. Tosca calls Mario to rise, then discovers to her horror that Scarpia has cheated her. The firing squad's bullets were real, and Mario is dead. Spoletta, who has found Scarpia's body, now comes rushing up with some soldiers to arrest Tosca. She kills herself by jumping off the ramparts of the fortress.

Madama Butterfly

Madama Butterfly (Cio-Cio-San)	*Soprano*
Suzuki, her servant	*Mezzo-soprano*
Kate Pinkerton	*Mezzo-soprano*
B. F. Pinkerton, Lieutenant in the U. S. Navy	*Tenor*
Sharpless, U. S. Consul in Nagasaki	*Baritone*
Goro, a marriage broker	*Tenor*
Prince Yamadori	*Baritone*
The Bonze, Butterfly's uncle	*Bass*
The Imperial Commissioner	*Bass*
The Registry Officer	*Baritone*
Trouble, Butterfly's child	. . .

Butterfly's Relatives and Friends, Servants

Time: the present (i.e., 1904).
Place: Nagasaki.

ACT I

Pinkerton, a lieutenant in the U. S. Navy, has arranged with the Nagasaki marriage broker Goro to marry a fifteen-year-old girl, Butterfly (or Cio-Cio-San). By Japanese law, the groom is free to dissolve the marriage whenever he wants to, and though Pinkerton is clearly fascinated by his child-bride, it is obvious that he doesn't take the marriage seriously. He says as much to Sharpless, the American consul, who warns him that Butterfly is in earnest and tragedy may ensue. But Pinkerton pays no attention. When the brief ceremony is over, Butterfly's uncle, a Buddhist priest, arrives in a fury, revealing that the girl has renounced her people's ancient faith and taken the white man's god. The family, horrified, deserts Butterfly. She weeps bitterly, but Pinkerton comforts her, and soon all is forgotten as the two express their love.

ACT II: PART 1

Pinkerton has been gone for three years. Everyone—even her faithful maid Suzuki—tells Butterfly that he has forsaken her, but she steadfastly insists that he will come back, as he promised, "when the robins make their nest." Goro keeps urging her to marry his wealthy client Prince Yamadori. And even Sharpless suggests that she accept this offer, since he knows that though Pinkerton is, in fact, coming back, he is bringing an American wife with him. Sharpless tries to prepare Butterfly for this blow, but before he can do so, she reveals that she has had a child by Pinkerton, and the consul leaves without delivering his message. The harbor cannon then announces the arrival of a ship. It is Pinkerton's, the *Abraham Lincoln*. With Suzuki's help, Butterfly decorates the little house with flowers. Then, with Suzuki and with the child, Butterfly prepares to await Pinkerton's arrival.

ACT II: PART 2

Dawn. Butterfly has waited all night. Suzuki persuades her to go and rest, and in her absence from the room, Pinkerton and Sharpless arrive. They break the news to Suzuki and try to enlist her help in persuading Butterfly to give up the child to Kate, Pinkerton's new wife, who has also come but is discreetly outside in the garden. Pinkerton then leaves: the memories of the house, his remorse are too much for him. Kate speaks with Suzuki, then goes out again. Butterfly enters and, horror-stricken, learns the truth. When Kate repeats her request, Butterfly answers that she will give the child to his father if Pinkerton will come back for him in a half hour. The visitors leave. Butterfly blindfolds the child, then commits hari-kiri. She dies just as Pinkerton rushes in, calling her name.

La fanciulla del West

Minnie	*Soprano*
Jack Rance, Sheriff	*Baritone*
Dick Johnson (Ramerrez)	*Tenor*
Nick, bartender at the "Polka"	*Tenor*
Ashby, Wells Fargo Agent	*Bass*
Sonora	*Baritone*
Trin	*Tenor*
Sid	*Baritone*
Handsome	*Baritone*
Harry } *Miners*	*Tenor*
Joe	*Tenor*
Happy	*Baritone*
Sid	*Baritone*
Larkens	*Bass*
Billy Jackrabbit, an Indian	*Bass*
Wowkle, Billy's squaw	*Mezzo-soprano*
Jake Wallace, camp minstrel	*Baritone*
José Castro, a member of Ramerrez's gang	*Bass*
Pony Express rider	*Tenor*
Men of the Camp	

ACT I

Evening at the Polka Bar in a Gold Rush settlement in the Sierra Nevada Mountains of California. Nick, the bartender, enters carrying a lit candle and lights the lamps, revealing Sheriff Jack Rance having a quiet smoke alone. Joe, Harry, and Handsome enter noisily and are joined by Sid for a bit of rowdy gambling at the faro table. Rance wonders what is keeping Minnie. Sonora presses Nick to confirm that he is Minnie's favorite. Nick slyly admits it, and the delighted Sonora orders cigars for the house. A moment later Trin asks Nick the same question, receives the same answer, and orders whiskey for all. Jake Wallace, the camp minstrel, enters singing a heart-felt song of home. The miners join in and Larkens, moved by the words, bursts into tears. A hat is passed among the miners and Larkens is sent off. The card game begins again but is interrupted by accusations of cheating. Rance restores order. Nick and Sonora start an argument over which of them is the object of Minnie's affections. Sonora draws a gun, but to the joy of all present, Minnie enters and separates the two rivals. Minnie holds a Bible class for the miners. When the class is over, Rance tells Minnie in vain of his love for her. Dick Johnson arrives and engages Minnie in conversation. Rance's suspicions are aroused when he hears that this is not the first time the two have met. As Johnson and Minnie waltz in the dance-hall, the Wells Fargo agent Ashby announces that Castro, an accomplice of the notorious bandit Ramerrez, has been captured. Recognizing Ramerrez (Johnson) inside the bar, Castro does his best to confuse Ashby and offers to lead a posse in search of the criminal, thus affording Johnson time and opportunity to steal the miners' gold. Left alone, Minnie and Johnson talk, and he learns that Minnie herself guards the treasure. Impressed by her devotion to the miners, Johnson abandons his planned theft. Minnie invites Johnson to her cabin to continue their talk undisturbed. Johnson praises Minnie's beauty and sensitivity. Unaccustomed to such flattery, Minnie hides her face in her hands.

ACT II

After a brief scene between Wowkle and Billy Jackrabbit, Johnson arrives at Minnie's cabin. He is in high spirits and discovers Minnie is dressed in her finest. Minnie tells Johnson how she first came to the mining camp and of the pleasures of her solitary life. She rebuffs Johnson's initial request for a kiss but relents when he asks a second time. Johnson prepares to leave, but a blizzard is now raging outside, so Minnie offers him her bed for the night while she curls up in front of the fire. The two are rudely awakened by knocking. Through the door Nick warns Minnie that Ramerrez has been seen in the vicinity. Not wishing to found alone with Johnson, Minnie urges him to hide behind the bed curtains before admitting Nick, Rance, Ashby, and Sonora. Minnie is shocked when Rance shows her a picture given to him by Johnson's "woman" and tells her that

Johnson is none other than the bandit Ramerrez. When the four men leave, Johnson tries to reassure Minnie that his feelings for her are genuine but she imperiously orders him to go. He leaves.

A shot rings out and Johnson falls back against the door with a thump. Minnie drags the injured man inside and confesses her love, even though she has learned his true identity. Mustering all her strength, she helps him up a ladder into the loft to hide. Rance enters, his gun drawn, and ransacks the cabin in a vain effort to find Johnson. Suddenly he seizes Minnie and kisses her. Minnie protests and manages to break free. A drop of blood from the loft falls onto Rance's hand. Immediately realizing the situation, he orders Johnson down and Minnie helps the wounded man to a table where he faints from loss of blood. To save Johnson's life, Minnie offers to risk her fate and that of the man she loves in a game of cards. If she loses, she will be Rance's and Johnson will be brought to justice. If she wins, Johnson will be allowed to go free. Rance agrees. The game proceeds, and as Rance seems to win the third and decisive hand, Minnie pretends to faint and furtively draws winning cards from her stocking, where she had wisely hidden them before the game began. Rance leaves in disgust, as Minnie embraces the unconscious Johnson.

ACT III

Dawn in a clearing in the forest. Rance and Nick are seated by a fire discussing Johnson and Minnie. Shouting is heard in the distance; and Ashby, who has been sleeping nearby, jumps up and exclaims that the posse is closing in on Johnson. A few members of the search party enter, and Ashby tells them Johnson must be taken alive. Ashby mounts his horse and leads the other miners back to the posse. Rance cannot help but be delighted at the prospect of Johnson's being captured and hanged. Sonora gallops in, to announce that Johnson has been caught.

A noisy crowd gathers. As Billy Jackrabbit slings a rope over a branch of a tall tree, Ashby charges Rance and the miners with administering justice. Johnson asks them to finish the job quickly, but first he begs them to let Minnie believe he got away free, to live the better life she had made him long for. This tenderness toward Minnie enrages Rance. He strikes Johnson and urges the men to carry out the sentence. Minnie arrives on horseback, carrying a pistol. She places herself between Johnson and the mob, to foil the lynching. Rance orders the men to proceed, but Minnie reminds the miners of all she has done for them and pleads for Johnson's life. She insists that he is a man redeemed and deserves another chance. Minnie's words have their effect; the crowd gradually yields, and Sonora cuts Johnson loose and turns him over to Minnie. The lovers bid farewell and go off to begin their new life together.

La rondine (first version)

Magda de Civry, mistress of Rambaldo	Soprano
Lisette, her maid	Soprano
Ruggero, a young man from Montauban	Tenor
Prunier, a poet	Tenor
Rambaldo, a Parisian banker	Baritone

Yvette	Friends of Magda	Soprano
Bianca		Soprano
Suzy		Mezzo-soprano

Perichaud	friends of Rambaldo	Baritone
Gobin		Tenor
Crebillon		Bass

Georgette	Grisettes	Soprano
Gabriella		Soprano
Colette		Mezzo-soprano

Rabonnier, a painter	Baritone
A student	Baritone
Majordomo	Bass
Whistler	

Ladies and Gentlemen, Students, Artists, Grisettes,
Dancers, Flower Girls and Waiters.

ACT I

*M*agda, mistress of the rich Parisian banker Rambaldo, is pouring tea for her three guests: Yvette, Bianca, and Suzy. Prunier is entertaining them with his thoughts on love. He tells the ladies that romantic love has become a regular epidemic in Paris, and he begins singing a sentimental ballad to which Magda improvises a second verse. Everyone is charmed by Magda's efforts, and Rambaldo presents her with a pearl necklace. Lisette bursts in to announce a stranger, asking for Rambaldo. Rambaldo asks Magda's permission to receive the son of an old school-friend. The talk in the salon again turns to love, and Magda describes a youthful flirtation with a charming young man.

Prunier offers to demonstrate his skills as a palmist to the ladies and while the reading is going on, Lisette shows the young Ruggero Lastouc into the room, where he is greeted by Rambaldo. Prunier, reading Magda's palm, tells her that she is like a swallow, eager to migrate across the ocean toward the sun, toward true love. When all learn that Ruggero has not been to Paris before, they offer suggestions for how he should spend his first evening in the city. The *Bal Bullier* is highly recommended, and the young man takes his leave. Soon after, Magda's guests also leave and she debates whether or not to go out. Remembering Prunier's palm reading, she decides to go to *Bullier* herself and hurries off to change.

Lisette, too, has plans for the evening. She enters dressed in her finest and joins the waiting Prunier. He makes some adjustments to her costume and they depart. Magda reappears, now dressed as a simple *grisette*. Studying her disguise in the mirror, she feels confident no one will recognize her.

ACT II

An animated crowd fills *Bullier* that evening. Magda catches the attention of some young men who crowd around her, hoping to win her favor. She manages to escape them and makes her way to Ruggero's table where she apologizes for disturbing him and promises that she will leave as soon as the pack of admiring gentlemen stops watching her. Ruggero urges her to stay and tells her that her shyness reminds him of the girls' behavior back in Montauban. He asks her to dance and is impressed by her grace and skill. The dance floor soon becomes crowded. Prunier and Lisette appear, arguing over his constant efforts to refine her manners and appearance. Magda and Ruggero return to their table, where their conversation soon leads to a reciprocal confession of love, sealed by a passionate kiss. Lisette has spied the amorous couple and is sure the young woman is Magda, her mistress. Prunier pretends not believe her and takes Lisette to the lovers' table, where Magda is able to carry off the deception. The two couples sit together and toast their love with champagne. Rambaldo enters, and Magda hurriedly begs Ruggero to leave her alone for a few minutes. Rambaldo confronts her and Magda confesses all. Rambaldo asks her to come away, but she refuses and tells him of her love for Ruggero. Rambaldo leaves and Magda is alone in the deserted hall. Ruggero returns and the two of them go off together, deeply in love.

ACT III

Magda and Ruggero have been leading a blissful life on the Riviera. Ruggero tells her that he has written his family, asking their consent to his marriage. Ruggero paints a idyllic picture of wedded happiness; Magda, knowing that she would be unacceptable to his family, listens uncomfortably. Ruggero goes to see if an answer has arrived. Magda is torn between her desire to tell Ruggero the truth about herself and her wish to avoid hurting him. Lisette and Prunier enter. Prunier has tired of her resistance to his "improvements," and Lisette wishes only to return to Magda's service. Magda happily agrees. Prunier informs her that Rambaldo is willing to take her back on any terms.

Ruggero returns with a letter from his mother, which he gives Magda to read. As her voice trembles, Magda reads the mother's hopes that her son's bride will be a virtuous and worthy woman. Magda can keep silent no longer and reveals her past to Ruggero. He listens, stunned, while she tells him that she can never be his wife. Despite Ruggero's pleas, Magda insists he return home. Ruggero slumps down, devastated. Magda goes off, with Lisette in attendance.

Il tabarro

Michele, barge-owner	*Baritone*
Luigi, a stevedore	*Tenor*
Il Tinca (the Tench), a stevedore	*Tenor*
Il Talpa (the Mole), a stevedore	*Bass*
Giorgetta, Michele's wife	*Soprano*
La Frugola (the Rummager), Talpa's wife	*Mezzo-soprano*

Stevedores, a Song-Vendor, Midinettes, an Organ-Grinder
and His Assistant, Two Lovers

The time is the present.
The place is Paris, a quay along the Seine.

A barge is tied up at a Paris quay. As the stevedores unload it, the boss Michele talks briefly with his young wife Giorgetta, complaining of her coldness. Then, as work ends, Giorgetta offers wine to the men; and when a strolling musician stops and plays, she dances with Luigi, the youngest of the stevedores. With him, too, she tells of the joys of living in Paris, instead of the cramped, unsettled life on the barge. When they are alone, it becomes clear that they are lovers; they arrange to meet that same night, after Michele has gone to sleep. Giorgetta will strike a match as the signal that the coast is clear. Luigi leaves. Again Michele tries to stir Giorgetta from her frustrating estrangement, even reminding her of their dead child. Giorgetta goes into the cabin. Now convinced that she has a lover, Michele remains on deck, musing bitterly. He strikes a match to light his pipe. Thinking this is the signal, Luigi steals aboard. Michele catches him, forces a confession from him, and strangles him, concealing the body in his cloak. When Giorgetta, uneasy, comes out of the cabin, Michele opens his cloak and Luigi's body rolls at her feet.

Suor Angelica

Sister Angelica	*Soprano*
The Princess	*Contralto*

The Abbess	*Mezzo-soprano*
The Monitress	*Mezzo-soprano*
The Novice Mistress	*Mezzo-soprano*
Sister Genovieffa	*Soprano*
Sister Osmina	*Soprano*
Sister Dolcina	*Soprano*
The Nursing Sister	*Mezzo-soprano*
The Alms-Collectors	*Sopranos*
The Novices	*Sopranos*
The Lay Sisters	*Soprano and Mezzo-soprano*

The time is toward the end of the seventeenth century.
The place is a convent in Italy.

*I*n a little convent, daily life seems to flow peacefully: the nuns pray, do penance, perform their simple tasks, even dream briefly of unfulfilled, innocent desires. Only Sister Angelica seems profoundly restless: for seven years, ever since she has been here, she has had no news of the outside world. But then a visitor arrives, and Sister Angelica is summoned to the parlatory. The visitor is her aunt, a stern, austere aristocrat, who has come chiefly to settle a matter of inheritance. Almost marginally, she informs Angelica that her child—the child of sin and the reason why the family put Angelica in the convent—has died. The Princess leaves, and Angelica—half-crazed with grief—prepares a poisonous drink from some herbs and drinks it. Realizing her sin, she begs the Madonna to save her; and as the other sisters look on, a miracle occurs: the Madonna appears with Angelica's child, who will lead her to Paradise.

Gianni Schicchi

Gianni Schicchi	*Baritone*
Lauretta, his daughter	*Soprano*
Relatives of Buoso Donati:	
Zita, known as "the old one," cousin of Buoso	*Contralto*
Rinuccio, her nephew	*Tenor*
Gherardo, Buoso's nephew	*Tenor*
Nella, his wife	*Soprano*
Gherardino, their son	*Contralto*
Betto di Signa, Buoso's brother-in-law, poor and badly dressed	*Bass*
Simone, Buoso's cousin	*Bass*
Marco, his son	*Baritone*
La Ciesca, Marco's wife	*Mezzo-soprano*
Maestro Spinelloccio, doctor	*Bass*

Ser Amantio di Nicolao, notary	*Baritone*
Pinellino, cobbler	*Bass*
Guccio, dyer	*Bass*

The time is around the end of the thirteenth century
or beginning of the fourteenth, in Florence.

A large bedroom in the house of Buoso Donati, a rich Florentine, who has
just died. The corpse lies in a huge four-poster bed in the background; the
bed's curtains are drawn. Buoso's relatives are mourning his death, but
then a rumor begins to circulate among them that Buoso's considerable
fortune has been left not to his family but to some monks. The relatives
break off their laments and search desperately for the will. Young Rinuccio finds it, and, before giving it to his aunt Zita, asks her permission to
marry his beloved Lauretta, daughter of the upstart Gianni Schicchi. Zita
says that if they receive their inheritance, Rinuccio can marry anyone he
pleases. But, as a reading of the will quickly reveals, it is indeed the monks
who inherit everything. Rinuccio then secretly sends for the shrewd Schicchi, who can, perhaps, save the situation, even though the relatives object
to this plan. Schicchi arrives with Lauretta, and is ill-received by Zita.
Lauretta pleads with her father to help the family anyway, and he agrees.
His plan is simple: he will impersonate Buoso, dictate a new will, and
leave everything to the relatives, who then, one by one, offer him handsome bribes if he will favor them in the will. The notary arrives and Schicchi dictates the testament, leaving the bulk of the estate to "his good friend
Gianni Schicchi." The relatives are helpless, since their—and Schicchi's—
deceit is a grave crime. Once the notary has gone, there is a terrible rum-
pus, whereupon Schicchi chases them all out of the house, which is now
his. Only Rinuccio and Lauretta remain, embracing, dreaming of their
love. Schicchi, in an aside to the audience, insists that Buoso's money
could hardly be used for a more worthy purpose.

Turandot

Princess Turandot	*Soprano*
The Emperor Altoum	*Tenor*
Timur, exiled Tartar king	*Bass*
The Unknown Prince (Calaf), his son	*Tenor*
Liù, a slave girl	*Soprano*
Ping, Grand Chancellor	*Baritone*
Pang, Grand Purveyor	*Tenor*
Pong, Grand Cook	*Tenor*
A Mandarin	*Baritone*

The Prince of Persia, the Executioner, Servants,
Handmaidens, etc.

In Peking.
In legendary times.

ACT I

𝒯he cold and beautiful Princess Turandot is destined, by a sacred oath, to
be the bride of the royal suitor who can successfully answer three riddles
which the Princess asks him. So far all of Turandot's suitors have failed;
and for failure the punishment is death, by beheading. In fact, as the opera
begins, the Imperial City is preparing for the execution of the latest unlucky
aspirant, the Prince of Persia. In the milling crowd appears Timur, the
defeated Tartar king, old and blind, led by his faithful slave girl, Liù. As
the guards roughly handle the mob, the old man falls to the ground. A
stranger helps him up and recognizes him. The stranger, the Unknown
Prince, is Timur's son, who was believed killed in battle. As they exchange
stories, Timur describes Liù's affectionate care, and the prince asks her
why she has voluntarily shared such hardship. In a voice filled with love,
Liù answers, "because, one day, you smiled at me." The moon rises: the
hour for the execution has come. The crowd begs for mercy for the young
victim, but Turandot orders the executioners to proceed. The crowd follows the executioner and the victim, leaving Timur, Liù, and the Prince
alone. At his first sight of the icy Turandot, the Prince has fallen madly in
love and is eager to try his luck. Timur and Liù attempt to dissuade him,
and so do the three grotesque ministers, Ping, Pang, and Pong, who appear
just as the Prince is about to strike the gong, signaling that a new suitor
has appeared. All pleas are ineffectual, and, calling Turandot's name, the
Prince strikes the gong.

ACT II

Ping, Pang, and Pong meet to lament the state of affairs in Peking, where
beheadings are becoming more and more frequent. Each minister speaks
nostalgically of his native region, to which he longs to return. But it is
time for the Prince to face the supreme trial. The aged Emperor tries also
to dissuade him, but the Prince is adamant. Turandot herself appears and
vows that no one shall ever possess her, since she is avenging the cruel
murder of her ancestress at the hand of the Tartars long ago. One by one,
Turandot asks the riddles, and each time the Prince guesses the correct
answer. Defeated, Turandot begs her father not to give her to the stranger,
but the Emperor says that the sacred vow must be fulfilled. Finally, Turandot turns to the Prince and asks him if he wants to have her by force.
He answers that he wants her love, and offers to release her from the vow
if she can discover his name before dawn.

Act III

No one is sleeping in Peking, as the Princess has commanded that the stranger's name be discovered by dawn. Otherwise heads will roll. The three ministers try to lure the Prince with offers of lovely maidens, wealth, glory; he refuses all of them. Then guards drag in Timur and Liù. Turandot appears and orders Liù to be tortured. But Liù explains that her love gives her the strength to resist, and when she feels herself weakening, she seizes a dagger and commits suicide. The crowd is aghast, and, with Timur, all follow the poor girl's body as it is carried off. Left alone with Turandot, the Prince reproaches her and, at the same time, insists that love can make her human. He kisses her. Turandot returns the kiss, but is then overcome with shame at her own weakness. She admits that she loves the Prince, but begs him to go away. Instead, he places his life in her hands, revealing that his name is Calaf, son of Timur. Dawn comes at last. The court and the crowd gather to hear Turandot's defeat or victory. She announces that she does indeed know the stranger's name, but then, vanquished, she murmurs, "His name . . . is love!" Calaf rushes to her, as the crowd cheers.

INDEX

Numbers in *italics* refer to illustrations; numbers in **bold** refer to major discussion.